Studies in Accounting and Finance

Contemporary Issues and Debates

Editors

Arun Kumar Basu
Professor of Commerce, University of Calcutta

Malayendu Saha
Professor of Commerce, University of Calcutta

INDIAN ACCOUNTING ASSOCIATION
CALCUTTA BRANCH

PEARSON

Delhi • Chennai • Chandigarh

ISBN 978-81-317-5445-0

First Impression

Published by Dorling Kindersley (India) Pvt. Ltd, licensees of Pearson Education in South Asia.

Head Office: 7th Floor, Knowledge Boulevard, A-8(A), Sector-62, Noida 201309, UP, India.
Registered Office: 11 Community Centre, Panchsheel Park, New Delhi 110 017, India.

Typeset by—County Caramels, Ghaziabad

Printed in India by India Binding House.

Contents

Preface *ix*

About the Editors and Contributors *xv*

1. The IFRS Revolution—Move Towards One Worldwide Language for Financial Reporting
Arun Kumar Basu **1**

1.1 Introduction 1

1.2 Rationale for a Single Set of Global Accounting Standards 2

1.3 The IASB—An Overview 4

1.4 IFRS—Form, Quality and Content 6

1.5 Worldwide Adoption of IFRS 10

1.6 Some Unfinished Business 14

1.7 Conclusion 15

2. Full Cost Accounting—A Stepping Stone for Corporate Sustainability Reporting
Kanika Chatterjee **19**

2.1 Introduction 19

2.2 Inadequacies of Traditional Accounting vis-à-vis Sustainable Development 21

2.3 FCA as a Pre-requisite for Mainstream Sustainability Reporting Practice 22

2.4 Traditional Versus Emerging Views of Full Cost Accounting 25

2.5 Definition and Nature of FCA 27

2.6 Business Case for FCA 28

2.7 Approaches to Internalization of Externalities for FCA Implementation 29

2.8 Appropriate Methodology for FCA Adoption 31

2.9 Conclusion 37

3. Intangible Assets—New Paradigm Initiatives
Malayendu Saha **41**

3.1 Introduction 41

3.2 Awareness for Intangible Assets 43

3.3 Literature Review 44

3.4 Definition and Recognition of Intangible Assets 45

3.5 Measurement and Valuation of Intangible Assets 48

3.6 Accounting and Reporting of Intangible Assets 51

3.7 Conclusion 56

4. Accounting for Financial Instruments—A Commentary on the Contemporary Principles, Standards and Related Issues
Prithul Chakraborty **59**

4.1 Introduction 60

4.2 Evolution of Accounting Standards on Financial Instruments—A Chronicle 62

4.3 Rules and Principles of the Prevailing Accounting Standards—An Overview and Search for Similarities and Differences between IASB Standards and FASB Standards 64

4.4 Controversial Issues on Prevailing Accounting Standards 68

4.5 Reform Initiatives Taken by the Standard-setting Bodies 73

4.6 Conclusion 77

5. Corporate Governance and Corporate Reporting Practices—An Overview of the Conceptual Landscape
Pintu Sarkar and Swagata Sen **81**

5.1 Overview of Corporate Governance 81

5.2 What is Corporate Governance? 83

5.3 Benefits of Good Corporate Governance 84

5.4 Evolution of Corporate Governance Practices—An Overview 85

5.5 Synoptic View of the Genesis of Corporate Governance in India 90

5.6 Corporate Governance and Corporate Reporting 92

5.7 Conclusion 95

6. XBRL and Financial Reporting Taxonomy—A Revolution in Preparation, Communication and Analysis of Electronic Financial Reports
Sunil Kumar Gandhi **97**

6.1 Introduction 97

6.2 Evolution of XBRL 98

6.3 Concepts of Related Terminologies 99

6.4 Tools Used in XBRL Reports 100

6.5 Advantages of XBRL Reporting 101

6.6 XBRL Adoption by Different Countries (Source: www.edgar-online.com) 101

6.7 Conclusion 103

7. ESOP Valuation and Disclosures in India
Satyajit Dhar and Subhabrata De **109**

7.1 Introduction 109

7.2 ESOP Accounting 110

7.3 ESOP Valuation 111

7.4 Regulatory Framework for ESOP Accounting in India 114

7.5 Disclosure of Stock Option Value by Indian Companies 116

7.6 Conclusion 122

8. Transition from AS 14 to IFRS 3—The Roadmap to Accounting for Business Communications
Tanupa Chakraborty **125**

8.1 Introduction 125

8.2 Provisions of AS 14: Accounting for Amalgamations 128

8.3 Salient Features of IFRS 3—Business Combination and Its Comparison with AS 14 131

8.4 Challenges Inflicted by IFRS 3 132

8.5 Conclusion 133

9. Fair Value Accounting—A Discussion for Development of a Conceptual Framework
Ananda Mohan Pal **135**

9.1 Introduction 135

9.2 Fair Value Recognition 136

9.3 Developments on Fair Value Measurement and Application 138

9.4 Modification of Income Statement 140

9.5 Problems with Fair Value Accounting 141

9.6 Conclusion 141

10. IFRS for SMEs vs Full IFRSs—A Comparison of Form and Contents
Gautam Mitra and Ashish Kumar Sana **143**

10.1 Introduction 143

10.2 How SMEs are Defined? 145

10.3 The Rationale for Having Two Sets of Standards—IFRSs and IFRS for SMEs 147

10.4 Evolution of IFRS for SMEs—A Historical Perspective 147

10.5 IFRS for SMEs—The Key Characteristics 149

10.6 IFRS for SMEs IFRSs and Full IFRSs—Similarities and Differences 152

10.7 Conclusion 154

11. Obstacles to the Development of Optimal Accounting Standards—Accounting and Political Issues
Arnab Deb Narayan Roy **159**
11.1 Relevance of Optimal Accounting Standards 159
11.2 Uniform Accounting System and Government Involvement in Accounting Regulation 161
11.3 Contrast Between Financial Reporting and Tax Accounting 162
11.4 Problems in Achieving International Harmonization in Financial Reporting 163
11.5 Factors That Affect Standard Setter's Performance 163
11.6 How Accounting Credibility May Suffer? 168
11.7 Complication from Reflexive Intervention by Capital Market in Standard Setting 174

12. The Philosophical Aspects of Accounting Ethics
Radhanath Pyne **181**
12.1 Ethical Theories and Accounting Ethics 181
12.2 Applied Areas of Accounting Ethics 185
12.5 Conclusion 190

13. A Note on Global Financial Crises (From an Indian Perspective)
Syamal K. Ghosh **197**
13.1 Introduction and Background 197
13.2 Financial Crisis or Financial Meltdown—Definition 199
13.3 Where Are We Now? 199
13.4 How Does the Bursting of a Bubble Hurt? 200
13.5 Curative Measures 201
13.6 How Are We Doing Here, in India? 205
13.7 Concluding Observations 208

14. M–M Hypothesis of Dividend Irrelevance in the Backdrop of Taxation in India
Snehamay Bhattacharyya **211**
14.1 Introduction 211
14.2 Modigliani and Miller (M–M) Hypothesis 212
14.3 World Scenario on Dividend Taxation 213
14.4 History of Dividend Tax in India 214
14.5 Testing of Validity of M–M Hypothesis 216
14.6 Observations 216
14.7 Conclusion 217

15. Performance of NGOs—A Study on Some Selected Districts in West Bengal
Dhrubaranjan Dandapat and Bhaskar Bagchi **219**

15.1 Introduction 219
15.2 Activities of NGOs in West Bengal 220
15.3 Performance Evaluation Techniques 222
15.4 Methodology 224
15.5 Performance Evaluation of Selected NGOs 224
15.6 Findings of the Study 229
15.7 Conclusion 230

16. Personal Carbon Trading—A Lifestyle-based Carbon Control Mechanism
K. C. Paul **233**

16.1 Introduction 234
16.2 Approaches to Mitigating Measures 235
16.3 Lifestyle-based Carbon Control 240
16.4 Personal Carbon Trading 241
16.5 Conclusions 245

17. GARCH Models—A Key to Capture Volatility of Financial Data
J. K. Das and Sharad Nath Bhattacharya **249**

17.1 Introduction 249
17.2 Characteristics of Financial Data—A Discussion 251
17.3 Modelling Volatility Clustering and Non-linear Dependence 254
17.4 Multivariate GARCH 267
17.5 Conclusion 268

Index **277**

Preface

This book provides important recent contributions from leading scholars to the literature of accounting and finance. The articles contained in the book offer insightful commentary on some of our pressing issues, such as globalization of accounting standards, accounting for financial instruments, fair value accounting, accounting for intangibles, corporate governance and accounting, accounting for social and environmental costs, accounting for employee stock option plans, obstacles to the development of high-quality accounting standards, small company reporting, accounting ethics, technology reporting and global economic meltdown. The first article by **Arun Kumar Basu**, one of the editors of this volume, describes a journey into the world of International Financial Reporting Standards (IFRSs). IFRSs are the means by which the International Accounting Standards Board (IASB) seeks to realize its objective of delivering a universally accepted common financial reporting model. The IASB model is currently being used in more than 100 countries around the world, and in many other countries, the process of adoption of the model is well under way. The benefits of having a universally accepted common financial reporting language are many and varied. There are, however, some obstacles to the development of such a language. In this article, the author analyses the key features of the IASB financial reporting model and examines its prospect of becoming the *lingua franca* of the accounting world. The article concludes with several issues and challenges and presents the means by which these can be addressed.

The second contribution by **Kanika Chatterjee** builds up a case in defence of *full cost accounting* as an essential and significant improvement over the traditional system that fails to take account of externalities arising in the form of adverse social and environmental impacts of doing business. Chatterjee's paper explores the concept of full cost accounting and discusses the issue of what could be an appropriate full cost accounting method for a bank. The paper also highlights significant implementation issues.

The third contribution by **Malayendu Saha**, one of the editors of this volume, explores the issue of recognition, measurement and reporting of intangibles. The emergence of the knowledge-based economy has brought significant changes in the way companies conduct their operations and create wealth. In many companies, intangible assets such as creativity, patents, brands, R&D, copyrights, franchises, relationships and customer base have become the most important factors of business success. However, accounting has failed to cope with this new reality. The current accounting model, which is designed to serve the accounting and reporting needs of a manufacturing-based economy, fails to describe companies whose principal wealth-creating assets are intangibles. In this article, the author explores the efforts currently under way to identify the changes that are needed in our current accounting model to support the new business reality.

The fourth contribution, from **Prithul Chakraborty**, is a critical evaluation of the rules and principles of accounting for financial instruments as provided by the prevailing accounting standards of the US Financial Accounting Standards Board (FASB) and the IASB. The standards on financial instruments deal principally with accounting for all types of financial instruments such as debt securities, loans and structured products like collateralized debt obligations. Establishing accounting standards on financial instruments has always been a challenging job for the accounting standard setting bodies. There has been controversy regarding the appropriate accounting for financial instruments. The prevailing standards appear to be very complex, and they fail to address many fundamental issues. Efforts are currently under way to develop a universally agreed framework for recognition, measurement and reporting of financial instruments. In this article, the author argues that the converged standard should be robust enough to capture the underlying economic reality of the transactions involving the use and application of financial instruments. He also argues in favour of simplifying the requirements relating to classification and measurement of financial instruments.

The fifth contribution, by **Pintu Sarkar** and **Swagata Sen**, describes the role of corporate governance in corporate financial reporting. Corporate governance is about how a company is managed. It is about commitment to values and ethical conduct of business operations. It has been observed that there is a link between poor corporate governance and financial reporting frauds and irregularities. In this article, Sarkar and Sen explore the concept of corporate governance and examine how corporate government practices have evolved over time. They review the various benefits that can be derived from having a good corporate governance system and specifically mention its importance in preserving and enhancing the quality of corporate reporting. The article concludes by giving an indication of what needs to be done to promote a good corporate governance system.

Sunil Kumar Gandhi reviews the eXtensible Business Reporting Language (XBRL), which is an XML-based markup language for electronic transmission of business and financial data, in his article. One of the central features of XBRL is that it can be easily adjusted to meet company-specific requirements. XBRL does not treat financial information as a block of text. Instead, it provides a computer-readable tag to identify individual pieces of financial information. The new reporting language is expected to generate huge benefits at all stages of generation, transmission and analysis of financial information. Gandhi's article discusses the origin and evolution of XBRL and explores the various issues related to this emerging business reporting languages such as the terminologies and the tools used, current state of application, etc. The author ends his article by presenting an optimistic view of the future of XBRL.

The next article, by **Satyajit Dhar** and **Subhabrata De**, explores employee stock option (ESO) valuation and reporting practices by Indian companies. Employee Stock Option Plans (ESOPs) are contracts between a company and its employees that give employees the right to buy a specific number of the company's shares at a fixed price within a certain period of time. Companies use ESOPs to compensate, retain and attract employees. One of the major problems with ESOPs relates to their treatment concerning the accounts. There are conflicting viewpoints as to how option grant value should be determined and how that value should be expensed in the profit and loss account. Although the leading accounting standard-setting bodies of the world have formulated guidelines on accounting for ESOPs, problems persist. In this article, the authors examine these and other related issues and present an overview of corporate practices in India with regard to ESO valuation and disclosures.

The eighth article, by **Tanupa Chakraborty**, deals with business combinations. A business combination is a process of bringing together different businesses into a single reporting entity. Business combinations involve a variety of issues. In this article, Chakraborty focuses on accounting and reporting issues concerning business combinations. She explores those issues in the context of convergence of Indian accounting standards with IFRSs. The accounting standard currently in force in India on the subject of business combinations is *AS 14: Accounting for Amalgamation.* The corresponding international standard is *IFRS 3: Business Combinations.* There are some significant differences between these two sets of standards. Chakraborty explains these differences and reviews the challenges accountants in India will have to face when they will be required to account for business combinations in accordance with the requirements under IFRS 3.

The contribution by **Ananda Mohan Paul** is about fair value accounting. The issue of fair value measurement has gained widespread prominence in recent years. Accounting standard setters both at national and international levels are now taking steps to extend the application of fair value principle to an increasing number of assets and liabilities in the belief that it will provide more transparency in financial reporting. The IASB has issued numerous accounting standards that require or permit the use of fair value measurements in financial reporting. In this article, Paul explores the recent developments in the spheres of application and measurement of fair value in accounting and tries to establish logical links between the conceptual issues and technical developments. He argues that the measurement issue should be properly addressed in the remodelled IASB conceptual framework for financial reporting.

The contribution by **Gautam Mitra** and **Ashish Kumar Sana** is a comparative study of full IFRSs and IFRS for Small and Medium-sized Enterprises (IFRS for SMEs).The IFRS for SMEs is the first international accounting standard developed by the IASB to serve the accounting and reporting needs of non-public companies. Although the new standard incorporates the principles that are based on full IFRSs, the accounting and reporting requirements have been simplified to a great extent to suit the entities within its scope. The article by Mitra and Sana explores the central features of IFRS for SMEs and provide an overview of the main differences between this standard and the full IFRSs.

The article by **Arnab Deb Narayan Roy** examines the obstacles in the development of optimal accounting standards. Accounting standards should be of high quality if they are to generate full and fair disclosure of relevant information in corporate financial reports. The quality of accounting standards may be impaired if they are slanted in favour of any one economic interest by compromising accounting logic. Those responsible for setting accounting standards must strive to maintain independence from those governed by their financial accounting and reporting requirements. The overriding consideration in the development of accounting standards should be the delivery of a better system of financial reporting by companies. A new standard should be promulgated only if it adds to the quality of financial reporting. However, this ideal situation does not always prevail. In this article, the author describes the attributes of good accounting standards and examines the problems encountered in maintaining a set of optimal accounting standards.

The article by **Radhanath Pyne** relates to the philosophical foundation of accounting ethics. In the aftermath of the recent high-profile accounting and audit failures, there has been an international concern over the poor standards of accounting ethics. Accountants are required to adhere to high ethical standards if they are to safeguard the accuracy and integrity of financial accounting and reporting. Accounting ethics, which primarily deals with moral values and judgements, is usually categorized as a field of applied ethics. In this article, the author explores different ethical theories and develops their linkages with accounting ethics. The article also explores the theories of moral behaviour as they relate to practising accountants and identifies the major stimuli that germinate unethical institutions among accountants. Pyne concludes his article by providing a brief outline of what he thinks should be done to curb unethical behaviour by accountants.

Shyamal K. Ghosh in his contribution discusses global financial crises from an Indian perspective. Economic history is replete with instances of economic meltdown of various kinds and shades in different parts of the world. Some of these have even had a global reach. Ghosh explains the symptoms of a financial crisis or meltdown and cites some instances of major financial crises that we have witnessed since the beginning of the twentieth century. He then examines the present crisis that started in the United States owing to excessive deregulation of the financial markets and the effect of speculative lending. Ghosh argues that although India has been affected by the recent global financial meltdown, she has been able to avert a major disaster. He provides a detailed analysis of how this has been possible.

Snehamay Bhattacharyya's article examines the Modigliani–Miller (M–M)'s dividend irrelevance theory in the backdrop of taxation in India. The study reveals that the theory does not hold good in India. The M–M theory says that there is no effect from dividends on a company's capital structure or stock price. The underlying assumption is that investors can affect their return on a stock regardless of the stock's dividend. M–M assume that there is no personal income tax payable by the shareholder. There is an alternative assumption that dividends and capital gains are taxed at the same rate. The M–M theory does not imagine a situation where dividend distribution tax is payable by the company that pays the dividend. According to the taxation rule currently prevailing in India, companies that distribute dividends are required to pay tax on such distributions. This is why the theory does not hold good in India, even though dividends and capital gains are similarly taxed in this country.

The article by **Dhrubaranjan Dandapat** and **Bhaskar Bagchi** is an exercise in NGO performance measurement. NGOs are legally constituted not-for-profit organizations that usually operate independently from any government. They are established to accomplish a variety of purposes. Since different NGOs are governed by different objectives, there is no standard technique for assessment of their performance. In this article, the authors provide a brief description of the activities performed by NGOs and explore the various approaches that can be adopted to evaluate their performance. The authors argue that the evaluation of an NGO should be done at least from two perspectives: performance measurement of programmes and organizational evaluation. The article presents the survey results of performance evaluation across selected NGOs in certain districts of West Bengal. The performance evaluation has been done based on the former perspective.

The last two articles address issues that are not directly connected with accounting and finance. One of them deals with personal carbon trading while the other one is concerned with statistical models used in accounting and finance research. The article by **K. C. Paul** deals with an emerging new concept of 'personal carbon trading (PCA)' or 'personal carbon allowances'. PCA has come to be regarded as a radical proposition in the sphere of reduction of carbon emissions. Schemes of PCT allow the carbon emission costs to be included in routine business decision making. This is expected to promote energy efficiency and behavioural changes. There are, however, some outstanding issues that need to be addressed before the concept can be implemented as a policy option. In this article, the author first makes an assessment of the approaches currently available to mitigate the problem of reducing carbon emissions and then explores the concept of PCT. The article also explores the merits and demerits of the various PCT models and examines their applicability. The author argues that certain behavioural changes are needed if PCT is to emerge as a viable alternative mechanism to contain greenhouse gas emissions.

The last contribution, by **J. K. Das** and **Sharad Nath Bhattacharyya**, discusses the properties of the statistical models accounting and finance researchers use in the analysis, interpretation and forecasting of financial data. The contribution focuses on models judged to be useful for financial data with heavy tails and volatility clustering. Emphasis, in particular, is laid on univariate GARCH-type model that takes conditional variance into account. The authors argue that volatility forecasting models are extremely data specific, and it may not be possible to identify any particular model with superior forecasting power than the others.

We first would like to thank the Executive Committee of the Indian Accounting Association, Calcutta Branch, for undertaking the venture of publishing an edited volume on contemporary issues in accounting and finance and choosing us as its editors. Our heartfelt thanks also go to each of the contributors to this volume for their spontaneity and willingness to share ideas with the readers and for their ungrudging patience and cooperation in revising their papers, when asked for. We are very much aware of the amount of work that reviewers have done for this volume and greatly appreciate their input. In preparing this volume, we were helped by the suggestions from colleagues in the Department of Commerce at the University of Calcutta. We are thankful to all of them. We would like to convey a special word of thanks to Professor Bhabatosh Banerjee, Professor Sudipti Banerjea, Professor Jita Bhattacharyya and Professor Dipti Kumar Chakraborty for encouraging us in this venture.

The book is intended for a wide-ranging audience. We expect the book to be of interest to business executives, accounting and finance practitioners and researchers. It will be relevant to students of M.Com., MBA, M.Phil. and Ph.D. programmes in accounting and finance. It will also be relevant for CA and ICWA students.

Despite our best efforts, there may be errors and omissions. As editors, we accept full responsibility for all the errors and omissions in the manuscript.

About the Editors and Contributors

Ananda Mohan Paul, author of 'Fair Value Accounting—A Discussion for Development of a Conceptual Framework', is a selection grade lecturer in the Department of Business Management at the University of Calcutta.

Arnab Deb Narayan Roy, author of 'Obstacles to the Development of Optimal Accounting Standards—Accounting and Political Issues', is a selection grade lecturer in the Department of Commerce at Umes Chandra College, Kolkata.

Arun Kumar Basu, author of 'The IFRS Revolution—Towards One Worldwide Language for Financial Reporting', is a professor in the Department of Commerce at the University of Calcutta.

Bhaskar Bagchi, co-author of 'Performance of NGOs—A Study of Selected Districts of West Bengal', is a senior lecturer in the Department of Commerce at Alipurduar College, Jalpaiguri, West Bengal.

Dhrubaranjan Dandapat, co-author of 'Performance of NGOs—A Study of Selected Districts of West Bengal', is a professor in the Department of Commerce at the University of Calcutta.

J. K. Das, co-author of 'GARCH Models—A Key to Capture Volatility of Financial Data', is an associate professor in the Department of Commerce at the University of Calcutta.

Kanika Chatterjee, author of 'Full Cost Accounting—A Stepping Stone for Corporate Sustainability Reporting', is a reader in the Department of Commerce at the University of Calcutta.

K. C. Paul, author of 'Personal Carbon Trading—A Lifestyle-based Carbon Control Mechanism', is a professor of commerce and coordinator of MBA Programme in the Department of Commerce with Farm Management at Vidyasagar University, Midnapore, West Bengal.

Malayendu Saha, author of 'Intangible Assets—New Paradigm Initiatives', is a professor and coordinator of MBA (Finance) Programme in the Department of Commerce at the University of Calcutta.

Pintu Sarkar, co-author of 'Corporate Governance and Corporate Reporting Practices—An Overview of the Conceptual Landscape', is a selection grade lecturer in the Department of Commerce at Shibpur Dinabandhu Institution College, Shibpur, Howrah.

Prithul Chakraborty, author of 'Accounting for Financial Instruments—A Commentary on the Contemporary Principles, Standards and Related Issues', is a professor in management studies at JIS College of Engineering, Kalyani, Nadia.

Radhanath Pyne, author of 'The Philosophical Aspects of Accounting Ethics', is a selection grade lecturer in the Department of Commerce at S. A. Jaipuria College, Kolkata.

Satyajit Dhar, co-author of 'ESOP Valuation and Disclosures in India', is a reader in the Department of Business Management at the University of Kalyani, Kalyani, Nadia.

Sharad Nath Bhattacharyya, co-author of 'GARCH Models—A Key to Capture Volatility of Financial Data', is a senior lecturer at Army Institute of Management, Kolkata.

Snehamay Bhattacharyya, author of 'M–M Hypothesis of Dividend Irrelevance in the Backdrop of Taxation Laws in India', is a selection grade lecturer in the Department of Commerce at the University of Calcutta.

Subhabrata De, co-author of 'ESOP Valuation and Disclosures in India', is an assistant professor in the Department of Commerce at Kanchrapara College, Nadia.

Sunil Kumar Gandhi, author of 'XBRL and Financial Reporting Taxonomy—A Revolution in Preparation, Communication and Analysis of Electronic Financial Reports', is a professor in the Department of Commerce at the University of Kalyani, Kalyani, Nadia.

Swagata Sen, co-author of 'Corporate Governance and Corporate Reporting Practices—An Overview of the Conceptual Landscape', is a professor in the Department of Commerce at the University of Calcutta.

Syamal K. Ghosh, author of 'A Note on Global Financial Crises (From an Indian Perspective)', is a guest faculty in the Department of Commerce at the University of Calcutta. Formerly, he was a professor of finance at IIM Calcutta; a senior professor at the Institute of Management Technology-Ghaziabad; Dean, P. C. Chandra School of Business, Kolkata and Dean, International College of Financial Planning, Delhi.

Tanupa Chakraborty, author of 'Transition from AS 14 to IFRS 3—The Roadmap to Accounting for Business Communications', is a senior lecturer in the Department of Commerce at the University of Calcutta.

CHAPTER 1

The IFRS Revolution—Move Towards One Worldwide Language for Financial Reporting

Arun Kumar Basu

ABSTRACT

The advent of International Financial Reporting Standards (IFRS) is a landmark event in accounting history. It has brought accountants from various parts of the world closer to speaking a common language for communicating financial information. IFRS is a country-neutral financial reporting framework developed and maintained by the International Accounting Standards Board (IASB), a London-based worldwide accounting standard-setting body. The main objective of the IASB is to develop a single set of high quality, understandable and enforceable standards for financial reporting and promote their worldwide acceptance and observance. There are more than 100 countries around the world that are currently using the IASB financial reporting framework and in many other countries the process of adoption of this framework is well under way. This article describes a journey into the world of IFRS. It examines the rationale for a global financial reporting language and explores how IFRS is heading for creating such a language.

1.1 Introduction

The emergence of International Financial Reporting Standards (IFRS) as the dominant global accounting framework is a revolutionary event in the history of accounting. This is an event that has dramatically transformed the landscape of corporate financial reporting throughout the world. It seems that the stage has been set for the creation of one global financial reporting framework that will be used by companies across the world in the preparation and presentation of their general purpose financial statements. The need for having a single set of global accounting standards has been felt for a long time. It has been argued that a common set of high-quality global accounting standards would increase transparency and comparability in financial reporting and facilitate efficient allocation of global capital. There have, however, been disagreements on translating the idea of having a common set of global accounting standards into a practical reality. The increasing acceptance of IFRS among countries throughout the world has prompted many to believe that a global consensus on a single set of accounting standards will be reached through this IFRS route. IFRS is a country-neutral financial reporting framework developed and maintained by the International Accounting Standards Board (IASB), a London-based worldwide accounting standard-setting body. The aim of the IASB is to develop 'a single set of high quality, understandable and enforceable global accounting standards that require transparent and comparable information in general purpose financial statements'.[1] The IFRS revolution actually began in 2002 when the European Union (EU) adopted a new accounting regulation that would require all EU-listed companies to follow, with effect from 2005, the standards promulgated by the IASB in their consolidated financial statements. Today, there are more than 100 countries, including 27 EU countries, which either require or permit the use of IFRS. A number of other economically significant countries, such as Brazil, Canada, China, India, Japan and Korea, have undertaken programmes to migrate to IFRS. The IASB expects that by 2011 more than 150 countries will have adopted IFRS.[2] Even the United States, which has long insisted on accepting US GAAP as global GAAP, is increasingly being inclined to embrace IFRS. The US Securities and Exchange Commission (SEC) has already taken a decision to allow non-US companies to file their financial statements based on IFRS without reconciling back to US GAAP. The SEC is also considering adopting IFRS and potentially abolishing US generally accepted accounting principles (GAAP). According to 2008 *IFRS Survey* by Deloitte & Touche LLP (2008), about 40 per cent of the Fortune Global 500 companies currently use IFRS. The document further maintains that the percentage will significantly increase over the next couple of years since most companies outside the United States that currently use their domestic accounting standards will be required to move to IFRS. Efforts are now being made to speed up the initiatives to expedite the process of adoption of IFRS. The Group of 20 (G-20) nations called on international accounting bodies 'to redouble their efforts to achieve a single set of high-quality, global accounting standards within the context of their independent standard-setting process and complete their convergence project by June 2011' (Lamoreaux 2009).

This paper describes our journey into the world of IFRS. It describes the operation of the IASB and renders an account of how IFRS is heading for creating a uniform global financial reporting regime. The rest of the paper is organized as follows. Section 1.2 examines the rationale for a single set of global accounting standards. Section 1.3 renders an overview of the IASB and its activity. Section 1.4 examines the form, quality and content of IFRS. The next section, Section 1.5, provides a brief description of the current status of worldwide adoption of IFRS. Section 1.6 focuses on the problem areas. The last section, Section 1.7 concludes the discussion.

1.2 Rationale for a Single Set of Global Accounting Standards

A single set of global accounting standards brings uniformity all over the globe in the matters of preparation and presentation of financial statements. As a result, companies operating in different countries are able to compete on the same level playing field (Anderson 1993). Uniformity in financial reporting practices gives rise to increased comparability of financial reporting information across jurisdictions. The globalization of world's capital markets has made it imperative to develop a single set of globally accepted accounting standards that will provide in a comparable and consistent manner transparent representations of the underlying economic reality of the transactions undertaken by enterprises operating in different countries. A single set of globally accepted accounting standards is critical in increasing the efficiency of the global capital markets and improving the allocation of global capital. Jacob and Madu (2004: 367), describes the importance of a common set of global accounting standards as follows:

> It is a foregone conclusion that the world needs a set of high-quality international accounting standards that would result in relevant, transparent, comparable, and decision useful information. Investors, creditors, and others who make similar decisions would clearly benefit from this. The capital markets are demanding this and the bureaucrats and politicians, who have dragged their feet in the past, are now actively supporting and urging their development.

Sir David Tweedie, the IASB chairman, argues:

> As the world's capital markets integrate, the logic of a single set of accounting standards is evident. A single set of international standards will enhance comparability of financial information and should make the allocation of capital across borders more efficient. The development and acceptance of international standards should also reduce compliance costs for corporations and improve consistency in audit quality.[3]

Diversity in financial reporting practices among countries has been a continuing cause of concern for the participants in the global capital markets.[4] Inconsistencies in financial reporting practices among countries have impeded financial statement comparability. Inefficiency in the transmission of financial information has brought about a negative impact on the allocation of global capital. Investors involved in evaluating cross-border investment alternatives have greatly been handicapped by the existence of international diversity in financial reporting practices. The international diversity in financial reporting practices has also created problems for companies seeking to explore cheaper sources of capital in foreign markets. If the accounting world can agree on a common set of accounting standards, financial statement comparability will improve, which in turn will increase the efficiency of cross-border investment decisions. Companies seeking multi-market listings will not be required to prepare different sets of financial statements for different markets. As a result, their capital raising costs will reduce. A single set of high-quality global accounting standards will substantially ease the process of managing foreign operations. Multinational companies (MNCs) will particularly be benefited by a common set of accounting standards as this will substantially reduce the costs of preparation of their consolidated financial statements. The preparation of consolidated financial statements by an MNC requires reconciliation of the financial statements of their foreign subsidiaries. This tends to be a costly exercise when the financial statements of the foreign subsidiaries are prepared under different financial reporting frameworks. MNCs will also be able to reduce their administrative costs to a significant extent if there is one accounting language company-wide.

Multinational accounting firms are expected to gain immense benefits from having a common set of global accounting standards. The international diversity in accounting rules tend to impose several restrictions on the cross-border mobility of accounting professionals.

Uniformity in accounting rules will increase the mobility of accounting personnel, which will enable multinational accounting firms to deliver audit, assurance and other professional accounting services at a lower cost.

Securities market regulators are expected to derive huge benefits from having a common set of globally accepted accounting standards. International inconsistencies in financial reporting practices create a lot of problems for the securities market regulators that are required to interpret financial statements submitted by foreign issuers. A common financial reporting language will enable them to adopt a consistent approach towards foreign issuers. As a result, these regulatory burdens will reduce substantially.

A common financial reporting language will lead to better cross-border mergers and acquisitions (M&A) decisions. Mergers and acquisitions across national borders have increased substantially in recent years. Today, they account for a major part of foreign direct investment (FDI). Accounting information plays a very important role in negotiating cross-border M&A deals. The diversity in accounting practices among countries often makes the proper assessment of the financial position of targets difficult. Accordingly, problems are encountered in determining appropriate purchase price. The use of a common financial reporting language by companies across the world will make things easier for those involved in making cross-border M&A deals.

Thus, it is clear that a common set of global accounting standards benefits all. The standards have, however, to be of high quality if they are to deliver the desired benefits. The standards should be able to provide a consistent basis for recognition, measurement, presentation and disclosure of transactions and events in financial statements. Moreover, the standards should be properly interpreted and rigorously applied in all jurisdictions.

High-quality financial reporting depends not only on the quality of accounting standards, but also on many other factors. According to a recent document published by the International Chamber of Commerce (ICC), to achieve a high-quality reporting, it is necessary to have an underlying infrastructure of strong corporate governance practices, effective regulatory oversight and enforcement, effective auditing, management commitment to transparency and support from users of financial information (ICC 2005).

1.3 The IASB—An Overview

The International Accounting Standards Board (IASB) is a London-based independent, full-time accounting standard-setting body of the International Accounting Standards Committee (IASC) Foundation. It is funded by contributions from the major accounting firms, financial institutions and industrial companies throughout the world; central and development banks; and other international and professional organizations. Its members are chosen for their expertise in accounting. The IASB was originally formed in 1973 as the International Accounting Standards Committee (IASC) to develop quality accounting standards and to promote their worldwide acceptance and observance. It had been in operation for nearly three decades, during which period it had developed 41 accounting standards covering a wide range of financial accounting and reporting topics. During this period, the IASC had also developed a conceptual framework, *Framework for the Preparation and Presentation of Financial Statements*, which states the basic principles for accounting standards. In 2000, the IASC members voted a new IASC Constitution, giving effect to a major restructuring. The new constitution came into effect in April 2001 when the IASB replaced the IASC. The restructuring has allowed the body to strengthen its position as a global accounting standard setter.

The reconstituted standard-setting body consists of 15 members.[5] To achieve a balance of perspectives and experience, a minimum of five members of the IASB are selected from persons having audit backgrounds, a minimum of three with experience in financial statements, a minimum of three from among the users of financial statements, and at least one with an academic background. The members are responsible for preparing exposure drafts, revising old standards and announcing new ones. As the IASB aims at bringing about changes in national standards, it establishes contacts with national standard setters through a liaison person in the Board. The new constitution requires that seven IASB members have formal liaison responsibility with national standard setters in Australia–New Zealand, Canada, France, Germany, Japan, the UK and the USA. Regular joint meetings of the chairs of those standard setters and the IASB are held to assess current situations.

The IASB adopted all the IASC standards that were in force at the time it began its operations. These pronouncements continue to be designated as 'International Accounting Standards (IASs)'. The new standards being developed by the newly constituted body are designated as 'International Financial Reporting Standards (IFRSs)'. Currently, the IASB's inventory of accounting pronouncements comprises 29 IASs, 9 IFRSs and 26 interpretations. The IASB has also retained the conceptual framework developed by its predecessor body. But the document is now being reformatted in order to enhance its usefulness.

The IASB has an interpretative body known as 'International Financial Reporting Interpretations Committee (IFRIC)', which is designed to help the IASB improve financial reporting through timely identification, discussion and resolution of financial reporting issues within the framework of IFRS. It develops authoritative interpretations of existing standards which are referred to the IASB for discussion and approval. If the interpretations are approved, they become part of IFRS. Complying with the interpretations is obligatory on the part of companies reporting under IFRS.

The IASB publishes its pronouncements in English, which is its official language. The pronouncements are translated into other languages for use in countries where English is not in use. There is in place a well-organized and rigorous system of translating the pronouncements. Currently, the translated versions of IFRS are available in about 40 languages. Although sufficient care is taken to prevent distortions, translation problems persist. This is because, certain English words, phrases, and terms cannot be translated into other languages.

The IASB is considered to be a well-equipped standard-setting body having the ability to develop high-quality accounting standards. It meets all the characteristics of a high-quality standard setter as outlined in the US SEC *Concepts Release*.[6] These characteristics include:

- An independent decision-making body
- An active advisory function
- A sound due process
- An effective interpretative function
- Independent oversight representing the public interest
- Adequate funding and staffing

The IASB works in a very transparent manner. It follows an international due process in setting its standards. The process is elaborate, and it involves accountants, financial statement users, the business community, market regulators, academics, and other interested individuals and agencies from around the world. The IASB *Due Process Handbook* (IASC Foundation 2006) provides a detailed description of the consultative arrangements followed in developing accounting standards. There are several stages in the due process of setting standards. They include preparation of discussion documents, publication of exposure drafts and final issuance of standards. The process does not come to an end with the promulgation of standards. The IASB holds regular meetings with interested parties to assess the unanticipated issues arising from implementation of the standard.

The IASB is currently enjoying a strong global support. Its mission of making one global accounting framework a practical reality has been supported by many worldwide organizations and agencies, including the United Nations (UN), the World Bank, the Organization for Economic Co-operation and Development (OECD), the World Trade Organization (WTO), the European Union (EU), the International Organization of Securities Commission (IOSCO) and the International Forum on Accountancy Development (IFAD). Most of these organizations have taken active interest in promoting measures for facilitating the process of adoption of IFRS.

A major problem with the IASB is that it has no enforcement authority. Since it is a private sector body, it cannot compel countries to comply with its standards. For achieving compliance, the IASB has to depend on the follow-through of the accounting regulators in individual countries.

1.4 IFRS—Form, Quality and Content

The term IFRS[7] is used to refer collectively to the entire body of pronouncements that the companies adhering to the IASB financial reporting framework are required to follow in the preparation and presentation of their general purpose financial statements. These pronouncements consist of IASs promulgated by the IASC and subsequently adopted by the IASB, IFRSs promulgated by the IASB, Interpretations of the Standing Interpretations Committee (SIC) and Interpretations of the IFRIC. IFRS contains requirements relating to layout and presentation of financial statements, recognition and measurement of financial information, and disclosure of information in general purpose financial statements. IASB standards are principle-based requirements in that they establish broad principles rather than detailed rules. The standards have few 'bright line' application rules. The principle-based system 'requires a clear hierarchy of overarching concepts, principles that reflect the overarching concepts and further limited guidance (ICAS 2006).' Principle-based standards focus on reporting the economic substance of transactions and their application requires greater use of professional judgement.

Layout and presentation of financial statements is an important issue in financial reporting. It involves consideration of how information should be displayed in the financial statements. The principal IASB accounting standard that deals with layout and presentation of financial statements is revised IAS 1 (IASB 2007). The standard seeks to ensure comparability both with the firm's own financial statements of previous periods and with the financial statements of other enterprises. It requires the financial statements to present fairly the financial position, financial performance and cash flows of the entity. The essence of fair presentation lies in representing faithfully the transactions and events in accordance with their economic reality, and not merely their legal form. It is reasonably assumed that complying with all applicable IFRS will result in fair presentation (Tiffin 2007).

IFRS financial statements are prepared on a going concern basis unless management intends to either liquidate the business or discontinue operation. Except for cash flow information, the accrual basis of accounting is followed in the preparation of financial statements. According to IAS 1, a complete set of financial statements includes the following components:

- Statement of financial position
- Statement of comprehensive income
- Either a statement of changes in equity (SOCE) or a statement of recognized income or expense (SORIE)
- Notes, including a summary of the significant accounting policies

According to the standard, comparative information is to be provided for the previous reporting period (IAS 1.36). IAS 1 does not prescribe any specific formats for the financial statements. But it sets out their minimum contents. There are requirements relating to the information to be displayed on the face of the financial statements. *The statement of the financial position* is to present the assets, liabilities and equity of the entity. Certain key items are specified in the standard and it allows the entity to decide on what additional items it should include depending on the nature of the business.

The statement of comprehensive income is to include all non-owner changes in equity. Comprehensive income consists of profit or loss for the period and other comprehensive income, i.e., gains and losses that are not included in profit or loss. The statement of changes in equity is required to present the total comprehensive income for the period, effects of retrospective applications or restatements, and transactions with owners in their capacity as owners.

The statement of cash flows is designed to show the entity's cash flow of the period. It requires details of historical changes in cash and cash equivalents. A distinction is to be made between cash flows from operating, financing and investing activities. The notes summarize the significant accounting policies used by the entity and provides other explanatory details. They are an integral part of the financial statements.

The central focus of IFRS is on recognition and measurement of financial information. There are requirements relating to recognition and measurement, which prescribe how entities should recognize their transactions and events and how those transactions and events should be quantified in monetary terms. Recognition and measurement are very crucial issues in accounting. This is because they affect the way periodic profits are computed and net asset values are determined. The IASB adheres to a historical cost–dominated mixed-attribute measurement model. However, there are indications that tend to suggest that the IASB is increasingly being inclined to prescribe fair value as the basis of measurement of assets and liabilities. There are provisions for fair value measurement in many of its standards. There are provisions for fair value measurement in respect of financial instruments (IAS 39), investment property (IAS 40), net assets of an acquiree in a business combination (IFRS 3) and biological assets (IAS 41). More recently, the IASB has published an exposure draft (ED) of proposed guidance on how fair value should be measured where it is required by existing standards (IASB 2009a). If the proposed guidance is adopted, it will settle much of the controversy that surrounds IFRS fair value measurement requirements. The IASB ED on fair value measurement has been prepared based on the principles that govern fair value measurement requirements under US FASB Standard SFAS 157 (FASB 2006).

Disclosure requirements are concerned with the information that an entity is required to provide on a supplementary basis in order to make financial reporting full and fair. There are two types of disclosures: protective disclosures and informative disclosures. Protective disclosures are aimed at protecting users from unfair treatment. The objective of making informative disclosures is to enhance the decision-usefulness quality of information. IFRS disclosure requirements are focused mainly on the second type of disclosures. The IASB has promulgated some standards that are all about disclosure. Examples include IAS 24, Related Party Disclosures and IFRS 7, Financial Instruments: Disclosures. The former standard requires disclosure of information about related party relationships and about transactions and outstanding balances between an entity and its related parties, while the latter prescribes disclosure requirements that are aimed at enhancing users' understanding of the significance of financial instruments to an entity's financial position, performance and cash flows. The IASB has many recognition-measurement standards that also contain requirements relating to disclosures. In many of its recently promulgated standards, the IASB has placed greater emphasis on disclosures.

1.4.1 The Conceptual Foundation of IASB Standards

The IASB conceptual framework—*Framework for the Preparation and Presentation of Financial Statements*—provides theoretical inputs necessary to develop high-quality, coherent and consistent accounting standards. The conceptual framework (IASB 1989) identifies the objectives of financial statements, sets forth the assumptions underlying financial statements, determines the kinds of financial statements that are to be prepared, explains the qualitative characteristics of financial reporting information, defines the basic elements of financial statements, specifies the criteria as to the recognition and measurement of the elements of financial statements and outlines the concept of capital that an entity should adopt. The conceptual framework is founded on the notion of giving primacy to the balance sheet (statement of financial position). Accordingly, assets and liabilities have come to be viewed as the primary focus of financial reporting. The idea underlying the awarding of primacy to the balance sheet is that the sanctity of the balance sheet is to be maintained by shifting the volatility to the income statement.

According to the framework, the purpose of financial statements is to provide information about the reporting entity that is useful to all stakeholders of the entity. The framework considers capital providers as being the primary users of financial statements. This is because capital providers are the ultimate risk takers of the entity. It is, however, asserted that the provision of financial statements that meet the needs of capital providers will also meet the needs of a broad range of other users. To realize the objective of financial reporting, it is necessary to provide information about an entity's assets, liabilities, equity, income and expenses (including gains and losses), contributions by and distributions to shareholders, and cash flows.

Although the conceptual framework is intended to guide accounting standard setters, it is also capable of assisting those responsible for the preparation and presentation of financial statements. The preparers of financial statements are likely to encounter financial reporting issues that are not specifically addressed in the prevailing standards and interpretations. They have to use judgement in developing appropriate accounting policies to deal with those issues. While using judgement, they are to give due consideration to the definitions, recognition criteria, and measurement concepts for assets, liabilities, income, and expenses provided in the framework.

There are aspects of the IASB conceptual framework that are not fully developed. There are also some inconsistencies in the ways in which conceptual issues are dealt with. As a result, the framework often fails to provide sufficient direction for the development of standards. The framework's definition of assets and liabilities appears to be flawed. The most glaring defect of the framework lies in the way in which it approaches the measurement issue. The IASB has admitted that there are shortcomings in the existing framework and has undertaken, in collaboration with the US FASB, a project to rebuild it.[8]

1.4.2 Mini IFRS

IFRS is a rigorous set of standards tailored for companies that are exposed to the capital markets. The standards are not relevant to small- and medium-sized entities (SMEs), which are estimated to represent more than 95 per cent of all companies. Most of these entities do not have the resources to adopt the full set of IFRS. To serve the needs of SMEs, the IASB has developed a simplified version of IFRS (IASB 2009b). SMEs are defined in different jurisdictions in different ways. The IASB in its new standard defines SMEs as entities that do not have public accountability and publish general purpose financial statements. The mini IFRS is about 15 per cent of the length of full IFRS (PwC 2009). It simplifies the principles of recognition and measurement of assets, liabilities, revenues and expenses. It also reduces disclosure requirements to a great extent. Topics that are not relevant to SMEs have been excluded. If it is found that a transaction or event being encountered by an entity is not addressed by the IFRS for SMEs, judgement will then be used in determining an appropriate accounting policy for that transaction or event. The entity may also refer to the main body of IFRS for guidance in the matter. But this is optional. IFRS for SMEs may be adopted by a country or jurisdiction even if it has not adopted the full IFRS. Sir David Tweedie, IASB Chairman, in a Press Release dated 9 July 2009 said:

> The publication of IFRS for SMEs is a major breakthrough for companies throughout the world. For the first time, SMEs will have a common high quality and internationally respected set of accounting requirements. We believe the benefits will be felt in both developed and emerging economies (<http://go.iasb.org/IFRSforSMEs>)

The IASC Foundation is developing comprehensive training material to support proper implementation of the IFRS for SMEs.

1.4.3 First-time Adoption of IFRS

As an entity moves from domestic GAAP to IFRS, it has to adhere to certain formalities. IFRS 1 deals with those formalities (IASB 2001). The overriding principle of IFRS 1 is full retrospective application of all applicable IASB pronouncements. According to the standard, a first-time adopter is required to prepare an opening IFRS statement of financial position (balance sheet) as a starting point for its IFRS reporting. The statement has to be prepared in accordance with the recognition and measurement rules prescribed under all applicable IASB pronouncements. The standard requires disclosures that explain how the transition from previous domestic GAAP to IFRS has affected the reported financial position, financial performance and cash flows of the entity. Limited exemptions are granted in specified areas where the cost of complying with the requirements would exceed the benefits to users of financial statements.

1.5 Worldwide Adoption of IFRS

IFRS is being implemented by countries in two different ways: outright adoption and convergence. Outright adoption occurs when a country abandons its domestic standards in favour of a full set of IFRS. This is known as the 'big bang' approach. The adoption of IFRS in its entirety involves incurring one-time costs, the magnitude of which may at times be quite high. If the adoption route is adopted, adequate preparation is needed. Outright adoption may be risky if all the parties involved in financial reporting are not familiar with the new system. Migrating to IFRS may be more than a technical change in many jurisdictions. It may involve adoption of a completely new culture and new ways of doing things. However, for jurisdictions that do not have their own standard-setting machinery, direct adoption appears to be the only alternative.

Under the second approach, domestic standards are adjusted on a step-by-step basis to make them compatible with IFRS. This is a time-consuming process but it does ensure a smooth and least costly transition for both preparers and users of financial statements. As mentioned earlier, IFRS is currently being used in more than 100 countries. In approximately two-thirds of these countries, IFRS reporting is a requirement for all domestic, listed companies. In other countries, reporting under IFRS is a permissible alternative. An endeavour is now being made to offer a brief description of the current status of worldwide adoption of IFRS. The adoption status is shown by continent/region.[9] We begin with Europe, which has been well ahead of the rest of the world in the matter of adoption of IFRS.

1.5.1 Europe

Europe has been at the forefront of continents in the matter of implementation of IFRS. In an effort to create a single European securities market, the European Union published the IAS Regulation (EC) 1606/2002 in 2002, which required EU-listed companies to use IFRS in the preparation and presentation of their consolidated financial statements as from 2005. The EU countries have also the option to use IFRS in the preparation of financial statements of unlisted companies and also in the preparation of unconsolidated financial statements. A number of EU countries (e.g., Denmark, Greece and Italy) have extended IFRS requirements to the individual financial statements of listed companies. In many EU countries (e.g., Ireland, Spain and UK), moves are currently underway to align domestic GAAP with IFRS.

In Europe, IFRS is being used not only in EU member countries but also in several other jurisdictions. IFRS has been adopted in countries such as Albania, Georgia, Macedonia and Moldova. Russian Federation permits IFRS for listed companies and it has made IFRS a requirement for Russian commercial banks in respect of stand-alone financial statements. In 2004, the Ministry of Finance announced detailed plans for full adoption of IFRS. The plans have not yet been implemented. Full transition to IFRS is expected to take place from 2011.

1.5.2 Asia

IFRS has been implemented in many parts of Asia. There are many Asian countries where IFRS is required for both consolidated and stand-alone financial statements. They include Armenia, Israel, Kazakhstan, Lebanon, Pakistan, Philippines and Turkey. There are some countries and jurisdictions in Asia that have domestic accounting standards which closely mirror IFRS. Examples include Hong Kong and Singapore. Moreover, in a number of Asian countries, the process of adoption of IFRS is currently in progress. For example, in India the process of adoption of IFRS will begin in April 2011. It was earlier announced by the Institute of Chartered Accountants of India (ICAI) that IFRS would be mandatory in India for financial statements for the periods beginning on or after 1 April, 2011. But the Ministry of Corporate Affairs (MCA) has announced a revised timeline for the adoption of IFRS in India. According to the revised schedule, IFRS adoption in India will take place in a phased manner. Companies with net worth of Rs. 1,000 crores and those which are part of BSE Sensex, NIFTY and companies listed in overseas stock exchanges will be required to adopt Indian accounting standards converged with IFRS from April 2011. All companies with net worth between Rs. 500 crores and Rs. 1,000 crores should adopt the converged standards from April 2013. The adoption date for all companies with net worth of Rs. 500 crores or less will be April 2014.

The MCA has also announced a revised timeline for adoption of converged standards by insurance companies, banking companies and non-banking finance companies (NBFCs). The process will begin with insurance companies who will be required to adopt converged standards from April 2012. For banks and non-banking finance companies the timeline will be April 2013.

Since Indian accounting standards have been developed after giving due consideration to the prevailing international standards, there is a great deal of similarity between the two sets of standards. The few gaps and inconsistencies that are still present can be eliminated without much difficulty. Therefore, India's transition to IFRS is not going to be a difficult task. Even then, the ICAI is taking all possible measures to ensure that the necessary infrastructure is in place before IFRS is fully implemented in India.

Korea and Japan have also announced that they will embrace IFRS. Companies (other than financial institutions) in Korea are currently permitted to use IFRS. According to the Roadmap announced in 2007, the adoption of IFRS will be mandatory for all listed companies from 2011. Japan will take a little longer to move to IFRS. The Business Accounting Council (BAC), a key advisory body to the Commissioner of the Financial Services Agency (FSA), approved in June 2009 a roadmap for the adoption of IFRS in Japan. The roadmap provides for early adoption of IFRS by listed companies beginning 1 April 2009 and it proposes mandatory adoption from 2016. Since Japan is the second largest economy in the world, its decision to go for mandatory adoption of IFRS will further accelerate the movement towards global accounting standards. While commenting on the Japanese roadmap of adoption of IFRS, Sir David Tweedie said[10]:

> This is a landmark decision, both for Japan and for IFRSs. For Japan, it signals the eventual adoption of IFRSs. For the IASB, adoption of IFRSs by the world's second largest national economy underscores the truly global nature of IFRSs and the acceptance of these standards by all major economies.

China has discarded its old accounting system and is adopting IFRS. It is doing so by issuing its own national interpretation of IFRS. In February 2006, the China Accounting Standards Committee (CASC) adopted a comprehensive set of New Chinese Accounting Standards (CAS) that cover nearly all topics addressed in IFRS. The standards have become mandatory for listed companies with effect from 1 January 2007. Listed companies are currently being required to adhere to these standards. The standards will gradually be extended to other entities. Since China is not a market economy, there are some difficulties in adopting IFRS in full. The differences that exist between 'pure' IFRS and its Chinese equivalent are not quite significant. One major difference relates to related party disclosures. The IASB standard on related party disclosures (IAS 24) generally requires related-party transactions to be disclosed. Because most Chinese companies are state-owned, they are in a sense related. If the requirements laid down in IAS 24 were to be implemented in China, the size of annual reports would be unduly lengthy. Accordingly, a modified version of the standard has been adopted.

1.5.3 Africa

Most of the economically significant countries in Africa, especially those having stock exchanges, have adopted IFRS. The countries that have already made IFRS reporting mandatory include Botswana, Kenya, Malawi, Namibia, South Africa, Swaziland, Tanzania, Uganda, Zambia and Zimbabwe. In some of these countries, local adaptations have been made. But these adapted versions are not much different from pure IFRS.

South Africa is one of the early adopters of IFRS. Listed companies in this country have been applying IFRS for a considerable period of time. Countries that are now adopting IFRS are looking to published financial statements of South African companies to obtain an indication of how IFRS financial statements are prepared. South Africa has actively participated in the IASB project on extractive industries.

There are some African countries that require IFRS for certain categories of entities. Morocco is an example in this respect. According to the prevailing rule, Morocco permits IFRS for consolidated financial statements, but it is a requirement for consolidated financial statements of banks and other financial institutions. A similar situation prevails in Mozambique. In this country, IFRS is not generally required. But it is obligatory when it comes to financial institutions and large investment companies.

1.5.4 North America

North American countries have been rather slow to embrace IFRS. In Canada, public accountable enterprises will be required to report under IFRS from 1 January 2011. Mexico has undertaken a plan to migrate to IFRS from 2012. The United States (US) has not yet adopted IFRS. The US happens to be largest economy in the world and it has the largest capital market of the world in terms of market capitalization. If IFRS is to establish itself as a truly global financial reporting language, it is to gain acceptance in the US. Since 2002, the US Financial Accounting Standards Board (FASB) and the IASB have been working towards promoting convergence between US GAAP and IFRS. The ultimate goal of this convergence is to produce a single, high-quality set of accounting standards for global use. The two boards have coordinated and integrated their operations in order to end inconsistencies between US GAAP and IFRS. Under the Norwalk Agreement reached between the FASB and the IASB in 2002 and subsequent memoranda of understanding (MoUs), the boards are taking the best solution from either US GAAP or IFRS or jointly developing entirely new standards where none has satisfactory solutions. As a result of the convergence initiatives, many of the inconsistencies between the two sets of standards have been removed. In view of this, the US SEC has removed the US GAAP reconciliation requirement in respect of foreign companies that report under IFRS. The new rule has become effective for fiscal years ending after November 2007. Foreign companies that elect to submit IFRS financial statements must state explicitly and unreservedly in the notes to their financial statements that their financial statements are in compliance with IFRS as issued by IASB.

The SEC has also issued a road map that could lead to regulations requiring the US companies to file their financial statements using IFRS by 2014 or by 2011 for companies that volunteer (SEC 2008). It has expressed the belief that a staged transition would help mitigate the costs of the shift to issuers and the resource demands on auditors, consultants and others. The proposal of the SEC was initially announced at its open meeting on 27 August 27 2008. It was formally confirmed in a notice-and-comment release issued on 14 November 2008.

1.5.5 South America

Countries in South America with strong ties with the UK have been using IFRS for a long time. In the remaining parts of the continent, US GAAP has been the principal driving force in regulating corporate financial reporting. But things are now changing. IFRS has started to make its presence felt in a big way. As most Latin American countries are now working towards implementation of IFRS, it is expected that within a few years, the whole continent will adopt IFRS. The Latin American countries that have already embraced full IFRS include Costa Rica, Dominican Republic, Nicaragua, Panama, Peru and Venezuela (Hannon 2005). IFRS is going to be implemented in Chile from 2009. Brazil is moving to IFRS from 2010. The Securities and Exchange Commission of Brazil issued in 2007[11] a rule requiring listed companies to publish their consolidated financial statements according to IFRS, starting with reporting periods ending in 2010. Use of IFRS will be optional for these companies from 2007 through 2009.

1.5.6 Australia

Australia is a pioneering country in the matter of adoption of IFRS. One of the objectives of the Australian Accounting Standards Board (AASB), which is the body responsible for developing accounting standards for Australian companies, is to participate in and contribute to the development of a single set of accounting standards for worldwide use. The AASB has implemented IFRS in Australia through the promulgation of Australian equivalents of IFRS (A-IFRS). A-IFRS reporting began in Australia in 2005. Currently, Australia has a differential reporting regime. Full A-IFRS reporting is applicable to entities in respect of which there are users who are dependent on general purpose financial statements for information which will be useful to them for making economic decisions. There are some differences between A-IFRS and IFRS. The AASB is working on a project to judge whether the differences that currently exist between A-IFRS and IFRS could be abolished altogether.

New Zealand has adopted a version of IFRS (New Zealand Equivalents to IFRS), which is required for all companies unless they are not issuers, are not overseas owned and are not large. The NZ-IFRS and IFRS are similar but not the same. Even then, New Zealand is regarded as an IFRS-compliant country.

Worldwide adoption of IFRS is taking place at a fairly rapid pace. The pace is expected to accelerate further once the US SEC takes its final decision as to mandatory adoption of IFRS by US domestic companies.

1.6 Some Unfinished Business

The IASB is working hard to provide the world with a common language for financial reporting. Its progress to date is quite satisfactory and the worldwide adoption of IFRS is on track. The time has now come when the IASB should pay greater attention to improving the quality of its pronouncements. Although the IASB standards currently in force are considered to be comprehensive enough to help generate high-quality financial reporting information, gaps and inconsistencies do persist. Many are inclined to believe that IFRS has not yet become the 'gold standard' of financial reporting and that further steps are needed to bring about improvement in its quality. There are several areas where improvement is necessary. The IASB appears to be undecided as to how it should approach fair value measurement. Its prevailing revenue accounting standard does not provide adequate guideline for enterprises that generate revenue from complex processes. The existing IFRS requirements relating to consolidation has several problems associated with them.

There are a number of IASB standards that permit alternative accounting treatments. Permitting alternative accounting treatments may impede comparability. It may also create opportunities for earnings management. When alternative treatments are permitted, entities may be induced to choose the treatment that makes their financial figures more attractive. The IASB is aware of this possibility. It has eliminated alternative treatment from many of its standards. Efforts are being made to eliminate the remaining ones to the extent feasible.

There are aspects of accounting requirements under IFRS that appear to be complex and obscure (Ernst & Young 2009). Complexity in accounting requirements impedes transparency. It is true that complex transactions require complex solutions. But unnecessary complexity should be avoided. Efforts should be made to keep things as simple as possible. Complexity in IFRS is currently encountered especially in the spheres of accounting for financial instruments, share-based payments and post-employment benefits including pensions. IAS 39, which deals with derivatives, is possibly the most complex IASB standard currently in force. IFRS is generally principle based. But IAS 39 has been developed in a different way. The standard contains huge prescriptive rules. As a result, it has become too complex.

IFRS reporting requires huge disclosure requirements many of which are indeed very complex. The IASB has undertaken initiatives to address the complexity issue. Efforts are being made to make accounting standards more user friendly. The newly developed IFRS for SMEs has eased the problems of financial reporting for thousands of companies around the world.

As economies are becoming more and more knowledge driven, greater emphasis is being placed on knowledge-based assets. In many enterprises, knowledge-based assets have become the key driver of value. But the existing accounting system fails to reflect these assets on the balance sheet. Under the existing system, expenditures on knowledge assets are expensed when incurred. The IASB has an accounting standard on intangible assets (IAS 38) but that standard is not adequately geared for addressing the issues of knowledge-based assets in a systematic and rational way. The IASB needs to work through the issues and formulate appropriate mechanisms for increasing the visibility of knowledge-based intangible assets.

The financial reporting framework developed by the IASB is focused on the form and content of the basic financial statements. It does not deal with the information that the companies provide on a supplementary basis outside the basic financial statements in order to provide a cohesive picture of their status and performance. It is now being believed that information outside the basic financial statements has a very important role to play in providing an improved understanding of the current events and future prospects of the business. The size of corporate annual reports has expanded considerably in recent years. Much of this has occurred in response to the growing need for accommodating information not encompassed by the basic financial statements. But since information outside the basic financial statements is the exclusive domain of company management, there is lack of uniformity among companies in the way in which this information is provided. The IASB should think of developing a standardized framework for providing additional information so as to make the information comparable across companies.

If IFRS emerges as global accounting standards, it will mean assumption of monopoly power by the IASB. It has been argued from some quarters that monopoly in accounting standard setting may give rise to some problems. If lower quality standards are promulgated, that will impair the quality of financial reporting. It is also feared that lack of competition in accounting standard setting may retard innovation and progress (Hail et al. 2009: 7). This is an issue that needs to be addressed.

There are a number of countries where there is a local version of IFRS. In many countries, IFRS requirements have been modified in order to reflect local conditions. Even the EU has its own version of IFRS. Local variation of IFRS may undermine the comparability of financial statements. Since users cannot be expected to keep track of the jurisdictional versions of IFRS, efforts should be made to ensure that IFRS is used in the form issued by the IASB.

1.7 Conclusion

IFRS has made great strides in establishing itself as the *lingua franca* of the accounting world. IFRS reporting has already begun in many parts of the world. Currently, there are more than 12,000 companies in approximately 110 countries that are reporting under IFRS. However, much remains to be done to realize the goal of having a truly global financial reporting regime. IFRS is still to gain acceptance in some parts of the world. Uncertainties still prevail as to the US adoption of IFRS. Although the US SEC has removed reconciliation requirement for foreign private issuers that file their IFRS financial statements, it is still not clear when and how US companies will be allowed to use IFRS. US GAAP and IFRS represent two different financial reporting regimes. Much of US GAAP is rules-driven, while IFRS is predominantly a principle-based requirement. It is difficult to bring the two regimes together in a converged way.

Achieving comparability in financial reporting among countries is a very important goal. To realize this goal, it is essential to adhere to a common set of accounting standards. But having a common set of standards is not sufficient. To achieve comparability in financial reporting, it is also necessary to have uniformity in the way the applicable standards are implemented. As there is no global enforcement authority, difficulties are being encountered in achieving uniformity in the application of IFRS. Concerted efforts are needed to address the application problem. It has to be ensured that countries reporting under IFRS have in place an appropriate matching infrastructure of strong corporate governance practices and effective regulatory oversight and enforcement. Without this, the desired goal of having international comparability in financial reporting cannot be achieved.

If the IASB is to function as truly global accounting standard-setting body, it has to be ensured that its independence is not jeopardized. One of the preconditions for maintaining independence is to have a stable funding mechanism. According to the prevailing system, IASB has to depend on voluntary contributions from private companies, accounting firms, international organizations and central banks. It may be equitable if funds are procured through imposing levies on IFRS-user companies based on turnover or some other financial reporting variable. There are powerful lobbying groups that tend to exert pressures on the IASB to bend accounting standards in favour of a particular interest. Most recently, the IASB had to modify its accounting rule relating to fair value accounting under pressure from the EU regulators. This is not a good sign. If this is allowed to continue, the quality of IFRS will be impaired and, as a result, investors' interests may be jeopardized.

The setting of accounting standards is an ongoing and constantly evolving process. Standards have to be revised and upgraded on a regular and timely basis to keep pace with the evolving business environment. Standard setters should always strive for delivering the best system of financial reporting by companies. This is not an easy task especially when the standards being developed and maintained are designed to serve the information needs of the participants in the global capital markets. As the IASB is emerging as the sole accounting standard setter of the world, it will have to assume greater responsibility and serve the interests of all by keeping its financial reporting framework compatible and consistent with latest developments.

Notes

1. The International Accounting Standards Board (IASB) Web site—www.iasb.org
2. *Emerging Markets Weekly*, Issue #3, February 2008.
3. Statement before the Committee on Banking, Housing and Urban Affairs of US Senate, Washington DC, 14 June 2006. http//www.iasb.org
4. There are a variety of factors that are responsible for international diversity in financial reporting. Interested readers may refer to Gray (1988), Cook and Wallace (1990), Meek and Saudagaran (1990), Basu (1995; 2008), Doupnik and Salter (1995), Gernon and Meek (2001), Iqbal (2002), Nobes and Parker (2002), Larson and Street (2006) and Pounder (2009) for obtaining a greater insight into the nature and causes of inter-country financial reporting diversity.

5. Following a decision at the January 2009 Trustees meeting, the IASB will be expanded to 16 members by 2012.
6. SEC Concepts Release: *International Accounting Standards 2000* (February). www.sec.gov./rule/concept
7. In its narrower sense, IFRS refers to the individual new numbered series of standards being promulgated by the IASB.
8. Basu (2009) provides a detailed analysis of the IASB–FASB joint project to remodel the conceptual framework of accounting.
9. Detailed information about the adoption of IFRS by country can be had from a recent publication by PricewaterhouseCoopers (PwC 2009a).
10. The Ministry of Corporate Affairs (MCA) has revised the timeline for the adoption of IFRS in India. According to the revised schedule, IFRS adoption in India will take place in a phased manner.
11. IASB Announcements and Speeches, 12 June 2009: 'Japan takes major steps towards IFRS adoption'. www.iasb.org
12. *Source*: The Securities and Exchange Commission of Brazil, Rule No. 457. www.cvm.gov br

References

Anderson, A. (1993). 'The Globalization GAAP'. *Management Accounting*, August, pp 52–54.

Basu, A. K. (1995). *International Accounting Harmonisation*. DSA in Commerce, University of Calcutta, Kolkata, India.

———(2008). *Accounting Standards and the Standard Regime in India*. IAA Research Foundation, Kolkata, India.

———(2009). 'Remodelling the Conceptual Framework of Accounting: Perspective and Prognosis'. In U. Bhattacharyya (ed.), *Studies in Accounting, Finance and Management: Contemporary Issues*. Netaji Subhas Open University, Kolkata, India.

Cook, T. E. and Wallace, O. R. S. (1990). 'Financial Disclosure Regulation and Its Environment: A Review and Further Analysis'. *Journal of Accounting and Public Policy*, vol. 9, pp 79–110.

Deloitte & Touche LLP (2008). *2008 IFRS Survey: Where Are We Today*? Deloitte Development LLC. http://www.iasplus.com/dttpubs/2008ifrssurvey.pdf

Doupnik, T. S. and Salter, S. B. (1995). 'External Environment, Culture, and Accounting Practice: A Preliminary Test of a General Model of International Accounting Development'. *International Journal of Accounting*, 30(2).

Ernst & Young (2009). *International GAAP 2009*. John Wiley & Sons.

Financial Accounting Standards Board (FASB) (2006). *SFAS 157: Fair Value Measurements*. FASB, Norwalk, CT.

Gernon, H. and Meek, G. K. (2001). *Accounting : An International Perspective*. McGraw Hill, New York.

Gray, S. J. (1988). 'Towards a Theory of Cultural Influence on the Development of Accounting Systems Internationally'. *Abacus*, vol. 24, pp 1–15.

Hail, L., Leuz, C. and Wysocki, P. D. (2009). *Global Accounting Convergence and the Potential Adoption of IFRS by the United States: An Analysis of Economic and Policy Factors*. Available at SSRN:http://ssm/con/abstract=1357331

Hannon, N. (2005). 'XBRL and IFRS in Latin America'. *Strategic Finance*, 1 February.

Institute of Chartered Accountants of Scotland (ICAS) (2006). *Principles not Rules: A Question of Judgement*. ICAS, Edinburgh, UK.

International Accounting Standards Board (IASB) (1989). *Framework for the Preparation and Presentation of Financial Statements*. IASB, London.

———(2001). *IFRS 1: First-time Adoption of International Financial Reporting Standards*. IASB, London.

———(2007). *IAS 1: Presentation of Financial Statements*. IASB, London.

———(2009a). *Exposure Draft (ED/2009/5): Fair Value Measurement.* IASB, London.

———(2009b). International *Financial Reporting Standards for Small and Medium-sized Entities.* IASB, London.

IASC Foundation (2006). *Due Process Handbook for the International Accounting Standards Board (IASB)*. IASCF, London.

International Chamber of Commerce (ICC) (2005). *Improving the Quality of Financial and Business Reporting*, ICC, Paris, France.

Iqbal, Z. M. (2002). *International Accounting: A Global Perspective.* South Western, Cincinnati, OH.

Jacob, R. A. and Madu, C. N. (2004). 'Are We Approaching a Universal Accounting Language in Five Years?'. *Foresight*, vol. 6, no. 4, pp 356–363.

Lamoreaux, M. (2009). 'G-20: Achieve Single Set of Global Accounting Standards by June 2011'. *Journal of Accountancy*, September (editorial).

Larson, R. K. and Street, D. L. (2006). 'Roadmap to Global Accounting Convergence'. *The CPA Journal, October* pp 36–43.

Meek, G. K. and Saudagaran, S. M. (1990). 'A Survey of Research on Financial Reporting in a Transnational Context'. *Journal of Accounting Literature*, vol. 9, pp 145–182.

Nobes, C. W. and Parker, R. (2002). *Comparative International Accounting* (7e), Prentice Hall, London.

Pounder, B. (2009). *Convergence Guide Book for Corporate Financial Reporting.* John Wiley & Sons, Inc.

PricewaterhouseCoopers (PwC) (2009). *IFRS Adoption by Country.* http://www.pwc.com/_US/us/issues/ifrs-reporting/assets/ifrs_country_adoption.pdf

———(2009a). *IFRS for Small and Medium-sized Entities Pocket Guide Book.* http://www.pwc.com/en_GX/gx/ifrs-reporting/pdf/IFRSSME09.pdf

Securities and Exchange Commission (SEC) (2008). *Roadmap for the Potential Use of Financial Statements Prepared in Accordance with International Financial Reporting Standards (IFRS) by US Issuers.* www.sec.gov/rules/proposed/2008/33-8982.pdf

Tiffin, R. (2007). *The Complete Guide to International Financial Reporting Standards* (2e). Viva Books Pvt. Ltd.

CHAPTER 2

Full Cost Accounting—A Stepping Stone for Corporate Sustainability Reporting

Kanika Chatterjee

ABSTRACT

As a strong behavioural driver within a company, corporate accounting and reporting should recognize extra-organizational concerns as social and environmental impacts of doing business, because of the widening sphere of corporate responsibility to an increasing number of stakeholderships under the imperative of sustainable development. Corporate sustainability management relies heavily upon business initiatives in redefining 'sustainable' enterprise performance through a balanced interpretation of the social, environmental and economic aspects.

Against this background, full cost accounting (FCA) helps reckon the 'full' social and environmental costs of a particular activity or product to society and ecosystems, so that externalities, i.e., costs not conventionally borne by the responsible entity, can be effectively internalized as the costs of doing business. FCA champions the idea of 'total' capital (natural, social, human, manufactured and financial) maintenance, by reflecting what it would cost an accounting entity at the end of the accounting period, to return the planet and biosphere to the state existing at the beginning. FCA can revolutionize the intellectual foundation of accounting through enhanced visibility of life-cycle costs from a buyer's standpoint at the time of purchase, and from the producer's standpoint when deciding to commence production.

This paper seeks to (i) distinguish between the contemporary and traditional notions of FCA, (ii) identify emerging approaches to internalize externalities for FCA, (iii) clarify the FCA methodology, (iv) outline the potential benefits of FCA to build a strong business case for its adoption, and (v) highlight various implementation issues surrounding FCA by referring to the celebrated real-world case of Ontario Hydro.

2.1 Introduction

As a socio-technical system within organizations, an accounting information system is recognized as a strong driver of individual and collective human behaviour. Despite this reality, historically, the social and environmental impacts of engaging in business were overlooked and squarely excluded from the purview of accounting information systems (unless an entity's profitability was affected), because of the predominant financial focus of accounting under the yoke of financial capitalism. The omission of such impacts appeared justifiable on the basis of a straightforward economic logic that expresses the long-range sustainability perspective of an enterprise in terms of the need for investment, inducing the accumulation of capital that encourages higher profit levels.

In present times, with the business community being steadily recognized as an influential social institution and an indispensable partner in delivering the social/environmental realities associated with sustainable development, the so-called extra-organizational non-financial concerns, commonly known in economics as 'externalities', are widening the sphere of corporate responsibility to an extensive circle of stakeholders. A focus on profits is often presented as a short-termist, myopic perspective that is either indispensable or immoral, depending upon the polarity of viewpoints adopted. A compromise between these two extreme views gives rise to the concept of 'enlightened capitalism' that underscores two important ideas: (i) it is possible to increase profits by improving social and environmental performances, and (ii) the strategic objective of long-term profitability is considerably undermined by pursuing short-term profit maximization. Thus, adoption of a sustainability vision that recognizes the need to integrate social, environmental and economic performance criteria can reinforce environmental and social sustainability (Sen 2001; Stiglitz 2002), bringing in its fold, pervasive benefits at the planetary and societal levels.

Academia posits that a sustainable global economy can emerge only through an era of intense technological, economic, social and political metamorphosis (Elkington 2001) with current unsustainable patterns of wealth creation, measurement and distribution as a key driver of action. The dysfunctional economic prosperity of today's civilization is based upon rampant destruction of natural and social capital in the mindless chase towards global financial capitalism. This has caused a yawning divide between the powerful rich and the disfranchised poor. Acts of terror staged globally show us that absolute and relative poverty are critical issues that cannot be ignored in the near future. Current patterns of wealth creation under global financial capitalism inherently spiral off into a vicious circle of worsening environmental and social problems, obliging large business enterprises like multinational corporations (or MNCs) and national governments—the two most dominant social institutions of our time—to expedite the transition towards sustainable development.

The pursuit of sustainability couches the development debate within a global context, in which continuous fulfilment of the survival needs of both human and non-human society on this planet is the ultimate goal of all human endeavours, including business. When this global ethic applies to a business enterprise, corporate sustainability becomes a guiding principle asking corporate managers to anticipate and meet the needs of the present generation of a firm's direct (e.g., shareholders, employees and customers/clients) and indirect stakeholders (e.g., pressure groups, communities, etc), such that its ability to meet those of future stakeholders (i.e., unborn generations) is not compromised (Dyllick and Hockerts 2002: 131). Corporate evolution towards sustainability relies on proactive, integrated and collaborative managerial initiatives. Accordingly, accountants as information service providers within the managerial team are compelled to shun their traditional mind-set obsessed with the demands of financial capitalism, and recognize their obligations that are implicit in the imperative of sustainable development. This required shift should transform the accountant's traditional role in respect of: (i) measurement of a firm's impacts arising out of resource consumption for business activities by including wider environmental/social issues at the global and planetary scale, and (ii) reporting of these impacts through a balanced interpretation of sustainability in terms of integrating the triple bottom line (TBL) aspects—social, environmental and economic—of enterprise performance.

2.1.1 Major Objectives of the Present Study

Against this background, the following are the major objectives of this paper:

1. To identify the inherent inadequacies in traditional accounting systems vis-à-vis the prerequisites of sustainability.
2. To establish the need for FCA adoption as a foundation for transforming sustainability reporting into a mainstream corporate communication tool.
3. To distinguish between the emerging notion of FCA and its traditional connotation.
4. To delineate the goal and nature of FCA.
5. To build a business case defending FCA adoption in the future.
6. To identify potential approaches for internalization of business-related externalities for FCA application.
7. To articulate an appropriate FCA methodology relevant for business.
8. To highlight significant implementation issues regarding FCA by showcasing the experiences of Ontario Hydro, a Canadian enterprise, acclaimed to be the pioneer of FCA in the world of business.

2.2 Inadequacies of Traditional Accounting vis-à-vis Sustainable Development

Traditional accounting paradigms based upon economic theories of efficiency, optimality, and profit maximization are inadequate to meet the contemporary challenges of sustainability-oriented decision making. In this regard, Gray (1997) maintains that "the emptiness of financial accounting theory, the perniciousness of an accounting-centred world and the criminally vacuous economic theory on which it is based" are easy targets for criticism within the traditional accounting literature at a time of mounting concern about the ill-managed adverse ecological and social impacts of doing business under free-market financial capitalism.

The principal reason that can explain the perceived gap in the traditional accounting paradigm is the interrelatedness of accounting and accountability (Gray and Bebbington 1996). If accountability relationships evolve in terms of the three main participants in the accounting information process—(1) the *accountees* (to whom accounts must be given), (2) the *accountors* (whom the accountees hold accountable), and (3) the *accountants* (who develop and use accounting techniques for a healthy accountability relationship between these two parties)—then accounting is bound to change accordingly. Environmental accountability represents one such novel challenge for dealing with this crisis, as also do many other major social and ethical concerns like fair trade, exploitative marketing, gender discrimination, abuse of child labour and money laundering. The crisis in accounting further intensifies if together with new accounting issues, new accountees emerge on the scene, demanding their right to know. More and more parties to an accountability relationship imply a larger and more diverse population of stakeholders, i.e., all those individuals and groups whose benefits and costs are affected favourably or adversely by the objectives, decisions and actions of an organization. Thus, the widening spectrum of environmental and social concerns is leading to a steady increase in the stakeholder population.

This brings two important issues to light. Firstly, an *increasing number of accountees* (i.e., stakeholders) are becoming *more aware of their claims* (to decision-relevant information) and are, therefore, demanding fair and transparent *information about many new aspects* (i.e., ethical violations and failures) regarding enterprise performance. In this respect, adverse environmental aspects, e.g., climate change, water scarcity, loss of habitat and biodiversity, and dwindling natural resources, figure prominently when it becomes necessary to assess whether stakeholder utility or welfare is negatively affected; in that case, the question of claiming compensation by those harmed ought to arise in accordance with the ethical tenet of distributive justice. Secondly, traditional corporate accounting and reporting systems have not yet been subject to fundamental restructuring to support the sustainable development ethic, but continue to reflect their obsession with a narrow view of social and economic reality anchored on unsustainable production and consumption, which is passé. This, of course, is a matter of short-sighted convenience for the accountants, who first developed accounting systems for those items that were easiest to measure, i.e., sums of money, and physical (or tangible items). Intangible items, being contentious, and hence, difficult to measure, have not been handled deftly or have often been totally omitted because they are even more difficult and costly to account for. Thus, accountants have largely concentrated on accounting for the easiest items first.

These two issues point to two major causes behind the crisis in the accounting profession (Lesourd and Schillizi 2001: 102): (1) It cannot and does not feel entitled to acknowledge new stakeholders as new accountees (such as local communities, consumers and the global community); and (2) It is yet to develop fully the right techniques to account for, measure and report to these new stakeholders. Certainly, the second cause induces the first because it undermines the profession's expertise in the face of heightening societal expectations. This crisis also locks accounting and financial analyses in competition with one another. With the increasing prominence of environmental stakeholders, and the advent of environmental accountability and accounting, four types of difficulties crop up:

1. A common framework with standard accounting practices
2. Measurement problems
3. Integration problems
4. Scope or boundary of a firm's environmental accountability

To cope with these difficulties, the horizons of traditional accounting needs to be broadened, thus calling for a three-stage adaptation (Lesourd and Schillizi 2001: 103) in terms of (i) introducing hitherto hidden environmental costs and benefits into accounting practice, (ii) measuring the environmental impacts of the firm's activities and products, and (iii) integrating the financial and ecological consequences of the firm's activities.

2.3 FCA as a Pre-requisite for Mainstream Sustainability Reporting Practice

Giving shape to a sustainable future requires aspirant firms to address the twin challenges of internalization/inclusion and integration as part of organizational learning. Inclusion calls for the progressive engagement of a wide range of external and internal stakeholders, understanding their priorities and meeting their various legitimate needs, including their 'right to know'. The integration challenge takes the form of 'silo-busting', i.e., eliminating the tendency to compartmentalize sustainability thinking, prevalent in most companies today, which is driven by isolated concepts and techniques in vogue, such as corporate social responsibility (CSR), environment, health and safety (EHS), information technology (IT), total quality environmental management (TQEM), shareholder value added (SVA), life cycle analysis (LCA), FCA, corporate environmental reporting (CER), and sustainability accounting and reporting (SAR). In a bid to firmly integrate TBL thinking into corporate strategy and governance, most leading companies across the world have to dismantle their silo-type thinking patterns (Elkington 2004: 14–15). Thus, TBL thinking must be used prudently, and not rendered ineffective by perpetuating parallel activities in silos, devoid of integration. In the TBL conference held in 2003 in Australia and New Zealand, on the theme "Beyond the Triple Bottom Line—Boards, Brands and Business Models", the message that came across unequivocally was that the challenges of integration for promoting corporate sustainability will essentially converge in four key areas:

- Balance sheets focusing on transparency, accountability, reporting and assurance
- Boards underscoring ultimate accountability, corporate governance and strategy
- Brands engaging suppliers, investors, customers and consumers directly in sustainability issues
- Business models urging a movement from the external dimensions of corporate existence to the very DNA of business

These integration challenges for sustainable business may be presented in the form of a 2 × 2 matrix (Exhibit 2.1) by combining the currency of the challenges (shown as the rows) and the source of their solutions (depicted by the columns).

Exhibit 2.1: Matrix Showing Integration Challenges

	Governance-based	Market-based
Emerging challenges	Boards	Business models
Existing challenges	Balance-sheets	Brands

Source: Elkington, 2004, p.15

The matrix above shows that increasing attention needs to be directed towards developing the four kinds of clusters indicated in terms of the role of social entrepreneurs in developing out-of-the-box, leap-frog strategies, business models, product and process technologies, as well as impact measurement and reporting methodologies for addressing the unserved needs of more and more customers constituting the base-of-the-pyramid (BOP) (Prahalad 2005).

The matrix also helps us establish the measurement of the triple bottom line (TBL) as an important management tool for corporate sustainability whereby physical and financial activities of a company can be integrated. It is a challenge facing both the business and the accounting professions to create appropriate metrics to gauge corporate sustainability and to find new forms of accounting and accountability (Elkington 1999). Although this appears to be a major challenge and an uphill task today, experimentation in sustainability accounting, auditing and reporting through the next few decades would pave the way for decisive future action (Elkington 1997: 93) in this direction. Traditional accounting indicators, procedures as well as the guiding rules and principles are strictly regulated by external legislation and professional standards. This, however, is not the case for environmental and social accounting enshrined under sustainability accounting and reporting. Here, indicators are usually determined within the company in the absence of any widely accepted accounting standards or metrics to measure and account for environmental and social activities, or the broader economic impact of doing business. The result is bad information quality vitiating the quality of reports to users (Cerin 2002).

Ever since the early 1990s, when the Association of Chartered Certified Accountants (ACCA) in the UK published the pioneering work of Rob Gray (1990) entitled The *Greening of Accountancy: The Profession After Pearce*, a substantial body of research has emerged on the role of accountancy in sustainable development. Undoubtedly, much of this research has focused on the reporting aspects of environmental accounting. However, the genesis and development of the ISO 14000 family of standards (ISO 1995) for managing and evaluating environmental performance since 1995 has stimulated a growing awareness of the management accountant's role in implementing corporate environmental management systems (SMAC 1997).

Traditionally, costs have had a strong influence on most corporate decisions, irrespective of whether they relate to financial, social or environmental performance. Lately, much of the focus on TBL has been directed on accounting for the environmental dimension. In this respect also, Bennett and James (1998: 20) argue that most of the 'work in the field of environment-related management accounting is that of providing decision-makers and others with a better representation of reality through more accurate knowledge of environmental costs'. The aim of environmental cost accounting as one of the pillars of the TBL is 'to identify where a company is in terms of its environmental impacts, to determine appropriate sustainability targets or standards to aim for, and to work out the most cost-effective way for the company to close that "sustainability gap"' (Howes 2002). In this connection, Parker (1999) found that the environmental accounting techniques such as cost identification and analysis were still in an embryonic stage as compared with the widespread application of environmental policies, environmental management systems (EMS), environmental impact statements (EIA) and environmental audits (EA). Environment-related management accounting focused on managing the environmental costs of doing business has the potential to demonstrate the impact of using natural capital on the income statement, besides helping to identify cost reduction and other improvement opportunities, prioritizing environmental actions, guiding product-pricing mix, enhancing customer value and supporting the development of sustainable business.

Thus, the TBL concept underlying the sustainability reporting framework suggests that an inclusive cost management methodology in the nature of FCA would be required to internalize external costs. FCA enables prices to reflect full environmental costs, which would then flow into the consumption and production chain to reinforce progressively more sustainable patterns of behaviour (O'Dwyer 2001). This view is reinforced in the reporting principle of 'completeness' as provided by the Global Reporting Initiative (GRI) Sustainability Reporting Guidelines 2002 (GRI 2002: 30)—'The process for determining a complete scope may include, for example, the results of lifecycle analysis of products or services and assessment of the full range of direct and indirect social or ecological impacts of the reporting organisation'. As such, FCA is an accounting model providing details on all costs associated with producing a product or service and, hence, enables intending firms to be ready for compliance with the GRI framework.

2.4 Traditional Versus Emerging Views of Full Cost Accounting

The term 'full cost' is by no means a brand new addition to the vocabulary of cost management. As a matter of fact, in traditional cost accounting, the classical approach to analysing overhead costs is also referred to as the 'full cost' or absorption approach in sharp contrast with the increasing relevance of the contribution approach and the activity-based approach in present times. However, it is important to understand that the traditional accounting systems have applied the term 'full cost accounting' to refer to full private (or bottom-line) costs of an activity or an enterprise. It does not account for externalities (i.e., social and environmental impacts), which are treated as costs for which an enterprise is not responsible. These were considered (i) insignificant based on the assumption of infinite supply of natural resources on the planet, (ii) an unavoidable price that society must pay for industrial progress, (iii) irrelevant to the core business processes as well as the bottom-line, and (iv) difficult to estimate and assign as financial values.

Exhibit 2.2 (a): Traditional Approach to Full Cost Accounting

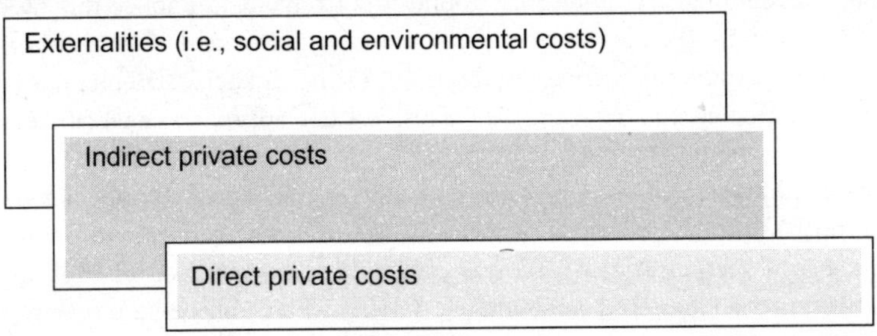

Exhibit 2.2 (b): Emerging Approach to Full Cost Accounting

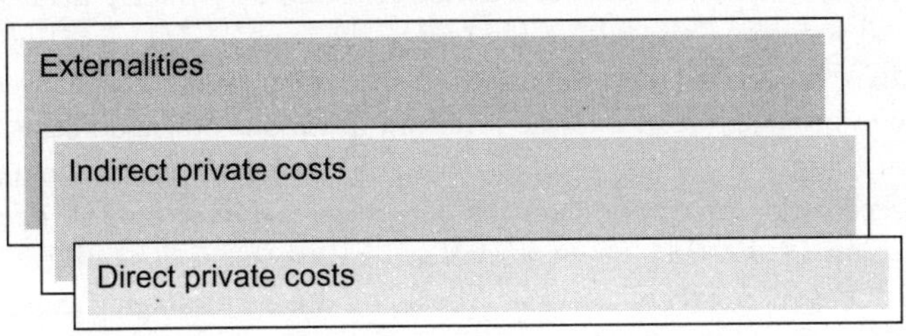

A good example of exclusion of externalities from traditional accounting is that the adverse ecological impacts of climate change and social impacts in the form of health hazards resulting from carbon emissions from automobiles are neither included in the price that consumers pay for petroleum (a revenue cost) nor included as part of the capital cost of acquiring and using a car. In its extended and correct formulation, FCA should refer to all the social and environmental costs of a particular activity or product to the enterprise, to society and to ecosystems. Thus, FCA envisages the need to internalize externalities for reckoning the costs of doing business. Exhibit 2.2 (a) and (b) highlight the difference between traditional and contemporary conceptions of FCA. It will be observed that the shaded area(s) shows the inclusion of cost categories within the analytical framework of costs in business. The unshaded area shows that costs are actually incurred in the course of business operations, but not recognized and charged to the firm.

The new-generation FCA is steadily becoming a significant issue in environmental cost accounting, as an indispensable tool for sustainability-oriented decision making. It serves to enhance the visibility of costs incurred over the entire life-cycle of a product, both from a buyer's viewpoint at the time of purchase, and from the producer's standpoint at the time of deciding to go in for production. Visibility helps improve the accuracy of accounting information by refining cost identification and measurement. Quite often, a manufacturer's costs of waste management (or rather mismanagement!) remain concealed in indirect overhead accounts; these costs are neither activity-based nor product-based. This makes it possible to conveniently allocate a part of the hazardous waste cost of an activity or product to another product that is in no way involved with the release of the hazardous/toxic materials. At the other end of the value chain spectrum are the lowest visibility costs, i.e., costs to society that are downstream costs and hence, difficult to measure. For this reason, conventional accounting has found it convenient to impose this burden on to the community as its overall problem of waste management, not particularly distinguishing one polluter from another. Consequently, they remain undisclosed in the financial statements of the producer as well as the consumer. In this respect, the inclusive FCA approach can help revolutionize the intellectual foundation of the accounting discipline.

The growing popularity of FCA is testified by the several dedicated publications on FCA that the accounting profession has produced over the last decade. The earliest and the most significant effort in sensitizing the accounting profession as well as the corporate sector in this respect is that of the Canadian Institute of Chartered Accountants (CICA) who published a research report in 1997 entitled *Full Cost Accounting from an Environmental Perspective* to encapsulate how to account for internal and external costs and how FCA information can be rendered useful for external and internal users (CICA 1997). The document reported extensively on the Ontario Hydro initiative to develop FCA. The focus of the report was on reorganizing existing costs rather than on internalization of externalities, and so, despite the title of the report, the issue of FCA was not really addressed. However, the CICA report did help in directing the attention of the accounting profession towards FCA and in bringing the idea to the forefront in various public domains. A second major attempt in this direction was that of the Financial and Management Accounting Committee of the International Federation of Accountants (IFAC) which examined the role of the management accounting profession in the field of environmental management. The IFAC report defined a 'cost spectrum' that included external costs and the methodology of costing externalities. However, similar to the CICA study, this report refrained from offering any concrete suggestions for progress in this area. Thirdly, the Society of Management Accountants of Canada (SMAC) has published management accounting guidelines or statements on environmental management accounting. These guidelines draw heavily upon the USEPA cost distinctions, and also outline the Ontario Hydro

FCA experiment. This document is significant in that it contains a discussion on the definitional aspects of FCA. In the UK, the Association of Chartered Certified Accountants (ACCA), in the year 2001, came up with a major publication *Full Cost Accounting: An Agenda for Action* for providing guidance to the accounting profession about how to address the issue of FCA, and participate in its developmental process during these formative years.

2.5 Definition and Nature of FCA

Ever since 1992, when Agenda 21 was formalized as part of the Rio Declaration at the UN Conference on Environment and Development (UNCED), to define the responsibility of business in progressing towards sustainable development, there has been much contemplation about the nature and intent of FCA from several authoritative bodies.

Applying the Hicksian concept of capital maintenance to the preservation of natural capital, Gray (1992) defines FCA as approximating with a 'parallel accounting system which provides calculations of what additional costs must be borne by the organisation if the organisational activity were not to leave the planet worse off, i.e., what it would cost at the end of the accounting period to return the planet and biosphere to the point it was at the beginning of the accounting period'.

One of the pioneer accounting bodies to propel the FCA movement, the CICA (1997: xii) define FCA from an environmental perspective 'as the integration of an entity's internal costs (including all internal environmental costs) with the external costs relating to the impacts of the entity's activities, operations, products and/or services on the environment'.

World Resources Institute, one of the frontrunners in promoting sustainable practices in business globally, capture the viewpoint of FCA that is emerging among accounting practitioners, in the following words (CICA 1997: 88): 'Within the accounting profession, FCA means that all manufacturing, sales and administrative costs are allocated to products. Recently, a number of environmental and business leaders have also used FCA to describe the practice of introducing environmental costs once considered external into corporate decision making. This broader interpretation encompasses the range of private and social costs imposed throughout a product's life cycle, from raw material extraction to product disposal'.

Taking a process perspective of cost management, the International Federation of Accountants (IFAC 1998: 11) view FCA as a 'commonly accepted term applied to the identification, evaluation, and allocation of a combined and potentially complex set of conventional costs, environmental costs and social costs'.

2.5.1 Fundamental Goal of FCA

From an environmental perspective, FCA signifies a process of integration of an entity's internal costs (including all internal environmental costs) with the external costs relating to the impacts of the entity's activities, operations, products and/or services on the environment.

For example, the cost of health-care that arises from pollution-induced respiratory disease is not borne by the organizations that emit pollution and so, they are externalities from the perspective of the pollution emitters. FCA seeks to identify these types of external impacts associated with polluting activities and to estimate the size of these impacts. By this token, a fundamental aim of FCA is to ensure that goods and services are appropriately priced to reflect their true costs through the inclusion of environmental and other social costs.

Regarding the level of cost analysis, it is worth noting that the FCA logic is intended for integrated with national, financial, as well as managerial/cost accounting, depending on the type of accounting system involved. With FCA, natural resources could be factored into calculations of a country's GDP and also redefined as assets on company ledgers, and environmental costs could be built into a product's cost. Within each level of accounting system, the FCA may be used to refer to either the full private (or bottom line) costs to an enterprise of an activity, or more precisely, the full social and environmental costs to society of the activity including externalities (such as health impacts resulting from ozone depletion). Negative externalities are costs not borne by the responsible entity.

The term environmental costs can be used to describe both *private* environmental costs, i.e., the costs that directly impact a firm's bottom line, as well as *public* or *social* environmental costs, i.e., the costs to society as a whole. To date, attempts to focus on improvements in tracking and allocation of environmental costs within management accounting frameworks have focused predominantly on private costs. However, some companies have stepped forward to estimate and include social or 'full' costs in their internal management information systems.

2.6 Business Case for FCA

FCA is one the vital concepts that seeks to work through the current business mechanism for the pursuit of more environmentally sensitive and socially just futures (Bebbington et al. 2001: 13). An early adoption of the FCA approach can be beneficial for business enterprises, irrespective of their history, nature or size. Some of the easily recognizable benefits are as follows:

1. It fosters an organization-wide commitment and participation towards managing sustainability extending beyond the confines of the Environment, Health and Safety (EHS) department.
2. It redirects the attention of the dedicated corporate EHS/environmental management/sustainability departments seeking to manage their costs from a perspective of *who* is providing the service to a perspective of *what* service is being provided to *which* facility, business or other staff unit.
3. It provides an opportunity to corporate EHS/environmental management/sustainability departments to evolve from their earlier misconceived status as an evil, 'other overhead' line item to being increasingly perceived as a customer-oriented, value-added participant in their organization and in the business value chain.
4. It can provide a more accurate picture of the costs and benefits of a product, project, facility or organization.
5. Hence, it provides a powerful incentive to search for the most economic ways to mitigate environmental damage and social harm.
6. It underscores choices that explicitly consider present and future environmental and social impacts of alternative decision options or projects.

7. As a result, resource consumption patterns in businesses are expected to become more efficient and effective.
8. It enables the environmental and social costs of doing business to be assigned, communicated and managed more accurately and transparently.
9. Accordingly, if FCA gains popularity as a standardized approach to cost management, it should help level out the playing field when evaluating demand and supply options in respect of achieving corporate sustainability.

However, the many advantages that FCA can bring to an organization must be weighed against the necessary challenges that must be encountered, at least during the early stages of FCA adoption. In fact, these formidable challenges can be the major deterrents in accepting and adopting FCA despite its potential advantages. These include:

1. **Psychological barrier:** FCA implementation will necessitate radical changes in the accepted accounting practices within a company; hence resistance to change must be managed.
2. **Resource barrier:** A cost managemnt initiative towards designing and implementing FCA would require significant investment of time and other resources to determine whether there will be worthwhile results, no matter whether the market will permit its implementation.
3. **Information barrier:** Evaluations based on FCA may be severely constrained because of the inadequacy of accurate information that forms the basis of this tool.
4. **Leadership barrier:** The favourable results obtainable from adopting FCA may be undermined due to lack of credibility arising out of an absence of management buy-in of the philosophy of corporate sustainability in general, and FCA, in particular.

Fortunately, these implementation barriers are slowly being overcome as organizations learn how to modify their efforts to match their specific company culture and processes.

2.7 Approaches to Internalization of Externalities for FCA Implementation

There are four recognizable ways in which externalities may be internalized for the sake of FCA implementation (Bebbington et al. 2001: 15–22; UNCTAD 1996: 76–77):

1. The *democratic/accountability* approach represents the first move towards sustainability by way of permitting and encouraging members of society to make more sustainable choices and take fewer unsustainable decisions for which the pre-condition would be information for accountability. Effective social and environmental accountability is essential for democracy. At the organizational level, this accountability would be achieved through the development and mandatory application of social and environmental reporting by all organizations predicated upon a society that is increasingly informed with members acting in a more ethical manner. Boycotts, green consumerism, socially responsible investment and action on companies by pressure groups are typical examples of how this approach works. In these ways, some degree of 'getting the prices right' would be achieved because certain economic options that are cheaper but les ethical would be eschewed, while the volumes of production of some goods and services would decline so that current economies of scale would be lost. Some products and services would be driven away from the market, while others would become expensive as costs would become internalized at different points in the life cycle of the product. Economies would, thus, shift both in emphasis and direction.

2. The essence of the *full privatization* approach (Pearce et al. 1989) is that all environmental elements must be embedded in price. Thus, for example, a company's use of air for pollution, water for cooling, silence for making noise, land for waste disposal and natural habitats for mining must be charged to the company. In this way, the use of all these endowments is paid for, so that the organization seeks out cheaper (i.e., less environmentally damaging) options. This, in turn, causes either a reduced demand (and hence, less environmental pressure) or substitution of other goods and services up to the point where society signals that it is compensated for the consumption/destruction of the environmental good that was previously a free, collective 'common' good. The most visible example of privatizing environmental rights is the emissions trading schemes, granting of land and mining rights, privatization of water, determination of society's 'willingness to pay' values for environmental resources such as continuance of natural habitats, sites of natural beauty and 'debt-for-nature swaps'.
3. The *structural change* approach is the most diverse and includes the use of market instruments and law as a means of achieving environmental and social responsibility. The essence of this approach lies in recognizing that markets are governed by constraints and rules and are not anarchic institutions. The structures within which markets operate (e.g., the rules of limited liability, audit, taxation, natural justice, stock market listing, etc.) are regulated by governments. Hence, the most obvious way to encourage more sustainable behaviour is to change the 'rules of the game' within which private enterprises perform by initiating reforms in the structure of the economic environment within which business operates. Some of the mechanisms that are employed here are environmental taxes, environmental grants, environmental regulations, environmental fines and penalties, environmental quotas and removal of assets from economic activity through establishment of heritage assets. The impact of these mechanisms on the economy for 'getting the prices right' is very similar—certain prioritized environmental and social 'negatives' are discouraged and/or environmental and social 'positives' are encouraged.
4. The *shadow price* approach deals less with real cash effects than with potential cost and price changes. The earlier approaches produce impacts that are manifested in demand shifts, reductions in supply, cost increases or direct manipulation of the economics. But, in this approach, the concern is with what would have been incurred if the organization had been sustainable. At the corporate level, this approach can take any one of three forms: rearrangement, redefinition and reporting of actual costs (USEPA 1996); use of economic valuation systems to produce a social cost benefit statement as undertaken by BSO/Origin (1990; 1991; 1992; 1995); or the use of existing market prices to calculate the cost that an organization would have had to bear if it had acted in a sustainable manner during the accounting period. This is the 'sustainable cost approach' used by Rubenstein (1994) and Forum for the Future (2000) and also by Ekins (2000) under the label 'sustainability gap analysis'. All these attempts to produce and report on the 'shadow prices' of environmental and social interactions are intended to change perceptions and attitudes, and hence, could be considered to be an extension of the first approach.

Any system that aims at 'getting the prices right' by depicting the environmental and social aspects of economic activity, and hence, is designed to embrace FCA, will have to adopt at least some aspects of all four non-discrete approaches to internalizing externalities (Bebbington et al. 2001: 22).

2.8 Appropriate Methodology for FCA Adoption

The implementation of FCA in business enterprises requires four distinct phases:

1. Definition of the *cost objective* (e.g., a product, production process, waste disposal option, part of an economic entity, an entire entity or an industry). This is the foremost requirement of FCA. It is necessary to ascertain specifically the purpose behind calculation of fuller costs—particular product or process, comparative analyses of two or more products and processes, an organization's entire set of activities, the activities of an entire industry, or all or some activities within a geographically defined area. The nature of the cost objective will be dictated by the particular purpose of an FCA analysis. For example, a stated purpose of Ontario Hydro's FCA experiment was to quantify for Canadian regulators, the social and environmental impacts that arose from hydroelectric power production in Canada for the benefit of export to the US. In many other cases, FCA has been used as an input for strategic choice in decisions about production processes, waste disposal options and product development. There are some organizations that have focused on particular externalities associated with their entire operations.
2. Specification of the *scope/limits* of analysis (i.e., what subset of all possible externalities are to be identified) is concerned with which externalities need to be measured in the FCA analysis, in light of the chosen cost objective. For example, if we were to identify the externalities associated with an entity's use of electricity, the following layers would be discernible: (i) the entity's use of electricity directly in organizational activities to the extent that impacts are not captured at all or are not fully captured by the accounting system (e.g., the electricity used for running a photocopier in the office and the generation of consumed toner cartridges, creates a pollution externality to the extent that the pollution impact of the toner cartridges is not included in the waste disposal costs); (ii) impacts arising out of the generation and distribution of electricity that has been used by the organization (e.g., pollution impact of non-renewable fossil fuels use such as coal or petroleum). This externality is not created by the accounting entity itself but by the supplier to the organization. Once the organization uses electricity powered by fossil fuels, it creates, via its demand, the externalities generated by the electricity supplier, too. Hence this externality could be viewed as relating to the organization's operations as a second-level impact. If we peel the layer of the impact one step backwards, then the construction of the power plant and the machinery used to build the power plant to make electricity production possible also generate externalities. In this way, one may regress endlessly to track down the externalities linked to an activity such as electricity use for running office equipment.

   Although it may be a valuable and insightful exercise to include all possible layers of impacts in the FCA analysis, it may be far from practicable considering the problems of data availability. For example, the data regarding externalities arising out of construction of power plant is far too complex so as to be available. Also, the ascertainment of the percentage of external upstream impacts would be difficult. Moreover, the farther we move upstream with respect to the cost objective being analysed, the smaller will be the impact arising from the next layer. Thus, a long regress along the supply chain to uncover externalities may be an intellectually stimulating exercise that adds to the accuracy of analysis, but may not be necessary considering the significance of the impacts arising from a product/process. For many externalities, this 'tailing off' impact may be noticeable. This calls for the need to scope the FCA analysis. The boundaries may be established with reference to the layers of impact required for analysis or the significance threshold (calculated in terms of toxicity or size of impact) that must be exceeded for an impact to be included in the analysis. The selection of the boundary is dependent on the purpose of analysis. Impacts deemed to have a negligible impact on the outcomes of an FCA-related decision can be safely omitted from the calculations. However, in setting the dividing line of significance of impact, stakeholder engagement may prove indispensable as the case of Proctor and Gamble's disposable nappies shows. Gray et al. (1993: 174–75) document a life cycle analysis of disposable nappies and conventional cloth nappies to reveal that Proctor and Gamble's boundaries of analysis were not wide enough to consider the adverse impacts arising out of sourcing the wood pulp for the disposable nappies from their suppliers, Stora, who, in turn, were dealing unjustly with the Sami, Europe's last of the indigenous people who live in the forests from which the wood pulp for the disposable nappies was being obtained. Proctor and Gamble missed this vital fact because the boundaries of analysis were not correctly set, and so, the company's claims about the environment friendliness of this product came in for severe public criticism.

3. Identify and *measure external impact* (which involves making the link between a cost objective and the externalities arising from the cost objective). The third step deals with generating data that is appropriate to the cost objective chosen and within the boundaries specified by the analysis, in order to identify the impacts arising from the cost objective, a significant amount of information that is not readily available. Essentially, data need to be gathered on two aspects: (i) data on the cost objective itself and (ii) data on the externalities associated with the cost objective. Much of the information required to determine the activity aspects of a cost objective may be available from extant information systems of the organization. To that extent, existing accounting systems may be useful for FCA. In some instances, however, there will be resource flows in and out of an organization which are not priced, and hence not reflected by the current accounting system. These resource flows need to be identified and captured outside the accounting information systems. For this, it is necessary for an organization to have a well-developed environmental information system that generates life cycle assessment data on a continuous basis.
4. Attachment of cost to external impact (i.e., monetisation of the externalities, or determination of the fuller cost associated with, but which are not already captured by, the current accounting for a cost objective).

In order to lend transparency to the corporate practice of measuring and reporting 'full' costs, the USEPA (1996) has developed the following four-tiered system of examining costs:

- *Tier 0* costs represent **Conventional Capital and Operating Costs** (such as equipment, materials and labour)
- *Tier 1* costs represent **Hidden Costs** (such as monitoring, paperwork and reporting requirements)
- *Tier 2* costs include **Contingent Costs** (such as penalties, fines and future liabilities)
- *Tier 3* costs represent **Less Tangible Costs** (such as corporate image, community relations and consumer response)

The spectrum of environmental costs based upon the degree of difficulty to measure is shown in Exhibit 2.3. Clearly, Tier 0 costs are the easiest to measure while Tier 3 costs are the most difficult. All of these costs are private costs borne by the company. This analysis does not include the social costs or externalities not directly borne by the company. Once environmental costs have been identified and quantified or estimated, they need to be allocated to the originating activities. By allocating these costs, a company will motivate managers and decision makers to find creative pollution prevention (P2) alternatives, which will lower these costs.

Exhibit 2.3: The Spectrum of Environmental Cost

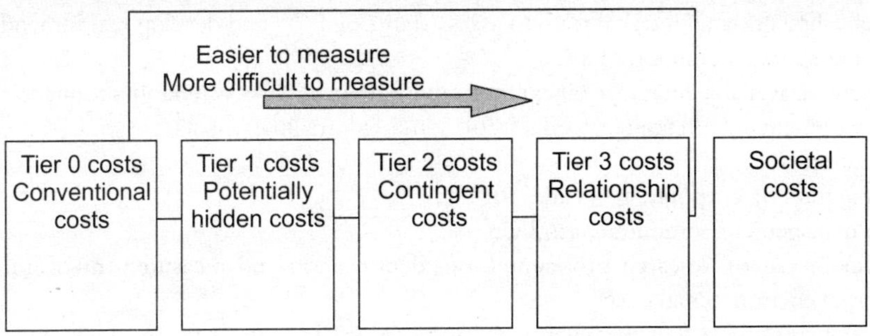

Source: USEPA (1995).

In its correct formulation, FCA should refer to all social costs. Once we move beyond the concept of private costs to the quantification and allocation of full social costs, we face a serious challenge of devising an appropriate approach to assign costs to social and environmental intangibles (or what economists refer to as public goods) such as clean air and water, a beautiful landscape, virgin ecosystems, species existence and genetic diversity of flora and fauna. Some environmental impacts can be estimated or measured by adopting an anthropocentric stance, and arriving at estimates of human health-related costs or impacts on the economy. However, many impacts such as the costs of species extinction or ecosystem loss are difficult to determine because the impacts on the human community are either indirect or not pervasive enough to be distinguished. Recognizing and devising operational approaches to factor these externalities would definitely make long-term sense because today's external costs usually become tomorrow's internal costs as a result of scientific evidence, social pressure, government policy or legal restriction. In fact, instances where there is a large discrepancy between internal and external costs are probably good indicators of areas where regulations are expected to appear.

2.8.1 Classic FCA Experiment at Ontario Hydro

Created in 1906, Ontario Hydro is a self-sustaining, government-owned company and the biggest power utility in North America in terms of installed generating capacity, and is acclaimed to have developed and implemented an advanced system of FCA.

According to the Ontario Hydro Corporate Guidelines for Full Cost Accounting (Ontario Hydro 1995) 'FCA is a means by which environmental considerations can be integrated into business decisions. FCA incorporates environmental and other internal costs, with external impacts and costs/benefits of Ontario Hydro's activities on the environment and human health. In cases where the external impacts cannot be monetized, qualitative evaluations are used'.

The USEPA (1996: 4) outlines the major achievements of Ontario Hydro's experiment with FCA during the period 1980–95 as follows:

1. Calculation of externality data to support exports of electricity power
2. Estimation of annual environmental spending using guidelines containing over 130 categories
3. Adoption of approach for assessment of external impacts and costs
4. Establishment of an internal team to assess status of FCA and develop recommendations
5. Clear corporate definition of FCA
6. Review of available literature on external environmental costs of energy production
7. Development of preliminary values for some externalities associated with the company's operations
8. Preparation of corporate guidelines for FCA
9. Top management commitment to FCA
10. Development of research programme on identification and measurement of internal and external environmental costs
11. Development of sustainable energy development (SED) criteria for including environmental considerations in financial evaluation and investment decisions
12. Arrangement of training and seminars on FCA
13. Arrangement ofoutreach activities beyond the company to foster widespread adoption of FCA
14. Application of FCA in planning at the corporate and lower levels of the organization

Exhibit 2.4: Ontario Hydro's FCA Approach

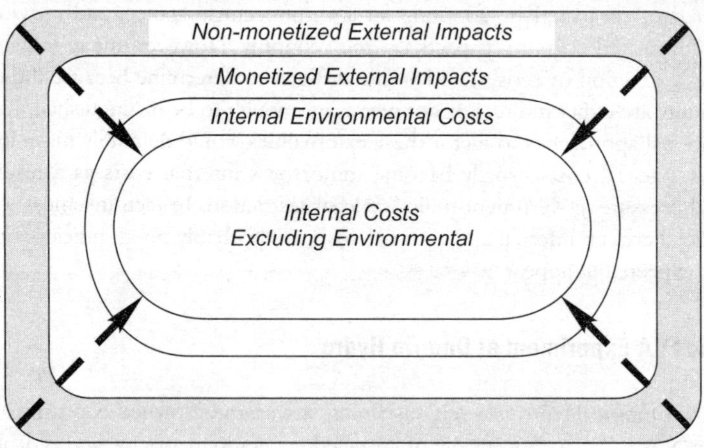

Source: USEPA (1996: 9).

TABLE 2.1

Internal and External Environmental Costs of Ontario Hydro

External Environmental Costs	
Examples:	
Depletion of natural resources	Long-term waste disposal
Noise and aesthetic impacts	Uncompensated health effects
Residual air and water emissions	Change in local quality of life
Internal Environmental Costs	
Direct or Indirect Environmental Costs	**Contingent or Intangible Environmental Costs**
Examples:	**Examples:**
Waste management	Uncertain future remediation or compensation costs
Remediation costs or obligations	Risk posed by future regulatory changes
Compliance costs	Product quality
Permit fees	Employee health and satisfaction
Environmental training	Environmental knowledge assets
Environmentally-driven R&D	Sustainability of raw material inputs
Environmentally-related maintenance	Risk of impaired assets
Legal costs and fines	Public/customer perception
Environmental assurance bonds	
Environmental certifiction/labelling	
Natural resource inputs	
Recordkeeping sand reporting	

Ontario Hydro follows generally accepted models of full cost accounting that divide environmental costs into (i) internal costs not related to the environment, (ii) externalities/environmental costs, (iii) monetized external impacts, and (iv) non-monetized external impacts. Identifying, measuring and allocating environmental costs, including environmental impact costs are the primary challenges in any FCA exercise. These are shown in Exhibit 2.4, which summarizes Ontario Hydro's FCA approach. The exhibit reveals that the long-term goal for Ontario Hydro is to internalize external impacts into corporate planning and decision making. Environmental costs can be grouped in many ways but typically fall into two main categories of internal environmental costs and external environmental costs. The distinction between internal and external environmental costs is illustrated in Table 2.1.

The total area of the box in Table 2.1 represents the entire spectrum of environmental costs that can be incurred as a result of the production or existence of the firm. The internal environmental costs to the firm are composed of direct costs and indirect costs, and contingency costs. These are those costs that are borne by the firm. Direct costs can be traced to a particular product, site, type of pollution, or pollution prevention programme (e.g., waste management or remediation costs at a particular site), whereas indirect costs such as environmental training, R&D, and record keeping and reporting are allocated to cost centres such as products and departments or activities, because there is no direct causal link. Similarly, contingent or intangible environmental costs are potentially future internal costs insofar as they may impact the effective operations of the firm. For example, a contingency cost may come in the form of changes in product quality as a result of regulatory changes that affect material inputs, methods of production or allowable emissions.

At present, internal environmental costs are directly related to the bottom line of the firm, and include items such as remediation or restoration costs, which are internal and more easily identifiable than external environmental costs. Internal costs can usually be estimated using the standard costing models that are available to the firm and can be allocated to a cost centre. For example, waste management expenses are considered internal environmental costs in that they are manageable, can be allocated to specific budgets within specific departments and can be reported with relative certainty in the financial statements of the firm. External costs, on the other hand, are typically less tangible, are difficult to measure in monetary terms and are generally borne outside the firm. Within the existing financial reporting framework, CICA (1997) applies the term *environmental losses* to this category of environmental costs. These include '*damages* that have to be paid to others, as a result of damage to the environment that resulted in bodily injury to humans, damage to the property of others, economic damage to others, and damage to natural resources'. While environmental externalities can potentially be the larger of the two cost components (and typically more ambiguous), internal costs of environmental management can also be extensive, are not always clearly defined, and tend to pose considerable allocation problems.

The USEPA (1996) case study of the Ontario Hydro FCA model reveals a number of important points that must be considered to make FCA effective:

- FCA must be positioned as an approach, which makes good business sense in promoting integration of environment and business issues. Steps must be taken to demonstrate the benefits of understanding the environmental impacts and costs (internal and external) associated with business activities.
- It is important to implement FCA as a central component of a company's overall Environmental Management System (EMS). In this regard, it is important to develop some high level FCA Guidelines and link them to the EMS.
- The process of changing corporate culture and attitudes are key to fostering support and commitment to FCA; however, this is often a slow and tardy process. The challenge is to develop an appreciation for the business case for FCA and sustainable development.
- FCA is multi-disciplinary by its very nature. The successful development and implementation of FCA requires a team approach with input from a wide variety of professionals in the organization such as, scientists and planners, environmental economists and accounting-based disciplines. FCA is not solely an accounting system issue. Rather, it is a framework that can be used to consider the broader financial and environmental implications of doing business.
- The process of identifying, quantifying and where possible, monetizing environmental impacts and costs (internal environmental costs and externalities), and integrating information into

decision-making processes is data-intensive. Data must be analysed consistently if it is to be meaningful in decision making and the promotion of sustainable development.

- There is a need to integrate environmental and financial staff in the organization. Many of the capital investment decisions are made within the financial area of the organization. If investments are to be considered on more than just private costs, there must be communication and collaboration between the financial and environmental decision-makers in the organization.

2.9 Conclusion

The present write-up represents a modest endeavour to build a case in defence of FCA as an essential and significant improvement over extant cost management methodologies that omit and/or undermine today's inevitable need to account for externalities arising in the form of adverse and mostly irreversible ecological and social impacts of business processes, projects and products. FCA purports to concretize an approach to account for externalities and internalizing hitherto excluded business costs for the purpose of strategic decision-making, project selection, product development and pricing. The business case for FCA adoption appears strong in the face of severe climate change threats, and mounting stakeholder pressure on the business community to protect their 'right to know' in terms of fuller disclosure of business impacts on the ecosystem and society through informative and authenticated sustainability reports. However, there are problems galore in devising both a workable and credible FCA system. The Ontario Hydro experiment with FCA during the last quarter of a decade can serve as a benchmark for companies aspiring to undertake this momentous challenge in the near future.

In presenting the positive aspects of FCA, we do not intend to conceal the many problems and difficulties that organizations will have to face when they embark on this journey. Two kinds of problems are identifiable. Generic problems associated with FCA include the difficulties of estimating the costs of environmental damage. There is no easy way to calculate many environmental and social costs, and in many instances, it can become a question of personal values. Additionally, detailed FCA would require an understanding of the life cycle environmental impacts of a product, process or activity. Life cycle assessment (LCA) is the tool being developed to provide information on life cycle impacts, although at present, there is no accepted methodology for LCA.

Specific difficulties associated with developing FCA include (i) comparing present and historical measures (financial accounts are used to do historical analyses); (ii) making international comparisons if different countries arrive at different methods for full cost accounting; (iii) consistency among companies because of the absence of rules regarding how an entity is to do its internal cost accounting and absence of audit on cost accounting data; (iv) translating costs into prices is not straightforward in a competitive global market—there is usually an incentive to 'cheat' and exclude some environmental or social costs as excluding costs will lead to lower prices and competitive advantage; (v) lack of internal incentives in changing accounting and financial practices because where budgetary constraints exist there are incentives to reduce, rather than increase, costs.

Given these difficulties, the onus falls on legislators, accounting standard-setters, environmental service providers, environmental consultants, corporate sustainability managers, accountants and a wide spectrum of corporate stakeholders to work in concert to make FCA a living reality in the years to come.

References

Bebbington, J., Gray, R., Hibbitt, C. and Kirk, E. (2001). *Full Cost Accounting: An Agenda for Action.* Certified Accountants Educational Trust of the Association of Chartered Certified Accountants (ACCA), London.

Bennett, M. and James, P. (1998). *The Green Bottom Line: Environmental Accounting for Management; Current Practice and Future Trends.* Greenleaf Publishing, Sheffield, UK.

BSO/Origin (1990). Annual Report.

———(1991). Annual Report.

———(1992). Annual Report.

———(1995). Annual Report.

Canadian Institute of Chartered Accountants (CICA) (1997). *Full Cost Accounting from an Environmental Perspective.* CICA, Toronto.

Cerin, P. (2002). 'Characteristics of Environmental Reporters on the OM Stockholm Exchange'. *Business Strategy and the Environment,* 11, 298–311.

Dyllick, T. and Hockerts, K. (2002). 'Beyond the Business Case for Sustainability'. *Business Strategy and the Environment,* 11, 130–141.

Ekins, P. (2000). *Estimating Sustainability Gaps for the UK.* Forum for the Future, London.

Elkington, J. (1997). *Cannibals with forks: The Triple Bottom line of 21st Century Business.* Oxford: Capstone.

Elkington, J. (1999). 'Triple Bottom Line Revolution—Reporting for the Third Millennium'. *Australian CPA,* November.

———(2001). *The Chrysalis Economy: How Citizens, CEOs and Corporations can Fuse Values and Value Creation.* Capstone, London.

———(2004). 'Enter the Triple Bottom Line'. In A. Henriques and J. Richardson (eds.), *The Triple Bottom Line: Does It All Add Up?* Earthscan, London.

Forum for the Future (2000). Annual Report.

Global Reporting Initiative (GRI) (2002). *Sustainability Reporting Guidelines,* 2002. http://www.globalreporting.org

Gray, R. H. (1990). *The Greening of Accountancy: The Profession After Pearce.* Certified Accountants Publications Ltd., London.

———(1992). 'Accounting and Environmentalism: An Exploration of the Challenge of Gently Accounting for Accountability, Transparency and Sustainability'. *Accounting, Organizations and Society,* 17(5), 399–425.

———(1997). Article Review Section. *Social and Environmental Accounting Journal,* 17(1), (April).

Gray, R. H., Bebbington, J. and Walters, D. (1993). *Accounting and the Environment.* London: Pant Chapman.

Gray, R. and Bebbington, J. (1996). 'Sustainable Development and Accounting: Incentives and Disincentives for the Adoption of Sustainability by Transnational Corporations'. In *International Accounting and Reporting Issues,* 1995 Review, UNCTAD/DTCI/25, Geneva.

Howes, R. (2002). *Environmental Cost Accounting: An Introduction and Practical Guide.* Chartered Institute of Management Accountants (CIMA), London.

International Federation of Accountants (IFAC) (1998). *Environmental Management in Organizations: The Role of Management Accounting.* IFAC, New York.

International Organisation for Standardisation (ISO) (1995). *ISO 14000: 199X, ISO/TC/207/SCI/WG2.* February 1995. ISO, Geneva.

Lesourd, J. B. and Schillizi, S. G. M. (2001). *The Environment in Corporate Management: New Directions and Economic Insights.* Edward Elgar, Cheltenham, UK.

O'Dwyer, B. (2001). 'Business, Accountancy and Sustainable Development'. *Accountancy Ireland,* 33, 20–23.

Ontario Hydro (1995). *Corporate Guidelines for Full Cost Accounting.* September 1995.

Parker, L. (1999). *Environmental Costing: An Exploratory Examination*. Melbourne: Australian Society of Certified Practising Accountants.

Pearce, D., Markandya, A. and Barbier, E. B. (1989). *Blueprint for a Green Economy*. Earthscan, London.

Prahalad, C. K. (2005). *The Fortune at the Bottom of the Pyramid: Eradicating Poverty through Profits*. Philadelphia University of Pennsylvania, Wharton School Publishing. (www.whartonsp.com)

Rubenstein, D. (1994). *Environmental Accounting for the Sustainable Corporation*. Quorum Books, London.

Sen, A. K. (2001). *Development as Freedom*. Oxford University Press, Oxford.

Society of Management Accountants of Canada (SMAC) (1997). *Accounting for Sustainable Development: A Business Perspective*. SMAC, Hamilton, Ontario.

Stiglitz, J. E. (2002). *Globalization and its Discontents*. Allen Lane, London.

United Nations Conference on Trade and Development (UNCTAD) (1996). *Self-regulation of Environmental Management: An Analysis of Guidelines Set by World Industry Associations and Their Member Firms*. UNCTAD (Division on Transnational Corporations and Investment), Geneva.

United States Environmental Protection Agency (USEPA) (1995). An Introduction to Environmental Accounting as a Business Management Tool: Key Concepts and Terms. EPA-742-R-95-001 (May 1995).

———(1996). *Environmental Accounting Case Studies: Full Cost Accounting for Decision Making at Ontario Hydro*. USEPA.

CHAPTER 3

Intangible Assets—New Paradigm Initiatives

Malayendu Saha

ABSTRACT

Intangible assets have gained prominence in the past few decades due to transformation in approaches by the global corporate entities. The technological revolution also has brought intangible resources into the fore of the business environment. Some immaterial components of companies, such as relationship with the business partners, brand awareness, products or services, human resources, corporate cultures and organizational capital have become more significant for the companies to sustain in this global competitive environment. The traditional accounting and management instruments have been making continuous endeavour to capture these new initiatives and to account for them. While some researchers have perceived that accounting of intangible asset will fulfil the accuracy requirement of the accounting functions and reports, whereas, others have observed that accuracy should be traded-off with relevance and reliability. Further, the economic effects of intangible asset on corporations have shown that accounting or not disclosing for such resources amounts to miscommunications regarding the activity and financial state of a business to its shareholders. This paper aspires to explore the current range of thinking relating to intangible assets and how such resources should be valued, recognized and presented in the corporate financial reporting. However, the challenges remain: How to determine intangible assets in a meaningful manner? How to report such assets and what are the possible consequences of alternative accounting treatments?

I can make a whole lot more money skillfully managing intangible assets than managing tangible assets —**Warren Buffet**, CEO Berkshire Hathaway

3.1 Introduction

With transformation from industrial economy, characterized by a seller's market and industrial mass production, to knowledge economy, where companies have to compete in open global business market, there is a growing need for continuous innovation, customer centricity and high-quality customer services. At present, more and more resources are put into the preparation of operated activities (like research and development, brand building, establishing good customer relationships, employee education, flexible supply chain networks or information technology infrastructure) than for their execution (such as producing, selling and delivering products and services). As such the corresponding expenses incurred as investment, if not capitalized, may distort the income statement, as is usually the state due to the current accounting regulations. The present companies have acknowledged this as the fundamental reason for better representation of intangible assets in their financial statement.

The importance of intangible assets, the immaterial value of companies such as relationships with the business partners, brand awareness, products or services, human resources, corporate cultures and organizational capital, has greatly increased. These assets are inherently different from physical and financial assets and are also responsible for generating vast economic value and growth at the corporate and national levels. Unlike financial and physical assets, intangible assets are hard for the competitors to imitate, which make them a powerful source of sustainable competitive advantage. Measuring the values of such intangible assets is the holy grail of accounting, controlling and effective management systems. Despite their widely accepted relevance, intangibles still appear to be poorly understood and not sufficiently investigated and analysed both by academics and practitioners. The traditional accounting and management instruments also fail to capture these new values and report on them. It is expected that it is time now to expand accounting, controlling and management systems to a new level to enable companies to optimize, manage and report in the present value creating activities and processes.

This paper is motivated by the present stand-off between the accounting approach to measuring and reporting intangible investment, and the desire by many, both at the level of the enterprise and the business unit and their stakeholders, for more. There is resistance from the accounting standards setting authorities, both nationally and internationally; there is also likewise opposition from many managers and analysts to more explicit reporting of these investments as intangible assets on the balance sheet. Underlying this problem leads to an uneasy and complex relationship between the accounting and economic frameworks. Accounting treats these investments as long-lived assets only when (a) the expenditures are expected to give rise to future economic benefits, (b) the firm has control over the benefits because of a past transaction, and (c) the benefits are probable and can be reliably measured. From an economic perspective, intangible investments are any expenditure not immediately embodied in physical matter, but which are intended to generate long-term benefits. This uncertainty creates an obvious problem for accounting, which is charged with the responsibility of reporting accounting numbers that can be relied on to make investment decisions, decreases the effectiveness of accounting and increases the scope for financial misrepresentation or fraud. Since many deliberations have already been made referring to its various aspects, contributing to the development of a new accounting system is not the objective of this paper, rather it aspires to discuss on the plethora of proposed methods and theories on intangible assets over the last few years.

The paper is organized as follows. Section 3.2 discusses successive awareness for intangible assets as an innovative source of capital value and growth to various stakeholders comprising the academicians, policy makers and corporate executives as well. Section 3.3 makes a review of some relevant issues in literatures on some selected intangible assets. Defining intangible assets for accounting and subsequently recognizing those assets for better reporting are dealt with in Section 3.4. Section 3.5 critically reviews the promising initiatives for measurement and valuation of such assets to fill the information vacuum. In Section 3.6, an in-depth study considering the IFRS, US GAAP and Indian GAAP on the accounting and reporting of intangible assets is made.

3.2 Awareness for Intangible Assets

The assets composition of business enterprises, at the beginning of the 1990s, showed a significant rising trend in the value of intangible assets. This not only attracted the attention of researchers and erudite authorities, but also the policy makers and corporate executives. They, however, succeeded in creating awareness for intangibles as the new source of corporate value and growth and also the serious information deficiencies related to these assets. Baruch Lev (2002) opined that intangibles are inert by themselves—they neither create value nor generate growth; they need to be combined with other production factors. The corporate accounting and reporting system should be such that it provides a more holistic view to the stakeholders to evaluate the performance of the total value creation system of the entity. As the company environment is constantly changing, the value-creating constellation cannot remain fixed, rather it has to be continually adapted and executed in the corporate reporting practices.

At the beginning of the twenty-first century, the role of the intangibles as value and growth creator was accepted among economists, investors and managers. The inadequate information about corporate intangible asset and its economic impact had caused abnormally high volatility of stock prices, resulted in undue losses to the investors, led to excessive trading gains to corporate insiders and destroyed customers' confidence. Generally, purchased intangibles are capitalized at cost, and the costs associated with developing internally generated intangibles are expensed as incurred. However, when it comes to recording of internally generated intangibles, very little had changed during the last 70-plus years. The consequences related to the non-reporting of intangibles are numerous, and are ultimately related to the fact that financial reports of knowledge-based entities do not meet the criteria of either relevance or reliability. Arguments about the inability of current US Generally Accepted Accounting Principles (GAAP) to measure the activities of knowledge-based, hi-tech, research-dependent entities are coming at a time when the accounting profession is under fire from the Securities & Exchange Commission (SEC), the International Accounting Standards Board (IASB), and—in the wake of Enron—World.com and others—the polity at large (Gelb and Siegel 2000). The dollar amount of unrecorded intangibles had changed enormously. For example, knowledge capital estimates for Microsoft were $ 211 billion, Intel, $ 170 billion; GE, $ 112 billion; and Merck, $ 110 billion, to name just a few.

It is, thus, needless to mention that the accounting profession is under enormous pressure and is also facing significant challenges. One such problem is to respond effectively to the criticisms of how intellectual and other capital is to be recognized and measured. A continued failure to effectively address this issue undermines the credibility of reported earnings and, therefore, the association between such earnings and stock market valuations (Gelb and Siegel 2000). The 'intangible movement', however, has succeeded in creating awareness and active discourse about the economic role of intangible assets and their consequences.

3.3 Literature Review

In this section, we review some of the studies on specific intangibles and the effects of accounting treatment. These studies found that (a) omissions of capital accumulation distort the measures of productivity and earnings and lessen the predictive value, and (b) capitalization, on the other hand, provides a more accurate description of the firm's position and economic performance resulting in stronger indications from financial point of view. The following sub-sections discuss some of the intangible assets.

3.3.1 Research and Development

Research and development (R&D), technological change and economic growth have a strong relationship with each other—as most of the studies opine. The studies have also empirically established such relationships at the firm, industry and national levels. Most of the studies have concluded that R&D results in subsequent gains in productivity, earnings, and shareholder value (Barth et al. 2001; Deng and Lev 1999; Gelb and Siegel 2000; Griliches 1995; Lev and Sougiannis 1996). These studies conclude that expenditures on R&D and technological change promote economic growth and also recommend that these expenditures should be capitalized in order to present more truthful representation of the totality of a firm's assets and their contribution to the future growth of the firm (Amir and Lev 1996). According to Healy et al. (1997), there is trade-off between objectivity and relevance in reporting R&D in the pharmaceutical industry. Lev and Sougiannis (1999) found that low book-to-market (B/M) companies had large R&D capital, while high B/M firms had low R&D investment. They also reported that R&D capitai was significantly associated with subsequent returns, after accounting for other fundamentals like beta, size, book-to-market, leverage and P/E ratios.

3.3.2 Computer Technology

The level of intangible capital investments that have accompanied computerization of the economy is probably far larger than the direct investments in computers. According to Yang and Brynjolfsson (2000), complimentary intangible investments are around ten times larger than the hardware investments and accounting for these intangible investments will help in modifying productivity measures substantially. However, the omission of this capital accumulation, no doubt, distorts measures of productivity and income. Unmeasured intangibles include software and software development, training costs, organizational restructuring, business process redesign, and reallocation of decisions rights and incentive systems (Amir and Lev 1996). In addition to productivity measures, non-disclosure of these investments on financial reports distorts earnings. Aboody and Lev (1999) found that software companies that expensed all software costs had positive abnormal return drifts for at least three years after expensing whereas capitalizing firms did not, indicating a distortion of information.

3.3.3 Patents

Patent application citations, references cited in patent documents and other references have been found to be significantly associated with market-to-book ratios and stock returns for technology and science-based companies (Deng and Lev 1999). According to Gelb and Siegel (2000), firms whose patent portfolios contain a large number of frequently cited patents are generating innovative technology that is likely to yield important inventions and successful products.

3.3.4 Human Resources

There is no doubt that the human resources are the most important assets of an organization. According to Becker and Huselid (1998), the financial performance of an organization is very much dependent on the ability of its human resources. They found a strong relationship between the quality of a firm's human resource management systems and its subsequent financial performance. They argue that human assets should be viewed as an investment rather than an expense. This is important because the increasing use of technology not only requires greater level of human capital but a better valuation of such assets. This leads to a stronger signal in validation of accounting and financial reporting for a better representation of the firm's position and economic performance.

Most of the studies have demonstrated that capitalization of intangible assets results in significant improvement in the predictive power and assists to portray more accurate picture of the firms' future financial performance and better future investment allocation decisions. Thus, it is expected that the recent standards should make provisions for the capitalization of intangible assets whether purchased or internally generated.

3.4 Definition and Recognition of Intangible Assets

Definition, in this context, refers to the way the concept of intangible assets is envisaged and perceived by the accounting system of the different countries. There are generally two important approaches: (1) actual definitions, which is referred to as 'conceptual'; and (2) lists of intangible assets, a kind of 'inventory'. The conceptual approach is then divided into three categories: (1) definitions by opposition (fixed assets other than tangible or financial), (2) tautological definitions (an intangible asset is characterized by lack of physical substance, and in order to be included in the balance sheet under 'intangible fixed assets', an asset must be intangible) and (3) real definition, i.e., a genuine conceptual effort to determine an intangible asset.

Most of the regulations, except the International Accounting Standard Board (IASB), define intangibles by means of lists comprising the types of intangible items that can be recorded as an asset. The Board does not give a list of intangible assets, but includes a list of intangible items that fail the recognition criteria. Though efforts are made in certain standards to define intangibles, it can be inferred that there is a link between the desire to establish a conceptual framework and the existence of a conceptual definition approach to intangible assets. Thibierge (1996) attributes the lack of overall homogeneity among accounting standards to the absence of any conceptual framework with a solid theoretical basis. According to Lacroix (1996), the fragmented approaches mentioned previously encourage the development of more general criteria for recording intangibles. She identifies generally used recognition criteria for recording intangibles in the consolidated financial statements and shows that it is possible to make a difference between purchased intangibles, which mainly refer to the 'market' criterion, internally generated research and development, which uses the identifiability criterion plus the two exclusion criteria, and internally generated other intangible assets, which are mostly related to the exclusion criteria (Fig. 3.1). An item should meet the following four fundamental recognition criteria to be recognized as an element in financial statements (SFAC 2):

- It has a relevant attribute measurable with sufficient reliability
- The information about it is capable of making a difference in user decisions
- The information has representational faithfulness and verifiability
- The information must be neutral (FASB 1980)

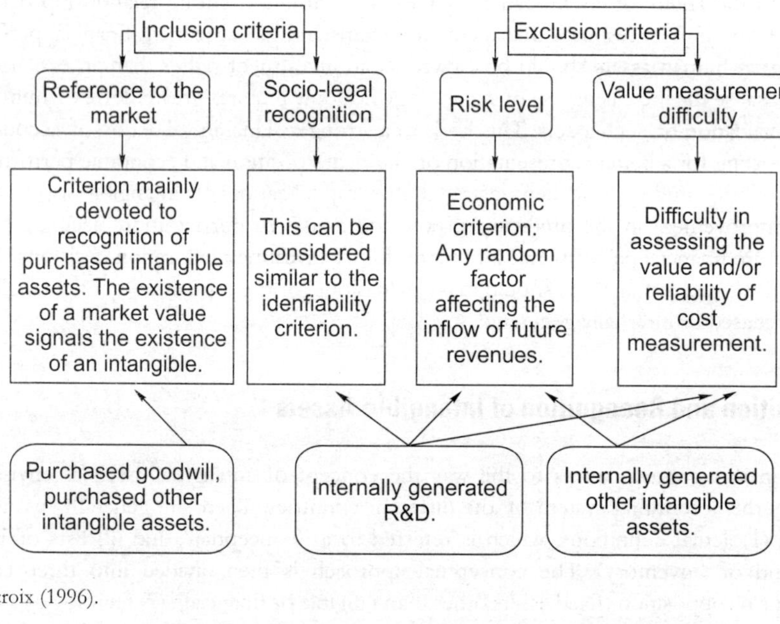

Source: Lacroix (1996).

Figure 3.1 A broad classification of intangible asset

Recognition of elements in financial reports is also subjected to decisions about trade-offs between relevance and reliability. This decision is generally resolved based on proof and verifiability of the element. Extant literature indicates recognition by the professionals in respect to investment in R&D, advertising, human resources and other intangibles that meet the definition for classification as assets and the criteria for measurement (Gelb and Siegel 2000). The Board, for example, used evidence provided by publications in scholarly journals in reaching their conclusions concerning the relevance of goodwill (SFAS 141). Market reaction is another professionally accepted medium for providing evidence (Ofer and Siegel 1987).

Types of Acquisition	Measurement of Recognition
Separately acquired intangible assets.	At cost with cost comprising the purchase price (including import duties, non-refundable purchase taxes and trade discounts and rebates) and any cost directly attributable to preparing the asset for its intended use (e.g., costs of employee benefits, professional fees, testing of asset's functionality).
Intangible assets acquired in a business combination.	At fair value on acquisition date.
Intangible assets acquired free of charge, or for nominal consideration, by way of a government grant.	At fair value.
Internally generated intangible assets satisfying the recognition criteria.	At cost with cost determined as the sum of expenditure incurred from the date when the intangible asset first meets the recognition criteria; i.e., past expenses are not to be recognized as an asset.
Intangible assets acquired in exchange for non-monetary assets.	At fair value. However, the carrying value of the asset given up is used if the exchange lacks commercial substance or the fair value of neither the asset received nor the asset given up is reliably measureable.

Source: IASB 138: Intangible assets.

Figure 3.2 Recognition of intangible assets

The recognition of an intangible asset (Fig. 3.2) also requires an enterprise to demonstrate that the item needs to qualify: (a) definition of an intangible asset and (b) recognition criteria set out in this Statement. Generally, past expenses cannot be capitalized at a later date. However, subsequent expenditure on an intangible asset after its purchase or its completion should be recognized as an expense when it is incurred unless it is probable that the expenditure will enable the asset to generate future economic benefits in excess of its originally assessed standard of performance and the expenditure can be measured and attributed to the asset reliably. Probability shall be assessed using reasonable and supportable assumptions and the best estimate by the management of the economic conditions that will exist over the useful life of the asset. If these conditions are satisfied, the subsequent expenditure should be added to the cost of the intangible asset. The probability recognition criterion is always considered satisfied for separately acquired intangible assets and also intangible assets acquired as part of a business combination. Generally, specific rules are applied in respect of internally generated intangibles, internally generated goodwill, internally generated brands, mastheads, publishing titles, customer lists and items similar in substance. Research expenditure is not recognized, however, specific recognition criteria are applied to development expenditure. In case, where the research phase of an internal project cannot be distinguished from the development phase, then expenditure on the project is classified as research and considered as expensed.

In IFRS 3 and IAS 38, the IASB sought to clarify the assessment of identifiability of an intangible asset, whether acquired in a business combination or otherwise. An intangible asset now is considered identifiable if it arises from contractual or legal rights or is separable either individually or together with a related contract, asset or liability. IFRS 3 has broadened the recognition criteria by adding contractual or legal rights as a specific alternative to separatability. Probability of future economic benefits is also assumed for intangibles acquired in a business combination under IFRS 3. Thus, an acquirer recognizes an intangible item separately from goodwill at the acquisition date, if the definition of an intangible asset is met and the asset's cost (its fair value) can be measured reliably. Consequently, an in-process research and development project that meets the definition and can be measured reliably should be recognized separately from goodwill. The new version of IAS 38 provides additional guidance in respect of control criterion in the definition and probability recognition criterion for intangibles acquired separately or in a business combination. These changes, however, do not affect the recognition criteria for internally generated intangibles.

3.5 Measurement and Valuation of Intangible Assets

The unique ability of intangibles to enable a company to withstand pressures and sustain in this competitive environment is responsible for their remarkable ascendance to the role of premier corporate entities. Questions generally arise—How to measure the intangibles? The adage, 'What's not measured is not managed and what's not managed cannot be disclosed is true for individuals and business enterprises as well. The main problem, however, is that it is not possible to measure the social phenomena with anything close to scientific accuracy. This creates a basic inconsistency between manager's expectations, the promise made by the method developers and what the systems can actually achieve.

The specific attributes of intangibles—partial excludability, high risk and non-tradability—render the measurement and valuation of intangibles a daunting task (Lev 2004). For example, given the high technological uncertainty, cash flows from patents are hard to predict, and consequently patent valuation is often of questionable reliability. Even more challenging is to value an employee-training programme, given the usually high labour turnover. How to value a brand that is constantly threatened by competitors' product? How can the value of a biotech company with a large investment in early stage research and development that has uncertain prospects be ascertained? Truly, all investments in intangibles such as research and development, brand enhancement, employee training and system development are expensed in corporate financial report: such investments are not considered assets that promise future benefits. Lev opined that the measurement and valuation of the benefits of the intangibles are more challenging as well. The high profits and large market share of Microsoft are jointly contributed by highly trained employees, superior technology (research and development) and an effective sales and promotion effort. But, how to allocate the Microsoft's total output (revenues and profits) among the various intangibles (research and development, human capital, brand) responsible for it or how to determine the brand value?

One of the most common frameworks for intangibles comes from the EU's MERITUM (Measuring Intangibles to Understand and Improve Innovation Management) project, commonly known as the three C's which comprises of human capital, structural capital and relational capital. The human capital, which may either be unique or generic, refers to the knowledge, skills, experiences and abilities of people. Structural capital is comprised of organizational flexibility, documentation service, the existence of a knowledge centre, the general use of information technologies, organizational learning capacity, etc. Resources linked to the external associations of the firm with customers, suppliers or R&D partners are termed as structural capital. It comprises that part of Human and Structural Capital as are involved with the company's relations with stakeholders (investors, creditors, customers, suppliers, etc.), along with their perceptions about the company. Examples of this category are image, customers' loyalty, customer satisfaction, links with suppliers, commercial power, negotiating capacity with financial entities, environmental activities, etc. There are other methods of valuing intangible assets, all of which are variations of the three basic approaches to valuation, namely: (i) cost approach, (ii) market approach and (iii) income approach. Under cost approach, it is possible to value intangible assets on the basis of their 'cost to create' or the amount to be expended to either reproduce (exactly duplicate) or to replace (create a functional equivalent) the asset. The method takes into account the current costs, rather than looking at the past expenditures. The main drawback is that it fails to account for the economic benefit to the asset owner through its use. The market approach considers the comparable market transactions. Also known as the 'sales comparison' approach, this is where fair value is determined by making comparisons with the annual sales of comparable assets. However, for numerous types of intangible assets, it is uncommon for the asset to be sold separately from the other assets of a business. It is, thus, often difficult to find examples of prices paid in outright sales for comparable assets. The income approach aims in quantifying income from having these assets. The approach considers the net present value of the stream of future benefits accruing to the owner of the assets through a capitalization process.

The measuring approaches as suggested by Luthy (1998) and Williams (2000) are segregated into four categories (Fig. 3.3). The market capitalization method (MCM) aspires to determine the value of its intellectual capital or intangible assets by measuring the difference between market capitalization of the company and its stockholders' equity. As per the return on assets method (*ROA*), the average pre-tax earnings of a company for a period of time are divided by its average tangible assets. The outcome is compared with the industry average and then the difference is multiplied by the company's average tangible assets to calculate the average annual earnings from intangibles. Dividing the above-average earnings by the company's average cost of capital or an interest rate, an estimate of the value of its intangible assets or intellectual capital can be derived. According to direct intellectual capital method (*DICM*), the various components of intangible assets are identified and subsequently evaluated either individually or as an aggregated coefficient. Under scorecard method (*SC*) the various components of intangible assets or intellectual capital are first identified with their indicators and indices and reported in scorecards. Economic value added (*EVA*) [calculated as net operating profit after tax (NOPAT) – (Capital × Cost of Capital)] is another financial performance measure that aims to capture the true economic profit of an enterprise. It focuses on maximizing the shareholders wealth and helps management in creating value for shareholders.

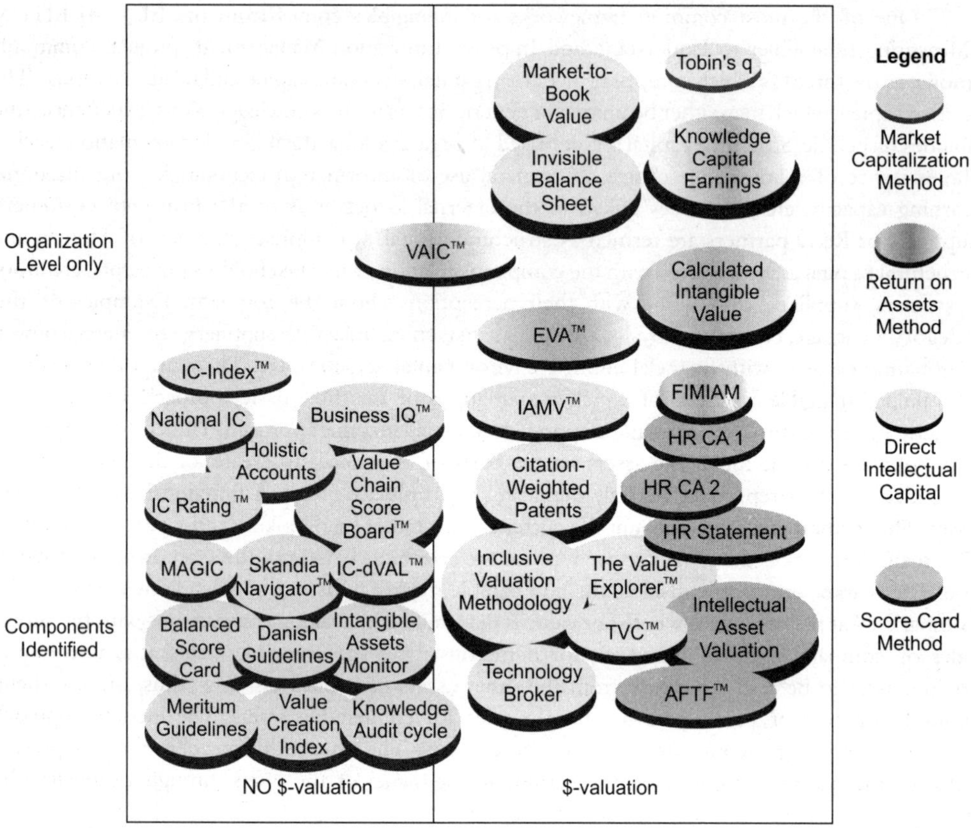

Source: Luthy (2000).

Figure 3.3 Thirty-four intangible assets measuring models

The International Valuation Standards Board issues Guidance Notes (GNs) on the application of the fundamental principles of a specific asset type or for a specific valuation purpose. GN 4, '*Valuation of Intangible Assets*', provides guidance on the main recognized methods used for the valuation of intangible assets. This guidance note provides additional guidance for valuations undertaken for inclusion in financial statements prepared in accordance with IFRSs and include:

- IFRS 3 (Business Combinations) and IAS 38 (Intangible Assets) to deal with initial recognition of intangible assets arising from a business combination;
- IAS 36 (Impairment of Assets) to discuss intangible assets measured at fair value less costs to sell for impairment testing purposes;
- IFRS 5 (Non-current Assets Held for Sale and Discontinued Operations) to consider intangible assets whose carrying amount is intended to be recovered principally through a sale transaction rather than through continuing use; and
- IAS 38 to consider intangible assets carried under the revaluation model.

In IFRSs, for valuation of intangible asset, the definition is restricted to 'identifiable' assets. Goodwill is treated separately from other intangible assets according to the standard. Under IAS 38, only intangible assets for which fair value can be determined by reference to an 'active market' may be carried on in the balance sheet under the revaluation model.

3.5.1 Intangible Assets Arising from a Business Combination Recognized in Accordance with IFRS 3 and IAS 38

IFRS 3 and IAS 38 require that intangible assets arising from a business combination be recognized at their fair value on the date of acquisition and suggests that there need to be sufficient information for the fair value to measure such assets. Moreover, while assessing the fair value, the level of aggregation implicit in those transactions should be considered and compared to the appropriate level of aggregation in estimating the fair value of the subject asset or assets. The standard, however, does not address specifically whether similar or identical intangible assets should be aggregated for the purpose of initial measurement. In practice, certain types of similar intangible assets that together form a portfolio of similar intangible assets are frequently aggregated for ease of valuation. In such aggregation, the nature of the underlying assets and their characteristics, appropriate for such valuation purposes, should be documented in the valuation report.

3.5.2 Valuations in Accordance with IAS 36, 'Impairment of Assets'

IAS 36 provides that intangible assets are required to be shown in the balance sheet at not more than their recoverable amount. The standard frames 'the impairment test', which the reporting entities must perform in order to ensure that their goodwill and other identifiable intangible assets are not represented in the balance sheet at more than their 'recoverable amount'. Thus, as per the standard, the impairment test must be conducted annually for the following:

- Identifiable intangible assets with an indefinite life and not amortized
- Purchased goodwill
- Identifiable intangible assets amortized over a finite life when one or more indicators of impairment as defined by IAS 36 are present.

3.6 Accounting and Reporting of Intangible Assets

Despite their widely accepted relevance, intangibles still appear to be poorly understood and not sufficiently investigated and analysed both by academics and practitioners. The perceived vacuum in the official accounting measures in relation to intangible investment has spawned divergent views. One such view seeks an internally consistent system of accounting rules but a solution that has scant regard to the economics of the expenditures under consideration (e.g., Canibano et al. 2000). An accounting-based solution has also not been pursued by accounting standards bodies due to political interventions and inability of accounting to solve the 'intangibles' problem divorced from the economic context. The recent developments and phenomena have further amplified the importance of intangibles to managers, intermediaries and investors. In this perspective, the accounting standards revolution in Europe requiring the implementation of International Accounting Standards/ International Financial Reporting Standards (IAS/IFRS) has accentuated the measurement and reporting of intangibles in European companies' financial statements. The European Union (EU) agreed to the IFRS, in 2002, as the common financial reporting language for the listed companies. The decision of the EU has been regarded as a catalyst for change and many countries across the world have also chosen to accept IFRS as the gateway to a single global set of accounting standards with easier access to global capital market and increasing allocation of global capital. The principles-based standards of IFRS are aimed at (a) promoting confidence in the reliability and transparency of financial reporting, (b) making better cross-border investment decisions, (c) improving in the quality of cross-border mergers and acquisitions decisions, (d) helping in easy preparation of consolidated accounts by multinational companies, and (e) contributing towards promoting economic growth and employment throughout the world.

A comparison between IAS/IFRS and the US Financial Accounting Standards (US GAAP) also reveals some differences in the treatment and capitalization of intangible assets, and potentially a different degree of disclosure between the two sets of rules, with consequences in terms of appreciation of these resources (Fig. 3.4).

Moreover, the awareness to make company information available in a widespread and timely fashion and the need for a detailed and rapid benchmarking between business reports of different entities are paving the way for new technological tools such as the eXtensible Business Reporting Language (XBRL), which can be usefully applied also to information on intangibles.

3.6.1 IAS 38 Intangible Assets

IAS 38 deals with accounting for intangible assets in detail. According to the standard, an intangible asset refers to an identifiable non-monetary asset without physical substance. The term identifiable here signifies that the asset is either separable, which means, it can be sold apart from the firm's other assets, or it crops up from contractual or other legal rights. These essential criteria of intangibles are additional to those applicable to other types of assets, namely, that there must be probable future economic benefits that are attributable to the firm and the cost of the asset can be measured reliably. Intangibles resulting from exchange of assets are treated at par with asset purchases and are usually recognized at fair value. When intangible assets are acquired or purchased separately, the probability of generating future benefits is always considered to be satisfied, the argument being that the rational firms would only outlay the costs if they were reasonably certain to obtain the future benefits and be recognized in the balance sheet, initially at their cost price. However, in certain restrictive circumstances, they may be revalued (Austin 2007). The standard also specifically prohibits capitalization of the costs of some internally generated intangible assets, even if they meet the development criteria. Moreover, there are certain other intangible assets which do not meet the identifiability criteria, for example, the costs of ongoing training or recruitment programs, advertising, relocation, start-up, pre-opening and pre-operating costs.

Subject	IFRS	US GAAP	Indian GAAP
Intangible assets	An intangible asset is recognized separately from goodwill if it represents contractual or legal rights or is capable of being separated or divided and sold, transferred, licensed, rented or exchanged. Acquired in-process research and development (IPR&D) is recognized as a separate intangible asset if it meets the definition of an intangible asset and its fair value can be measured reliably. Non-identifiable intangible assets are subsumed within goodwill.	The requirements for recognizing intangible assets separately from goodwill are similar to IFRS. However, under US GAAP, the acquired IPR&D is expensed immediately unless it has an alternative future use.	An intangible asset is recognized in amalgamations accounted under the purchase method using the fair value, if it is probable that the future economic benefits that are attributable to the asset will flow to the enterprise and the cost of the asset can be measured reliably. However, the fair value of intangible assets with no active market is reduced to the extent of capital reserve, if any, arising on the amalgamation.
Acquired intangible assets	Capitalized if recognition criteria are met; amortized over useful life. Intangibles assigned for an indefinite useful life are not amortized but reviewed at least annually for impairment. Revaluations are permitted in rare circumstances.	Similar to IFRS, except revaluations are not permitted.	Capitalized if recognition criteria are met; all intangibles are amortized over useful life with a rebuttable presumption of not exceeding 10 years.
			Revaluations are not permitted.
			In case the life of an intangible asset is ascertained to be more than 10 years, then impairment testing is compulsorily required irrespective of the triggering event.
Internally generated intangible assets	Research costs are expensed as incurred. Development costs are capitalized and amortized only when specific criteria are met.	Unlike IFRS, both research and development costs are expensed as incurred, with the exception of some software and Web site development costs that are capitalized.	Similar to IFRS.
Impairment of long-lived assets held for use	Impairment is a one-step approach under IFRS and is assessed on the basis of discounted cash flows. If impairment is indicated, assets are written down to higher of fair value less costs to sell and value in use. Reversal of impairment losses is required in certain circumstances, except for goodwill.	Impairment is a two-step approach under US GAAP. Firstly, impairment is assessed on the basis of undiscounted cash flows. If less than carrying amount, the impairment loss is measured as the amount by which the carrying amount exceeds fair value. Reversal of losses is prohibited.	Similar to IFRS, except reversal of impairment losses for goodwill is required in certain circumstances.

Figure 3.4 Differences between IFRS, US GAAP and Indian GAAP on intangible assets

Intangible assets, externally acquired or purchased from outside, usually have identifiable costs and discernible benefits, and have difficulties in accounting. Moreover, intangible assets developed within the firm over a period of time (the internally generated intangibles) have traditionally been ignored, that is, not recognized in the financial statements. The reason behind such omission has been due to a perceived lack of a relation between their costs and specific future revenue. For example, expenditures incurred in developing brand assets were not adequately covered by early accounting standards. To guide and justify accounting of these intangibles, companies fell back on broad principles of asset determination and recognition as developed partially for such purposes. These conceptual statements usually gave the option of capitalizing or expensing some intangibles, depending on the interpretation of the firms in the definition of assets.

3.6.2 Acquisition as Part of a Business Combination

There are restrictions while recording internally generated intangible assets applied at the individual company. However, the rule changes when the assets of a firm are acquired as a part of 'business combination'. The most common form of business combination is takeover, when the parent company acquires all or a majority of the shares of another company, the subsidiary. As the parent and subsidiary now form a group of companies, a third set of financial statements is required, which adds the income and expenses, assets and liabilities of all the individual companies in the group to produce a consolidated income statement and a consolidated balance sheet. IAS 38 provides additional guidance in respect of (a) intangibles purchased as part of a business combination, (b) intangibles acquired by way of government grant or (c) intangibles exchanged. The significance is that the standard allows intangibles, which may not have passed the recognition test at the individual subsidiary company level (and are therefore excluded in the subsidiary's accounts), to be recognized when the assets of the subsidiary are added to those of the parent to form the consolidated balance sheet. The intangibles of the subsidiary are now recognized because the parent has obtained control of the assets, including intangibles, when the ownership interest in the subsidiary company was acquired. The previously unrecognized intangibles are now treated similarly to purchased or externally acquired intangibles and if the fair value of these separable intangible assets can be reliably measured, they can be reported in the consolidated balance sheet. The recognition of the separable intangible assets at their fair value would likely to contradict the IAS 38 requirement to initially record intangible assets at cost. However, the presumption is that the company was acquired by the parent at market price and the intangibles were purchased at fair value.

3.6.3 Revaluing Intangible Assets

According to IAS 38, after recognition, intangible assets may be measured using either a cost model or a revaluation model. If the cost model is selected, then after initial recognition, such asset shall be carried at cost less accumulated amortization and impairment losses. If the revaluation model is selected, the intangible asset shall be carried at its fair value less subsequent accumulated amortization and impairment losses. Fair values are to be determined from an active market and are to be reassessed with regularity sufficient to ensure that, at the balance sheet date, the carrying amount does not differ materially from its fair value. An active market is referred to one in which all the assets traded are homogenous, there are many buyers and sellers, and where the prices are available to the public. As a result of a revaluation, if the carrying amount of an intangible asset is increased, such increase shall be credited directly to equity under the heading of revaluation surplus. However, such increase shall be recognized in profit or loss to the extent that it reverses a revaluation.

3.6.4 Amortization and Impairment

IAS 38 also requires an entity to assess the useful life of its intangibles with finite and indefinite lives. An indefinite life refers to when 'there is no foreseeable limit to the period over which the asset is expected to generate net cash flows for the entity'. Amortization applies to those with finite lives and requires an estimate of the useful life of the asset. There is a rebuttable presumption that the maximum amortization period is 20 years. Those with indefinite lives are not systematically amortized but must be assessed at least annually for possible impairment adjustments. IAS 3 (Business Combinations) prohibits the amortization of goodwill. As the cash flows generated by goodwill is attached to the other assets rather than goodwill, its impairment is more complex. The test for goodwill impairment compares the current market value of the subsidiary's equity with the balance sheet value of its equity plus the goodwill arising on the original acquisition. If the current market value is below the balance sheet value of the equity (plus goodwill), then the value of the investment in the subsidiary has fallen and the goodwill is impaired.

Introduction of new accounting rules and regulations through IFRS in recent years had a major impact on the reporting of intangible assets in the balance sheet and profit and loss account. Until 2001, corporate entities were not obliged to recognize acquired intangible assets separately from goodwill. IFRS 3 now recommends that, on acquisition, intangible assets should be separately disclosed on the acquiring company's balance sheet providing they satisfy the required criteria and the value of intangible asset can be determined reliably. Strong advocates of 'fair value reporting' believe that the changes should go further and that all of a company's tangible and intangible assets and liabilities should regularly be measured at fair value and reported on the balance sheet, including internally generated intangibles such as brands and patents, so long as valuation methods and corporate governance are sufficiently rigorous. Some go as far as to suggest that 'internally generated goodwill' should be reported on the balance sheet at fair value, meaning that management would effectively be required to report its own estimate of the value of the business at each year end together with supporting assumptions. However, the current international consensus is that internally generated intangible assets should not be recognized on the balance sheet. Under IFRS, certain intangible assets should be recognized, but only if they are in the 'development' (as opposed to 'research') phase, with conditions on, for example, technical feasibility and the intention and ability to complete and use the asset.

The revised IAS 36 also introduces new disclosure requirements, the principal one being the disclosure of the key assumptions used in the calculation. Increased disclosure is required where a reasonably possible change in a key assumption would result in actual impairment. The most famous impact of new reporting standards has been on management accountability. Greater transparency, rigorous impairment testing and additional disclosure should mean more scrutiny both internally and externally.

3.7 Conclusion

The limitations of the existing accounting models are exposed with the growth in intangible assets. The innocent non-accountants and the managers, investors and financial analysts as well, are constantly asking the question: If intangibles are so important, why aren't they on the balance sheet? This debate surfaced energetically over a decade, but without any concrete conclusion. The practice did not become widespread till the recent accounting standards reflect the current consensus, which advocates that the internally generated intangibles cannot be usually included in the balance sheet. Intangibles, as per the consensus, do not meet accountants' test for balance sheet recognition, as such assets are frequently diffused in nature and not readily separable from other assets or from the business as a whole. The nebulous property rights surrounding many intangibles mean that the company may not exercise the effective control required for an asset. Moreover, being unique, there is no active secondary market of similar assets to which the accountants can refer to for a market price. So, the valuation of intangibles necessarily involves subjective evaluations of future cash flows.

The debate about whether the firm should value the intangibles in the balance sheet is fading out in recent times—the new challenge is disclosure. At present, firms have very little awareness on what information they should usually disclose to enable outsiders to evaluate their intangibles. The new regulation requires the companies to report in depth and more comprehensively not only about all their intangible assets and but also about their capabilities to create and exploit such assets. It entails them to report about strategies, management challenges and about the actions taken to create, manage and exploit intangible assets based on knowledge resources. It, therefore, forces the corporate entities to reveal much more in advance about their intentions, how they want to create value with activities related to intangibles. So the concept results in a much better degree of transparency, but less rigid, which also means in more opportunities to 'play with the numbers and reports'.

The best solution should be a combination of both the approaches: recognition of intangible assets in financial statements including the ones that have not been acquired but created in-house (to enable investors to better assess the past performance of companies) and in addition to the financial statements, a supplement report which is reporting on the potential available and in creation to enable for future performance (which is then measured against financial results in the future). Unless equity analysts and other outsiders can use the data regarding information of the various aspects of the functioning of the companies, attempts to improve disclosure will be frustrated. The future, it is believed, will show us, which of these concepts will be better to 'invite' companies to manage their intangible assets more accurately. It is going to be fascinating to observe how and in what dimension the debate proceeds.

References

Aboody, D. and Lev, B. (1999). 'The Value Relevance of Intangibles: The Case of Software Capitalization'. *Journal of Accounting Research*, 36 (Supplement 1999).

Accounting Standards Board (ASB) (1997). *FRS 10. Goodwill and Intangible Asset.* Accounting Standards Board, London. Vol. December.

Amir, E. and B. Leve (1996). 'Value Relevance of Non-Financial Information, The Wireless Community Industry'. *Journal of Accounting & Economics* (22): pp 3–30.

Austin, L. (2007). 'Accounting for Intangible Assets. Business Review'. *Internal Valuation Standards Committee*, 9(1).

Barth, M. and Glinch, G. (1998). 'Revalued Financial, Tangible and Intangible Assets: Association with Share Prices and Non Market Based Value Estimates'. *Journal of Accounting Research*, 36, pp 199–233.

Barth, M., Kasznik, R. and McNichols, M. (2001). 'Analyst Coverage and Intangible Assets'. *Journal of Accounting Research*, 39, pp 1–34.

Becker, B. and M. Huselid (1997). 'High Performance Work Systems and Firm Performance: A Synthesis of Research and Managerial Implications'. *Research in Personnel and Human Resources* (4): pp 2–34.

Deng, Z. and Lev, B. (1999). 'Science and Technology as Predictors of Stock Performance'. *Financial Analysts Journal*, May/June, pp 20–32.

Financial Accounting Standards Board (FASB) (1974). *Accounting for Research & Development Costs.* Statement of Financial Accounting Standards 2. Stamford, CT: FASB.

Financial Accounting Standard Board (FASB) (1980). 'Quantitative Characteristics of Accounting Information'. *Statement of Financial Accounting Concepts* No. 2, Stamford CT: FASB.

———(1978). *Objectives of Financial Reporting by Business Enterprises.* Statement of Financial Accounting Concepts 1. Stamford, CT: FASB.

———(2001a). *Goodwill and Other Intangible Assets.* Statement of Financial Accounting Standards No. 142. Stamford, CT: FASB.

———(2001b). *Business Combinations.* Statement of Financial Accounting Standards No. 141. Stamford, CT: FASB.

Gelb, D. S. (2002). 'Intangible Assets and Firms' Disclosures: An Empirical Investigation'. *Journal of Business, Finance, and Accounting.* (29): pp 457–476.

Gelb, D. and Siegel, P. (2000). 'Intangible Assets and Corporate Signaling'. *Review of Quantitative Finance and Accounting.* (15): pp 307–323.

Griliches, Z. (1995). 'R&D and Productivity: Econometric Results and Measurement Issues'. *Handbook of the Economics of Innovation and Technological Change*, Paul Stoneman, (ed.) Oxford, UK: Blackwell.

Healy, P., Myers, S. and Howe, C. (1997). 'R&D Accounting and the Relevance—Objectivity Trade-off: A Simulation Using Data from the Pharmaceutical Industry'. Working Paper, POPI Center, MIT Sloan School.

International Accounting Standards Board (IASB) (2004). (revised). *Intangible Assets.* International Accounting Standards No. 38. IASB, London, UK.

International Accounting Standards Committee (1997). 'Exposure Draft'. *E 60, Intangible.* International Accounting Standards Committee, London. Vol. September.

———(1998a). *IAS 38 Intangible Assets.* International Accounting Standards Committee, London. Vol. September.

———(1998b). *IAS 36, Impairment of Assets.* International Accounting Standards Committee, London. Vol. September.

Lacroix. M. (1996). 'Les actifs incorporels: etude compare de la doctrine compatable francaise et international'. CREGE, University Montesquieu, Bordeaux IV, France, Research paper.

Lev, B. (2002). 'Intangibles at a Crossroads: What's Next?' *Financial Executive Magazine*, April, pp 121–127.

———(2004). 'Intangibles: Management, Measurement and Reporting'. *Accounting Review.*

Lev, B. and Sougiannis, T. (1996). 'The Capitalization, Amortization, and Value-Relevance of R&D'. *Journal of Accounting and Economics*, 21, pp 107–137.

———(1999). 'Penetrating the Book-to-Market Black Box: The R&D Effect'. *Journal of Business, Finance, & Accounting*, April/May.

Luthy, D. H. (1998). *Intellectual Capital and Its Measurement.* Utah State University, Logan, UT.

Mathews, M. R. and Higson, A. W. (2000). *Potentially Dysfunctional Impacts of Harmonising Accounting Standards: The Case of Intangible Assets.* Discussion paper Series No. 199, Massey University School of Accountancy.

Nakumara, L. (2001). 'What is the U.S. Investment in Intangibles?' Presented at the 4th Intangibles Conference of The Vincent C. Ross Institute of Accounting Research. University Stern School of Business, New York.

———(2003). 'A Trillion Dollars a Year in Intangible Investment and the New Economy'. In J. Hand and B. Lev (eds.), *Intangible Assets: Values, Measures and Risks.* Oxford University Press, pp 19–47.

Ofer, A. and Siegel, D. (1987). 'Corporate Financial Policy, Information, and Market Expectations: An Empirical Investigation of Dividends'. *The Journal of Finance*, 42, pp 889–911.

Rivett, K. and Line, D. (2000). 'Discovering New Value in Intellectual Property'. *Harvard Business Review*, January–February, pp 55–66.

Sougiannis, T. (1994). 'The Accounting-based Valuation of Corporate R&D'. *The Accounting Review*, 69, pp 44–68.

Stittle, J. (2004). 'UK Corporate Reporting of Human Capital: A Regulatory Failure to Evolve'. *Business and Society Review*, 109, pp 311–337.

Thibierge, C. (1996). *Le Traitement Comptable des elements incorporels, un apercu des pratiques en Europe.* Research paper, CREFIGE, Dauphine University, Paris.

Yang, S. and Brynjolfsson, E. (2001). 'Intangible Assets and Growth Accounting: Evidence from Computer Investments'. 4th Intangibles Conference, Stern School of Business, New York University.

CHAPTER 4

Accounting for Financial Instruments—A Commentary on the Contemporary Principles, Standards and Related Issues

Prithul Chakraborty

ABSTRACT

The impact of financial instruments on the financial position, performance and earning potential of an enterprise has become more significant in the wake of globalization of capital markets and change in market regulations accompanied by increasing volatility in trading of financial instruments and, of course, by the onset of derivatives and other complex financial instruments in the markets. This has led to an urgent need for evaluation of the managerial performance in respect of the use of the financial instruments held by an enterprise. For this, proper recognition of financial assets and liabilities, periodical measurement of their values and adequate disclosure of the impact of changes in their values on the enterprise's earnings are very much imperative. The accounting standard-setting authorities of different countries including International Accounting Standards Board have already issued a number of accounting standards in this respect. Because of the wide existence of array of risks to which the financial instruments are exposed in the ever-changing market scenario, an incessant brain storming is still going on among the accounting standard-setters, professionals and academics across the globe in the matter of formulation and dissemination of pragmatic standards to ensure providing more relevant, reliable, comprehensive and comparable accounting information relating to financial instruments to all sections of the financial statement users' community. In this paper, an attempt has been made to critically review the rules and principles of accounting for financial instruments as provided by the prevailing internationally recognized accounting standards along with a focus on the reform initiatives being taken by the international accounting standard-setting bodies to issue more comprehensive, proactive and sensible accounting standards and principles for financial instruments.

4.1 Introduction

Accounting for financial instruments has become the most talked-about topic today among the accounting professionals and academics particularly in the context of a high level of uncertainty in the financial markets being caused by the transformation from regulation to liberalization and from planned economy to market-oriented economy across the globe. The uncertain financial markets bring about a wide range of risks in the forms of change in interest rate, foreign exchange rate, and security price and so on to the business enterprises. Such risks may pose a threat to the survival of an otherwise successful business. In this critical scenario, the stewardship function assigned by the owners of a business enterprise upon its management puts before the latter a mission to manage those risks effectively and efficiently in order to satisfy the formers' interest, i.e., maximization of the value of the business and thereby maximizing the owners' wealth. The proper and prudent use of the assets and liabilities of the firm is the essence of the management's success in performing this task. Financial instrument being a contract that simultaneously gives rise to a financial asset of one enterprise and a financial liability of another enterprise is more vulnerable to risks than all other assets and liabilities of a firm. Financial instrument leads to a contractual obligation of one party to deliver cash or any other financial asset to a second party and a corresponding contractual right of the second party to receive that cash or financial asset in exchange for no consideration other than release from the obligation. Therefore, apart from the aforementioned risks, financial instruments are also exposed to liquidity risk and default risk stemming from both macroeconomic factors as well as idiosyncratic factors. The impact of financial instruments on the financial position and earning potential of an enterprise has become more significant in the wake of globalization of capital markets and change in market regulations accompanied by the increasing volatility in trading of financial instruments and, of course, by the onset of derivatives and other complex financial instruments in the markets . Because of their flexible character, in addition to the normal use as sophisticated tools for hedging risks, derivatives are being increasingly used by the business firms and financial institutions for earning excessive profits through speculation resulting in often financial disasters to the investors.

In view of the foregoing, understanding the performance of the financial instruments has become a great challenge particularly in the perspective of all the developments and changes taking place in the financial markets. At present, no business entity exists without the financial instrument, be it as simple as cash in hand, loans and receivables or high-end innovative and complex instruments like derivatives. Therefore, efficient management of the financial instruments has now become a vital concern of not only the managers but also the present and prospective investors of all business enterprises and even the regulators and policy makers. In this backdrop, accounting for financial instruments has assumed a paramount importance to the interested parties because of its significant role in creation of a communication framework to provide relevant, reliable, comprehensive and comparable information on certain crucial issues like the following:

- Impact of the financial instruments on the financial position and performance of an entity
- Nature and extent of risks arising from the financial instruments to which the entity is exposed during the reporting period and at the reporting date
- Effectiveness of the strategy taken by the entity for mitigating such risks

The growing complexity, diversity and volume of the financial instruments have led to an urgent need for evaluation of the managerial performance in respect of their use and for this, periodical measurement of the values of the financial assets and liabilities and proper disclosure of the impact of changes in their values on the firm's earnings are very much essential. With a view to address the above-mentioned issues, an overwhelming urge has been witnessed among the accounting standard-setters of different countries of the world since the last decade to formulate and promulgate accounting standards and principles in the matter of recognition, classification, measurement, presentation and disclosure of financial instruments. An incessant brain storming is still going on among the accounting standard-setters, professionals and academics all over the world in the matter of formulation of appropriate accounting principles relating to financial instruments which would be universally acceptable to all concerned. Previously, most financial instruments were measured at historical cost. But as the increasing uncertainty of the markets causes the financial instruments to be more complicated and highly exposed to a wide array of risks and effective mitigation of such risks becomes an essential condition for sustainable financial growth of an enterprise and since this requires proper reporting of the economic value of financial instruments which the traditional accounting fails to provide, the accounting standard-setters feel the need to introduce market-based valuation of the financial instruments which invites fair value approach for measuring financial instruments. But adoption of fair value approach in financial instruments accounting gives rise to a number of valid questions in the minds of the preparers and users of financial statements regarding the appropriateness of such approach to the valuation of all financial instruments under all circumstances, reasonable basis of determination of fair value, frequency of such valuation particularly when this market-based value is subject to ever-changing market forces, proper mode of presentation of changes in fair value in the income statement, verifiability, reliability and relevance of the accounting numbers based on such value and so on.

A modest endeavour has been made in this paper to critically review the rules and principles of accounting for financial instruments as provided by the prevailing internationally recognized accounting standards and to focus on the reform initiatives being taken by the international accounting standard-setting bodies to issue more pragmatic standards and principles relating to accounting for financial instruments. The rest part of the paper is organized as follows: Section 4.2 discusses the evolution of the accounting standards on financial instruments with special reference to the international accounting standards (IASs) and generally accepted accounting principles of the USA (US GAAPs) and the development taking place in India in this field. The third section, Section 4.3, provides an overview of the rules and principles under the prevailing accounting standards pointing out the areas with similarities and differences between the IASs and US GAAPs. The controversial issues arising from the present accounting standards are deliberated in Section 4.4 while Section 4.5 focuses on the initiatives taken recently by the standard-setting bodies for sorting out those controversies and developing more pragmatic and rational rules and principles for accounting for financial instruments. The final section, Section 4.6, draws conclusion with a few suggestions that may be considered by the standard-setters in their effort to make the accounting standards more conducive to fulfilment of the multi-dimensional expectations of the users of the financial statements.

4.2 Evolution of Accounting Standards on Financial Instruments—A Chronicle

The history of accounting for financial instruments shows that initially, the measurement of financial instruments was dependent on whether the instruments were of short or long term. While the value of the short-term instruments was reported at the lower of cost or market price, the long-term instruments were valued at cost only. But this simple accounting rule failed to keep pace with the increasing complexity and multiplicity of financial instruments and structured financial transactions. Moreover, previously, derivatives were not recognized on balance sheet because of nearly zero cost being incurred at the time of entering into a derivative contract. In consequence thereof, a number of accounting scandals leading to excessive speculative trading on securities, unforeseen losses on derivatives, off-balance sheet financing, etc. have been witnessed in different parts of the world. This has created an impulse among the accounting principle makers to promulgate appropriate accounting norms and principles for financial instruments.

In respect of promulgation of the principles relating to accounting for financial instruments, the pioneering role has been played by the Financial Accounting Standards Board (FASB) of the USA since the mid-1980s when it commenced a project on financial instruments accounting. Initially, as and when a crisis arose relating to reporting of financial instruments, the FASB used to provide guidance for its immediate solution in a piecemeal fashion. The early 1990s saw for the first time comprehensive accounting principles for financial instruments when a number of Statements of Financial Accounting Standard (SFAS) are issued by the FASB mandating recognition and disclosure of various kinds of financial instruments in the financial statements. Two important standards are SFAS107, *Disclosure about fair value of financial instruments* (issued in 1991) and SFAS119, *Disclosure about derivative financial instruments and fair value of financial instruments* (issued in 1994). It is for the first time when SFAS 107 provides a definition of fair value and requires disclosure of all recognized financial assets and liabilities at fair value. With the passage of time, since there is a change in value of the underlying variable (e.g., rate, price or index) of a derivative instrument and this change leads to a positive or negative value to the derivative instrument, it needs to be recognized in the financial statement. Considering this, SFAS 119 requires disclosure of fair value estimates of derivative financial instruments. In addition thereto, FASB issues some more accounting standards like SFAS 105, *Disclosure of information about financial instruments with off balance sheet risk and financial instruments with concentrations of credit risk* (issued in 1990), SFAS 115, *Accounting for certain investments in debt and equity securities* (issued in 1993), SFAS 123, *Share-based payments* (issued in 2004), and SFAS 133, *Accounting for derivative instruments and hedging activities* (issued in 1998). SFAS 115 provides for mixed measurement approach allowing certain classes of financial assets to be measured at fair value and certain class at amortized cost. SFAS 133 requires for the first time that a firm should record all derivatives as either assets or liabilities at fair value in the statement of financial position.

The International Accounting Standards Committee (IASC), the predecessor of the present International Accounting Standards Board (IASB), starts to play a pivotal role in the matter of formulation and dissemination of accounting principles for financial instruments since the second half of the last decade. Initially, it issues two important international accounting standards on financial instruments: (i) IAS 32, *Financial Instruments: Disclosure and Presentation* (issued in 1995) and (ii) IAS 39, *Financial Instruments: Recognition and Measurement* (issued in 1999). IAS 32, passing through several amendments since its issue in 1995, defines the key financial instrument terms and provides the requirements for basic financial reporting disclosure and presentation for financial instruments. On the other hand, IAS 39 focuses on two important areas: (i) principles relating to accounting for financial instruments including derivatives, if not designated for hedging, which cover recognition and derecognition of financial instruments, their classification and measurement and accounting treatment of gains or losses from changes in values of the financial instruments, and (ii) principles relating to hedge accounting which deal with recognition and derecognition of hedging instruments and hedged items, eligibility criteria for hedge accounting and accounting treatments for different types of hedging relationships. In August 2005, the IASB issues IFRS 7, *Financial Instruments: Disclosure*, to replace IAS 32 insofar, as it provides the disclosure requirements. The remaining part of IAS 32 that provides principles and guidance for presentation and classification of financial instruments (e.g., debt or equity, compound financial instruments and so on) is still in effect and renamed as *Financial Instruments: Presentation.* Moreover, IFRS 7 supersedes the disclosure requirements of IAS 30, *Disclosures in the Financial Statements of Banks and Similar Financial Institutions* (issued in 1990) and introduces new disclosure requirements which are not only bank-specific but also applicable to all types of companies irrespective of whether those companies are financial or non-financial, and hold large or small portfolios of financial instruments. IFRS 7 requires disclosure of not only valuation information of the recognized financial instruments, both those measured at fair value and those at amortized cost, but also the qualitative information of those financial instruments like their liquidity risk, credit risk and so on.

A notable point is that while the IAS 32 and IFRS 7 are similar to their US counterparts SFAS 107 and SFAS 119, IAS 39 is similar to SFAS 115 and SFAS 133 with certain minor differences among them. In fact, when IAS 39 was on anvil and deliberations were carried on by the IASC in this regard, the FASB had already issued formal guidance on recognition and measurement of financial instruments. Therefore, much of the provisions of IAS 39 are found to be similar to those of the FASB standards. The standards issued by the IASB are now recognized as GAAPs by many countries of the world including the European Union that requires the firms of its member countries to prepare their financial statements in accordance with the IASB standards. In their efforts to bring about a harmonization between the US GAAPs and IASB standards regarding measurement and disclosure of financial instruments, both the FASB and the IASB have already initiated a joint project to promulgate uniform standards.

Previously, there was no laid down accounting principles for financial instruments in India, except AS 13 providing principles for investment accounting, AS 11 relating to accounting for the effects of changes in foreign exchange rates and a few Guidance Notes issued by the Institute of Chartered Accountants of India (ICAI) on Guarantees and Counter Guarantees given by the Companies, Accounting for Securitization, Accounting for Equity Index Futures, Accounting for Equity Index Options and Equity Stock Options, etc. In most of the cases, those accounting standards and guidance notes are not in consonance with their international counterparts. This has impeded the comparability of the financial statements of the Indian business enterprises and financial institutions with their foreign counterparts which is not favourable to them in achieving a niche in the global competitive market. Therefore, the Council of the ICAI has issued AS 30, *Financial Instruments: Recognition and Measurement*, AS 31, *Financial Instruments: Presentation* and AS 32, *Financial Instruments: Disclosure*. AS 30, AS 31 and AS 32 are formulated substantially as replicas of IAS 39,

IAS 32 and IFRS 7, respectively, with a view to accomplish the objective of bringing synchronization between international accounting standards and Indian accounting standards.

4.3 Rules and Principles of the Prevailing Accounting Standards—An Overview and Search for Similarities and Differences between IASB Standards and FASB Standards

In order to provide appropriate basis for measurement of the financial instruments for reporting in the balance sheet and to provide the principles for recognition of gains or losses on changes in values of the financial assets and liabilities in the income statement, both the IASB and FASB standards have given more emphasis on the nature, character and purpose of holding of the instruments by the entity. From this point of view, the financial instruments are classified into four distinct categories by IAS 39 and three categories by SFAS 115. While the three categories recognized by both the standards are: (i) Financial Assets and Liabilities Held at Fair Value through Profit or Loss (HaFV) or Held for Trading (HFT) instruments, (ii) Held-to-Maturity(HTM) Investment and (iii) Available for Sale (AFS) Financial Assets , the fourth category only specific to IAS 39 is Loans & Receivables (L&R). Given below are some ideas regarding the nature and characteristic of the above-mentioned categories of financial instruments as postulated by the accounting standards:

- *Held at Fair Value through Profit or Loss (HaFV)*: The financial assets and liabilities that are held for trading (HFT) in the near short run with an intention to make profit out of short-term price changes are brought under this category. This category incorporates derivative instruments also if these instruments are not designated as hedging instruments.
- *Held-to-Maturity Investments (HTM)*: These are the non-derivative financial assets generating determinable cash flows and having a fixed maturity date till when the holder of the assets has a positive intention and ability to hold the assets. Investments that have no fixed and determinable maturity date (e.g., equity) cannot be classified under this category.
- *Available-for-Sale Financial Assets (AFS)*: This is the residuary class encompassing all non-derivative financial assets that are not classified under any other categories. Investments in other firms neither held for making short-term profit nor being held till maturity (e.g., debt securities) are likely to be brought under this category.
- *Loans and Receivables (L&R)*: Financial assets of this category have the same criteria as HTM assets. However, L&R originated by enterprise should not be quoted in an active market and the entity should not have any intention to sell these assets in near future (i.e., the assets should not be of HFT nature). L&R is relevant not only for the banks and financial institutions, but also for manufacturing firms as L&R result from supply of money (e.g., loan by a bank) as well as supply of goods and services (i.e., trade receivables).
- Though not explicitly specified by the standards, there is one more category of financial liabilities that is *financial liabilities at amortized cost.*

At the time of entering into a financial contract, the firm must have to carefully choose the appropriate category for each financial asset and liability because sometimes this classification is irrevocable in nature and this choice of category significantly affects the valuation of the instruments, their mode of presentation and recognition of changes in their carrying amounts in the income statement.

4.3.1 Measurement Principles for Financial Instruments

Applicability of a particular basis of measurement, be it amortized cost or fair vale, should depend on the nature and characteristics of the financial assets and liabilities to be measured, restrictions on the sale of those assets, availability of most advantageous market for those assets and liabilities and the purposes for which they are held by an entity. That is why both the IASB and the FASB standards provide for mixed-measurement or 'part fair value, part amortized cost' model for determination of the carrying values of the financial instruments. In general, fair value approach should be adopted for measurement of the financial assets and liabilities of HaFV category which are basically held for trading in the near short run. The financial assets of AFS category, although unlike the first category not meant for trading in immediate future, are also required to be measured at fair value because in case of such assets, there is a high probability that the changes in their value caused by changes in different external factors would be realized at any moment. The other categories of financial assets (L&R and HTM investments) and financial liabilities should be measured at amortized cost using the effective interest method. There are two logics behind adopting amortized cost basis in respect of such financial instruments: (i) the timing and size of the future cash flows to be generated by these instruments are predictable because they are contractual in nature and held for a certain period of time and (ii) there is no active market for these instruments and, therefore, determination of reliable fair value for those instruments would be a matter of intricacy.

However, IAS 39 provides a unique requirement that at the time of initial recognition of the financial assets and liabilities, all financial assets and liabilities should be measured at fair value irrespective of their categories. Here, fair value is equivalent to transaction price or market price (i.e., the consideration given in respect of financial asset and consideration received in respect of financial liabilities) provided that the transaction is not between related parties and not made under any distress. In the case of a financial instrument being exchanged for other financial instrument (otherwise than for cash), the initial measurement should be on the basis of the fair value of that other financial instrument. Transaction costs incurred by the entity at the time of entering into a contractual arrangement (e.g., fees and commissions paid to agents, brokers and dealers, transfer taxes, etc.) are included in the transaction price for initial measurement of all financial assets and liabilities except those of HaFV category.

4.3.2 Treatment of Gains and Losses

The principles for recognition of gains or losses on changes in values of financial assets and liabilities as promulgated by the standards are basically related to one issue, i.e., whether MTM (Marking to Market) accounting is relevant for the financial assets and liabilities or not. MTM accounting requires carrying of an asset or liability in the balance sheet at a fair value instead of amortized cost. Therefore, MTM accounting is relevant for the financial assets and liabilities of HaFV category and AFS assets, since these instruments are carried at fair value, but not relevant for L&R and HTM assets which are carried at amortized cost.

Fair value being a market price-based measurement, tends to change because of changing market forces. Therefore, MTM valuation results in gain or loss due to change in fair value of the financial instruments. We find a consistency between the IASB standards and the FASB standards regarding recognition of gain or loss arising out of such MTM valuation of HaFV and AFS assets. The financial assets and liabilities of HaFV category are marked to market every trading day since these are held for short-term trading purpose and, therefore, gain or loss arising from such MTM valuation should be recognized in the income statement. On the other hand, AFS assets are required to be marked to market only at the time of financial reporting (say, every half-year) and gain or loss on such assets should be recognized in an appropriate equity reserve account like investment revaluation reserve account (or Other Comprehensive Income as per FASB standards) until such financial assets are derecognized. On derecognition of the assets, the amount of such gains or losses accumulated in the equity reserve account should be transferred to the income statement.

But in respect of the financial assets and liabilities carried at amortized cost, a gain or loss may arise at the time of their derecognition by way of a difference between the carrying amount of such assets/liabilities and the consideration received/paid at the time of extinguishment or discharge or other derecognition of the assets/liabilities. Such gain or loss is recognized in the income statement through amortization process.

4.3.3 Treatment of Impairment Losses

In respect of the financial assets reported at amortized cost and the financial assets of AFS category, there may be impairment or decline in value of such assets due to certain events like financial difficulty or delinquency on the part of the debtor, concession made by the lender, a high probability of bankruptcy of the borrower, etc. These are called loss events that occur after the initial recognition of the assets. In order to bring the effect of such impairment in the income statement, the IAS 39 provides a unique requirement that an entity should determine at the end of each reporting period whether there is any objective evidence (i.e., observable data) of such impairment and the loss event(s) has (have) an impact on the estimated future cash flows of the financial assets. If it is so, the impairment loss should be recognized in the income statement. The amount of such loss is measured as the difference between the asset's carrying amount and the present value of estimated futures cash flows (excluding future credit losses) discounted at the original effective interest rate of the financial asset. However, the standards permit recognition of impairment losses which have already been incurred and not future potential losses.

4.3.4 Hedge Accounting

The use of hedge accounting allows an entity to reflect the effectiveness of a hedge relationship in the financial statements by offsetting the unfavourable change in the value of an asset or liability (i.e., *hedged item*) with the gains/losses from a position in a derivative instrument(s) [i.e., *hedging instrument(s)*]. The hedge accounting principles promulgated by the accounting standards call for modification of the usual accounting treatment of the hedging instruments and hedged items in order to properly recognize the offsetting effects on profit or loss of changes in the fair values of the hedging instruments and changes in fair values/future cash flows of the hedged items which are attributable to the risk being hedged. Since the hedging instruments are treated by the accounting standards as HFT assets, these instruments are measured at fair value and require regular MTM. Gains or losses on such MTM valuation are to be recognized in income statement. On the other hand, the hedged items include any asset, liability, firm commitment or net investment in foreign operations. Such assets or liabilities may be measured at fair value or amortized cost. Changes in fair value or future cash flow make the firm exposed to a wide variety of risks through changes in interest rate, foreign exchange rate, equity price, commodity price, etc. The impact of such changes on the income statement may be immediate or in future.

Although there is a marginal difference between IAS 39 and SFAS 133 in terms of classification of the hedge relationships, a consistency is found between the two standards in respect of accounting rules for different types of hedges. Both the accounting standards classify the hedging relationship into three categories, viz., (i) hedge of the exposure to changes in fair value of the hedged item (called *Fair Value Hedge*), (ii) hedge of the exposure to changes in cash flows of the hedged item (called *Cash Flow Hedge*), and (iii) hedge of the foreign exchange exposure to net investment in foreign operations (called *Net Investment in Foreign Operations Hedge*).

In case of fair value hedge, the gain or loss from change in fair values of the hedging instrument should be recognized in the income statement and the gain or loss arising due to change in fair value of the hedged item (including HTM securities which are normally measured at amortized cost) attributable to the hedged risk should be adjusted with the carrying amount of the hedged item and be recognized in the income statement. However, SFAS 133 requires the net difference between the change in fair value of the hedging instrument and the change in fair value of the hedged item (i.e., the ineffectiveness of the fair value hedge) to be recorded through income statement.

On the other side, hedge effectiveness has a significant effect on accounting for a cash flow hedge. Hedge effectiveness is determined by the extent to which the variation in the value of the hedged item is safeguarded by the hedging instrument. The gain or loss from change in fair value of the hedging instrument which is pertaining to the effective portion of the hedge should be initially recognized in an appropriate equity reserve account like Hedging Reserve Account (but in Other Comprehensive Income as per SFAS 133) and the ineffective portion of change in fair value of the hedging instrument should be recognized directly in the income statement of the current period. The main objective of carry forward of the unrealized gain or loss on the effective portion of the hedge is to offset the variation in forecasted cash flow of the hedged item at a later date. The accumulated amount of such gains/losses is transferred to the income statement in the period in which the hedged transaction affects the earnings.

The accounting treatments of hedge of a net investment in foreign operations are similar to that of cash flow hedge both under IAS 39 and SFAS 133.

A notable point is that hedging of unrecognized firm commitment to buy or sell an asset at a fixed price is classified by SFAS 133 as a fair value hedge and as a cash flow hedge by IAS 39. Even in respect of the unrecognized firm commitment with foreign exchange exposure, the SFAS 133 specifically provides that it should be treated as fair value hedge. On the other hand, both IAS 39 and SFAS 133 agree to treat the hedging of AFS securities involving foreign currency exposure to the enterprise as fair value hedge and the accounting treatment for this kind of hedge is similar to that of a fair value hedge in both the standards.

4.4 Controversial Issues on Prevailing Accounting Standards

A study of the prevailing standards relating to accounting for financial instruments reveals that the principles require substantial changes to the traditional systems, methods and documentation in the matter of recognition, valuation and disclosure of financial instruments and also require changes to the way the enterprises view and manage risks. Since financial instruments are complex instruments having exposure to different kinds of risks which need to be managed in different ways, the managers as well as investors are interested to predict their future performances on the basis of their past and present performances. For presenting the past performance of the financial instruments, the measurement of the instruments was traditionally made at amortized cost. But the uncertain market has a substantial impact on the economic value and performance of the financial instruments and their inherent risks. The traditional historical cost accounting is too unfit to properly depict such values and risks. Therefore, both the FASB and the IASB standards have given much emphasis on fair value accounting for financial instruments along with continuation of the amortized cost-based accounting in respect of certain instruments where adoption of fair value basis is either irrelevant or infeasible in evaluating present performance and estimating future performance.

The accounting standards prefer amortized cost basis of measurement when the instruments are held to maturity in order to generate predictable future cash flows because in this case, temporary changes in fair value have no impact either on the current operations of the entity or on prediction of the future cash flows. But when the entity is actively engaged in trading activities and thereby being exposed to opening and closing market risk positions, short-term changes in fair value become a crucial factor in presenting the current earning position of the entity and estimating the future performance of the financial instruments. The standard setters are of the opinion that fair value can measure the performance of financial instruments in a better manner than the cost-based measure because fair value absorbs the effect of all economic events occurred during the reporting period. In a vibrant economic environment, any measurement based on amortized cost must inevitably be out-dated as unlike fair value, it fails to provide up-to-date measure of an entity's financial position and performance. Moreover, fair value accounting attempts to regulate the pricing mechanism of trading financial instruments and bring a greater transparency in reporting their values in the financial statements which is very much imperative in curbing the unhealthy speculative trading in such instruments and improving the pricing efficiency of the market which is an essential condition for economic development of a country.

A lot of debates are there as to whether fair value–based hedge accounting affects the risk management behaviour of a firm or not. In mid-1990s the banking organizations in the USA criticized the FASB's proposal for fair value–based hedge accounting on the ground that it failed to properly reflect the risk management activities of the banks and it triggered excessive volatility in comprehensive income that caused investors to overstate their risk assessment. On the contrary, a number of empirical studies do not support any significant effect of fair value–based hedge accounting on volatility in income statement (Park 2004; Singh 2004; etc.). But hedging instruments, which are basically derivative instruments, cause new risks that cannot be appropriately addressed to or recognized under traditional cost accounting. In order to ensure transparent use of the derivative instruments for managing or hedging risks more effectively, fair value–based hedge accounting is needed. Hedge accounting based on fair value approach helps a firm in identifying its underlying risk exposure in a better way and in choosing the best hedging alternative (Melumad et al. 1999). If changes in fair value of the hedged item caused by the entity's risk exposure are recognized in the income statement, volatility in income statement will depict the income volatility associated with market-based risk factors and it will provide proper information regarding the risk management activities of the firm. Accounting principles for fair value hedge as provided by the standards require inclusion of fair value changes for all financial instruments in the income statement and thereby providing more complete proxy for the systematic risks. At present, the financial enterprises start to realize the importance of fair value–based hedge accounting through their experience that earning would be less volatile over time if the net effect of changes in fair values of the hedging instruments and the hedged items is recognized in the income statement.

But the present accounting standards relating to financial instruments are exposed to a number of controversial issues some of which are highlighted in the following.

- It is always desirable that accounting rules and principles should ensure a proper balance between complexity and explicability of the information presented in the financial statement because all its users may not have the required knowledge and skill in studying and analysing the accounting numbers. Unfortunately, the rules provided by the present accounting standards are too stringent, rigid and tough to understand, interpret and apply and to provide intricate information in an intelligible manner. It requires high level of professional expertise both for the preparers and users of financial statements which is not available under all circumstances. Moreover, the standards provide stringent rules on hedge accounting that call for formal designation and documentation of hedge relationship, documentation of risk management objectives and strategy of the firm, identification of the hedging instruments, hedged items and nature of the risks being hedged and assessment of hedge effectiveness. This involves a lot of hurdles including non-availability of proper documents or its availability at high cost. Because of such high costs and complications, the managements of the enterprises have to make a trade-off between the cost of maintaining hedge accounting and the potential benefit achieved by reduction in income statement volatility that would otherwise arise.
- According to the IASB, the current accounting standards provide neither a clear measurement objective nor a robust measurement framework. The standards provide for the use of mixed measurement model or 'part amortized cost, part fair value' model for valuation of financial instruments which not only increases the complexity of financial reporting but also reduces the comprehensibility of the accounting information. Sometimes identical assets held by two companies are measured in different ways. For example, a particular bond held by an investment bank as trading asset in order to gain a profit from changes in its price is required to be measured at fair value through profit or loss whereas the same bond held by a retail banking company as HTM asset in order to receive a stable flow of income over the period till its maturity is to be measured at amortized cost. The employment of different measurement criteria for the same asset may reduce the comparability between the financial statements of the two companies. Moreover, while using the financial statements for decision-making purpose, the investors are to devote considerable time and attention to study the choices made by the management for determining the basis of measurement of financial instruments. Naturally, the investors find it difficult to concentrate on other relevant issues pertaining to their decision-making process.

- Relevance and reliability are two essential criteria of fair value–based information. While relevance signifies the potential of fair value to impact the decisions of the financial statement users, reliability ensures that the reported fair value represents what it is purported to represent (Barth et al. 2001). One cannot expect information to be reliable unless it is relevant; similarly an unreliable information can never be relevant. Therefore, while using the financial statements, the users want to see a proper balance between the relevance and reliability of the accounting numbers. In order to ensure relevance of the accounting information, the users like to know whether the fair value–based accounting numbers disclosed in the financial statements would be more informative and have more impact on the share price or return of the firm as compared to the traditional historical cost–based accounting information. At the same time, both the financial statement preparers and users are interested to know whether the fair value can be estimated with more reliability and less bias. In order to assess whether best measurement of the financial instruments is possible under fair value accounting and whether such measurement is sufficiently reliable or not, a cost-benefit trade-off between relevance and reliability is essential.

  A widely accepted way of assessing the relevance of the disclosed accounting information is to ascertain its incremental association with the share price or share return of the firm. A number of empirical studies (Barth 1994; Barth et al. 1995; etc.) suggest that the valuation information of financial assets and liabilities based on fair value are incrementally associated with the entities' share prices after controlling for other accounting and market information. These studies also reveal that fair value–based measures of net income are more volatile than historical cost–based measures but that incremental volatility has very trivial reflection in the share prices. On the other hand, accounting information would be relevant if such information help in understanding the timing and quantum of the potential cash flows of the financial instruments and their exposure to credit risk and liquidity risk. Fair value may be considered as relevant to a lender, while assessing the loans granted by it to a business enterprise, if the future potential of the asset to generate cash flows and the ability of the borrowing firm to meet its obligation can be accurately represented by the fair value. But fair value becomes irrelevant for the financial assets which the firm has no intention to sell and/or for which there is no knowledgeable and willing counterparty in the market. Rather, in this case, amortized cost, including allowances for impairment loss in financial assets, provides the users with more relevant information on potential cash flow performance of the instruments.

  So as far as reliability of fair value–based accounting information is concerned, it may be stated that current fair value of financial instruments and movement in such values during the accounting period or between two reporting dates cannot faithfully present the transactions in financial instruments and their impact on the financial position and performance of the firm unless the instruments are held by the firm for the purpose of trading in the near short run. Furthermore, the reliability of accounting information under fair value accounting can be gauged by the cost of fair value measurement. This cost is incurred by the investors and other users of financial statement when some or even many of the financial instruments cannot be measured with adequate accuracy in consequence of which the financial position and earning potential of the firm cannot be reliably and properly reflected in the financial statements (SEC 2005). Some experts opine that fair value being based on current market conditions may fail to contribute to a reliable understanding of the actual cash flows that would be achieved by entering into the transactions particularly under the rapidly changing market conditions. This reliability cost is further multiplied in the absence of any deep, liquid and vibrant markets for the financial instruments, non-existence of ideal market conditions and non-availability of knowledgeable, independent and economically rational market participants. Under this situation, management is compelled to estimate the fair value of such instruments either by using current fair value of any surrogate financial instrument or by using discounted cash flow technique or option pricing model which are highly subjective and potentially unreliable and biased. Thus, fair value measurement of financial instruments leaves the users with a critical task of making a cost-benefit trade-off between relevance and reliability of accounting information.

- Moreover, estimation of fair value may cause manipulation or discretion by the management. For instance, management may be tempted not to use certain unfavourable information privately held by them as inputs to fair value estimation process. This may give rise to two serious problems: (i) adverse selection and (ii) moral hazards. In the absence of adequate and plausible information, the market tends to value the apparently identical financial instruments held by two firms similarly while assessing their fair values. This may lead to adverse selection problem if one of the firms has portfolio of higher quality financial assets than the other (Landsman 2006). On the other side, the problem of moral hazards arises when the managers tend to use their private information to manipulate fair value of the financial instruments in order to fulfil their own interest (Landsman 2006). This may lead to mispricing of stocks of the firms (i.e., a deviation of the market price of the stock from its fair price) and inaccurate portrayal of the financial position of the firms to the users of the financial statements. Therefore, fair value accounting for financial instruments sets before the accounting standard-setters a challenge of determining how much latitude or freedom is to be given to the managers in their use of private information in fair value estimation process so that the problems of adverse selection and moral hazards can be mitigated.
- The existing accounting standards call for inclusion in the income statement of the effect of changes in fair value of the financial instruments resulting from market price movement even though no actual transaction takes place for the instruments. Thus, gains or losses are recognized in the income statement just when market rates change and not when such gains are realized or losses are suffered. Recognition of unrealized gain/loss in the income statement may lead to greater volatility and unpredictability in earning. This is substantiated also by the findings of a number of empirical studies (Barth et al. 1995; Hodder et al. 2006). Presenting changes in fair value in the income statement affects both relevance and reliability of accounting information (Maines and Wahlen 2006) and also has a significant association with the share prices and annual share returns of the firms (Stella and Smith 2009). This may go against the desire of the investors/shareholders for smooth earning growth and growth in share return, putting the firm and its management reputation at risk. However, the proponents of the fair value measurement hold the view that the objective of financial statement is not to smoothen the profit figures but to depict the economic reality of the firm to enable the users to make economic decision (Mc Bride 2006). Moreover, the outcome of many researches'

documents is that that the recognition of unrealized gains in the income statement has no significant influence over the decision making of the investors (IASCF 2008).

- For effective hedge, change in fair value of the hedging instrument should be directly correlated with the change in fair value or cash flow of the hedged item. But in the event of any mismatch between the aforesaid changes in values of the hedging instrument and hedged item, the net effect thereon represents the hedge ineffectiveness which is recognized in the income statement. Regular monitoring of the effectiveness of the hedge throughout the hedge period is a condition to be fulfilled for carrying on hedge accounting. When a hedge fails the effectiveness test, the hedge accounting is discontinued prospectively. A hedge is considered to be effective if the hedge is expected to achieve offsetting of changes in fair value or cash flow of the hedged item attributable to the hedged risk during the period of hedge (prospective test) and if the actual results of the hedge (i.e., gain or loss on hedging instrument/loss or gain on hedged item) are within the range of 80 per cent to 125 per cent (retrospective test). But this norm of hedge effectiveness cannot be maintained by a firm in case of a surrogate or proxy hedge, because in this case, in absence of a hedging instrument on the underlying hedged asset, the firm has to use any hedging instrument on different asset the price of which, although moves in tandem with the price of the hedged asset, is not perfectly correlated to that price. This results in hedging ineffectiveness beyond 80 percent to 125 per cent range and, therefore, the firm may not be successful in applying hedge accounting.
- Criticisms against IAS 39 and SFAS 133 find a new dimension when the recent turbulence of the financial markets brings a lot of controversies to the forefront holding some of the requirements of those standards responsible for the financial ferment. *First*, the banks have to follow the capital adequacy norms as set by their regulating authority. During the recent financial crisis period, there was a continuous fall in market prices of the securities. Since these securities were held by the banks as HFT assets, these were measured at falling market prices as per the requirement of IAS 39 and SFAS 133. In consequence thereof, the banks had to witness substantial erosion in their capital adequacy ratio. This had adversely affected the banks' ability to lend which, in turn, aggravated the recessionary condition of the economy. *Second*, the concern about the IASB's role in exacerbating the financial crisis became more serious in October 2008 when all of a sudden the IASB made an amendment to IAS 39 allowing reclassification of certain financial assets from HFT category to L&R category. As a result of such amendment, the sub-prime mortgages which could no longer be traded due to illiquid market had been reclassified as L&R by the banks. On such reclassification, those assets became subject to management impairment review as per requirement of IAS 39. Impairment decision is largely influenced by the management discretion and, therefore, the managers of the banks got an opportunity to suppress the impact of impairment on the income position of the banks. Beside this, such reclassification helped the banks avoid MTM valuation of the sub-prime mortgages and thereby offering a scope of protecting their capital adequacy ratio in an unhealthy manner. Thus, the amendment had served the short-term interests of the banks at the cost of its financial distress in the long run and, at the same time, debarred the investors from getting real information about the financial position of the banks. *Third*, the HTM assets are measured at amortized cost rather than at fair value because these assets are held for long term without any intention to sell in near future. But, in practice, no firm can hold a financial

asset till maturity under all circumstances. The reality witnessed during the recent economic crisis reveals that the firms holding assets of HTM category are very much inclined to reclassify them as HFT assets to meet their short-term need for fund. But the requirements of the prevailing standards are too inconvenient to enable those firms to make such reclassification in tune with the demand of the situation. Further, the recent financial crisis shows that there are not enough knowledgeable and willing customers to buy toxic assets; but still the firms holding such assets have to use fair value basis for their measurement resulting in flawed or imperfect valuation.

4.5 Reform Initiatives Taken by the Standard-setting Bodies

The standard setters have already started to realize the complexity and other shortcomings of the existing accounting standards relating to financial instruments, particularly the drawbacks of the mixed-measurement model. Recognizing the worldwide importance of the issue, the Financial Instruments Joint Working Group (JWG) has been formed comprising representatives of the accounting standard-setting bodies of the UK, the US, Canada, France, Germany, Japan, Australia, New Zealand and many other countries. The JWG has issued a draft standard[1] in December 2000 that proposes radical changes to accounting for financial instruments. These include adoption of comprehensive fair value measurement model virtually for all financial instruments, recognition of all changes in fair value in the income statement, preclusion of special accounting for financial instruments used for hedging and detailed disclosure about the methods and assumptions used to determine the fair value of financial instruments, financial risk positions of an entity, and its objectives and policies for managing such risks.

Both the IASB and the FASB have agreed that some of the stringent, fuzzy and inexplicable provisions of their accounting standards were responsible for the recent financial disaster. This is clear from the following statement made by Sir David Tweedie, Chairman of the IASB, while introducing the IASB Exposure Draft of proposals to improve financial instruments accounting in July 2009:

> The financial crisis has demonstrated that investors need to be given a better understanding of information presented in the financial statements about financial instruments held or issued by a company. Making it easier for investors to understand financial statements is an essential ingredient to the recovery of investor confidence.

As part of the Memorandum of Understanding, *A Road map for convergence between IFRS and US GAAP 2006–08*, the IASB and the FASB have undertaken a joint project on Accounting for Financial Instruments including Accounting for Hedging Activities with a view to significantly improve the decision usefulness of financial instrument reporting and issuing a simplified common accounting standard for financial instruments that would be universally applicable. The major objectives of the project are to reconsider the recognition and measurement of financial instruments, address the issues pertaining to impairment of financial instruments, improve financial reporting of hedging activities to make the accounting model more comprehensible for the users and to increase convergence in accounting for financial instruments.[2] In order to improve the quality of the reporting for financial instruments, the Boards have agreed to develop a new standard for derecognition of financial instruments, require measurement of all financial instruments at fair value with recognition of the realized and unrealized gains and losses in the income statement in the period in which they occur and to eliminate the need for special hedge accounting requirements. As an outcome of the joint effort of the two Boards, the IASB has issued the March 2008 Discussion Paper, *Reducing Complexity in Reporting Financial Instruments*,[3] which the FASB has also published for comments by its constituents.

Considering that the main reason behind the complexity of the present standards is the multiplicity in designation and measurement of financial instruments, the IASB in its Discussion Paper, *Reducing Complexity in Reporting Financial Instruments*, has proposed for measuring all financial instruments in a uniform manner in order to make the financial statements more user friendly, consistent and transparent and to facilitate comparison between different entities and periods. The discussion paper has proposed for adoption of full fair value model for measurement of all types of financial instruments in the long run. It puts several arguments in favour of full fair value model some of which are as follows:

- Full fair value model would reduce the scope of ambiguity and confusion about measurement of financial assets and liabilities of different natures and characters.
- There would be no need for impairment testing and measuring impairment losses.
- Problems relating to reclassification of financial instruments would be eliminated.
- The balance sheet would reflect the value of a financial asset (liability) that would be received (paid) if an entity needs to sell (transfer) the asset (liability) at the balance sheet date and such information would be useful in ascertaining the true intrinsic value of the entity.
- Fair value, through indicating expected future cash flows, helps in predicting an entity's ability to take advantage of increase in value or to protect itself against decrease in value.
- Measuring all financial assets at fair value would help in providing information about anticipated future losses and improvements in credit risk of the assets since their origination.
- Measuring all financial liabilities at fair value would help entities with same credit ratings and obligations in reporting the liabilities at comparable amounts.

On the way to achieve the long-term objective of measuring all types of financial instruments at fair value, the IASB has offered a series of modifications[4] in IAS 39 in the interim period. This includes: (i) elimination of HTM and AFS categories, (ii) replacement of the existing mixed-measurement model with a fair value model with certain optional exceptions allowing measurement at cost, and (iii) simplifying existing requirements of hedge accounting.

The IASB has taken an endeavour to make a clear distinction between the instruments with highly variable cash flows and the instruments with fixed or only slightly variable cash flows so that fair value can be taken as the relevant measure for the former kind of instruments and amortized cost may be the appropriate alternative for measurement of the latter kind of instruments. In July 2009, the IASB issued an exposure draft standard, *Financial Instruments: Classification and Measurement*,[5] that divides all types of financial instruments into only two categories: (i) those measured at amortized cost and (ii) those measured at fair value. Only the financial instruments having basic loan features (i.e., the instruments with fixed or predictable cash flows in the form of payment of interest and principal instalments) and being managed on contractual yield basis will go under the first category while all other financial instruments will be brought under the second category. The IASB believes that the proposed reduction in classification of instruments will not only remove the complexity of classification but also succeed in achieving the long-term objective of application of the full fair value model.

However, full fair value model for measurement of all financial instruments is also subject to a number of valid criticisms in respect of the following:

- Inappropriateness of fair value measurement for a financial instrument held by an entity with an intention to earn a predictable cash flow on an ongoing basis till it matures.
- Increasing earning volatility through generation of unrealized gain or loss when measurement error in assets' fair value is not fully offset by measurement error in liabilities' fair value (Barth and Landsman 1995).
- Irrelevance of reporting change in fair value in the income statement if such change occurs due to short-term fluctuations in market prices that are beyond management's control.
- Too much dependence on the discretion or judgment of the management in estimating fair value in absence of any active market-based information that results in unreliable and biased value.
- Requirement of special supervisory expertise and understanding which may not be available under all circumstances.

So the standard setters should vigorously seek how best to minimize the aforesaid problems of full fair value approach for improving the decision usefulness of the accounting information to the investors and analysts. In paving the way towards universal application of fair value in the long run, the standard setters should emphasize three matters (i) clear definition of fair value, (ii) proper and simplified technique or approach for estimating fair value, and (iii) specific mode of presentation of changes in fair value in the income statement.

The IASB has already given due importance to the aforesaid matters. It joins hands with the FASB to examine the viability of full fair value model. A logical and feasible concept of fair value is the prerequisite for successful application of this model. The conventional concept of fair value is oriented towards the price at which an asset could be exchanged or a liability could be settled between knowledgeable, willing parties in an arms' length transaction. This concept implies existence of a perfectly efficient market where the participants are reasonably informed about the nature and characteristic of asset or liability and their potential values and behave in an unbiased manner in transacting such asset or liability. But since existence of a perfectly efficient market is a rare phenomenon, it has become necessary to replace this traditional concept of fair value by a more feasible one. The FASB issued its SFAS 157, *Fair Value Measurements*, in September 2006 that provides a more practical and logical definition of fair value (SFAS 157, Para-5) which focuses on the price that would be received to sell an asset or paid to transfer a liability (i.e., an exit price) in an orderly market (i.e., the principal market or, in its absence, the most advantageous market where the asset/liability would be sold/transferred at the most favourable price). This concept, of course, is based upon a hypothetical transaction (which should not be a forced transaction like a distress sale) at the measurement date, considered from the perspective of a market participant that holds the asset or owes the liability. This new concept of fair value helps in ascertaining future economic benefits associated with an asset and future sacrifices of economic benefits associated with a liability. For the sake of increasing convergence with the US GAAP, the IASB has already taken initiative to rejuvenate the concept of fair value in line with that of SFAS 157. The IASB has recently issued an

Exposure Draft on Fair Value Measurement[6] defining fair value, providing a framework for measuring fair value and requiring disclosure about fair value measurements which are largely consistent with SFAS 157. It is expected that the proposed guidelines on fair value measurement would help in introducing fair value accounting of financial instruments with less ambiguity and more simplicity.

The availability of inputs relevant for fair valuation of an asset or liability and the relative reliability of the inputs might have a bearing on selection of the appropriate valuation techniques. Therefore, the IASB exposure draft (ED/2009/5) also establishes a fair value hierarchy, mostly following the same as provided by SFAS 157, which involves the following three levels of inputs in order of their priority for use in fair valuation techniques:

Level 1 inputs are quoted prices (unadjusted) in active markets for identical assets or liabilities that can be easily accessed by the reporting entity at the measurement date.

Level 2 inputs are inputs other than quoted prices included in level 1 that are observable directly (i.e., prices) or indirectly (i.e., derived from prices) for the asset or liability. These include (i) quoted prices for similar assets or liabilities in active markets, (ii) quoted prices for identical or similar assets or liabilities in markets which are not active, (iii) other observable inputs for the assets or liabilities like interest rates, yield curves, prepayment speeds, default rates, etc.

Level 3 inputs are unobservable inputs for the asset or liability. These inputs are developed on the basis of the reporting entity's assumptions about the assumptions that market participants would make in pricing the asset or liability using the best information available in the circumstances.

While level 1 inputs provide the most reliable evidence of fair value and should be used to measure fair value whenever available, level 2 inputs should be used when level 1 inputs are not available. Level 3 inputs should be used to measure fair value to the extent that observable inputs are not available and under the situation when there is little market activity for the asset or similar asset at the measurement date. Thus, the fair value hierarchy reduces complexity in selection of reasonable and appropriate inputs to valuation techniques and thereby increasing reliability, consistency and comparability in fair value measurements.

The IASB exposure draft also proposes three approaches for estimation of fair value: (i) *Market approach* that uses prices and other relevant information generated by the market activities in respect of identical or comparable financial instruments; (ii) *Income approach* that uses discounted cash flow technique to convert estimated future cash flows or earnings into a single present value; and (iii) *Cost approach* that uses current replacement cost (i.e., the amount currently required to replace the service capacity of an existing asset) for determination of fair value. A firm should select that approach which is appropriate in the circumstances and for which sufficient and reliable inputs are available to measure the fair value. The exposure draft proposes for disclosure of information about the approach and inputs used to estimate the fair value of the assets and liabilities in order to provide transparency in the valuation process and to enable the users to assess the reliability of the fair value.

However, the IASB exposure draft remains silent about the mode of presentation of changes in fair value in the income statement. In order to provide decision useful information and to facilitate inter-firm and intra-firm comparison, all fair value changes should be reflected in income statement and recycling of such changes through other comprehensive income or equity reserve account should not be permitted. Otherwise, it may diminish the quality of financial reporting by distorting measurement of net income, earning per share and other performance metrics on which the investors have to rely while making investment decision. The IASB and the FASB should come out with certain specific and effective proposals in this respect. Otherwise, moving all financial instruments onto a fair value basis may just shift the accounting complexity from the balance sheet to the income statement.

In January 2007, the FASB took an initiative to address two critical issues relating to hedge accounting: (a) issues causing difficulties in hedge accounting and (b) potential approaches to accounting for hedging activities. Research on the first issue unearthed certain factors responsible for the difficulties in hedge accounting like strict documentation requirements, lack of clarity regarding designation and redesignation of the hedging instruments, method of assessing hedge effectiveness, consequences for failing to meet the criteria for hedge accounting and so on. To sort out these identified factors, the FASB has issued an Exposure Draft, *Accounting for Hedging Activities*, in June 2008. The exposure draft has received considerable response from different sections of the users' community that support the Board's proposal for a significant change in requirements for hedge accounting and simplification of accounting for hedging activities.

Thus, it is found that both the IASB and the FASB have given far-reaching emphasis on their scheme to develop comprehensive and simplified standards with an aim to provide greater transparency, relevance and reliability in the reporting of financial instruments.

4.6 Conclusion

Finally, it may be said that any change towards simplification is welcome when the benefits of such simplification outweigh the costs of such change. Full fair value model of accounting for financial instruments may ensure simplification in accounting principles through bringing uniformity in designation and measurement of financial instruments, but it may give rise to many new problems instead of optimally solving the present problems of accounting for financial instruments. It is true that uniformity may enhance the comparability of the financial statements. But the users' demand regarding financial statements is not confined to comparability only. They want financial statements to be more relevant, reliable, intelligible and also verifiable. Users may doubt whether full fair value model would be able to satisfy their aforesaid demands particularly when the financial instruments are neither traded in a liquid market nor held with the intention to trade. Moreover, it is apprehended that full fair value measurement may reflect complicated information in the financial statement that need to be supplemented by additional disclosure on explanation of various estimations being used and the factors responsible for changes in fair value. If this model is perceived by the management and the users of financial statements as not faithfully and transparently presenting the facts and underlying trends of performance, the financial statements may be relegated to the status of a mere compliance report. Finding no interest in such documents, the users will search for informal reports that may quench their thirst in a better way which would be detrimental to the fulfilment of overall accounting objectives. Therefore, unless all sections of the users of financial statements arrive at a consensus regarding the ability of full fair value model to provide decision useful information, the mixed-measurement model should be continued.

The silver lining is that with a view to reduce the complexity of accounting for financial instruments, significantly improving the quality of accounting information on financial instruments and, above all, with a view to increase the convergence in accounting principles for financial instruments, both the IASB and the FASB have already taken initiative to formulate a universally applicable accounting standard. Since the domain of the financial instruments is very large, complex and dynamic, these are not fit for classification and measurement by any hard and fast rule. Rather, application of professional judgment is more essential for such classification and measurement. The wise principle should be to use fair value approach only for the financial instruments which can be measured at fair value with reasonable certainty and cost, and all other financial instruments should be measured at amortized cost. Therefore, the standard-setters should explore the possibility as to whether the aforesaid demands of the users of financial statements can be better met through the mixed cost and fair value model with far-reaching modifications of the existing norms and principles. Towards this end, the standard setters should focus more on certain crucial issues like removing complexity and subjectivity of the existing valuation techniques, easing some of the onerous rules regarding recognition and derecognition of financial instruments, simplifying or eliminating the stringent requirements of the present accounting standards, reducing the level of detailed rules around hedge accounting and so on, so that the accounting standards can provide more user-friendly and, at the same time, more comprehensive, proactive and sensible norms and principles for accounting for ever dynamic and ever enigmatic financial instruments.

Notes

1. Draft Standard and Basis for Consultations, Financial Instruments and similar items, Financial Instruments Joint Working Group of Standard Setters. http://www.iasplus.com/resource/fijwg-1.pdf, accessed on 23 November 2009.

2. Accounting for Financial Instruments (formerly Financial Instruments: Improvements to Recognition and Measurement and including the Accounting for Hedging Activities Project)—Joint Project of the IASB and FASB. http://www.fasb.org/jsp/FASB/FASBContent_C/ProjectUpdatePage&cid=1175801889654, accessed on 23 November 2009.

3. Discussion Paper, Reducing Complexity in Reporting Financial Instruments, March 2008, IASB. http://www.iasb.org/NR/rdonlyres?A2534626-8D62-4B42-BE12-E3D14C15AD29/0/DPReducingComplexity_Reportingfinancialnstruments.pdf, accessed on 24 November 2009.

4. Can financial instrument accounting be simplified? *Banking & Capital Markets*; Pricewaterhouse Coopers. http://www.pwc.com/en-GX/gx/banking_capital_markets/pdf/simplify_fin_instruments.pdf, accessed on 23 November 2009.

5. Exposure Draft (ED/2009/7), Financial Instruments: Classification and Measurement, July 2009, International Accounting Standard Board. http://www.iasb.org/NR/rdonlyres/D1598224-3609-4F0A-82D0-6DC598C3249B/0/EdFinancialInstrumentsClassificationand-Measurement.pdf, accessed on 24 November 2009.

6. Exposure Draft (ED/2009/5), Fair Value Measurement, May 2009, International Accounting Standard Board. http://www.iasb.org/NR/rdonlyres/C4096A25-F830-401D-8E2E-9286B194798E/O/EDfairvalueMeasurement, accessed on 23 November 2009.

References

Barth, M. E. (1994). 'Fair Value Accounting: Evidence from Investment Securities and the Market Valuation of Banks'. *The Accounting Review*, January, pp 1–25.

Barth, M. E. and Landsman, W. R. (1995). 'Fundamental Issues Related to Using Fair Value Accounting for Financial Reporting'. *Accounting Horizons*, 9, pp 97–107.

Barth, M. E., Beaver, W. and Landsman, W. R. (2001). 'The Relevance of the Value Relevance Literature for Financial Accounting Standard Setting: Another View'. *Journal of Accounting & Economics*, 31, pp 77–104.

Barth, M. E., Landsman, W. R. and Wahlen, J. (1995). 'Fair Value Accounting: Effects on Banks' Earnings Volatility, Regulatory Capital, and Value of Contractual Cash Flows'. *Journal of Banking & Finance*, pp 577–605.

Financial Accounting Standards Board (FASB) (1991). SFAS No. 10: *Disclosure About Fair Value Financial Instruments*. FASB, Norwalk, CT.

———(1993). *SFAS No. 115*: *Accounting for Certain Investments in Debt and Equity Securities*. FASB, Norwalk.

———(1994). *SFAS No. 119*: *Disclosure About Derivative Financial Instruments and Fair Value of Financial Instruments*. FASB, Norwalk.

———(1998). *SFAS No. 133*: *Accounting for Derivative Instruments and Hedging Activities*. FASB, Norwalk.

———(2006). *SFAS No. 157*: *Fair Value Measurements*. FASB, Norwalk.

Hodder, L., Hopkins, P. and Wahlen, J. (2006). 'Risk-relevance of fair value income measures for commercial banks'. *The Accounting Review*, 81, pp 337–375.

International Accounting Standards Board (IASB) (1999). IAS 39: *Financial Instruments*: *Recognition and Measurement*. IASB, London.

———(2005). *IFRS 7*: *Financial Instruments*: *Disclosure*. IASB, London.

International Accounting Standards Committee Foundation (IASCF) (2008). *Framework for the Preparation and Presentation of Financial Statements*. IASCF, London.

Landsman, W. R. (2006). 'Fair Value Accounting for Financial Instruments: Some Implications for Bank Regulation'. Bank for International Settlements Working Papers No. 209, August 2006.

Maines, L. A. and Wahlen, J. M. (2006), 'The Nature of Accounting Information Reliability: Inferences from Archival and Experimental Research'. *Accounting Horizons*, 20(4), pp 399–425.

Mc Bride, P. (2006). 'Making a Statement: What are Financial Statements Designed to Do?'. *A Plus*, December, pp 42–44.

Melumad, N., Weyns, G. and Ziv, A. (1999). 'Comparing Alternative Hedge Accounting Standards: Shareholders' Perspective'. *Review of Accounting Studies*, 4, pp 265–292.

Park, J. (2004). 'Economic Consequences and Financial Statement Effects of SFAS No. 133 in Bank Holding Companies'. University of Wisconsin at Madison Dissertation.

Securities and Exchange Commission (SEC) (2005). Report and recommendations pursuant to Section 401(c) of the Sarbanes–Oxley Act of 2002 on arrangements with off-balance sheet implications, special purpose entities and transparency of filings by issuers. SEC, New York.

Singh, A. (2004). 'The Effects of SFAS 133 on the Corporate Use of Derivatives Volatility and Earning Managements'. Pennsylvania State University Dissertation.

Stella, S. and Smith, M. (2009). 'Value-Relevance of Presenting Changes in Fair Value of Investment Properties in the Income Statement: Evidence from Hong Kong'. *Accounting & Business Research*, 39(2), pp 103–118.

CHAPTER 5

Corporate Governance and Corporate Reporting Practices—An Overview of the Conceptual Landscape

Pintu Sarkar and Swagata Sen

ABSTRACT

The need to re-look at corporate governance has become imperative in view of the large number of scams, frauds and other irregularities which have swept the corporate entities around the world with India being no exception. In this backdrop, this paper endeavours to throw light on the interface between corporate governance and corporate reporting practices. Contextually, it has been unearthed that disclosure of true, fair, timely and relevant information is the hallmark of effective corporate governance system. Above all, the quintessential challenge for establishing and sustaining better corporate governance is the development of proper mindset of the people and the establishment of organizational culture with rock solid business ethics, which is supposedly to emerge from within.

5.1 Overview of Corporate Governance

Notwithstanding the fact that the ideology of governance is as old as human civilization, the issue of corporate governance stole the limelight ever since many frauds in multinational and global corporations leading to a string of collapses of high profile companies rocked the corporate world. *Oxford English Dictionary* defines 'governance' as the act, manner, fact or function of governing, sway, control. The term 'governance' owed its origin to the Greek word *kubernan*, meaning steering. It deals with the processes and systems by which an organization or society operates. The term 'corporate' is adjective meaning 'of or relating to a corporation', derived from the noun 'corporation'. Thus, etymologically, corporate governance may be described as the system by which companies are directed and controlled to the best interests of its shareholders and other stakeholders. It is generally understood as the framework of rules, relationships, systems and processes within and by which authority is exercised and controlled in corporations.

A corporation is an organization created (incorporated) by a group of shareholders who are the de-facto owners of the corporation. Once incorporated, it is an artificial being, invisible, intangible and existing in the contemplation of law having no soul to be damned and no body to be kicked. Apart from the shareholders possessing the substantial stake as bonafide owners, a corporation is a congregation of various stakeholders, namely, customers, employees, investors, suppliers and other creditors as well as the members of the community vis-à-vis society and government. In fact, a corporation is a legally enforceable mechanism established to allow different parties to contribute capital, expertise and labour, for the maximum benefit of all of them. A company's owners may number in the tens of thousands, diffused nationwide, more often worldwide in the present day of globalization, liberalization and privatization leading to cross-border investment. Besides the question of dexterity of individual shareowner, it is neither economically desirable nor practicable for them to participate in the day-to-day management of the corporation. So, they elect some representatives, collectively known as the board of directors, to oversee the management of the company on their behalf as agents and trustees. Although the main responsibility of stewardship and management of a company rests in the hands of board of directors, it generally delegates some of its powers by appointing managing, or whole-time or executive directors, manager, secretary and other executive officers for proper and smooth conduct of the business. Thus, within a legal framework, a company is managed by a triad of human agents—members in general meeting, the board of directors and the executives. The board, being a crucial part of corporate structure, acts as a fulcrum between the owners who provide capital (shareholders) and the people who use that capital to create value (the managers). Such distinguishing phenomena of divorce of ownership and controlling and management of corporate form of organization paves the way of possible conflict of interest between managers (agents) and shareholders (principals). Although, managers as agents of shareholders are likely to act in the interest of maximization of wealth of shareholders, in reality, managers enjoy substantial autonomy resulting into a natural inclination of abusing powers. There is, therefore, always a nagging suspicion that the executive may siphon off some part of the created wealth through excessive rewards to themselves and thus denying transmission of all created wealth to its rightful owners, i.e., shareholders. To describe this stalemate situation, Adam Smith (1776) opined: 'Being the managers of other people's money rather than their own, it cannot well be expected that they should watch over it with the same anxious vigilance which their partners in a private co-partnery frequently watch over their own.' This conundrum casts many doubts and raises the following relevant questions:

- How can one ensure that management is increasing the shareholder's wealth?
- Does management use the business as a place of profit for their personal benefit?
- Is the company protecting the interests of the minority shareholders?
- How can creditors be given assurance of financial strength?
- Are employee rights and benefits protected?
- Is the company discharging its social obligations?
- Is company disclosing transparent and timely information ensuring accountability of the stewardship functions of management?

Despite quite a handful of strict legislations relating to company formation, corporate administration and corporate finance, the above issues have continued to cause a considerable unrest and political controversy. The main concerns have centred on the apparent lack of effective control of publicly listed companies, which have manifested themselves in perceived excessive remuneration packages and mismanagement causing the ruin of many gigantic corporations like Polypeck (1990), Waste Management Inc. (1999), Xerox (2000), Enron (2001), Adelphia (2002), Merill Lynch (2002), AIG (2004) and Satyam Computer Services (2009).Thus, all the governments in the US, in the UK, in Europe and throughout the world felt the absolute essence of restoring public confidence to get rid of such corporate misgovernances emanating from agency problems. Warren Buffett once remarked, 'Both ability and fidelity of managers have long need of monitoring'. Corporate governance is a serious attempt in this direction to effectively control the remuneration of directors and activities of directors in their management of public companies to steer clear of high-profile corporate scandals. Thus, corporate governance extends beyond corporate law. Its objective is not mere fulfilment of legal requirements, but ensuring commitment on managing transparency for maximizing shareholder values. Corporate governance is based on the principles of integrity, fairness, equity, transparency, accountability and commitment to values. Good governance practices stem from the culture and mindset of the organization. As stakeholders across the globe evince keen interest in the practices and performance of companies, corporate governance has engaged on the centre stage. Besides, the subject of corporate governance leapt to the fore of every household in India from relative obscurity after the Satyam scam was let on to the public in January 2009 when Byrraju Ramalinga Raju, the then Chairman, Satyam Computer Services Ltd., mailed to SEBI his confession on accounting fraud at Satyam.

Against this backdrop, the present article tries to paint a rough sketch of the corporate governance and its relation with corporate reporting framework. With this end in view, the remainder of the paper is organized as follows. Section 5.2 is an attempt to define corporate governance in a nutshell. In Section 5.3, attention is focused on the possible benefits of good corporate governance. The following section, Section 5.4, looks briefly at the historical perspective of corporate governance internationally. Section 5.5 is devoted to rough out historical development of corporate governance in India. The penultimate section, Section 5.6, discusses the nature of symbiotic relationship between corporate governance and corporate reporting. The last section, Section 5.7, concludes the discussion.

5.2 What is Corporate Governance?

Corporate governance is the system by which companies are directed and controlled by the management in the best interest of the shareholders and others ensuring greater transparency and better and timely financial reporting. The Board of Directors is responsible for governance of their companies. Corporate governance is a set of structure and process of relationships between company's management, its board and its shareholders to enhance its competitiveness towards business prosperity and long-term shareholder value taking into consideration the interests of other stakeholders.

The Institute of Company Secretaries of India has very aptly defined corporate governance as 'the application of management practices, compliance of law in true letter and spirit and adherence to ethical standards for effective management and distribution of wealth and discharge of social responsibility for sustainable development of all stakeholders'.

In 1997, the Commonwealth Treasury went a little further in the context of the Corporate Law Economic Reform Program Paper (CLERP) No. 3, Directors' Duties and Corporate Governance, defining corporate governance as 'the term used to describe the rules and practices put in place within a company to manage information and economic incentive problems inherent in the separation of ownership from control in large enterprises. It deals with how, and to what extent, the interests of various agents involved in the company are reconciled and what checks and incentives are put in place to ensure that managers maximise the value of the investment made by shareholders'. 'Corporate Governance is needed to create a corporate culture of consciousness, transparency and openness. It refers to combination of laws, rules, regulations, procedures and voluntary practices to enable the companies to maximize the shareholders long-term value. It should lead to increasing customer satisfaction, shareholder value and wealth'.

In March 2003, the Australian Stock Exchange released its Principles of Good Corporate Governance and Best Practice Recommendations, which contained the following definition: 'Corporate governance is the system by which companies are directed and managed. It influences how the objectives of the company are set and achieved, how risk is monitored and assessed, and how performance is optimised. Good corporate governance structures encourage companies to create value (through entrepreneurism, innovation, development and exploration) and provide accountability and control systems commensurate with the risks involved. It is the process and structure used to direct and manage the business and affairs of the company towards enhancing business prosperity and corporate accountability with the ultimate objective of realizing long term shareholder value, whilst taking into account the interests of other stakeholders.

5.3 Benefits of Good Corporate Governance

Good corporate governance is of paramount importance in building market confidence and encouraging more stable, long-term international investment flows. Many countries see better corporate governance practices as a way to improve economic dynamism and, thus, enhance overall economic performance. Asian Development Bank defines good governance based on four pillars: transparency, accountability, predictability and participation, recognizing that 'their application must be country-specific and solidly grounded in the economic, social and administrative capacity realities of the country'. Studies in India and abroad revealed that markets and investors take notice of well-managed companies, respond positively to them and reward such companies with higher valuations. In fact, strong corporate governance is indispensable to resilient and vibrant capital markets and is an important instrument of investor protection. The major benefits of good corporate governance can be enumerated as follows:

- Good governance leads to good performance.
- It reduces risk as it allows decision making based on data.
- It creates an open and transparent system.
- It improves communication and breaks down systematic barriers to flow of information.
- It helps in creating a brand and creates comfort for all stakeholders and society.
- It ensures greater investor protection which, in turn, lowers the cost of capital and results in greater financial development and economic growth.

- Its mechanisms ensure better resource allocation and management, raising the return to capital.
- It can significantly reduce the risk of nation-wide financial crises.
- It can remove mistrust between different stakeholders, reduce legal costs and improve social and labour relationships and external economies like environmental protection.

5.4 Evolution of Corporate Governance Practices—An Overview

The emergence of corporate governance principally has its roots in the traditional problem of separation of ownership by shareholders and control by management. But with the passage of time, experiences gained from historical developments of corporate misdemeanour and with the revolution in the rising expectations of the society, a broader framework of corporate governance has been gradually evolved. The broader concept of corporate governance concentrates on bringing a balance between the economy and social goals and between individual and social goals with a view to ensuring efficient uses of resources by means of aligning as nearly as possible the interests of individuals, corporations and society. The gradual development of the discipline of corporate governance during the last six decades can be classified into the following phases:

Phase I: The Decade of Excessive Managerial Power—Between 1950 to 1959

From the mid-twentieth century, two factors were believed to be the main culprits of corporate mis-governance: (i) Abuse of enormous power of corporate executives: During this period market oligopolies created large companies, such as General Electric, General Motors and IBM, that were largely insulated from international competition, while the separation of ownership and control gave managers unlimited scope to act at their own sweet will. (ii) Lack of appropriate controlling and legislative framework: Critics viewed companies as running 'without any discernible controls', and assuming power that would 'rival the sovereignty of the state itself'. To steer clear of such albatross, managerial power was hamstrung by an antitrust policy and heightened pressure from international rivals. Most big mergers during this era were barred by the courts. Besides, competition in manufacturing did more to curb managerial power than all the anti-trust decisions of the era.

Phase II: The Decade of Conglomerates—Between 1960 and 1969

With business conditions conducive to growth, companies morphed into modern-day conglomerates. Initially, they were considered as a solution to the 'separation' problem as central managers in headquarters would monitor operating managers in far-flung divisions, allocating capital where returns were highest. But ultimately, inefficiencies emerged to creep into these gargantuan companies, creating the enemy of profits: corporate bloat. Quite a good number of hostile takeovers took place to capture weak units suffering from the syndrome of bloated profits.

Phase III: The Decade of Corporate Evils—Between 1970 and 1979

During this decade, corporations were broadly criticized for a number of perceived evils—excessive executive compensation, CEO domination, too few independent directors and too many inside and beholden directors, failure to act promptly and positively in times of crisis, and communicating inadequately with shareholders.

Phase IV: The Decade of Rising Insider Trading—Between 1980 and 1989

With the explosion in hostile takeovers, insider trading suddenly held out the potential for vast riches. Managers and Wall Street cronies who got wind of a buyout seized the opportunity to buy up stock before the deal was announced and sell it immediately after at a fabulous profit. It was about this time that stock options quickly gained in popularity, thanks to favourable accounting treatment and tax laws. Options appeared to be a solution of the 'separation' problem by turning managers into owners thereby providing an incentive to create shareholder value.

Many well-managed companies began to change the composition of their boards, placed more power in the hands of independent directors, and disclosed detailed information. In a number of high-profile cases, there were proxy fights, confrontations with institutional shareholders and CEO dismissals. What was really happening could be regarded as the beginning of efficient working of corporate governance system.

Phase V: The Decade of Exorbitant CEO Pay—Between 1990 and 1999

Instead of trying to create and enhance shareholder value, in many cases, top executives at the helm of the affairs began to fudge the numbers to fulfil their vested interests. As a consequence of it, earning restatements increased dramatically in the immediate aftermath of the 1990s. In the United Kingdom, there have been a number of scandals involving the likes of Guinness and Robert Maxwell and those highlighted the continuing ability of directors to involve public companies in management. Such collapses of gigantic companies do not only tell upon the interests of the stakeholders directly involved with these companies, but it also undermines the confidence of all investors of the worldwide capital market. These scandals unearthed the basic truth that effective control of the directors was not being carried out by the shareholders as a consequence of which governments and regulators were compelled to other means for effective control mechanisms.

Under such circumstances, the Cadbury Committee was set up by the Financial Reporting Council, The London Stock Exchange and the accounting profession in 1991. The Cadbury Committee Report was published in 1992 and recommended that the boards of listed companies should be required to comply with a code of best practices which should be included in their annual reports confirming the compliance or non-compliance with proper reasons. The main provisions of the code are as follows:

1. Independent non-executive directors should be appointed to the boards of listed companies.
2. The appointment of all executive directors should be vetted by a nomination committee made up of company's non-executive directors.
3. Executive directors should not be offered service contracts for more than 3 years, unless approved by the shareholders in a general meeting.
4. The remuneration packages of executive directors should be agreed by a remuneration committee, wholly or mainly comprising non-executive directors.
5. An audit committee consisting of a majority of non-executive directors should be formed to monitor the aspect of accounting, auditing and internal control of the company.
6. In order to promote the independent nature of the board the same person should not act as both chief executive and the chairperson.

The Cadbury Committee report could not address the problem of excessive remuneration of directors as it was mainly based on financial aspect of corporate governance. As a result, the Greenbury Committee was formed and it submitted its report in 1995 specifically on the aspects of directors' remuneration. The following are the salient provisions of the report:

1. The interests of both the shareholders and the directors should be considered by the remuneration committee at the time of determining the level of directors' remuneration.

2. Directors should never be given discounted share options and annual bonuses should not be pensionable.
3. Any long-term incentive schemes to be offered to directors should first be approved by the shareholders.
4. The annual accounts should contain an annual report of remuneration committee for consideration of shareholders.
5. An annual report of the remuneration committee should be included in the annual accounts and placed before the shareholders.
6. The report should contain a statement that full consideration has been given to the Greenbury code and should explain any instances of non-compliance.

With effect from December 1995, compliance with the Greenbury Report became a necessary prerequisite for obtaining a listing in the United Kingdom.

With a view to give effect to the prescriptions of Cadbury and Greenbury committee reports, the Hampel Committee was formed and it submitted its report on 28 January, 1998. The earth-shattering points of this report, basically relating to public listed companies were as follows:

1. Executive and non-executive directors should bear the corporate duties to the same tune and should be provided with more information and instruction as to their responsibilities.
2. Executive directors should have the necessary experiences to be able to understand the nature and extent of interests of the company for which they are acting.
3. At least one-third of the board should consist of non-executive and independent directors.
4. The same person should not hold the position of chairperson and chief executive.
5. The auditors should report on internal control privately to directors.
6. All companies should have nomination committees for recommending new board appointments.
7. Directors should be obliged to seek re-election every 3 years.
8. The remuneration of executive directors should not be excessive and should be based upon the recommendations of a remuneration committee made up entirely of non-executive directors.

In line with the Hampel Committee Report, the London Stock Exchange published a general code of good practice of corporate governance, more popularly known as the Combined Code of Best Practices which became mandatory for all companies listed after 31 December, 1998. Although it did not have the force of law, non-compliance could lead to the imposition of a fine by the London Stock Exchange and potentially led to a refusal to list. In the USA too, the Blue Ribbon Committee submitted its report in 1999 suggesting different measures for improving the effectiveness of corporate audit committees in order to ensure a comprehensive system of corporate governances.

Moreover, the Institute of Chartered Accountants in England and Wales (ICAEW) set up the Turnbull Committee to provide guidance to assist companies in implementing the requirements of the Combined Code relating to internal control. The report opined that the board of directors should include within its responsibilities:

1. An evaluation of the likely risks and categories of risk facing the company;
2. Ensuring the existence of effective safeguards and internal controls within the company to prevent or minimize risk;
3. Confirming the transparency of internal controls including an annual assessment of risk.

In May 1999, the taskforce appointed by the Organisation for Economic Cooperation and Development (OECD) brought out an outstanding piece of work on corporate governance, universally known as the *OECD Principles of Corporate Governance* which were basically based on the following four guidelines:

(i) Fairness to ensure the rights of shareholders, including minority shareholders.
(ii) Transparency or disclosure of adequate information on financial performance, governance and ownership.
(iii) Accountability for shareholder assets on the part of the Board of Directors.
(iv) Responsibility for ensuring that the enterprise is law abiding.

These guiding codes of best practices of corporate governance have since become an international benchmark for policy makers, investors, corporations and other stakeholders worldwide.

Phase VI: The Decade of Scandal—The First Decade of Twenty-first Century Commencing from 2000

At the turn of the century, a battery of corporate scandals blemished the very contextualities of accounting and auditing mechanism thereby devilishly shattering the public confidence in the corporate sector.

A glimpse of some of these corporate massacres can be gauged from Table 5.1.

As envisaged from Table 5.1, corporate America was blotted with many scandals during the last decade. A number of high-profile corporate scandals triggered an in-depth reflection on the regulatory role of the government on protecting the interest of stakeholders. The Enron scandal evoked a lot of doubts on the efficacy of the prevalent system and practices of corporate governance. As an aftermath of Enron debacle, the Federal Government of the USA was compelled to pass new tough regulatory measures against corporate misdeeds, whereby books of accounts were supposed to face unprecedented scrutiny in order to enhance transparency, re-establish corporate accountability and restore investors' confidence. In this backdrop, Sarbanes–Oxley Act (SOX) was introduced and passed by the US Congress in 2002 with the objective of protecting the investors from the fraudulent accounting practices of the corporations. The basic outline of SOX is as follows:

- Establishment of Public Company Accounting Oversight Board (PCAOB), where all accounting firms are required to get registered and submit, amongst other details, particulars of fees received from public company clients for audit and non-audit services and financial information about the firm.
- Accounting firms are prohibited from providing consultancy and any non-auditing services to their client organization.
- Stricter regulation and control of audit function by means of audit committees and inspecting accounting firms.
- Each member of the audit committee shall be an independent director.
- Every annual report must contain an 'internal control report' and the CEO/CFO shall prepare a statement to accompany the audit report certifying the appropriateness of financial statements.
- Penalty of corporate fraud may include a maximum of 20 years imprisonment for altering/destroying documents which are subject to federal inquiries.
- CEOs are liable to 10–20 years of imprisonment with fines of $1 million to $5 million if they certify falsified accounts.

TABLE 5.1

Some Notable Instances of Corporate Misgovernances

Name of Company	Year	Country	Name of Company	Year	Country
Micro Strategy	2000	United States	Merill Lynch	2002	United States
Unify Corporation	2000	United States	Mirant	2002	United States
Computer Associates	2000	United States	Halliburton	2002	United States
Xerox Corporation	2000	United States	Homestore.Com	2002	United States
One. Tel	2001	Australia	Nicor	2002	United States
Enron	2001	United States	Peregrine Systems	2002	United States
Adelphia	2002	United States	QwestCommunications	2002	United States
AOL	2002	United States	Reliant Energy	2002	United States
Bristol Myers Squibb	2002	United States	Sun Beam	2002	United States
CMS Energy	2002	United States	Tyco International	2002	Bermuda
Duke Energy	2002	United States	World Com	2002	United States
Dynegy	2002	United States	Royal Ahold	2003	Netherlands
El Paso Corporation	2002	United States	Paramalat	2003	Italy
Freddie Mac	2002	United States	Health South Corporation	2003	United States
Global Crossing	2002	Bermuda	Chiquita Brands International	2003	United States
K Mart	2002	United States	AIG	2003	United States
Merck & Co.	2002	United States	Satyam Computer	2009	India

In May 2003, the European Commission issued an action plan on *Modernising company law and enhancing corporate governance in the European Union*. The action plan contained 24 measures to be adopted before 2009.

On 1 November 2003, Financial Reporting Council (FRC) of UK issued a Combined Code on Corporate Governance. The Code aims to achieve more open and rigorous procedures for the appointment of directors and improved induction and development of non-executive directors. It recommended that half of the board members of a company should be independent non-executive directors and the non-executive directors should sit on the audit and remuneration committees. It also advocated that non-executive directors serving more than 9 years should no longer be considered to be independent. The Code also calls for formal evaluation of boards, committees and individual directors. In July 2006, FRC published an updated Code super-ceding and replacing the 2003 Code. It suggested that directors will be expected to apply the same standard of care when reviewing internal controls as when carrying out their general duties.

5.5 Synoptic View of the Genesis of Corporate Governance in India

The corporate world in India could not remain lackadaisical to the international developments. As a matter of fact, the history of corporate governance in India may be traced back to the year 1998, when Confederation of Indian Industry (CII) framed a voluntary code of corporate governance for listed companies. The striking points of this report can be summarized as follows:

- The board of any company having turnover of Rs. 100 crores or more should constitute at least 30 per cent professional non-executive directors and the chairperson should be a non-executive director.
- No director should be on the boards of more than 10 companies.
- Directors' remuneration should be enhanced by introducing incentive schemes.
- Measures for financial and non-financial disclosures and other significant information should be initiated.
- The system of nominee directors should be discontinued.
- A compliance certificate, duly signed by the CEO and CFO, should be submitted to stock exchange as per rules.

The Securities and Exchange Board of India (SEBI) appointed a committee on corporate governance in May 1999, with 18 members under the chairmanship of Kumar Mangalam Birla with a view of promoting and raising the standards of corporate governance. The report of the Birla committee is indeed a veritable landmark in the evolution of corporate governance in India. Based on the recommendation of this report, SEBI introduced Clause 49 of the Listing Agreement dealing with various norms of corporate governance to be compulsorily followed by every listed company with effect from the financial year 2000–01. The major recommendations of Birla Committee can be classified into two groups:

1. **Mandatory Requirements**

   (i) *Composition of the Board and its role*: BODs should comprise of executive directors and non-executive directors. A minimum of 50 per cent of directors should be non-executive if chairman is executive; otherwise one-third of such directors should be non-executive if the chairman is non-executive. Among such directors, the independent directors should not have any material or pecuniary relationship or transactions with the company, its promoters, management or subsidiaries.

   Board meeting should be held at least four times a year, i.e., once in every quarter. The board should decide the remuneration of non-executive director. The remuneration packages of all the directors should be fully disclosed. A director cannot be a member of more than 10 committees and he can act as a chairperson in maximum five committees across all companies in which he is a director.

   (ii) *Audit committee and its role*: The board of the company should set up a qualified and independent audit committee comprising minimum three members. The chairperson of the audit committee should be an independent director and should be present at the AGM of the company. The company secretary should act as the secretary to the audit committee.

   The audit committee should meet at least thrice a year and it has the authority to investigate any activity within its terms of reference. It can review any change in accounting policies and practice, adequacy of internal control system and financial and risk management policies of the company.

(iii) *Critical Information*: Management must disclose to the Board all information relating to material, financial and commercial transactions.

(iv) *Shareholder Communication*: A board committee should be formed to redress shareholders' complaints regarding transfer of shares and non-receipt of dividend, etc. There should be a separate section on corporate governance in the annual report with detailed compliance report.

2. **Non-mandatory Recommendations**

(i) Formation of remuneration committee

(ii) Declaration of financial performance

(iii) Non-executive chairperson

Following the Enron fiasco and subsequent enactment of Sarbanes–Oxley Act in the US, the Department of Company Affairs in India took another initiative by appointing Naresh Chandra Committee on 21 August 2002 to examine various issues of corporate governance in India, especially to examine the auditor–company relationship and regulate the role of auditors. Following are the distinguishing issues of this report:

- Prohibition of non-audit services and any direct financial interest or any other business relationship with the audit client by the audit firm
- Audit fee received from any one audit client and its subsidiaries should not exceed 25 per cent of the total revenues of the audit firm
- The minimum board size should be at least seven, of which four should be independent directors.

After a lapse of about 2 years, SEBI set up the second committee under the chairmanship of N. R. Narayana Murthy with a view of evaluating the adequacy of the existing practices of corporate governance. The committee issued two set of recommendations: the mandatory and non-mandatory recommendations. The mandatory recommendations focus on strengthening the responsibilities of audit committees, improving the quality of financial disclosures, including those pertaining to related party transactions and proceeds from initial public offerings, requiring corporate executive boards to assess and disclose business risks in the annual reports of companies, calling upon the board to adopt formal code of conduct, the position of nominee directors, and improved disclosures relating to compensation to non-executive directors and shareholders approval of the same. The non-mandatory provisions relate to moving to a regime providing for unqualified corporate financial statements, training of Board Members and evaluation of non-executive directors' performance by a peer group comprising the entire Board of Directors, excluding the director being evaluated. On the basis of the recommendation of this committee, Clause 49 of Listing Agreement was again revised by SEBI vide circular No. SEBI/CFD/DIL/CG/1/2004/12/10 dated 20 October 2004 to include the following major changes:

- CEO/CFO certification: In tune with the provisions of SOX Act, the revised clause requires CEO/CFO to certify to the Board the Annual financial statements in prescribed format.
- Management Discussion and Analysis Report of the Board to be submitted with annual report to shareholders.
- Quarterly compliance report to stock exchanges.

- Whistle Blower Policy: This is a concept being introduced for the first time in corporate governance borrowed from Western thinking. As per listing agreement, the company may establish a mechanism for employees, present or past, to report to management concerns about unethical behaviour, actual or suspected fraud or violation of company's code of conduct or ethics with adequate safeguard against any victimization.

Dr Madhav Mehra, the President of the World Council for Corporate Governance, UK added, 'Satyam gives India opportunity to lead the world by better enforcement of Clause 49 through proper selection, training, evaluation and monitoring of directors. The main problem of the Indian boards is their sameness. Same directors find seats on all the boards. That encourages cosy relationship. We need to encourage dissent, diversity, difference, dialogue and disclosure. To make it happen we do not need more laws but more training both of directors and investors'. Dr Mehra lamented, 'The institution of independent directors is a myth world over for two reasons: they depend on CEO for their remuneration. The dependence has only increased with phenomenal rise in their remunerations. It is difficult for people to understand something when their salary depends on not understanding it. Secondly as per a survey conducted by the WCFCG, the average time spent by independent directors in board meetings in a year is 14 hours. Better training will ensure that independents engage themselves in committee work such as audit committee, risk management committee, nomination committee and remuneration committee'.

Following the recent financial upheaval, the National Association of Software and Service Companies (NASSCOM) is set to focus on good corporate governance and ethics among its member companies. NASSCOM has constituted a Corporate Governance and Ethics Committee headed by N. R. Narayana Murthy with a view to strengthen the existing appropriate code of ethics, values and corporate code of conduct for the industry. The committee will work with authorities, policy makers and regulators in the areas of corporate governance and transparency.

A meticulous examination of the recommendations of the various reports reveals certain commonalities which are universal in nature. In fact, corporate governance is not a static concept which is bound to evolve continually under the dynamic environment and cannot remain within the four walls of any legislation.

5.6 Corporate Governance and Corporate Reporting

True, fair and transparent financial reporting is the rudimentary pillar for establishing and ensuring sound corporate governance. If we scan the history of corporate mis-governance, then it could clearly be established that whether it is Enron in the US or Satyam in India, the corporate fraud and scams are always associated with accounting misrepresentation and fraudulent financial reporting. For proper corporate governance, one of the most important and crucial requirements is the establishment of sound financial reporting supply chain. The financial reporting supply chain refers to the people and processes involved in the preparation, approval, audit, analysis and use of financial reports. All links in the chain need to be of high quality and closely connected to supply high-quality financial reporting. The cycle both starts and ends with the investors and other stakeholders, who want to make informed economic decisions about a company and, therefore, require financial information to do so. Subsequently, it is management that, under the general direction of the board of directors (supervisory board), prepares the financial information for eventual approval by the board and, in some countries, the general meeting of shareholders. The auditors interact with management and the board while auditing the financial information and provide independent opinions. The media and others distribute financial information, and analysts and credit-rating agencies evaluate it, to be used by the investors and other stakeholders. The natural law is that men learn from mistakes and design measures and implement such measures so that mistakes are not repeated. The same process is noticed in the area of corporate reporting. In the following paragraphs we would focus on how financial reporting system has responded in recent times after occurrence of innumerable cases of corporate mis-governance.

1. **Moving towards principle based standard:** The onset of new millennium intensified the age old debate regarding superiority of rule-based standard vs principle-based standard. Most of the accounting experts after the failure of large US corporate houses raised question about the effectiveness of rule-based standard framed by the FASB which, according to them, often make accountants mechanical in their approach and they seldom exercise personal judgment. This resulted in the initiative of having a global standard and which eventually lead to formulation of IFRS, where it is claimed that principle-based accounting standard would give way to rule-based accounting standard. The new standards are claimed to force the accountants to present financial reports in more transparent way.
2. **Universally accepted single accounting standard:** The prevalence of two major types of accounting standard, i.e., standards formulated by FASB and IASC, along with various national standards formulated by different national accounting bodies of different countries often confused the investors and other stakeholders of the companies especially in the era of globalized business. The acceptance of IFRS by almost all the countries from the year 2011 would ensure that from 2011 onwards, accountants all over the world would express themselves in one single language.
3. **Improvements to regulation governing financial reporting:** In the European Union, the change to IFRS has also changed the behaviour of company directors. Directors have struggled with IFRS and have therefore devoted more time to financial reporting. Within companies, another noted, the move to IFRS has encouraged organizations to review more closely the appropriateness of their accounting policies. At a practical level, due to mandatory compliance of the Code of Corporate Governance, almost all publicly listed companies are issuing financial reports within the time limit, as well as with improved presentation.
4. **Board of directors taking the responsibility of ownership of financial reporting process:** Boards of directors and management have increasingly taken ownership of the financial reporting process. It has been observed a regular review and sign-off by all levels of management and oversight by directors, and an improved scrutiny by boards of directors of the quality, accuracy and reasonability of financial information released to the public. In the US, despite its costs, the SOX legislation has made a positive contribution. CEOs were now more involved in financial reporting and the requirement that CEOs and CFOs sign-off on the financial reports increased the importance within companies of financial reporting and internal controls.
5. **Improved internal control and better technology:** Improved internal control over financial reporting is another positive development. Companies are now giving more emphasis on the role

of internal audit in order to improve the quality and accuracy of financial reporting. Adoption of modern technology in the sphere of financial reporting has also facilitated the proper governance of the companies. In this context, the adoption of XBRL (Extensible Business Reporting language) would be of great help. XBRL is going to revolutionize the business reporting. It will make sharing, communicating, transporting and accessing of information much more efficient and cost effective without any human interaction and computer platform. XBRL would also eliminate human errors like typing or retyping information for sharing, reporting and decision-making purposes.

However, the areas of concern in the sphere of financial reporting system still exists and due attention should be placed on these areas in order to ensure proper and effective governance. Some of these issues have been highlighted below:

(i) **Cost of transition to IFRS:** The transition to IFRS is a costly affair. Moreover, implementation of IFRS requires professionals with proper knowledge of IFRS. The IFRS has been introduced in too much haste. As IFRS involves sweeping change in financial reporting system, so the time spent in understanding and implementing new rules and regulations is taking time away from managing the business. Fifty years of change has taken place in ten years, which is creating indigestion and distorting reporting resources as a consequence.

(ii) **Complexity of financial reporting standard:** IFRS is adding to the complexities of financial reporting and for users of financial statements, it has really become a challenging task to read between the lines. Moreover, the very purpose of IFRS in formulating a principle-based standard gets diluted as some of the IFRS standards are too lengthy and elaborate and comprises hundreds of pages. Therefore, the objective of replacing rule-based standards by principle-based standards has not really been fulfilled which again may open the floodgates of misreporting in the future.

(iii) **Liability restricting process:** Financial statements usually accompany footnotes which are lengthy, elaborate and incomprehensible. This is surely a disclosure overload. The lawyers write these disclosures on behalf of the preparers of the basic financial statement, it is not plain business language and they are not easily understandable (Lyle 2004). Therefore, a lot of management reports are meant not to be understood. Even a simple press release takes hours of lawyers. This is simply because the directors are afraid of liability. Financial reporting could be improved by having less risk of litigation so that the report could be written by the board itself and in a freer style. Reporting needs to transform itself from an exercise of compliance to an exercise of communication so that it could be meaningful, cohesive and sufficient for making well-informed decisions.

(iv) **Problem of adoption of fair value:** Adoption of fair value creates room for manipulation as some items of the income statement as well as balance sheet are represented at estimated values. Therefore, the income statement and balance sheet should show the items which are voucher-backed and which are based on estimation (Chattopadhyay 2008).

(v) **Confusion with interim financial statement:** Directors of the company sometimes resort to window dressing of the un-audited interim financial statements like quarterly reports and half-yearly reports with a view of artificially boosting up the short-term image of the company. Therefore, questions now being raised about the veracity of the figures represented in the interim financial statements and also about the false impact they imprint on the mind of the stakeholders.

Basically, corporate governance is about promoting corporate fairness, transparency and accountability. Openness, integrity and accountability are the key elements of corporate governance. Corporate governance makes the whole structure of the company more accountable towards each of its stakeholders, whether it is majority or minority. These could only be ensured by making proper disclosure to the stakeholders about each strategic decision so that stakeholders and market can reward the good decisions and punish the bad decisions. Thus, corporate governance works as correcting mechanism for the company in case of wrong decisions and helps the company to take corrective life saving action on time. From macroeconomic perspective, full, timely and consistent disclosure of information by a corporate entity leads to market transparency which, in turn, promotes transparent and efficient markets leading to judicious allocation of economic resources.

5.7 Conclusion

As the very fact that corporate governance relates to relationships among parties and these relationships evolve over time under the constantly changing circumstances, so corporate governance is a dynamic phenomenon—an on-going process. Good corporate governance is a *sine qua non* for today's complex and dynamic business environment to ensure long-term sustainability. So, it should be monitored and reviewed regularly so that it synchronizes with the changing time and environment. Restricting corporate governance within the domain of certain regulations alone will, in fact, defeat the very purpose of corporate governance.

Corporate governance should be visualized as a way of life rather than a code. It is nothing but the moral or ethical or value framework under which corporate decisions are taken. It is about ethical conduct in business. It encourages ethical standards and sound business practices. Ethics defines what is good for the individual and for society and establishes the nature of duties that people owe to oneself and others in society. Quality of governance depends upon competence and integrity of directors, who have to diligently oversee the management while adhering to impeachable ethical standards. Strengthened systems and enhanced transparency can only further the ability. Transparency about a company's governance process is critical.

Implementing corporate governance structures are important but instilling the right culture is quintessential. Above all, the most important challenge for establishing and sustaining better corporate governance is the formation of the proper mindset of the people and evolving the right organizational culture which must come from within. The government or the regulatory agencies, at best, can provide the base where good corporate governance could be founded, but the primary responsibility for building the super structure rests on the stakeholders of the company, especially the members of the board of directors and the top management.

References

Agarwal, R. P. (2006). 'Lessons in Corporate Governance for the Corporate and Banking Sector'. *The Accounting World*, VI(III), pp 35–47.

Banerjee, B., Needles, B. E. Jr. and Figo, M. L. (2009). 'Corporate Governance in India: Issues and Practices of High-Performance Companies. *Indian Accounting Review*, June, pp 33–47.

Bhasin, M. (2008). 'Corporate Governance Scenario in India: Perspectives and Prospects'. *Chartered Secretary*, XXXVIII(2), pp 168–175.

Bhattacharyya, A. K. (2008). 'Corporate Governance and Audit', *Business Standard*, 2 June 2008, p 13.

Chattopadhyay, P. (2008). *Corporate Misgovernance.* Indian Accounting Association Research Foundation, Kolkata, India.

Das, S. C. (2006). 'Ethics in Governance Practices in Corporates—Some Issues and Implications'. *The Management Accountant*, 41(4), pp 279–281.

Fernando, A. C. (2006). *Corporate Governance: Principles, Policies and Practices.* Pearson Education, New Delhi, India.

Ghosh, S. K. and Budhia, S. (2005). 'Corporate Governance: How Effective Is It?' *Indian Accounting Review*, Indian Accounting Association Research Foundation, 9(2), December, pp 57–72.

Ghosh, T. P. (2003). *Accounting Standards and Corporate Accounting Practices.* Taxmann Allied Services Ltd., New Delhi.

Gollanpalli, S. (2003). 'Corporate Governance: A Global Perspective'. *Effective Executive*, V(10), pp 15–19.

Lyle, S. and Tophoff, V. (2004). *Financial Reporting Supply Chain.* IFAC.

Monks, R. A. G. and Minow, N. (2001). Corporate Governance. Blackwell Publishers Ltd., London, UK.

Nagarajan, N. R. (2006). 'Corporate Governance–Current Scenario in India'. *The Management Accountant*, 41(11), pp 867–871.

Prasad, K. (2006). *Corporate Governance.* Prentice Hall of India Pvt. Ltd., New Delhi, India.

Ravichandra, M.and Vasudevan, S. (2007). 'Corporate Governance and Accounting Standards—How to Make Use of Accounting Information for Investor Protection and Awareness'. *The Chartered Accountant*, 55(9), pp 1358–1372.

Satheesh, Kumar, T. N. (2006). 'Indian Family-managed Companies: The Corporate Governance Conundrum'. *The ICFAI Journal of Corporate Governance*, V(2), pp 41–55.

Shil, N. C. (2008). 'Accounting for Good Corporate Governance'. *JOAAG*, 3(1), pp 10–14.

Taxmann (2005). *Year Book Corporate Laws.* Taxmann Allied Services Pvt. Ltd., New Delhi, India.

Web sites

- http://images.businessweek.com/ss/05/04/crisis/source/1.htm
- http://www.cvc.nic.in
- www.corpgov.com

CHAPTER 6

XBRL and Financial Reporting Taxonomy— A Revolution in Preparation, Communication and Analysis of Electronic Financial Reports

Sunil Kumar Gandhi

ABSTRACT

In computer world, eXtensible Business Reporting Language (XBRL) is a markup language (and not a programming language), which has been developed to revolutionize online financial and business reporting. It is an extension of XML. From the stakeholders' point of view, a conventional report is static, non-interactive and less informative, and has become outdated. On the other hand, XBRL reporting is not just a replacement of the existing reporting system. It is a paradigm shift from 'readable information' to 'usable information'. When reports are prepared and filed in XBRL format, not only the summarized information is reported in the financial statements but also all the detailed information leading to the summarized information is available to the users of the report. In other words, every piece of information, reported on the face of the financial statements, will be linked to explanatory information, which can be retrieved by the users with the help of XBRL tags or labels. XBRL data are called 'interactive data' because users can interact with the online report and get information according to their needs. It is fast becoming a universal language.

6.1 Introduction

According to XBRL International (a not-for-profit consortium of approximately 550 companies and agencies worldwide working together to build the XBRL language and promote and support its adoption), 'XBRL (eXtensible Business Reporting Language) is a language for the electronic communication of business and financial data which is revolutionizing business reporting around the world. It provides major benefits in the preparation, analysis and communication of business information. It offers cost savings, greater efficiency and improved accuracy and reliability to all those involved in supplying or using financial data'. It is a not a programming language, rather it is a XML-based markup language, which has been developed to revolutionize online financial and business reporting. Online filing of a conventional financial report is not new, which is nothing but a soft copy of the paper version. From the stakeholders' point of view, a conventional report is static, non-interactive and less informative, and has become outdated. On the other hand, XBRL reporting is not just replacement of the existing reporting system. It is a paradigm shift from 'readable information' to 'usable information' (www.16thconference.xbrl.org). When reports are prepared and filed in XBRL format, not only the summarized information is reported in the financial statements but also all the detailed information leading to the summarized information is available to the users of the report. In other words, every piece of information, reported on the face of the financial statements, will be linked to explanatory information, which can be retrieved by the users with the help of XBRL tags or labels. XBRL data are called 'interactive data' because users can interact with the online report and get information according to their needs. According to the USA Securities Exchange Commission Chairman, Christopher Cox, 'The new system will make it easier both to file information with the Commission, and to use it. For investors and analysts, it will represent a quantum leap over existing disclosure technologies. For companies, it will mean easier and less costly compliance with SEC requirements' (www.edgar-online.com). He further added that, 'XBRL is fast becoming the universal language for the exchange of business information and it is the future of financial reporting. With Financial Explorer or another XBRL viewer, investors will be able to quickly make sense of financial statements. In the near future, potentially millions of people will be able to analyze and compare financial statements and make better-informed investment decisions. That's a big benefit to ordinary investors'.

The present study on XBRL is a knowledge-sharing initiative and it is not based on empirical data. It may be called 'Internet research'. Since XBRL taxonomy is yet to be implemented in India, getting empirical data is not possible. It is a study on various issues related to XBRL such as, the terminologies and the tools used, current state of application, etc. The rest of this paper has been divided into five sections. In Section 6.2, evolution of XBRL has been discussed. Section 6.3 covers concepts of related terminologies, Section 6.4 narrates tools used in XBRL reports, Section 6.5 discusses advantages of XBRL reports, Section 6.6 makes a survey of adoption of XBRL by different countries and Section 6.7 provides the concluding comments.

6.2 Evolution of XBRL

Development of XBRL can be traced to developments in two fronts. In the first front, the web-related Standardised General Markup Language (SGML) gave birth to two languages—Hyper Text Markup Language (HTML) in 1990, and eXtensible Markup Language (XML) in 1998. HTML is static and has predefined tags signifying how data elements are displayed and linked. But XML is dynamic which allows tags to be defined by the developer of the page. These tags describe what those data elements contain. XML supports 'metadata' which attaches meanings to the data by attaching hidden attribute tags. XBRL (original name was XFRML) was developed in 2000 while trying to use XML in financial reporting. On the other front, popularity of OLAP (On-Line Analytical Processing) system also gave impetus to the development of XBRL. OLAP, developed in

1993, is a database design in which data can be analysed from a multi-dimensional point of view for generation of strategic information. 'The key indicator of a successful OLAP application is its ability to provide information as needed, i.e., its ability to provide "just-in-time" information for effective decision-making. This requires more than a base level of detailed data' (www.trinity.edu).

Combination of these two ideas led to the development of XBRL. The most important feature of XBRL is that its source code is open and free of license fees. From very inception, XBRL has created ripples in the business world. Its advantage is so great that it is going to be the future mode of financial reporting.

6.3 Concepts of Related Terminologies

It is important to be acquainted with the terminologies used in XBRL. Some of the important key words are discussed below:

6.3.1 Taxonomy

In common parlance 'taxonomy' means classification and sub-classification. In the context of XBRL, taxonomy

- defines terms (also called elements/concepts/tags) such as 'Share Capital', 'Paid up Capital', Net Income', etc. to describe a particular reporting situation such as Indian Accounting Standards, US GAAP, etc. (called XBRL Schemas);
- establishes relationship between the elements (called XBRL linkbases);
- allows extension of elements by the reporting entity if the same is not available in the standard taxonomy.

According to XBRL International, 'Taxonomy is the set of technical definition files that allows business reporting concepts to be defined. It allows each concept to be described or an authoritative reference (such as an accounting or statistical standard) to be invoked. It allows the relationships between concepts to be defined. It also allows labels to be defined, in multiple languages, if necessary. Users of taxonomies can extend them to meet their own needs. For instance, if the generic element 'sales' were too general for specific needs, a user could extend the taxonomy with two new items 'equipment sales' and 'consumables sales'. Both would roll up to the 'sales' element. This allows users of XBRL to target their reporting messaging and avoid 'template reporting'.

These taxonomies can be global (say IFRS), country specific (say ICAI Taxonomy), industry specific (say ICAI's C and I taxonomy) or organization specific. One can use published taxonomies or make their own. An XBRL report is produced by mapping your data to the taxonomy of your choice and publishing the resulting document with reference to the taxonomy used (www.semansys.com).

It should be noted that taxonomy does not contain any factual financial information reported by the entities. It contains only the concepts (icai.org). For example, ICAI XBRL taxonomy.

6.3.2 XBRL Instance Document

A document created by using XBRL taxonomy is called instance document. It may contain full or part of a financial statement. Data needs to be tagged with XBRL taxonomy. To create an XBRL file, each piece of business data is matched with the XBRL concept describing that data. The data is surrounded by tags (information within angle brackets '<' and '>' containing the XBRL term). The tags can come from inside the financial system or can be applied by an add-on program or written by hand. A program can be developed using common programming languages such as Java, VB and VBA, and databases like SQL Server (www.xbrleducation.com). After creation, XBRL instance documents can be hosted as web pages, which can be viewed and analysed with the help of viewing software.

6.3.3 Approved/Recognized Taxonomies

XBRL International (www.xbrl.org) has a standard setting body called 'XBRL International Standard Board'. It sets standard, present version of which is 2.1. It also gives approval/recognition to the taxonomies defined by the accounting standard-setting bodies of different countries. The list of taxonomies approved/recognized by the XBRL International is given in the Appendix 1 and an example of XBRL taxonomy is given in Appendix 2.

It can be observed from the table in the Appendix that only some of the USA taxonomies have been approved by the XBRL International. All others are only recognized, and not approved.

6.4 Tools Used in XBRL Reports

Creating XBRL documents can be tedious and error-prone, if done manually. Fortunately, software tools are continually being developed and improved to help make the creation of valid XBRL documents easier (www.nysscpa.org).

For generation of XBRL financial reports, accountants need not know the complexities of XBRL. Software is available for the solution. Generally, two types of software are used—one for compilation of ordinary data into XBRL document by the companies and another for viewing the XBRL document by the users.

6.4.1 XBRL Composer

XBRL composer is a software which converts ordinary data into XBRL document based on taxonomies (technically known as 'XBRL instance document'). In other words, 'The XBRL Composer is a software product that can be used by anyone responsible for the production of business reports in XBRL format. The philosophy of the XBRL Composer is to serve many different types of users ranging from internal bookkeepers and business managers, to external software vendors who are seeking to deliver XBRL formatted outputs. The XBRL Composer allows for the use and combination of multiple taxonomies. Multiple taxonomies are necessary, to comply with various reporting standards' (www.xmlpitstop.com).

These composers can be used as add-ons to the existing application software like, electronic spreadsheet/database/accounting.

6.4.2 XBRL Viewer

XBRL Viewers help the users of a XBRL document to view it. The users can drill down to the related taxonomies for detail information. Some of the software has in-built provision to make further analysis from the available data. Data viewed from XBRL Viewers can be transferred to Excel or other databases. 'The XBRL file viewer tool is a simple standalone application that allows you to review every minor detail in an XBRL instance document' (www.reportingstandard.com).

XBRL Viewers are generally available free of cost. SEC has announced that the source code for the Interactive Financial Report Viewer that enables investors to analyse companies' interactive data filings is now available via its Web site for free use by the market.

6.5 Advantages of XBRL Reporting

XBRL reporting system has revolutionized financial reporting, and also use of those reports by the stakeholders. Advantages of it can be summarized as follows:

1. Interactive data will enable investors and other external users to make more productive decisions. Instead of wading through incomprehensible financial disclosure, investors can have access to meaningful information in a form which is more suitable for them.
2. From the accountants' point of view, it will enable them to prepare error-free accounts. Since accounting data are mapped into some recognized taxonomy, all errors are to be sorted out at this stage.
3. Auditors can detect errors in tagging financial data with the help of available application software. Adoption of XBRL will significantly lower both internal and external audit costs.
4. Objectives of any taxation system are accuracy and traceability on the basis of calculation, and compliance of rules and regulations. The accuracy will be provided by unambiguous data point definition as well as well defined sources of the information. Since most of the values used to calculate and report taxes are, in turn, derived, capabilities of the compliance system to trace such values all the way to the original or atomic information elements is essential. Finally, if the business rules and formulas used to assess taxes are documented, coded and understood, it is relatively straightforward to predict tax liability where and when a business transaction is taking place (www.ezinearticles.com/?XBRL-in-Tax-Compliance).
5. Real time analysis will help internal management to prepare reports for endless variety of internal management decisions.

   Thus, it will bring paradigm shift in the world of financial reporting.

6.6 XBRL Adoption by Different Countries (Source: www.edgar-online.com)

As of now, almost all the countries have recognized that XBRL is the business and financial reporting language of the future. Still its adoption by those countries is not uniform. Let us take a stock of the prevailing situation.

China—The China Securities Regulatory Commission has mandated XBRL filings for all public companies and sponsored related projects at the stock exchanges in China. There are currently reports from over 1,500 companies available in XBRL from the Shanghai and Shenzhen Stock Exchanges.

Japan—The Financial Services Agency has incorporated XBRL into EDINET, the statutory disclosure system. The Tokyo Stock Exchange has established an XBRL site to facilitate its use. The Bank of Japan is developing an XBRL system for gathering data from 500 financial institutions.

the Netherlands—In 'The Dutch Taxonomy Project', all governmental agencies are collaborating to use XBRL to reduce administrative burdens of businesses by 25 per cent in 4 years, an annual estimated commercial savings of 1 billion.

Spain—The Spanish Stock Exchange has already begun using XBRL for receiving and distributing public reports from more than 3,000 listed companies and currently has over 20,000 company reports available in the XBRL format. The Banco de Espana is also currently receiving regulatory data in XBRL from banks in the Spanish market and has also developed a Financial Information Exchange System to support XBRL reporting by credit institutions.

United Kingdom—Revenue & Customs (HMRC) began to accept corporate tax computations in XBRL online. The UK government plans to make XBRL mandatory for filing company accounts and tax returns in 2010.

United States—US Bank regulators moved to an XBRL format for specific regulatory reports for all US financial services company in October 2005 and are currently expanding the scope of this project to other reports. The Securities and Exchange Commission (SEC) directed Voluntary Filing Program since 2005. From the beginning of 2009, the largest companies would be required to provide financial information using interactive data, and within three years all public companies would follow suit. SEC's EDGAR (Electronic Data Gathering, Analysis and Retrieval) system is being replaced by IDEA (Interactive Data Electronic Applications).

India—The Reserve Bank of India is going to launch the Basel II reporting system using XBRL through the existing Online Returns Filing System (ORFS). A Committee has been constituted under the Chairmanship of Shri V Leeladhar, Deputy Governor for the purpose (www.rbi.org.in).

The Institute of Chartered Accountants of India constituted a Group on XBRL in January 2007, under the chairmanship of the President, ICAI. While building the taxonomy, three broad reporting categories have been considered, taking into account the different reporting requirements. These are

1. Commercial and industrial
2. Banking companies
3. Non-banking finance companies

Recently, the Group has finalized the draft general purpose financial reporting XBRL taxonomy for commercial and industrial companies and also for banking companies. These drafts cover the financial statements, viz., Balance Sheet, Statement of Profit and Loss, and Cash Flow Statement and the related non-financial information. The draft taxonomy has been developed conforming to Indian Accounting Standards and Company Law while adapting the architectural features of the IFRS general purpose taxonomy 2006. The ICAI has already issued Exposure Drafts for both types of companies. India has also launched XBRL India in collaboration with XBRL International, its Web site address being www.xbrl.org/in/(www.icai.org).

6.6.1 China and Japan—Ahead of USA

Brian G. Cartwright, General Counsel U.S. Securities and Exchange Commission, in his speech on 12 April 2008, said, "We'd like to think our capital markets are the most up-to-date on the planet, but when it comes to XBRL reporting, we're actually following in the footsteps of others. China, in fact, was the first country in the world to mandate XBRL reporting. China started in 2003 with 50 companies that voluntarily reported using XBRL. It's interesting that the Voluntary Filing Program we have here in the US includes about the same number of companies. In China today, the rules of both the China Securities Regulatory Commission and the Shanghai Stock Exchange require listed companies to file their quarterly, half-year and annual reports using XBRL. China's program now includes more than 800 companies. And China's far from alone. In Japan, the Financial Services Agency now requires approximately 5 thousand companies and 3 thousand investment funds to submit their quarterly, half-year and annual filings using XBRL. It's the same story in South Korea, where all publicly held companies are required to file financial statements using XBRL" (www.sec.gov).

6.7 Conclusion

It has already been proved that XBRL is versatile and very much useful for financial and business analysis to the investors and other stakeholders. Based on its success story, all the countries are coming forward to adopt this reporting language. Many countries have made its application mandatory, and others are in the pipeline. In the next few years it is going to be adopted by all the countries. Though India has made a late entry, still she is moving at a faster rate to catch up with others. We, the accountants in India, will have to make ourselves ready to take the challenge of introduction of XBRL in India.

Limitations of the study

Since the author of this paper does not have first-hand experience of preparing/handling XBRL reports, there may be lacking on conceptual issues.

Appendix 6.1

List of Taxonomies Approved/Recognized by XBRL International (December 2009)

Country/Jurisdiction	Taxonomy	Specification	Level	Status
Canada	GAAP Primary Financial Statements	2.1	Acknowledged	Draft
	Notes to Financial Statements	2.1	Acknowledged	Draft
China	China Listed Company Taxonomy Framework	2.1	Acknowledged	Draft
	China Fund Company Taxonomy Framework	2.1	Acknowledged	Draft
	China Financial Listed Company Information Disclosure Taxonomy	2.1	Acknowledged	Draft

Contd.....

Country/Jurisdiction	Taxonomy	Specification	Level	Status
Chile	General Purpose Financial Reporting for Profit Oriented	2.1	Acknowledged	Draft
IASB	IFRS 2009 Taxonomy	2.1	Acknowledged	Draft
	IFRS 2008 Taxonomy	2.1	Acknowledged	Draft
	IFRS 2006 Taxonomy	2.1	Acknowledged	Draft
	IFRS 2005 Taxonomy	2.1	Acknowledged	Final
	IFRS 2004 Taxonomy	2.1	Acknowledged	Final
International	Global Common Data Taxonomies	2.1	Acknowledged	Draft
	Microfinance Information Exchange (MIX)	2.1	Acknowledged	Draft
Ireland	GAAP Commercial and Industrial	2.1	Acknowledged	Draft
Israel	Israeli Annual and Periodic Reports General Purpose Financial Reporting, extension for International Financial Reporting Standards (IL-IFRS-GP)	2.1	Acknowledged	Draft
Japan	EDINET Taxonomy	2.1	Acknowledged	Final
Korea	GAAP Primary Financial Statements	2.1	Acknowledged	Draft
New Zealand	GAAP Commercial and Industrial (C & I)	2.1	Acknowledged	Draft
Spain	General Data Identification	2.1	Acknowledged	Final
	RSC Taxonomy for Corporate Social Responsibility	2.1	Acknowledged	Final
Taiwan	Taiwan Listed Company Financial Statements-(C & I)	2.1	Acknowledged	Final
Thailand	Listed Companies – Banking Services	2.1	Acknowledged	Draft
	Listed Companies – Commercial and Industrial	2.1	Acknowledged	Draft
	Listed Companies – Securities Companies	2.1	Acknowledged	Draft
United Kingdom	GAAP Commercial and Industrial	2.1	Acknowledged	Draft
United Sates	GAAP—Investment Management	2.1	*Approved*	Final
	XBRL US Accountants' Report Taxonomy 1.0	2.1	*Approved*	Final

Contd....

Country/Jurisdiction	Taxonomy	Specification	Level	Status
	XBRL US Country Taxonomy 1.0	2.1	*Approved*	Final
	XBRL US Currency Taxonomy 1.0	2.1	*Approved*	Final
	XBRL US Document and Entity Information Taxonomy 1.0	2.1	*Approved*	Final
	XBRL US Exchange Taxonomy 1.0	2.1	*Approved*	Final
	XBRL US GAAP Taxonomy 1.0	2.1	*Approved*	Final
	XBRL US Management's Discussion and Analysis Taxonomy 1.0	2.1	*Approved*	Final
	XBRL US Management Report Taxonomy 1.0	2.1	*Approved*	Final
	XBRL US North American Industrial Classification System (NAICS) Taxonomy 1.0	2.1	Acknowledged	Final
	XBRL US SEC Certification Taxonomy 1.0	2.1	*Approved*	Final
	XBRL US Standardized Industrial Classification (SIC) Taxonomy 1.0	2.1	*Approved*	Final
	XBRL US State-Province Taxonomy 1.0	2.1	*Approved*	Final
	GAAP—Commercial and Industrial (superseded by the 2008 version)	2.1	*Approved*	Final
	GAAP—Banking & Savings (superseded by the 2008 version)	2.1	*Approved*	Final
	GAAP—Insurance (superseded by the 2008 version)	2.1	*Approved*	Final
	GAAP—Brokers and Dealers (superseded by the 2008 version)	2.1	Acknowledged	Final
	GAAP—Pensions (superseded by the 2008 version)	2.1	Acknowledged	Final
	SEC Certification (superseded by the 2008 version)	2.1	*Approved*	Final
	Management Report (superseded by the 2008 version)	2.1	*Approved*	Final
	Accountants Report (superseded by the 2008 version)	2.1	*Approved*	Final
				Contd.....

Country/Jurisdiction	Taxonomy	Specification	Level	Status
	MD & A (superseded by the 2008 version)	2.1	*Approved*	Final
	ICI Mutual Fund Risk/Return SummaryTaxonomy	2.1	Acknowledged	Final
	XBRL US Schedule of Investments Taxonomy 2008	2.1	Acknowledged	Final

Source: www.xbrl.org.

Appendix 6.2

Example (Truncated) of XBRL Taxonomy for Banks Issued by ICAI


```
<?xml version="1.0" encoding="UTF-8"?>
<!-- Generated by Fujitsu XWand B0126T_02 -->
<!-- Created by IRIS Business Services (India) Pvt Ltd -->
<xs:schema targetNamespace="http://www.xbrl.in/in-gaap/2009-06-30"
attributeFormDefault="unqualified" elementFormDefault="qualified"
xmlns:xs="http://www.w3.org/2001/XMLSchema"
xmlns:in-gaap="http://www.xbrl.in/in-gaap/2009-06-30"
xmlns:link="http://www.xbrl.org/2003/linkbase"
xmlns:xbrldt="http://xbrl.org/2005/xbrldt" xmlns:ref="http://www.xbrl.org/2004/ref"
xmlns:xl="http://www.xbrl.org/2003/XLink"
xmlns:xsi="http://www.w3.org/2001/XMLSchema-instance"
xmlns:xbrli="http://www.xbrl.org/2003/instance"
xmlns:xlink="http://www.w3.org/1999/xlink">
    <xs:annotation>
    <xs:appinfo>
        <link:linkbaseRef xlink:type="simple" xlink:href="in-gaap-2009-06-30_pre.xml"
xlink:role="http://www.xbrl.org/2003/role/presentationLinkbaseRef"
xlink:arcrole="http://www.w3.org/1999/xlink/properties/linkbase"/>
        <link:linkbaseRef xlink:type="simple" xlink:href="in-gaap-2009-06-30_cal.xml"
xlink:role="http://www.xbrl.org/2003/role/calculationLinkbaseRef"
xlink:arcrole="http://www.w3.org/1999/xlink/properties/linkbase"/>
        <link:linkbaseRef xlink:type="simple" xlink:href="in-gaap-2009-06-30_def.xml"
xlink:role="http://www.xbrl.org/2003/role/definitionLinkbaseRef"
xlink:arcrole="http://www.w3.org/1999/xlink/properties/linkbase"/>
        <link:linkbaseRef xlink:type="simple" xlink:href="in-gaap-2009-06-30_lab.xml"
xlink:role="http://www.xbrl.org/2003/role/labelLinkbaseRef"
xlink:arcrole="http://www.w3.org/1999/xlink/properties/linkbase"/>
<link:roleType roleURI="http://www.xbrl.in/in-gaap/2009-06-30/role/Statutory"
id="Statutory">
        <link:definition>Statutory</link:definition>
        <link:usedOn>link:presentationLink</link:usedOn>
```

```
        <link:usedOn>link:calculationLink</link:usedOn>
        </link:roleType>
        <link:roleType roleURI=“http://www.xbrl.in/in-gaap/2009-06-30/role/
SourcesApplicationFunds”id=“SourcesApplicationFunds”>
        <link:definition>Sources Application Funds</link:definition>
        <link:usedOn>link:presentationLink</link:usedOn>
        <link:usedOn>link:calculationLink</link:usedOn>
    </link:roleType>
    <link:roleType roleURI=“http://www.xbrl.in/in-gaap/2009-06-30/role/TotalAssetsLiabilities”
```

Web sites

1. www.xbrl.org
2. www.xbrl.org/in/
3. www.edgar-online.com
4. www.xbrleducation.com
5. www.tryxbrl.com
6. www.w3.com
7. www.sec.gov
8. www.rbi.org.in
9. www.icai.org
10. www.rivetsoftware.com
11. www.reportingstandard.com
12. www.trinity.edu
13. www.16thconference.xbrl.org
14. www.semansys.com
15. www.nysscpa.org
16. www.xmlpitstop.com
17. www.ezinearticles.com

CHAPTER 7

ESOP Valuation and Disclosures in India*

Satyajit Dhar and Subhabrata De

ABSTRACT

Employee Stock Option Plans (ESOPs) are considered to be a highly appreciated tool for attracting and retaining top talent by the companies. Such a plan ties together the shareholder and management interests. Two alternatives for valuing employee stock option (ESO) are intrinsic value method and fair value method. Most companies like to measure compensation expense implicit in a stock option grant using the intrinsic value method, though they are required to disclose in their footnotes the fair value of employee stock options granted. The issue of whether the value of employee stock options (ESOs) should be recognized as expense has been subject of debate for decades. The anti-expensing lobby argues that there is no easy and proper accounting mechanism that captures the economic rationaie underlying stock option expensing. Questions that are raised on valuation of ESOs include: 'ESOs can't be valued', 'How can you value something that is not traded in an open market?' It is against this backdrop that the paper attempts to assess ESO valuation practices of Indian companies. In the process, it brings the use of managerial discretion over valuation model inputs into fore. Further, it surveys the ESO valuation and disclosure practices of companies in India. Lack of previous studies in this area provides incentive to undertake the study.

7.1 Introduction

Stock option plans are considered to be a highly appreciated tool for attracting and retaining top talent by the companies. Such a plan ties together the shareholder and management interests. The options can offer advantageous linkage between talent and pay at the onset of an employment

* An earlier version of the paper was presented at the *XXXII All India Accounting Conference* organized by Indian Accounting Association (Gwalior Branch) in association with the Institute of Commerce and Management, Jiwaji University, Gwalior during 14–15 November 2009 held at Gwalior, India.

relationship. Options prove efficient in matching managerial pay to ability and help a firm to find employees who are ready to link their pay with the firm's worth (Arya and Mittendorf 2005). An employee stock option plans (ESOP)[1] give employees the right to acquire shares of the company in the future at a predetermined price, even if the market value of the stock has increased from that of option's grant price. It may be noted that companies often will require the employee to hold the options for a period of time before being exercised. India's growing economy is being propelled by fast paced, talent-dependent service industries like Information Technology (IT). In this environment where top talent is very difficult to find and keep, stock options have become popular, primarily for retention purpose, in the 1990s and early 2000s. Industries where they are very common include IT, drugs & pharmaceuticals, banking & financial services and fast moving consumer goods. Now, other manufacturing companies are also being inclined to use this tool for retention of key employees.

Two alternatives for valuing employee stock options (ESOs) for accounting purposes are intrinsic value method and fair value method. Most companies like to measure compensation expense implicit in stock option grant using the intrinsic value method to avoid recognition of true cost of ESOs grant. Accounting standards of most of the countries permit use of intrinsic value method with proforma disclosure of the fair value of employee stock options. The issue of whether the value of ESOs should be recognized as expenses has been the subject of debate for decades.

Due to the features that a call option holder need not bear the downside risk and eligible to gain from upside, options are valuable. The same rule is applicable for ESOs. However, there being no active market of ESOs like market traded options, valuation of ESOs is a controversial issue.

Studies on ESOP in Indian context are very limited. Surprisingly, there is no study on ESO valuation and disclosure practice in India. Absence of extensive study on ESO disclosure practice prompted us to undertake a detail survey on reporting by Indian companies.

Against this backdrop, the paper attempts to assess ESO valuation practice of Indian companies. In the process, it brings use of managerial discretion over valuation model inputs into fore. Further, it surveys the disclosure practice of Indian companies on ESO valuation.

The rest of the paper proceeds as follows. Section 7.2 describes the accounting issues related to ESO grants. Valuation methods of stock options are presented in Section 7.3. A brief review of the regulatory framework for ESOP accounting currently prevailing in India is presented in Section 7.4. Section 7.5 outlines the results of a survey of ESO valuation and disclosure practices of Indian companies and Section 7.6 concludes the paper.

7.2 ESOP Accounting

Stock option accounting debates veered around two themes: first is 'intrinsic value' of the option and second is 'fair value'. Intrinsic value is the excess of the market price of the share under ESOP over the exercise price on the date of grant. If exercise price equals or is below the prevailing market price on the grant date, an option will have no value, i.e., intrinsic value is nil. The fair value of a stock option is the price that would be obtained for that option in an arm's length transaction between a willing buyer and a willing seller. The fair value shall be estimated using option valuation models that take into account various factors such as exercise price, expected dividend, expected volatility, risk-free interest rate for the expected term of the option. In valuation controversy, the anti-expensing lobby argues that there is no easy and proper valuation mechanism that measures the present value of an option at the time of grant. Sinnett (2003) documents all these opinion in this way: 'They can't be valued', 'How can you value something that is not traded in an open market?' 'Why would you want to value them?'

US GAAP pronouncements on ESOP are contained in APB Opinion No. 25 (1972), SFAS 123 (1993), SFAS 148 (2002) and SFAS 123(R) (revised 2004).

The Financial Accounting Standard Board (FASB) of USA recognized that the intrinsic value method does not capture the true value of employee stock options and issued a new standard, SFAS 123, in 1993 with the intent of conforming financial reporting to economic reality. SFAS 123 specified that options would be valued by using fair value and expenses must be recognized over the vesting period on the basing such fair value. But due to massive opposition, the FASB, however, permitted continuation of the old rule, i.e., use of existing intrinsic value method with a rider that fair value of value of ESOs should be disclosed in the footnotes. Subsequently, International Accounting Standard Board (IASB) issued in February 2004, IFRS 2, *Share-Based Payment*, and requires fair value–based accounting for share-based payment transaction. Thereafter, the FASB issued SFAS 123 (Revised) in December 2004 to eliminate APB Opinion No. 25's intrinsic value method and SFAS 123 prescribed footnote disclosures of fair value. SFAS 123 (Revised) requires all public entities to recognize as expense, the fair value of stock options issued to employees. FASB prescribes Black–Scholes model, Black–Scholes–Merton (BSM) model, Monte-Carlo model, Lattice model for valuation of employee stock option options, but showed no preference to any model.

After the formulation of IFRS 2, *Share-based Payment* and the revision of SFAS 123, the debate on accounting for employee stock option is shifting from *whether* to report options on income statements to *how* to report those (Kaplan and Palepu 2003).

In India, there is no accounting standard on ESOP accounting. Certain requirements are laid down in the SEBI Guidelines. The regulatory framework for ESOP accounting and disclosure in India is described in Section 7.4.

7.3 ESOP Valuation

Regular trade of stock options proves that option has some value. Economists have developed several models such as Black–Scholes model, Binomial model, BSM model, Lattice model, etc. to price option. Widely used model for valuation of stock options is Black–Scholes model. This model was modified by Robert Merton and incorporated the payment of cash dividends. The resulting model is Black–Scholes–Merton model (BSM Model). In the next subsections we describe the important valuation models.

In a seminal paper, Black and Scholes developed a precise model for determining the equilibrium value of an option (Black and Scholes 1973). The model has both the critical importance for valuing contingent claims and practical importance for identifying overvalued and undervalued options in the market.

In this context, the equilibrium value of an option, V_0 that entitle the holder to buy one share of stock is shown by Black and Scholes to be

$$V_0 = V_s N(d_1) - E/e^{rt} N(d_2)$$

where V_s is the current price of the stock

$N(d)$ is the cumulative normal productivity density function
E is the exercise price of the option

$$e = 2.71828, \text{ the base of natural logarithms}$$

r is the short-term annual interest rate continuously compounded
t is the length of time in years to the expiration of the option.

Black and Scholes model is based on a number of assumptions. These are: there are no transaction costs, the stock pays no dividend, only European options are considered.

7.3.1 Black–Scholes–Merton (BSM) Model

The BSM model (Merton 1973) was designed to value publicly traded option with short exercise periods. It is the moderate form of Black–Scholes model. The basic model assumes that the stock option does not pay dividends and the option can be exercised only at the expiration date.

The formula for the BSM model is

$$C = SN(d_1) - Xe^{-rt} N(d_2)$$

where S is the current price of the stock.

X is the exercise price of the option.

7.3.2 Lattice Model

A useful a very popular technique for pricing an option involves constructing a binomial tree (Cox et al. 1979; Rendelman and Bartter 1979). The model is based on a binomial probability distribution in which the underlying event has only two possible outcomes. In the case of employee stock options, the underlying event is the change in the stock price and related change in the intrinsic value of the option. During each period, the stock price can move either up or down when multiple periods are considered in sequence, a distribution of possible stock price is created. This binomial distribution is referred to as a lattice or tree, reflecting it appearance graphically. More branches are created as the time horizon lengthens. Each point of stock price on the lattice is referred to as a 'node'.

Baril et al. (2007) make a comparative study between two models—BSM and Lattice model—in the context of valuation of employee stock options. According to the study, the following are the major differences between the two models:

- Both models provide reasonable measures of fair value, incorporating the same information that market participants would use in valuing options in an exchange transaction. But lattice model can directly accommodate all the unique features of employee stock options, while the BSM model can accommodate these features indirectly.
- The BSM model assumes that both the risk-free interest rate and stock's price volatility remain constant, an unreasonable assumption for employee options with longer term. In contrast, the lattice model's greater flexibility enables users to assume different rate and volatilities for each time period. In fact, companies using the lattice model incorporate different scenarios along selected paths of the stock price tree.
- The BSM model may provide a satisfactory valuation in cases where employee stock option expense is immaterial.

In all valuation models, value of a stock option is computed by making certain assumptions about model inputs. Shaughnessy and Rashty (2007) summarize the assumptions that the management uses in determination of the share-based compensation. Such assumptions are made for

- expected life,
- volatility,
- interest rate,
- expected dividend and
- Income tax effects.

Certain empirical studies suggest that management of companies use considerable discretion in estimating option model inputs and consequently may distort the fair value estimate of stock option issued to employees. In the next subsection we review the literature relating to ESO disclosures and ESO valuation.

7.3.3 Literature Review

Different accounting standard-setting bodes recommended that firms should estimate the stock option expense by computing the fair value of the options granted during the year using an option pricing model.

Balsam et al. (2003) investigate whether footnote disclosures under SFAS 123 are managed in 1996. The authors find small, newly public firms and firms that provide high levels of CEO pay or stock option compensation allocate a small portion of the option value to the 1996 *proforma* expense. The findings of the study suggest that firms manipulated proforma stock option expenses when their estimate choices are not observable. Focusing on the four key option pricing model inputs—expected option life, expected stock price volatility, expected dividend yield and the risk free interest rate. Aboody et al. (2006) finds that firms understate option value estimates and proforma stock-based compensation expense disclosed under SFAS 123 (R). They also report that understatement of estimated option values is positively related with magnitude of such expenses, weaker corporate governance and excessiveness of executive pay. Further, the findings of the study indicate that firms use greater latitude in respect of the expected option life and expected stock price volatility input assumptions.

Hodder et al. (2006) find that firms use considerable discretion in estimating option model inputs when calculating the fair value of options. They also explore the consequences of such discretion. They conclude that firms exercise considerable discretion over all model inputs and this discretion results in material differences in ESO fair value estimates.

A study by Johnston (2006) examines the possibility of manipulating option pricing model assumptions, specifically, three option pricing model assumptions: (i) stock price volatility, (ii) dividend yield, and (iii) the risk-free interest rate. He divided the sample firms into 'recognizing firms' (i.e., the firms that voluntarily expense stock option) and 'disclosing firms' (firms that do not). He computed the expected volatility, expected dividend yield and expected risk-free interest rate assumptions for the recognizing and disclosing firms using industry averages and also computed the unexplained stock option expense for each observation by subtracting the expected expense from the reported expense. The analysis suggests that the understatement of stock option expense is significantly grater for firms that recognize the expense in their financial statements than for firms that only disclose the expense in the footnotes to their financial statements. Additional analysis reveals that recognizing firms assume a lower level of volatility than disclosing firms in the option pricing model calculations. The author finds no evidence that recognizing firms manage the dividend yield and risk-free interest rate assumptions more than disclosing firms.

Beams et al. (2005) investigate differences between firms that choose a zero volatility estimate and those that use a non-zero estimate in the calculation of their disclosed option values. Firms using the zero volatility assumptions understate fair value compared to fair value calculated using a peer group estimate of volatility. They further report that IPO firms using a non-zero estimate of volatility also understate the fair value of option like firms that use the zero volatility estimate.

Nelson and Mercy (2005) investigate the transparency of executive stock option disclosures of Australian firms for the financial years 2000 and 2002. They report low level of transparency in ESO-related disclosure by Australian firms and also find that the existence of compensation committee and size of the firm are positively associated with the level of transparency.

Libby et al. (2006) examine whether information in footnotes might lack reliability because auditors permit more misstatement in disclosed amount as opposed to recognized amount. Using the stock compensation and lease-related information, they find that auditors require greater correction of misstatement in recognized amount with an equivalent disclosed amount, as auditors view recognized amount as more material.

A study by Bassett et al. (2007) examines the role of corporate governance in ESO disclosures. The authors find that two corporate governance measures, viz. the quality of auditor and duality of the role of CEO and chair of the Board have dominant influence on such disclosure. They also report that firms do not fully comply with mandatory requirements on ESO disclosures but such firms voluntary provide other ESO disclosures.

Lam and Mensah (2007) examine the factors affecting firms' choice of ESO-related disclosure informativeness. They show that firms with executives who are excessively paid, poorly performing firms and firms substantially owned by insiders are more likely to choose less informative disclosure method. The authors also provide evidence that firms with higher accounting integrity command a higher market valuation.

In Indian context, studies on ESOP-related issues are very few. One study by Kumar (2004) investigated the effect of employee stock option plans on performance, productivity and risk. The author reports that existence of stock option plan does not necessarily improve productivity of sample firms. But, the author finds significant positive relationship between stock market performance and presence of option plans. Another study by Dhar and De (2009) reports the results of two surveys undertaken on ESOP disclosure. Two surveys relate to financial years 2002–03 and 2006–07. The authors report the cases of non-compliance with SEBI Guidelines but the findings indicate improvement in disclosure of sample companies in financial year 2006–07 as compared to that of financial year 2002–03.

7.4 Regulatory Framework for ESOP Accounting in India

The regulatory framework of accounting for ESOPs in India is at its infancy. There is no standard on the issue by the Institute of Chartered Accountants of India (ICAI). At present, ESOP accounting in India is governed by the SEBI Guidelines (Employee Stock Option Scheme and Employee Stock Purchase Scheme) issued in 1999 and the Guidance Note issued by the ICAI in 2003.

SEBI Guidelines *inter alia* provide accounting policies to be adopted for accounting compensation cost implicit in employee stock options. SEBI Guidelines permit accounting for ESOs either by fair value method or by intrinsic value method as per option of the company. According to the SEBI Guidelines, intrinsic value is the excess of the market price of the share under ESOP over the exercise price. An employee stock option has no intrinsic value where the exercise price is set equal to market price on the date of grant. The fair value of a stock option is the price that would be obtained for that option in an arm's length transaction between two willing parties, i.e., seller and buyer. The fair value shall be estimated using an option pricing model, e.g. Black–Scholes model or binomial model.

The **ICAI** Guidance Note entitles '*Accounting for Employee Share-based Payments*' (ICAI, 2003), establishes financial and reporting principles for Employee Share-based Payment Plans, Employee Stock Option Plan, Employee Stock Purchase Plans and Stock Appreciation Rights. The ICAI Guidance Note recommends that the fair value–based methods or intrinsic value method can be used for computation of cost associated with issuance of stock options. The Note further permits use of intrinsic value method with fair value disclosures. A number of aspects such as reload features, performance conditions, modifications to the terms and conditions of the grant of stock options, EPS, employee share-based payment plans with cash alternatives, etc. are dealt with in the Guidance Note. The Guidance Note being non-mandatory in nature, companies in India rarely comply with the requirements of Guidance Note. It may be noted that by 2011, Indian companies may be required to adopt international accounting standard including IFRS 2 Share-based Payments.

7.4.1 Disclosure Requirements as per SEBI Guidelines

SEBI Guidelines do not prescribe any valuation method to be adopted when determining the fair value of stock option but the guidelines do require companies to disclose the method used. As per the SEBI Guidelines, 1999, as amended in 2003, a company is required to make the stock option scheme related disclosure either in the Director's Report or in the Annexure to the Directors' Report. Such disclosure should include the following details:

(a) Options granted
(b) The pricing formula
(c) Options vested
(d) Options exercised
(e) The total number of shares arising as a result of exercise of option
(f) Options lapsed
(g) Variation of terms of options
(h) Money realized by exercise of options
(i) Total number of options in force
(j) Employee-wise details of options granted to
    (i) senior managerial personnel;
    (ii) any other employee who receives a grant in any one year of option amounting to 5 per cent or more of option granted during the year;

   (iii) identified employees who were granted option, during any one year, equal to or exceeding 1 per cent of the issued capital (exceeding outstanding warrants and conversions) of the company at the time of grant;

(k) Diluted Earnings per Share (EPS) pursuant to issue of shares on exercise of option calculated in accordance with Accounting Standard (AS) 20, Earnings per Share.

(l) Where the company has calculated the employee compensation cost using the intrinsic value of the stock options, the difference between the employee compensation cost so computed and the employee compensation cost that shall have been recognized if it had used the fair value of the options, shall be disclosed. The impact of this difference on profits and on EPS of the company shall also be disclosed.

(m) Weighted-average exercise prices and weighted-average fair values of options shall be disclosed separately for options whose exercise price either equals or exceeds or is less than the market price of the stock.

(n) A description of the method and significant assumptions used during the year to estimate the fair values of options, including the following weighted-average information:
   (i) Risk-free interest rate
   (ii) Expected life
   (iii) Expected volatility
   (iv) Expected dividends
   (v) Price of the underlying share in market at the time of option grant.

There is no requirement to audit such disclosures as those are part of the Directors' Report. Further, there is no review by any regulatory body to check the authenticity of such disclosure. Hence, completeness and correctness of such disclosure may not be taken for granted. In the next section we present the results of the survey undertaken to assess the practice of Indian company regarding stock option valuation related disclosure by Indian companies.

7.5 Disclosure of Stock Option Value by Indian Companies

The present study has been conducted to observe the valuation techniques and presentation of ESO-related information in the annual reports by the selected companies in India. So far, no study has been undertaken to assess the trend of ESOS reporting in India which is a recent addition in the area of financial reporting after the introduction of ESOP in India.

7.5.1 Sample Selection and Survey Procedure

The requirements of SEBI Guidelines on ESOP are applicable to the listed companies in India. Hence, we draw our sample from listed Indian companies that have issued shares pursuant to exercise of employee stock options till March 2008.Our initial sample consists of 213 companies. We have to exclude some companies from sample due to non-disclosure of ESOP-related data or non-availability of annual reports. Ultimately, we could include only 140 companies for final survey. We have obtained the name of these companies from Prowess, a database, maintained by CMIE LTD. The different pieces of information on employee stock options are hand picked from the annual

TABLE 7.1 Industry Classification of ESOP Companies

Industry Segments	Number of Companies	Percentage
Information Technology	50	35.71
Manufacturing—Drugs & Pharmaceuticals	19	13.57
Manufacturing—Others	27	19.29
Infrastructural construction	09	6.43
Banking & Financial services	07	5.00
Other services	28	20
Total	**140**	**100.00**

Source: CMIE PROWESS Database. Results computed.

reports of 140 companies for the financial year 2007–08. Proforma disclosure in the Directors' Report portion of the annual reports of the sample companies is the main source of these data. Additional pieces of information are also taken from narrative disclosure as contained in Notes to the Accounts. The survey procedures include close scrutiny of the annual reports of the sample companies. We have considered the following disclosure aspects for conducting survey.

(a) Place of disclosure

(b) Choice of valuation model and its disclosure.

(c) Disclosure of assumptions on valuation inputs, viz. risk-free interest rate, expected life, expected volatility and expected dividends.

We have hand-picked data relating to different employee stock option schemes, accounting policies followed by the sample companies and ESOP-related information from the annual reports of the sample companies. Table 7.1 gives classification of surveyed companies as per industry segment. Industry classification related information is obtained from CMIE Prowess database. It is observed that knowledge companies are more pro-active in administering ESOP schemes. Out of 140 companies, 50 companies (35.71 per cent) belong to information technology and 19 companies (13.57 per cent) to the pharmaceutical sector.

7.5.2 Place of Disclosure

As per SEBI Guidelines, the Board of Directors should disclose the details of ESOS either in the Directors' Report or in the Annexure to the Directors' Report. It is observed that out of 140 sample companies, 90 companies have disclosed ESOS-related information in Annexure to the Directors' Report, 47 companies presented it in the body of the Directors' Report, 03 companies disclosed it in the Corporate Governance (CG) Report. Figure 7.1 gives a pictorial presentation of the results of survey regarding places of disclosure. The companies that disclosed such information in the CG Report has preferred to deviate from the requirements of the SEBI Guidelines.

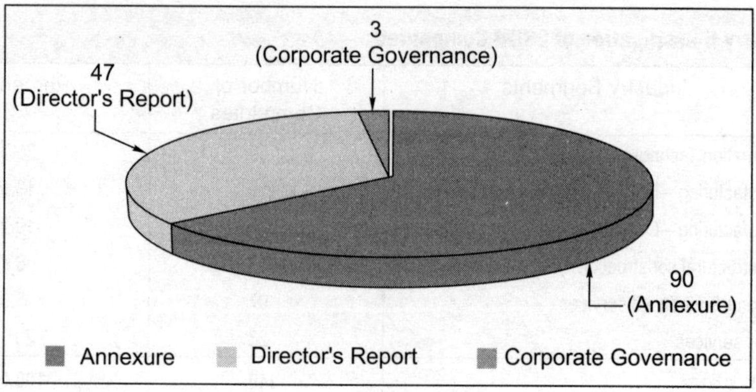

Figure 7.1 Place of disclosure

7.5.3 Valuation Model

As per SEBI Guidelines, a company is required to disclose the method and significant assumptions used to estimate the fair value of option granted during the year. It is observed that out of 140 surveyed companies, 50 (35.71 per cent) companies did not disclose the name of the valuation models. Our analysis revealed that surveyed companies followed most of the available valuation methods like Black–Scholes (B/S), BSM, binomial and lattice. Among the different valuation models, B/S is the most preferred model as 85 companies (60.71 per cent had used that model. We present the results of out survey in Fig. 7.2.

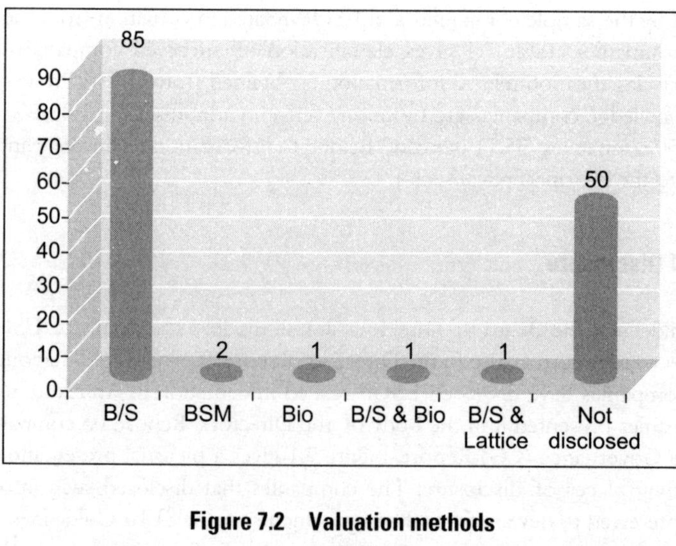

Figure 7.2 Valuation methods

TABLE 7.2 **Disclosure of Risk-free Interest Rate Assumption**

Disclosure Types	Number of Companies	Percentage
Disclosed as a single measurement	51	36.43
Disclosed in range	36	25.72
Mentioned only parameters, but no quantitative disclosure	09	6.43
No disclosure of risk-free interest rate	44	31.42
Total	**140**	**100.00**

Source: Annual Reports of Sample Companies, Results computed.

7.5.4 Valuation Assumptions and Their Disclosure

Option pricing models require firms to make several assumptions including life of the stock option, the volatility of the options, the risk-free interest rate and the expected dividend. Each of these assumptions affects the fair value of stock options, and it is very difficult to prescribe any rules to control wide disparity of such assumptions. Our survey reveals that the assumptions such as risk-free interest rate, expected life, expected volatility, expected dividends do vary widely among the sample companies.

1. **Risk-free interest rate:** As we have considered data partnering to financial year 2007–08, it is expected that there should not be any wide disparity regarding risk-free interest rate assumption. Our survey results indicate that risk-free interest rate assumption varies between 5.5 and 9.5 per cent. We have presented results of our survey regarding risk-free interest rate assumption in Table 7.2 along with disclosure on expected volatility assumption.

   Results of the survey presented in Table 7.2 reveals that 44 companies (31.42 per cent) avoided disclosure of assumption regarding risk-free interest rate in violation of SEBI Guidelines. Our scrutiny of annual reports also revealed that there are wide variations among the surveyed companies regarding the presentation of valuation inputs assumption. Some companies disclosed risk-free interest rate as point estimate and some companies disclosed the same as range estimate (e.g., 7.12–7.25). Nine companies disclosed the parameters used to estimate the risk-free interest but avoided disclosure of interest rates used for valuation. An example of such disclosure is cited below.

2. **Expected life of the option:** Like risk-free interest, there is wide disparity among the sample companies regarding disclosure of assumption on expected life of the option. Disclosure of assumed expected life of option was made in terms of years or in terms of months or in terms of days. Again some companies have given a range instead of single measurement. Furthermore, 42 companies (30 per cent) have not given any disclosure of expected life of option. Table 7.3 presents the result of the survey on expected life of the option disclosure.

TABLE 7.3 Disclosure of Expected Life of the Option

Disclosure Types		Number of Companies	Percentage
Disclosed in term of year	Point estimate	50	35.71
	Range estimate	31	22.14
Disclosed in term of months	Single estimate	04	2.86
	Range estimate	02	1.43
Days (point estimate only)		02	1.43
Disclosure of parameters only		09	6.43
Not disclosed		42	30
Total		**140**	**100.00**

Source: Annual Reports of Sample Companies, Results computed.

3. **Expected volatility:** Table 7.4 presents the findings on expected volatility disclosure. It is found that surveyed companies disclosed expected volatility-related information in form of point estimate or range estimate. Our survey revealed that a large number (59) of companies (42.14 per cent) disclosed no measurement in this respect. The assumption regarding volatility varies in a wide range and we have discussed this issue elsewhere in this paper. Thirty-one companies (22.14 per cent) disclosed range measurement instead of a single measurement. One company mentioned only parameters and avoided quantitative disclosure.
4. **Expected dividend:** Our finding (Table 7.5) reveals that the assumptions regarding expected dividend are disclosed by the surveyed firms as a percentage of face value, dividend per share and dividend per stock option. Few companies disclosed expected dividend yield related information as range estimate instead of point estimate. A large number of companies (48) disclosed no information in this regard.

TABLE 7.4 Disclosure of Expected Volatility

Disclosure Types Volatility	Number of Companies	Percentage
Point estimate	49	35.00
Range estimate	31	22.14
Disclosure of parameters only	01	0.72
No disclosure of risk-free interest rate	59	42.14
Total	**140**	**100.00**

Source: Annual Reports of Sample Companies, Results computed.

TABLE 7.5 Valuation Parameters for Fair Value Measurement

Expected Dividend	Number of Companies	Percentage
Point estimate	65	46.43
Not disclosed	48	34.28
Range estimate	13	9.27
Mention but no measurement	09	6.43
Per share measurement	04	2.87
Per option measurement	01	0.72
Total	**140**	**100.00**

Source: Annual Reports of Sample Companies, Results computed.

7.5.5 Use of Management Discretion on Valuation Inputs

Studies on valuation of stock options (Balsam et al. 2003; Hodder et al. 2006; Johnston 2006) reveal that in ample number of cases, management of sample companies use considerable discretion on valuation inputs. We have tried to assess the Indian scenario in this regard. Our survey results indicate that assumptions on risk-free interest rate and expected volatility vary in a wide range. Even 0 per cent volatility is assumed by the management of some companies. Similarly, the risk-free interest rate in the year under survey varies in the range of 5.5 per cent to 9.5 per cent. Hence, the use of management discretion on option valuation inputs may not be ruled out. We have presented the results in Table 7.6.

7.5.6 Disclosure of EPS

The listed companies are required calculate and disclose basic and diluted earning per share (EPS) in accordance with the accounting standard 20 (AS 20) from 1 April 2001. If an unlisted company voluntarily discloses EPS data, it should calculate and disclose earnings per share in accordance with this standard. An enterprise should present basic and diluted EPS with equal prominence for all periods on the face of the Profit and Loss. Negative basic and diluted EPS also be presented in the income statement. The SEBI Guidelines being introduced before 2001, require

TABLE 7.6 Variation in Stock Option Valuation

Valuation Inputs	Mean	Median	Range
Risk-free interest rate (%)	7.46	7.58	5.5–9.5
Expected volatility (%)	47.51	43	0–199

Source: Annual Reports of Sample Companies, Results computed.

the companies to disclose diluted EPS after taking into consideration dilutive impact of future issue of shares on exercise of option in accordance with IAS 33 'Earning per Share' (EPS) Subsequently, the mention of 'IAS 33' was replaced by 'AS 20'. In effect, a company is bound to consider the dilutive effect of options in force while calculating diluted EPS. A company is also required to disclose the impact on EPS due to adoption of 'intrinsic value' of stock option instead of 'fair value'. We have found that 113 (80.71 per cent) companies disclosed diluted EPS both as per AS 20 and basic and diluted EPS considering the non-adoption of fair value method. Out of 140 companies, 3 (2.14 per cent) companies followed IAS 33 instead of AS 20 for calculation of diluted EPS.

7.6 Conclusion

There is wide disparity among companies in relation to choice of valuation model inputs for disclosing fair value of options granted. Overall, it is observed that there are cases of non compliance with statutory requirements under the SEBI Guidelines concerning ESOP disclosures. It is interesting to note that international case studies (Botosan and Plumlee 2001; Chalmers and Godfrey 2005; Street and Cereola, 2004) document non-compliance with statutory option value disclosure requirements. Currently, developed countries are shifting to fair value accounting that requires expensing of stock option compensation based on fair value of options The Indian position will change from April 2011 when Indian companies will be required to follow the Indian accounting standards converged with IFRSs in the preparation and presentation on of financial statements. Consequently, the requirements of *IFRS 2: Share-based Payment* will be applicable and companies will be required to recognize implicit cost of option grant based on fair value.

Focusing on the four key option pricing model inputs—expected option life, expected stock price volatility, expected dividend yield, and the risk-free interest rate—for valuation of fair value of options, the study finds that assumptions regarding such model inputs vary widely among sample companies.

Such variation may be due to exercise of management discretion regarding opting pricing model inputs. Use of management discretion and lack of audit requirements adversely affect the overall reliability of disclosed stock option-based compensation expense for Indian firms. Till IFRS set of standards is adopted, ESOP related disclosure under SEBI Guidelines may be brought under audit to improve the transparency and reliability of such disclosures.

Notes

1. In the USA, the term ESOP is used for 'Employee Stock Ownership Plan', where an employee purchases shares of the company but such a plan has no 'option' feature. In India, the term ESOP is used to denote 'Employee Stock Option Plan'. In this paper we have used the Indian connotation of ESOP.

References

Aboody, D., Barth, M. and Kaasznik, R. (2006). 'Do Firms Understate Stock Option-based Compensation Expense Disclosed Under SFAS123'. *Review of Accounting Studies*, 11(4), pp 429–461.

Arya, A. and Mittendorf, B. (2005). 'Offering Options to Gauge Managerial Talent'. *Journal of Accounting and Economics*, 40, pp 189–210.

Balsam, S., Mozes, H. and Newman, H. (2003). 'Managing Proforma Stock Option Expense under SFAS No. 123'. *Accounting Horizon*, 17, pp 31–45.

Baril,C., Betancourt, L. and Briggs, J. (2007). 'Valuing Employee Stock Options under SFAS 123R Using the Black-Scholes-Merton and Lattice Model Approaches'. *Journal of Accounting Education*, 25, pp 88–101.

Bassett, M., Koh, P. and Tutticci, I. (2007). 'The Association between Employee Stock Option Disclosures and Corporate Governance: Evidence from an Enhanced Disclosure Regime'. *The British Accounting Review*, 39(4), pp 303–322.

Beams,J., Amoruso, A. and Richardson, F. (2005). 'Discretionary Reporting of Stock Options by IPO Firms'. *Accounting Horizons*, 19(4), pp 223–236.

Black, F. and Scholes, M. (May–June 1973). 'The Pricing of Options and Corporate Liabilities'. *Journal of Political Economy*, 81, pp 637–659.

Botosan, C. and Plumlee, M. (2001). 'Stock Option Expense: The Sword of Damocles Revealed'. *Accounting Horizons*, 15, pp 311–327.

Chalmers, K. and Godfrey, J. M. (2005). 'Stock Option Expense: A Material Concern'. *Journal of International Accounting*, Auditing and Taxation, 14, pp 157–173.

Cox, J., Ross, S. and Rubinstein, M. (1979). 'Option Pricing: A Simplified Approach'. *Journal of Financial Economics*, 7, 229–264.

Dhar, S. and De, S. (2009). 'ESOP Accounting in India: Measurement and Disclosure Issues'. *Journal of Business and Economic Issue*, 1(1), pp 26–42.

Hodder, L. D., Mayew, W., McAnally, M. L. and Weaver, D. (2006). 'Employee Stock Option Fair-Value Estimates: Do Managerial Discretion and Incentives?' *Contemporary Accounting Research*, 23(4), pp 933–975.

ICAI (2003). *'Accounting for Employee Share-based Payment'*. http://www.icai.org/post.html?post id=1414.

Jensen, M. C., Murphy, K. J., Wruck, E. G. (2004). 'Remuneration: Where We've Been, How We Got to Here, What Are the Problems, and How to Fix Them?' Harvard NOM Working Paper, available from the SSRN eLibrary. /http://ssrn.com/abstract=561305S

Johnston, D. (2006). 'Managing Stock Option Expense: The Manipulation of Option-Pricing Model Assumptions'. *Contemporary Accounting Research*, 23(2), pp 395–425.

Kaplan, S. R. and Palepu, G. K. (2003). 'Expensing Stock Options: A Fair-Value Approach'. *Harvard Business Review*, December, pp 105–109.

Kumar, R. B. (2004), 'Effect of ESOP on Performance, Productivity and Risk'. *IIMB Management Review*, 16, pp 9–20.

Lam, K. and Mensah, Y. M. (2007). 'Disclosure of the Fair Value of Executive Stock Options Granted to Top Executives'. *Employee Benefits, Compensation & Pension Law Absracts*, 8(35), pp 1–36.

Libby, R., Nelson, M. W. and Hunton, J. E., 'Recognition V. Disclosure, Auditor Tolerance for Misstatement and the Reliability of Stock Compensation and Lease Information', *Journal of Accounting Research*, 44(3), pp 538–560.

Merton, R. C. (Spring, 1973). 'Theory of Rational Option Pricing'. *Bell Journal of Economics and Management Science*, 4, pp 141–183.

Nelson and Mercy (2005). 'The transparency of Executive Stock Option Disclosures in Austratlian Annual Reports'. *Financial Reporting, Regulations and Governance*, 4(2), pp 1–35.

Rendleman, R. and Bartter, B. (1979). 'Two State Option Pricing'. *Journal of Finance*, 34, pp 1092–1110.

SEBI (1999). *SEBI (Employee Stock Option Scheme and Employee Stock Purchase Scheme) Guidelines, 1999.* http://www.sebi.gov.in/acts/cfdamend.pdf

Shaughnessy, J. and Rashty, J. (2007). 'Critical Accounting Estimates for Share Based Payment Arrangements'. *The CPA Journal*, June, pp 34–39.

Sinnett, W. (2003). 'Yes, Employee Stock Options CAN Be Valued'. *Financial Executive International.* www.fei.org

Street, D. L. and Cereola, S. (2004). 'Stock Option Compensation: Impact of Expense Recognition on Performance Indicators of Non-domestic Companies Listed in the U.S.'. *Journal of International Accounting, Auditing and Taxation*, 13, pp 21–37.

CHAPTER 8

Transition from AS 14 to IFRS 3—The Roadmap to Accounting for Business Communications

Tanupa Chakraborty

ABSTRACT

Business combinations, whether in the form of merger or acquisition or takeover have grown magnificently over the last one and half decades. Among the various research issues concerning business combinations, this paper focuses on its accounting and reporting aspects in reference to India. Till date, Accounting Standard (AS) 14 [Accounting for Amalgamations] issued by the Institute of Chartered Accountants of India (ICAI) has covered accounting and reporting of business combinations. But as India gears up to adopt International Financial Reporting Standards (IFRSs) with effect from 1st April 2011, the same shall be governed by IFRS 3 on 'Business Combinations'. Accordingly, this paper aims at preparing the roadmap for transition from AS 14 to IFRS 3 by describing and comparing the provisions of both the standards and highlighting the challenges to be faced by the accountants as a result.

8.1 Introduction

Deregulation of economies through liberalization and integration among world economies through globalization over the past two decades have brought forth dissolution of trade barriers and free flow of capital, labour and other resources, and goods or services across countries, and cut-throat competition among business houses. In its pursuit to survive and grow in this intensely competitive market, business firms have begun to adopt 'corporate restructuring' as a *sine qua non* for strategic value creating initiative. As a result, the business world has witnessed a phenomenal growth in various forms of corporate restructuring over the past one and half decades. As for example, in the USA alone, the domestic mergers and acquisitions activity, one of the most common forms of corporate restructuring, has grown rapidly from around $200 billion in 1992 to about $1.4 trillion in 2007 [*Source:* Securities Data Corporation].

'Growth' may be perceived as creating an image of aggressiveness, strategic opportunism and empire building, and amassing vast economic powers for the business entity. Growth is essential for sustaining the viability, dynamism and value-enhancing capability of a company. A growth-oriented company is not only able to attract the most talented executives, but is also able to retain them as it provides opportunities for their job enrichment and rapid career development. As growth leads to higher profits and increase in shareholders' value, a company always strives to achieve growth either *internally or externally*. The internal process of growth, or as is popularly known as *organic growth*, can be achieved through *capacity expansion* in existing line(s) of business thereby resulting into increased assets, sales and profit or by way of *diversification*, i.e., capacity building in related or totally unrelated lines of business or by *de-bottlenecking*, i.e., removing operational and financial constraints or by resorting to *greenfield expansion*, i.e., building a new plant or reinventing the entire manufacturing unit at a new undisturbed site or *brownfield expansion*, i.e., investing in a previously used site so as to derive logistics, cost and other advantages. But some serious demerits of organic growth are that it involves a substantial cash outlay and a long gestation period as a result of which the growth rate is very slow. So, when a company cannot grow internally due to either a lack of physical and managerial resources or paucity of time needed for internal development of facilities for growth, it may resort to external or *inorganic growth*. In inorganic growth, a company may grow by acquiring production facilities and other resources (human or physical or managerial) from another company or by combining its operations with another company, i.e., inorganic growth brings about a modification in the structure of a corporate entity. Since such corporate restructuring entails lesser cash payments and no gestation, it expedites growth and hence is the preferred route for growing than organic growth.

Corporate restructuring brings along with it the benefits of synergy, economies of scale, operating economies, increased market share, diversification of risk, tax savings, foreclosing competition, etc. It results in more intensive utilization of combined production capacities, purchasing set up, market coverage capacity, distribution channels, research and development (R&D) facilities, data processing systems, etc. and helps in avoiding or reducing overlapping functions and facilities, and enhancing managerial capabilities, creativity and innovativeness due to complementarity of resources and skills and a widened horizon of opportunities (Gole and Morris, 2007). This, in turn, enables the restructured entity to reduce operating costs and expand volume of production without a corresponding increase in fixed costs and hence improve profitability and cause its value to be more than the sum of independent values of the individual combining firms, a phenomenon which is technically known as *synergy*. Further, restructuring helps an entity to diversify the risks associated with its own cash flow streams by combining its operations with such other business(es) whose income streams are negatively correlated or uncorrelated, and also save taxes by setting-off accumulated losses and unabsorbed depreciation, if any, of the combining firms against the profits of the combined entity. Again, by increasing the combined firm's market share, corporate restructuring can limit the severity of competition and price war, and increased marketing costs.

The extent of benefits derived from corporate restructuring as an inorganic growth strategy may vary from one form to the other. The most common forms of corporate restructuring that have prevailed over decades are amalgamations (whether in the nature of merger or absorption/ purchase), acquisitions, takeovers and consolidations (Chakrabarti, 1998). '*Amalgamation*' is popularly understood to be a *fusion* of two or more companies. The fusion may take place either between existing and new companies or between existing companies themselves. Where a new company is formed as the *transferee company* to purchase two or more existing companies thereby necessitating liquidation of the existing companies (i.e., transferor companies), the amalgamation is said to be in the nature of *merger*. But amalgamation is of *absorption* variety when one existing company purchases another existing company without requiring the formation of a new company, though necessitating liquidation of an existing (i.e., transferor) company. Again, mergers can be *cogeneric* (i.e., where combining firms belong to the same industry) or *conglomerate* (i.e., where transferor companies belong to unrelated industries) in nature. Cogeneric mergers can be of *horizontal* type (i.e., merger between business competitors operating in the same kind of product/service or market or line of business) or of *vertical* form (i.e., merging companies providing complementary services at different stages of business process and hence can come with either backward or forward linkage depending on whether another firm involved in earlier or subsequent stages of the business process respectively are integrated with a firm). *Acquisition* is an act of acquiring effective control by one company (referred to as the 'acquirer' or 'acquiring/transferee' company) over the assets or management of another company (referred to as the 'acquiree' or 'acquired/transferor' company) without any combination of acquirer and acquiree. That is, acquisition is made possible by a purchase of either the whole or part of the assets of the acquiree, or the whole or a strategic stake in the acquiree (in case of which the acquisition is in the nature of *takeover*). Thus, unlike amalgamation, the acquiree or the transferor company is not dissolved and its independent and separate legal entity continues to exist, although there may be a change in the control of such company. *Consolidation* occurs whenever a group of companies is formed comprising a parent and one or more of its subsidiaries where the parent company acquires control of the composition of board of directors and of the financial and operating policy decisions of the subsidiary company through ownership of more than half of the voting power of the subsidiary. The new strategies of restructuring that have emerged in recent times include *hive off/slump sale* (i.e., disposal or sale of a productive unit to another company without any interruption in the smooth running of the company making such a sale), *brand acquisition* and *spin-off/demerger* (i.e., split of a division of a company into a new entity).

Any research on the age-old strategies of corporate restructuring (as discussed earlier) may focus on the basis for determination of the value of the transferor company(ies) that must be paid for on purchase and of the exchange ratio, or on means of financing the purchase deal, or legal aspects, or tax implications, or accounting and reporting issues, or on the performance of the transferee company post restructuring. Of these many issues, the present paper intends to discuss the accounting and reporting aspects of corporate restructuring threadbare with reference to India.

Till date, the Institute of Chartered Accountants of India (ICAI) has, from time to time, issued Guidance Notes, Statements on Accounting Matters and Accounting Standards (ASs) to bring about uniformity and consistency in the presentation of economic data contained in the financial statements of corporate enterprises so as to enable the users to understand and make proper use of such statements for their decision purposes. Accordingly, the ICAI has issued AS 14 on '*Accounting for Amalgamations*' and made it mandatory for all companies to follow the accounting procedure specified therein for amalgamations taking place on or after *1st April 1995*. It is noteworthy that AS 14 not just concentrates on amalgamations (though its title so reads) but also on other forms of business combinations like acquisitions or takeovers. However, consolidations are covered separately under AS 21. As India prepares itself to adopt wholly the single comprehensive set of high-quality generally accepted International Financial Reporting Standards (IFRSs), issued by the International Accounting Standards Board (IASB), with effect from *1st April 2011*, AS 14 will get replaced by '*IFRS 3: Business Combination*' (Ghosh, 2009). IFRS 3 straightaway uses an explicit title to cover all forms of corporate restructuring that result in bringing together of separate legal corporate entities into one reporting unit. Accordingly, IFRS 3 includes all such cases as business combinations where one or more companies become subsidiaries of another, net assets of one or more companies are legally merged into another, one combining entity transfers its net assets or equity interests of its owners to another combining entity, and all the combining entities transfer their net assets or equity interests of owners to a newly formed entity. However, consolidations will be guided by International Accounting Standard (IAS) 27 on 'Consolidated and Separate Financial Statements', in addition to IFRS 3.

Any business combinations may pose the following questions in the mind of an accountant:

(i) What are the broad principles for recognizing the assets and liabilities that are acquired in a business combination and at what values they should be carried in the acquirer's/transferee's balance sheet?
(ii) Should assets or liabilities arising out of pre-existing relationship between the transferor and transferee companies be recognized by the transferee company post combination?
(iii) Should the transferee recognize any such liability in business combination which relates to settlement of past dues, or remuneration to the past owners of the acquiree/transferor or its employees for future services?
(iv) How should the intangibles generated internally but not recognized by the acquiree prior to combination be treated?
(v) Are contingent liabilities of the acquiree recognized by the acquirer?
(vi) How are the 'reserves and surplus' of the acquiree treated in business combination?
(vii) How to account for the acquisition-related costs or expenses for business combination?
(viii) What constitutes 'purchase consideration' for business combination and how is its value determined?
(ix) How does 'goodwill' arise in a business combination and how it is measured?
(x) What specific disclosures are to be made by the acquirer post combination?

This paper aims at seeking an answer to the above-mentioned questions in the light of IRFS 3 and AS 14, and identifying the areas where IFRS 3 is an improvement over AS 14 and throws some additional challenges before the accountants.

The remainder of the paper is organized as follows. Section 8.2 examines the provisions of AS 14 while the requirements of IRFS 3 and its comparison with AS 14 are dealt with in Section 8.3. Section 8.4 highlights the challenges posed by IFRS 3. Finally, Section 8.5 concludes the paper.

8.2 Provisions of AS 14: Accounting for Amalgamations

AS 14 differentiates amalgamation in the nature of merger from amalgamation in the nature of purchase. An amalgamation is said to be in the *nature of merger* when (i) all the assets and liabilities of the transferor company become, after amalgamation, the assets and liabilities of the transferee company; (ii) shareholders holding not less than 90 per cent of face value of equity shares of transferor company (excluding those already held by transferee company, or its subsidiaries or nominees immediately before amalgamation) become equity shareholders of transferee company by virtue of amalgamation; (iii) consideration for amalgamation is discharged by the transferee company wholly by issue of its equity shares (excepting that cash is paid in respect of any fractional shares) to those equity holders of transferor company who agree to become equity shareholders of transferee company after amalgamation; (iv) business of transferor company is intended to be carried on, after amalgamation, by the transferee company, and (v) no adjustment is intended to be made to the book values of assets and liabilities of transferor company when they are incorporated in the financial statements of transferee company except to ensure uniformity of accounting policies (Bhattacharyya, 2006). An amalgamation which does not fulfil any one or more of these conditions is said to be in the *nature of purchase*. This type of amalgamation is effectively a mode by which one company acquires or takes over or absorbs another company and, in consequence, the shareholders of the acquired/transferor company do not continue to have a proportionate share in the equity of the acquiring/transferee company, or the business of the acquiree is not intended to be continued by the acquirer. AS 14 recommends *pooling of interests method* of accounting for amalgamation in the nature of *merger* and *purchase/acquisition method* for amalgamation in the nature of purchase.

The *Pooling of Interests method* applied in case of merger is so named because it involves a genuine pooling not merely of the assets and liabilities of the transferor companies, but also of the shareholders' interests and businesses of such companies into the transferee company. In this method of accounting, the identity of all the assets, liabilities and reserves (whether capital or revenue or arising on revaluation) of the transferor company is preserved after amalgamation and hence are recorded by the transferee company at their existing carrying amounts (excepting where suitable adjustments are to be made to bring uniformity in conflicting accounting policies adopted by transferor and transferee companies following amalgamation) and in the same form as they appear in the books of the transferor company on the date of the amalgamation (Lewis and Pendrill, 2000). As a result, the assets, liabilities and reserves balances in the books of the transferee company are mere aggregates of the corresponding balances in transferor and transferee (if existing) companies books before amalgamation thereby indicating total aggregation of financial figures. However, the balance of profit and loss account appearing in the financial statement of the transferor company is either aggregated with the corresponding balance of the transferee company, or, alternatively transferred to 'general reserve' (if any) of the transferee. In contrast, only those assets and liabilities of the acquiree as taken over are aggregated with their corresponding balances in the books of the acquirer under *purchase method* of accounting thereby indicating partial aggregation only (Banerjee, 2002). Accordingly, under the purchase method, the assets and liabilities of the acquiree/transferor company that are taken over are recorded by the acquirer/transferee company at their existing carrying amounts or, alternatively, the purchase consideration is allocated to individual identifiable assets and liabilities (including those not recorded in the financial statements of transferor company) on the basis of their fair values at the date of amalgamation. However, no reserves (including the balance of profit and loss account) of the transferor company, other than the statutory reserves like development allowance reserve, or investment allowance reserve, etc., are incorporated in the financial statements of acquirer. Statutory reserves of acquiree are credited in the books of acquirer, with the debit being given to 'amalgamation adjustment account' and recorded under 'miscellaneous expenditure' head of the balance sheet of acquirer. When the identity of statutory reserves is no longer required to be maintained under the relevant statute, both the reserve and amalgamation adjustment account should be reversed so as to eliminate such reserves from the books of the acquirer. If the scheme of amalgamation sanctioned under Companies Act, 1956 or any other statute prescribes a specific treatment for the 'reserves' of transferor company after amalgamation, the same should be followed.

In case of pre-existing inter-company debts, the transferee company sets off such mutual debts with the transferor company after amalgamation (irrespective of its nature) while in case of inter-company purchase and sale of goods prior to amalgamation, the transferee company cancels the amount of unrealized profit included in such stock. Again, if there is pre-existing intercompany investments, purchase consideration should be adjusted for such inter-company stock holdings on amalgamation (Banerjee, 2002).

The purchase consideration for amalgamation is the aggregate of shares and other securities issued and payments made in the form of cash or other assets by the transferee company to the shareholders of the transferor company. Any non-cash item in purchase consideration is to be measured at 'fair value' as may be fixed by any statutory authority, or determined by reference to the market value or net book value where market value cannot be reliably assessed. If any contingent consideration is payable on the occurrence of one or more future events, it is to be included in 'purchase consideration' provided such payment is probable and can be reasonably estimated at the date of amalgamation (Bhattacharyya, 2006). Goodwill does not arise in pooling of interests method used to account for amalgamation in the nature of merger. As a result, the difference between purchase consideration paid and the amount of share capital of the transferor company is adjusted in reserves of the transferee company. But in purchase method of accounting, the difference between the purchase consideration paid and the value of the net assets of the transferor company acquired by the transferee company is treated as goodwill (if the difference is positive) or capital reserve (in case the difference is negative) in the books of the transferee (White, Sondhi and Fried, 2004). The goodwill, if arising, is to be amortized to income on a systematic basis over a period of five years unless a somewhat longer period can be justified.

As regards *disclosures* to be made in the first financial statements of transferee following amalgamation, AS 14 prescribes that names and general nature of business of amalgamating companies, effective date of amalgamation for accounting purposes, method of accounting followed, and particulars of the scheme sanctioned under a statute are to be disclosed under both pooling of interests and purchase methods of accounting. In addition, description and number of shares issued, together with the percentage of each company's equity shares exchanged to effect the amalgamation, and the amount and treatment of any difference between consideration and value of net assets acquired are to be disclosed under pooling of interests method while the amount and a description of the consideration paid or contingently payable for amalgamation, and the amount of any difference between consideration and value of net identifiable assets acquired and its treatment including the period of amortization of any goodwill arising on amalgamation are required to be disclosed under purchase method. Further, if accounting adjustments are made to the existing carrying amounts of assets and liabilities of transferor under pooling of interests method, the effects of such changes on financial statements of transferee should be reported in accordance with AS 5 on 'Prior Period and Extraordinary Items and Changes in Accounting Policies'. Again, if the amalgamation is effected after balance sheet date but before the issue of financial statements of either party to the amalgamation, disclosure is to be made in accordance with AS 4, 'Contingencies and Events Occurring after the Balance Sheet Date', without reflecting the amalgamation in the financial statements.

Interestingly, AS 14 fails to address some of the research questions identified in the latter part of Section 8.1. As for example, AS 14 is silent regarding the treatment of internally generated intangibles, remuneration to past owners/employees of the transferee company and acquisition related expenses.

8.3 Salient Features of IFRS 3—Business Combination and Its Comparison with AS 14

IFRS 3, which comes into effect from the financial year 2011–12, applies the *'principle of control'* in determining whether any instance of 'business combination' has taken place (Ghosh, 2009). According to the standard, an entity (referred to as 'acquirer') can acquire or obtain control of one or more other business(es) [referred to as 'acquiree'] either by owning, directly or indirectly through subsidiaries, more than half of the voting power of the acquiree, or by acquiring power over more than half of its voting rights by virtue of an agreement with other investors, or the power to govern the financial and operating policies of the acquiree under a statute or an agreement, or to appoint or remove a majority of the members of the Board (i.e., Board of Directors) or the Governing Body of the acquiree, or to cast majority votes in a meeting of the Board or Governing Body of the acquiree. Any potential voting right of the acquirer in the acquiree arising out of conversion into equity shares of financial instruments like share warrants, share call options, debt, etc. issued by the acquiree and held by the acquirer should also be taken into consideration while evaluating 'control'. However, IFRS 3 requires former independence of the combining entities and hence leaves such business combinations from outside its purview in which all the combining entities or businesses are ultimately controlled by the same parties both before and after the combination and such control is not transitory. As for example, acquisition of a subsidiary by a holding company and combination of two companies belonging to the same group are not covered under IFRS 3.

Unlike in case of AS 14, IFRS 3 has dispensed with the pooling of interests method and recommended the use of purchase method (referred to as the *acquisition method* under IFRS 3) while accounting for business combinations. In acquisition method, all the identifiable assets and liabilities of the acquiree acquired and assumed by the acquirer are to be measured at their *fair values* as on the date of acquisition and carried to the acquirer's financial statement. This is in sharp contrast to AS 14 which requires that assets and liabilities may either be recorded at their existing carrying amounts or purchase consideration may be allocated to them on the basis of their fair values. IFRS 3 also calls for the recognition of identifiable intangibles like brand name, trademark, patent, literary and other artistic works, royalty agreement, customer list, etc. generated internally but not recognized by the acquiree excepting for expensing the costs incurred for its development. However, the acquirer is not required to recognize the assembled work force of the acquiree as any inherent intellectual capital acquired on business combination, and also any under-negotiation contract of the acquiree which may materialize in the post-combination period. Both their values are assumed to remain subsumed in 'goodwill' arising on such combination. Again, the acquirer and the acquiree may have pre-existing business relationship before the business combination takes place or they may enter into such relationship during the negotiation for such business combination. Some examples of contractual pre-existing business relation between the acquirer and the acquiree are franchisee arrangement, agency contract, operating or finance lease agreement, supply/service contract, etc. IFRS 3 requires that those assets and liabilities of the acquiree that, in effect, settles any past dues between the acquirer and acquiree, or remunerates employees or former owners of the acquiree for future services, or reimburses the acquiree or its former owners for paying the acquirer's acquisition related costs are not to be included in the list of assets acquired and liabilities assumed in business combination. As regards contingent liabilities of the acquiree, the acquirer is to recognize the same in a business combination if it is a present obligation arising out of past events and its fair value can be reliably measured as on the date of acquisition. Acquisition related costs or expenses such as fees paid for advisory, legal, accounting, valuation and other professional or consulting services, and general administrative expenses including expenses of maintaining an internal acquisitions department, etc. incurred by the acquirer to effect a business combination are to be expensed in the period in which these are incurred and the services are received. Thus, it is clear from the above discussion that IFRS 3 addresses even those issues which are left unanswered by AS 14.

The purchase consideration for business combination includes cash, cash equivalents or other assets transferred, or debt or equity instruments issued by the acquirer for acquiring the business of the acquiree. If any share based payment awards (e.g., stock options) held by the acquiree's employees are replaced by the acquirer's own share-based awards and if any amount is contingently payable to the acquiree's employees or management or selling shareholders, the same are to be included in consideration. Like AS 14, IFRS 3 requires measurement of fair value of consideration. Under IFRS 3, the acquirer must measure the difference between (i) the aggregate of acquisition–date fair value of the consideration transferred, fair value of any non-controlling interest (NCI) in the acquiree acquired, and acquisition-date fair value of acquirer's previously held equity interest in the acquiree in case the business combination is achieved in stages, and (ii) the net of acquisition–date fair values of the identifiable assets acquired and liabilities assumed. If the difference is positive, the acquirer recognizes it as goodwill on the acquisition date and if negative, the acquirer recognizes it as a gain in the income statement.

IFRS 3 asks for a more detailed disclosure in comparison to AS 14. Besides giving a general description of the business combination such as the name and description of acquiree's business, reasons for acquisition, acquisition date, etc., the acquirer must disclose in detail the fair values of each class of consideration transferred including any contingent consideration, fair values of each major classes of assets and any NCI acquired, and liabilities assumed, treatment of acquisition related costs, goodwill and the like (Deloitte, 2009).

8.4 Challenges Inflicted by IFRS 3

With an over-emphasis on fair valuation in IFRS set of standards, the challenges before the accountants are plenty. The most widely accepted definition of *fair value* is that it is the amount for which an asset could be exchanged or liability settled between two knowledgeable, willing parties in an arm's length transaction. Market value is the best reference of fair value, in the absence of which fair value is to be determined using an appropriate valuation model depending upon the intended use of the asset. So, a necessary pre-requisite to effectively accounting for business combinations under IRFS 3 is to have a sound knowledge of the entire set of IFRS standards, which, in turn, will help the accountant to recognize, measure and properly classify the assets acquired and liabilities assumed in a business combination and account for them applying appropriate IFRSs subsequently. Besides, the accountant must be well versed with the complex finance literature on valuation models in order to arrive at the fair valuation of assets and liabilities of the acquiree acquired by the acquirer. Further, with cross-border business combinations becoming more prevalent these days, the problem of translating assets and liabilities of the acquiree denominated in foreign currency into home currency of acquirer may arise. The challenge before the accountants is, therefore, stiff more so because IFRSs touch upon those grey issues which have been outside the knowledge domain of the accountants until before.

8.5 Conclusion

There is no denying the fact that investors, their advisors and other stakeholders face a difficult task in assessing how the businesses of the acquiree and the acquirer will combine and what will be its impact on post-combination performance. In this regard, IFRS 3 is expected to bring in more transparency in accounting and reporting for business combinations thereby enabling the market to have a greater insight into what has been acquired and judge the financial success or failure of acquisitions more quickly and accurately. But a few hurdles remain which need to be overcome for an effective implementation of IFRS 3 on all business combinations taking place from the financial year 2011–12 onwards.

References

Banerjee, B. (2002). *Regulation of Corporate Accounting and Reporting in India*, The World Press Pvt. Ltd., Kolkata, India.

Benston, G. J., Bromwich, M., Litan, R. E. and Wagenhofer, A. (2006). *Worldwide Financial Reporting—The Development and Future of Accounting Standards*, Oxford University Press, New York.

Bhattacharyya, A. K. (2006). *Indian Accounting Standards: Practices, Comparisons and Interpretations*, Tata McGraw-Hill, New Delhi, India.

Chakrabarti, P. (1998). 'Mergers and Acquisitions (M&A): An Accounting Approach'. In A. K. Basu, K. Mookerjee and S. Chakraborti (eds.), *Studies in Finance and Accounting*, Platinum Jubilee Commemorative Volume, Department of Commerce, University of Calcutta, Kolkata, India.

Deloitte (2009). *iGAAP 2010 : A Guide to IFRS Reporting*. LexisNexis, U.K.

Ghosh, T. P. (2009). *Understanding IFRSs*. Taxmann Publications (P) Ltd., New Delhi, India.

Gole, W. J. and Morris, J. M. (2007). *Mergers and Acquisitions: Business Strategies for Accountants*. John Wiley & Sons, New Jersey, USA.

Lewis, R. and Pendrill, D. (2000). *Advanced Financial Accounting*. Financial Times/Prentice Hall, Essex, U.K.

White, G. I., Sondhi, A. C. and Fried, D. (2004). *The Analysis and Use of Financial Statements*. John Wiley & Sons (Asia) Pte. Ltd., Singapore.

Web sites

www.icai.org

www.pwc.com

CHAPTER 9

Fair Value Accounting—A Discussion for Development of a Conceptual Framework

Ananda Mohan Pal

ABSTRACT

Broadly speaking, fair value refers to one in the family of current value measurement bases that should meet the criteria of reliability and relevance. The application of fair value in financial accounting is coined as fair value accounting. Historically, financial accounting is based on historical cost valuation. Fair value accounting is a journey towards replacement of historical cost value by fair value. This paper intends to understand how this change is accommodated within the basic accounting framework and reflected through the pronouncements of the standard-setting bodies as a basis for establishing the need for development of a comprehensive conceptual framework.

9.1 Introduction

Fair value refers to a well-defined value in the family of current values. As defined by the International Accounting Standards Board, *fair value is the price that would be received to sell an asset or paid to transfer a liability in an orderly transaction between market participants at the measurement date* (IASB 2009). Fair value accounting is application of fair value in accounting, i.e., recognizing and measuring *assets and liabilities* at fair value and recognizing and measuring *income* based on fair value of assets and liabilities. The recognition of assets and liabilities at fair value and of income based on fair value is a conceptual issue whereas their measurement is primarily a technical issue. This paper is intended to critically analyse the arguments in favour and against the conceptual issues regarding fair value recognition and to reconcile them with the developments in US GAAP and International Accounting Standards regarding fair value application and measurement. The paper has been arranged accordingly. In Section 9.2 fair value recognition has been taken up for analysing the issues regarding valuation and income recognition and in the subsequent sections the study would present the developments regarding fair value application and fair value measurement and try to establish a logical link between the conceptual issues with the technical developments.

9.2 Fair Value Recognition

Conventional financial accounting is characterized by the parameters of conservatism, reliability and integrity. These parameters differentiate conventional financial accounting from other disciplines of measurement. They provide strength in ensuing reliability by reporting of conservative income and wealth and by minimizing the risk of capital erosion. Yet they are responsible for holding financial accounting away from the relevance of information by recognizing the historical cost–based valuation. Financial accounting provides two major classes of information: about income and about wealth. The question of relevance arises more on information about wealth, about the value of assets and liabilities. It was argued in the past that business being a going concern, not meant for sale, its market value and consequently the market value of its assets and liabilities, is not very much important. For corporate enterprises, the argument encounters many questions. Even though the business is not readily available for sale, its ownership instrument is very much tradeable in the stock market. This market-generated ownership value of business sets the upper limit of relevant value for the business in the domain of market value. As one *CPA Journal* article contended: 'Perhaps the strongest argument for a move to fair value accounting is that historical cost financial statements do not provide information that is relevant to investors… The fair-value balance sheet provides information for investors who are interested in the current value of assets and liabilities, not the historical cost'. (Haldeman 2006) Balance sheet value is integrated with income measured in accounting through profit and loss account or other income accounts. Integration between valuation and income measurement implies that change in balance sheet values between two points of time is fully accounted for by the income measured for the period within. Thus, valuation and income measurement are both dependent on each other.

Although financial accounting is strengthened by the integration, particularly valuation is constrained by this interdependence. As income is distributable and distribution is not revertible, measurement of income has to comply with the principles of realization. Again, the principle of conservatism recognizes unrealized losses but not unrealized gains. However, the significance of valuation of assets and liabilities lies in relevance of such value to the users of accounting information. The paradox is that a current value (such as market value or use value or replacement value), which is more relevant to the users than the historical value may give rise to both unrealized gains and losses. As unrealized gains are not recognized by the principle of conservatism, the relevant value of assets or liabilities is ignored if it gives rise to unrealized gains. The problem boils down to the fact that integrity and reliability lie at one end and relevance lies at the other end. Historically, financial accounting prefers to stick to the first end of integrity and reliability compromising the other end of relevance. This bias gives rise to growing discontent to the users of valuation information.

Fair value movement refers to the process of change in financial accounting in the direction of fair value–based accounting shifting away from the historical cost–based accounting. The departure from historical cost–based accounting has been traditionally accepted only when current value appears to be less than the historical value. Such departure does no represent fair value accounting. Rather, the recognition of fair value even if it is higher than historical cost, giving rise to unrealized gains, along with ensuring uniformity in definition, measurement and disclosure of fair value, appears to commence the era of the fair value movement. Only the recent developments in GAAP have modified the rule of conservatism to recognize fair value in the valuation process (e.g., valuation of financial assets) in order to accommodate unrealized gains in the reported earnings and reported assets and liabilities in given circumstances. Although in US GAAP recognition of fair value has progressively been made by requiring application of fair value in different standards dealing with different accounting issues, a separate standard has been issued for fair value measurement. International Accounting Standard Board also recognized fair value in different standards and the setting of standard on fair value measurement is in process. The objective of issuing standard on fair value measurement is to establish reliability of fair value through its definition, measurement and disclosure. While these developments in GAAP make ways for reporting assets and liabilities at fair value giving rise to unrealized gains, questions may arise as to the logical validity of reporting unrealized gains in income accounts. Would income accounts no more require to oblige the principles of realization and conservatism? It may be pointed out at this juncture of controversy that there has been a simultaneous change in reporting of income accounts too. The income account has been divided into two parts. One part represents the traditional profit or loss account and the other part presents other comprehensive income which includes unrealized gains. The other comprehensive income is a change in equity that is not distributable by way of dividend. Thus, the issues cultivated in this section may be listed as: reliability of reported income and wealth, principle of realization and conservatism, relevance of valuation, integrity of valuation and income measurement and reliability of valuation. The inter-relationship among the above-mentioned issues is explained in the context of both historical cost–based value and fair value with the help of the following diagrammatic presentation. Figure 9.1 is on traditional accounting. It is observed in Fig. 9.1 that historical cost–based valuation fails to meet the attribute of relevance although it meets integrity and produces reliable income measurement meeting the criteria of realization and conservatism. Figure 9.2 is on accounting based on a fair value which is not as per standard. It is observed in Fig. 9.2 that a non-standard fair value accounting may meet the criteria of relevance and integrity but it cannot ensure reliability of both valuation and reported income. Figure 9.3 presents the fair value accounting as per standard. It is observed in Fig. 9.3 that with modified presentation of income statement and with application of fair value as per standard, the fair value accounting is supposed to meet the required criteria of relevance, reliability and integrity.

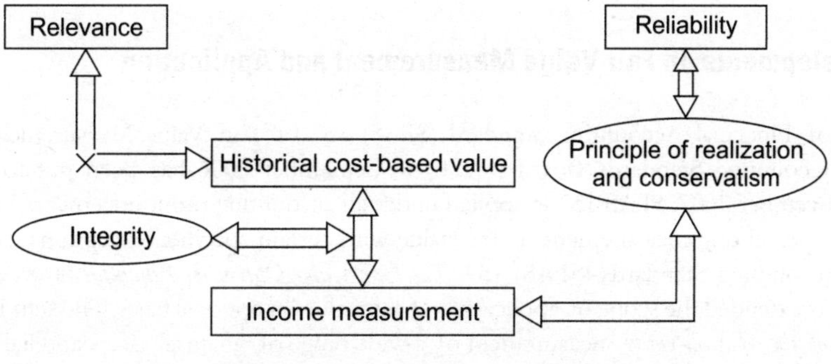

Figure 9.1 Traditional accounting

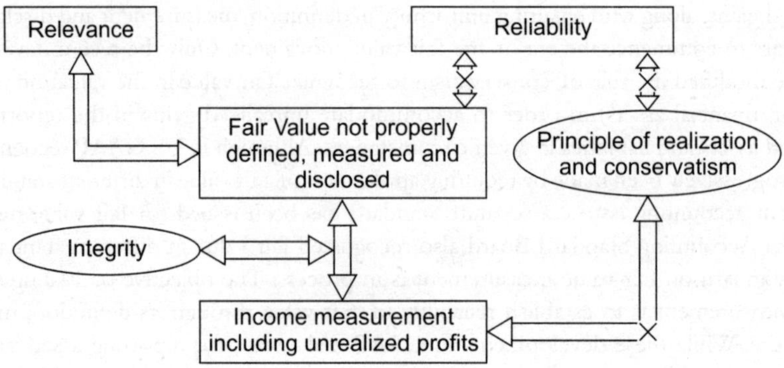

Figure 9.2 Accounting based on a fair value which is not as per standard

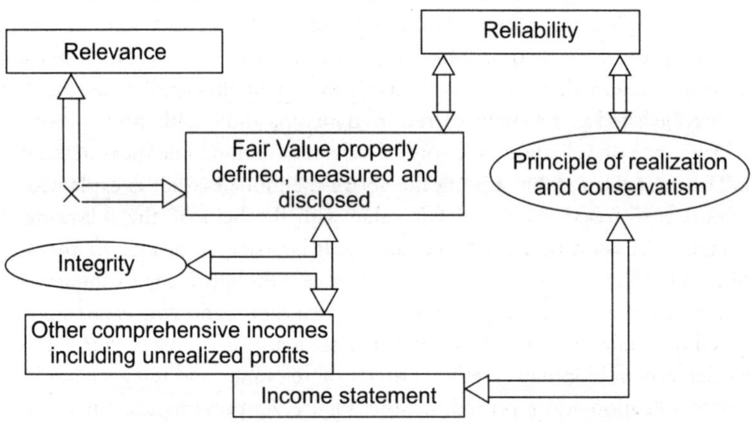

Figure 9.3 Fair value accounting (as per standard)

9.3 Developments on Fair Value Measurement and Application

Statement of Financial Accounting Standard (SFAS) 157 on Fair Value Measurement issued by Financial Accounting Standards Board (FASB) in September 2006 has been put to application from 15 November 2007. SFAS 157 is applied under all accounting pronouncements in US GAAP requiring or permitting measurement of fair value with certain specified exceptions. Statement of Financial Accounting Standards (SFAS) 159. *The Fair Value Option for Financial Assets and Financial Liabilities*, has extended the scope of application of fair value on optional basis. The standard permits, *at the option of the reporting entity*, measurement of a wide range of financial assets and liabilities at fair value. The IASB issued Discussion Paper on Fair Value Measurement in November 2006. The IASB decided to use US GAAP as the starting point of its own deliberation and included full SFAS 157 in the Discussion Paper. In October 2008, IASB published Expert Advisor Council's Report on *Measuring and disclosing the fair value of financial instruments in markets that are no longer active.* In April 2009, the FASB issued FASB Staff Position No. FAS 157-4 *Determining Fair Value When the Volume and Level of Activity for the Asset or Liability has Significantly Decreased and Identifying Transactions that are Not Orderly* (FSP).

The FSP provides guidance for

(i) measuring fair value when the volume and level of activity for the asset or liability have significantly decreased; and

(ii) identifying circumstances that indicate a transaction is not orderly.

In March 2009, the IASB issued *Improving Disclosures about Financial Instruments.* That document amended IFRS 7 *Financial Instruments: Disclosures* to enhance disclosures about fair value measurements of financial instruments. In May 2009, IASB issued the Exposure Draft for IFRS 10 on Fair Value Measurement. According to the fair value vision, the entire framework of transaction-based accrual accounting based on traditional concepts of revenue, expense and matching would be replaced by a system that measures net income by the difference in book equity—that is, the difference between the estimated fair values of assets and liabilities, adjusted for primary capital flows. However, the principle of such a single basis, full fair value model, is not yet generally accepted. Till now, both in US GAAP and in international accounting standards, application of fair value has been limited to financial instruments and other specified items. In practice, most of the balance sheet items for industrial and commercial companies are accounted for on a cost-based measure. Fair value accounting has become relatively more significant mainly to the financial companies having financial holdings. With rapid developments of derivative contracts, fair value seems to be the only realistic way of capturing the assets and liabilities arising from derivative transactions on to the balance sheet and making necessary disclosure of them.

9.3.1 US GAAP

SFAS 157 defined fair value, framed the fair value measurement process and expanded disclosure about fair value measurement. These are aimed for increasing consistency, comparability and ultimately, reliability of fair valuation. By the strength of reliability, fair value is supposed to consolidate its existing use in financial reporting. It provided a unique definition of fair value to be used for all the accounting pronouncements in US GAAP requiring measurement of fair value. Precisely, it is the exit price that would be received to sell the asset or transfer the liability at the measurement date. However, the valuation bases are multiple, three in number of approaches to precise. They are (i) market approach (comparable to net realizable value), (ii) income approach (comparable to present value) and (iii) cost approach (comparable to current cost value). The most important development in the fair value measurement project is the introduction of a framework for fair value hierarchy based on valuation inputs. There are three broad levels to the fair value hierarchy of inputs. Level-One inputs are quoted prices of identical assets or liabilities in the active market. Level-Two inputs are observable inputs other than quoted prices and Level-Three inputs are unobservable inputs. By disclosure of the fair value hierarchy of inputs, the relative reliability of the fair value estimate is indicated.

9.3.2 International Financial Reporting Standards (IFRSs)

IFRS (Exposure Draft) 10 on Fair Value Measurement has been issued in May 2009. According to IFRS (ED) 10, fair value is the price that would be received to sell an asset or paid to transfer a liability in an orderly transaction between market participants at the measurement date (an exit price). The Board considered it unnecessary to make a distinction between a current entry price and a current exit price in IFRSs with a market-based measurement objective (i.e., fair value), and decided to define fair value as a current exit price. Fair value measurement should assume that the sale of an asset or transfer of a liability takes place in the most advantageous market to which the entity has access. Fair value measurement is a market-based measurement, not an entity-specific measurement. Therefore, a fair value measurement uses the assumptions market participants would use when pricing the asset or liability. The exposure draft defines market participants as independent of each other (they are not related parties), knowledgeable about the asset or liability, and able and willing to enter into a transaction for the asset or liability. The exposure draft proposes that if location is a characteristic of an asset, the price in the most advantageous market should be adjusted for the costs that would be incurred to transport the asset to that market. Techniques used to measure fair value should be consistent with the market approach, income approach or cost approach. The Board noted that an entity's cost to replace an asset would equal the amount that a market participant buyer of that asset (who would use it similarly) would pay to acquire it (i.e., the entry price and the exit price would be equal in the same market). The fair value hierarchy gives the highest priority to quoted prices (unadjusted) in active markets for identical assets and liabilities (Level 1) and the lowest priority to inputs that are not based on observable market data (Level 3).

9.4 Modification of Income Statement

In order to retain integrity with conservative income measurement, recognition of fair value has mostly been limited to cases where fair value stands below historical cost–based value. For this reason, fair value has little reflection on financial reporting in a vast number of cases where fair value exceeds historical cost–based value. IAS 39 on Financial Instruments: Recognition and Measurement includes four categories of assets, assets held for trading, available for sale, held to maturity and loans and receivables, of which the first two categories are measured, in effect at market value and the last two are measured on an historical cost basis. In India there are provisions to recognize financial assets at fair value (AS 30, AS 31 and AS 32 in recommendatory nature w.e.f. 01 April 2009 and in mandatory nature w.e.f. 01 April 2011). In US, SFAS 159 makes it optional to use fair value for financial assets in replacement of the historical cost–based value. Thus, appreciation in the value of certain class of financial assets and corresponding recognition of revenue are allowed as per IFRS and US GAAP. This necessitates some modification in income measurement also. IAS 1 requires income account to be named as comprehensive income statement, which includes two separate divisions: profit or loss and other comprehensive income. Other standards issued by IASB require or permit certain gains or losses arising from fair value accounting to account through other comprehensive income. This division of total comprehensive income allows other comprehensive income part to maintain integrity with fair value of assets and liabilities keeping profit or loss part complying with the principles of conservatism and realization. However, standards on financial instruments allow accounting of unrealized gains or losses from investments held for trading through profit or loss, which appears to be a relaxation of the principle of realization.

9.5 Problems with Fair Value Accounting

By definition of fair value, the current market exit value appears to be weak in principle. *It is the value a business could have obtained from selling an asset at the balance sheet date, but this is therefore a value that it chose* NOT *to sell at.* (ACCA 2009) Probably the biggest problem with fair value is the widespread concern over the reliability of the values being used. Although few problems occur where there are quoted prices in liquid markets and transactions are taking place on a regular basis, moving from there to the models for valuation of unquoted instruments is a real step into uncertainty. Again, in cases where the markets become illiquid or even close down as experienced during the 2008 banking crisis in US and Europe, valuation based on few trades being done, becomes more uncertain and consequently, unreliable. Financial institutions have also complained that fair value accounting has effectively been driving business behaviour rather than reflecting it. During down markets, banks must write down assets to reflect current market value. These write downs reduce regulatory capital. To increase capital, some banks may sell undervalued assets into the depressed market. These sales place further downward pressure on asset values, which in turn may trigger further write downs and more sales. Similar concerns are expressed by the American Bankers Association in its letter to the SEC in September 2008: *The problems that exist in today's financial markets can be traced to many different factors. One factor that is recognized as having exacerbated these problems is fair value accounting* (American Bankers Association 2008).

9.6 Conclusion

Measurement of total comprehensive income allows integration of income with the fair value where the principles of conservatism and realization are duly applicable to profit or loss part. Separate presentation of unrealized gains through other comprehensive income and statement of changes in equity also helps to arrest loss of reliability of income reporting. IAS 1 is a development in that direction. To ensure reliability of fair value, one approach has been to define and measure it (as done by SFAS 157 and IFRS ED 10). The reliability varies with the level of inputs for measurement of fair value. By providing for the disclosure of input levels, the degree of reliability of fair value is intended to be indicated. As disclosure of weakness cannot overcome the weakness itself, the present study proposes that wherever there is need for disclosure of weakness, fair value should be opted for disclosure through notes and not for accounting. Thus, the other approach to ensure reliability of reporting of financial position is to restrict application of fair value only to items where measurement of fair value can be done reliably. Regarding application of fair value the study thinks that fair value has an important place in the accounting system—especially in the accounting for financial instruments. It is important that all derivatives are recognized at fair value, for instance. However, the scope of applying options in respect of use of fair value has reduced understandability, comparability and reliability of the accounting for financial instruments. The extent of the optional use of fair value should be reduced. The recent global financial crisis has highlighted the risks of using unreliable values in financial reporting. The present study suggests that the IASB should proceed to establish definitively its long-delayed conceptual framework for financial reporting duly addressing the criteria of reliability and relevance in valuation of balance sheet items and measurement of income in commensurate with fair value accounting.

References

The Association of Chartered Certified Accountants (ACCA) (2009). Policy Paper on Fair Value. www.accaglobal.com

American Bankers Association (2008). Letter to U.S. Securities and Exchange Commission, September 23, Washington, DC. [The relevant text has been quoted from the letter written by Edward L., Yingling, President and CEO, American Bankers Association, Washington, DC, to Mr. Christopher Cox, Chairman, U.S. Securities and Exchange Commission dated September 23, 2008].

Haldeman, R. G. Jr. (2006). 'Fact, Fiction, and Fair Value Accounting at Enron'. *The CPA Journal*, November, A Publication of the New York State Society of CPAs, New York.

IASB (2009). *Exposure Draft: Fair Value Measurement.* IASC Foundation, London.

CHAPTER 10

IFRS for SMEs vs Full IFRSs—A Comparison of Form and Contents

Gautam Mitra and Ashish Kumar Sana

ABSTRACT

The International Financial Reporting Standard for Small and Medium-sized Entities (IFRS for SMEs) is the first international accounting standard developed specifically to serve the financial accounting and reporting needs of private businesses. This self-contained accounting standard of about 230 pages was issued by the International Accounting Standards Board (IASB) in July 2009. The standard substantially eases the burden of IFRS reporting for entities whose securities are not publicly traded. It is estimated that over 99 per cent of private entities around the world will be eligible to use the standard. The standard can even be used in countries that have not adopted full IFRSs. The IFRS for SMEs (IASB 2009) incorporates the accounting principles that are based on full IFRSs. But the principles are simplified to a great extent to suit the entities within the scope of the standard. The standard removes some accounting treatments permitted under full IFRSs and eliminates topics and disclosure requirements that are not generally relevant to SMEs. In this paper, an endeavour is made to discuss the key characteristics of the IFRS for SMEs and to provide an overview of the main differences between the requirements of this standard compared to full IFRSs.

10.1 Introduction

The International Financial Reporting Standard for Small and Medium-sized Entities (IFRS for SMEs) is the first international accounting standard designed to serve the financial accounting and reporting needs of non-public companies. This self-contained accounting standard was issued by the International Accounting Standards Board (IASB) in July 2009. The IASB is the independent standard-setting body of the IFRS Foundation. Its members are responsible for the development and publication of IFRSs, including the IFRS for SMEs, and for approving Interpretations of

IFRSs as developed by the IFRS Interpretations Committee. The IASB was constituted in 2001 by reorganizing the International Accounting Standards Committee (IASC). It was the IASC which was in charge of development of accounting standards known as 'International Accounting Standards (IASs)' between 1973 and 2001. When the IASB took over standard setting from the IASC, it adopted all outstanding IASs issued by the latter. Many of these IASs continue to be in force. The new standards formulated by the IASB are known as 'IFRSs'.[1] Currently, 9 IFRSs and 29 IASs are in issue (see Appendix for a detailed listing of the standards).

The IASB standards set out recognition, measurement, presentation and disclosure requirements relating to transactions and other events and conditions that are important in general purpose financial statements. The concepts underlying IFRSs are set out in the IASB's 'Framework for the Preparation and Presentation of Financial Statements' (IASB 2001). The Framework deals with conceptual issues such as the objectives of financial statements, qualitative characteristics of financial statements, the elements of financial statements and their recognition and measurement, and the concept of capital and capital maintenance.

Today more than 100 countries around the world, including all EU countries, require or allow the use of IFRSs for the preparation and presentation of financial statements by publicly traded companies. Efforts are currently under way in a large number of countries to migrate to IFRSs from 2011. These include Canada, Korea, India, Japan, and much of South and Central America. Even the US Securities and Exchange Commission (SEC) is considering taking steps to allow US public companies to use IFRSs. According to a decision taken by the SEC, foreign private issuers are allowed to file financial statements prepared in accordance with IFRSs as issued by the IASB without reconciliation to US GAAP.

IFRSs are a robust set of standards that are meant for profit-seeking entities whose securities are publicly traded. The standards cover a wide range of issues and contain a large amount of implementation guidance. The disclosure requirements are also huge. It is difficult for small and medium companies to comply with these requirements. This is why the IASB has formulated a new accounting standard—IFRS for SMEs—that can be used by private business entities to generate high-quality transparent and comparable financial reports. Non-public companies account for more than 95 per cent of all companies.

The IFRS for SMEs is tailored exclusively for private companies. It is a stand-alone accounting standard that addresses almost all key recognition, measurement, presentation and disclosure issues involved in corporate financial accounting and reporting. The standard is much smaller in size and is organized by topic. It reduces disclosure requirements by nearly 90 per cent. According to the International Federation of Accountants (IFAC), the standard 'represents a very significant step on the path to global convergence of financial reporting practices by SMEs'. It further maintains that the standard 'will contribute to enhancing the quality and comparability of SME financial statements around the world and assist SMEs in gaining access to finance'.[2]

Introducing the IFRS for SMEs, Sir David Tweedie, IASB chairman, said:

> The publication of IFRS for SMEs is a major breakthrough for companies throughout the world. For the first time, SMEs will have a common high quality and internationally respected set of accounting requirements. We believe the benefits will be felt in both developed and emerging economies.[3]

The objective of this paper is to discuss the central features of the IFRS for SMEs and to provide a brief account of the key differences between the requirements of this self-contained standard compared to full IFRSs. The remainder of the paper is divided into six sections. Section 10.2 discusses the definition of SMEs. Section 10.3 examines the rational for having two sets of accounting standards: full IFRSs and IFRS for SMEs. Section 10.4 examines the evolution of the IFRS for SMEs. Section 10.5 examines the key characteristics of IFRS for SMEs. Section 10.6 renders a brief account of the similarities and differences between full IFRSs and IFRS for SMEs. Section 10.7 concludes the paper.

10.2 How SMEs are Defined?

Definitions of an SME vary widely across nations. Distinction between SMEs and non-SMEs are drawn on the basis of power consumption, number of workers, turnover, capital employed, etc. The IASB in its IFRS for SMEs has simplified the criteria to be used to define SMEs. It does not use any quantitative criterion. Instead, it focuses on two types of entities: (i) the unlisted companies and listed companies which have not yet attempted public issue of both equity or debt securities and (ii) entities other than those which hold assets in their fiduciary capacity, viz. banks, insurance companies, credit rating agencies, etc. It clarifies that in the nations where IFRSs have not yet been adopted, IFRS for SMEs may be applicable. It further states that if a subsidiary whose parent or group uses full IFRSs may use the IFRS for SMEs if that subsidiary itself does not have public accountability.

10.2.1 IASB Definition

In the IFRS for SMEs, IASB has defined SMEs. According to this definition, SMEs are those entities that:

(i) do not have public accountability, and

(ii) publish general purpose financial statements for external users.

An entity has public accountability if its debt or equity instruments are traded in a public market or it is in the process of issuing such instrument for trading in a public market. Public market implies a domestic or foreign stock exchange or an over-the-counter market, including local and regional markets, or it holds assets in fiduciary capacity for a broad group of outsiders as one of its primary businesses. This typically is the case for banks, credit unions, insurance companies, securities brokers/dealers, mutual funds and investment banks. If an entity holds assets in a fiduciary capacity as an incidental part of its business, that does not make the entity publicly accountable. Entities that fall into this category may include public utilities, travel and real estate agents, schools and charities.

General purpose financial statements are those that present fair financial position (balance sheet, operation results (profit and loss account) and cash flows for external capital providers and others. And examples of external users include owners who are not involved in managing the business. They include existing and potential creditors and credit rating agencies.

10.2.2 ICAI Definition of SMEs

The IFRS for SMEs is intended to be used by all countries that adopt IFRS. As the origin of this research is India, we intend to examine the SME definition of ICAI. The Council of the Institute of Chartered Accountants of India in its 236th meeting held on September 16–18, 2003 considered the accounting issues relating to SMEs and has classified all enterprises into three categories for the purpose of applicability of accounting standards: Level I, Level II and Level III enterprises. The criteria for classification of enterprises are mentioned below.

Level I Enterprises

Enterprises which fall in any one or more of the following categories, at any time during the accounting period, are classified as Level I enterprises: (i) Enterprises whose equity or debt securities are listed whether in India or outside India; (ii) Enterprises which are in the process of listing their equity or debt securities as evidenced by the board of directors' resolution in this regard; (iii) Banks including co-operative banks; (iv) Financial institutions;, (v) Enterprises carrying on insurance business; (vi) All commercial, industrial and business reporting enterprises, whose turnover for the immediately preceding accounting period on the basis of audited financial statements exceeds Rs. 50 crores. Turnover does not include 'other income'; (vii) All commercial, industrial and business reporting enterprises having borrowings, including public deposits, in excess of Rs. 10 crores at any time during the accounting period; and (viii) Holding and subsidiary enterprises of any one of the above at any time during the accounting period.

Level II Enterprises

Enterprises which are not Level I enterprises but fall in any one or more of the following categories are classified as Level II enterprises: (i) All commercial, industrial and business reporting enterprises, whose turnover for the immediately preceding accounting period on the basis of audited financial statements exceeds Rs. 40 lakhs but does not exceed Rs. 50 crores. Turnover does not include 'other income'; (ii) All commercial, industrial and business reporting. Enterprises having borrowings, including public deposits, in excess of Rs. 1 crores but not in excess of Rs. 10 crores at any time during the accounting period; and (iii) Holding and subsidiary enterprises of any one of the above at any time during the accounting period.

Level III Enterprises

Enterprises which are neither Level I nor Level II are called as Level III enterprises.[4]

It appears that there is a great similarity of approaches between the IASB and the ICAI in the matter of exclusion of companies which are either listed or intended to be listed shortly.

In India, enterprises in the first tier are required to apply IFRSs as adapted for the country. The remaining two tiers are composed of SMEs. According to the reporting requirements prevailing at the present time, simplifications and exceptions are allowed with respect to Level II and Level III enterprises.

10.3 The Rationale for Having Two Sets of Standards—IFRSs and IFRS for SMEs

Business transactions in general have become much complex and deserve intricate accounting standards to resolve their accounting issues. Accounting standards for complex transactions like derivatives or lease financing has raised controversies amongst the accountants. It has been observed that those standards are mostly required for enterprises who either go for (i) cross border business or (ii) their shares have participated in the derivative segment. SMEs in most of the cases do not have (i) group companies or (ii) shares in derivative segments. Obviously, these are not enough reasons to enforce all those detailed and complex accounting standards for their relatively simple and less voluminous set of transactions. Cost-benefit analysis of enforcing of accounting standards in SMEs has become a subject of long debate. There are arguments in favour as well as against the application of all accounting standards for SMEs. Four possible choices for SME accounting have been mentioned:

- Out of whole set of accounting standards, let a few accounting standards be eliminated and rest may be made applicable for SMEs.
- Let all accounting standards be made applicable to all enterprises, big, medium or small,
- A standard deals with three issues: recognition, measurement and disclosure. On recognition and measurement issues, let there be no disparity among enterprises, SMEs and non-SMEs. However, on disclosure issues, let there be relaxation for SMEs. In brief, let there be one set of accounting standards for SMEs which is derived from general set of accounting standards for all enterprises, big or small.
- Let's have two different sets of accounting standards. One set for SMEs and other for non-SMEs.

After a long debate, ultimately, the fourth one has been chosen.

10.4 Evolution of IFRS for SMEs—A Historical Perspective

The IFRS for SMEs has been developed over a fairly long period of time. In developing the standard, the IASB consulted extensively worldwide. A 40-member Working Group of SME experts advised the IASB on the structure and content of the IFRS at various stages in its development. The project to develop the standard was actually carried forward from the IASC agenda (IASB 2009a). The IASB deliberations on the subject started in 2003. At that time, the world standard setter made a survey as to whether it can prepare a comprehensive globally acceptable separate accounting standard for SMEs. In June 2004, a discussion paper was released with 117 comments. In April 2005, IASB questionnaire on recognition and measurement got 94 responses. An exposure draft (ED) on IFRS for SME was released in February 2007 (IASB 2007), which received 162 comments from different sections of the accounting fraternity. Field tests were conducted among 116 real SMEs in November 2007. In the month of May 2009, near final draft was posted on IASB web site. And the final IFRS for SMEs was issued only on 9 July 2009. In the same month, a survey made by Deloitte (United States) on finance professionals from 225 private companies found that more than 51 per cent of small- and mid-size private company respondents (revenue less than $1 billion) supported separate accounting standards for private and public companies. Evolution of IFRS for SMEs since 2003 is depicted in Exhibit 10.1. The IFRS for SMEs was issued in July 2009. Although the term 'SMEs' has been defined in the new standard, national accounting standard setters are free to decide which entities are permitted or even required to apply the IFRS for SMEs

Exhibit 10.1: Evolution of IFRS for SMEs since 2003

September 2003	Feasibility study conducted by World Standard Setters
June 2004	Discussion Paper was issued and received 117 comments
April 2005	Questionnaire on recognition and measurement (94 responses)
October 2005	Roundtable meetings on recognition and measurement (43 groups)
	Exposure Draft issued and received 162 comments
February–November 2007	Field tests were conducted on 116 real SMEs
March–April 2008	Board education sessions
May 2008–April 2009	Re-deliberations
May 2009	Near-final draft posted on IASB website
1 June 2009	Ballot draft sent to the Board
9 July 2009	Final IFRS for SMEs issued

IFRS for SMEs was approved for issue by 13 of the 14 members of the IASB. The only member, Mr Leisenring dissented. His observation about a separate set of IFRS for SME was '*neither necessary nor desirable*'. He offered a set of arguments against introduction of a separate set of IFRS for small enterprises despite having a full IFRS. His arguments were as follows:

1. Vast majority of accounting policy decisions of SMEs are straightforward and extensive reference to IFRS will not be required.
2. IFRS for SMEs would result into non-comparability. Not only SMEs accounts would be non-comparable, comparison of accounts between SMEs and non-SME's becomes difficult. Identical transactions may be treated differently by different SMEs and the treatments may be different from publicly accountable entities. This is inconsistent not only with IASB framework but also with pervasive principles of IFRS.
3. Simply on the basis of cost-benefit analysis no compromise should be made to recognition and measurement requirement. However, bearing in mind the special user's need, modification may be done on disclosure requirement.
4. IFRS for SMEs is inconsistent with the constitution of the IASC Foundation and the preface to IFRS. Those documents set out an objective of a single set of accounting standards taking into account the special needs of small- and medium-sized entities and emerging economies. It does not believe it implies separate sets of standards for entities in differing circumstances as indicated in paragraph BC-42 (basis for conclusioin-425; issued along with main standards).

However, despite protest from Mr Leisenring, IFRS for SMEs got final approval by all of 13 other members.

10.5 IFRS for SMEs—The Key Characteristics

The IASB currently has two financial reporting frameworks. The first one is represented by full IFRSs. It is meant for entities that have public accountability. The second one is represented by the stand-alone standard—IFRS for SMEs. The IFRS for SMEs has been written in clear, easily translatable language. The volume has been reduced by more than 85 per cent compared with the full IFRSs. Much of the implementation guidance has been omitted. The IFRS for SMEs is organized into 35 sections. Emphasis has been cast on fair value of assets and liabilities in most cases. Exhibit 10.2 depicts a brief summary that may be helpful in obtaining and understanding the original IASB version of IFRS for SMEs.

Exhibit 10.2: IFRS for SMEs

Section	Title	Remarks
1	Small and Medium Sized Entities	It offers a comprehensive definition of SMEs. It also resolves the conflict as to which entities may use full IFRSs and which entities may use IFRS for SMEs.
2	Concepts and Pervasive Principles	Qualitative characteristics of financial statement have been explained. Matters of significant attention are (i) recognition and measurement principles and (ii) principles of offsetting.
3	Financial Statement Presentation	Complete set of financial statement comprise: (i) a statement of financial position (balance sheet); (ii) either a single statement of comprehensive income or two statements: an income statement and a statement of comprehensive income; (iii) statement of changes in equity; (iv) statement of cash flows; and (v) notes. An entity may present only an income statement (no statement of comprehensive income) if it has no items of other comprehensive income (OCI). The only OCI items under IFRS for SMEs are (i) foreign exchange gains and losses and (ii) some changes in fair value of hedging instruments.
4	Statement of Financial Position	As an exception current/non-current split is not required if the entity concludes that liquidity approach offers a better disclosure. Flexibility exists to disclose sub-classifications either in the statement or in notes.
5	Statement of Comprehensive Income and Income Statement	Must segregate discontinued operations. No item shall be labelled 'extraordinary'. Unusual items can be separately presented.
6	Statement of Changes in Equity and Statement of Income and Retained Earnings	This statement of changes in equity would be omitted if the entity has no owner investments or withdrawals other than dividends and elects to presents a combined statement of income and retained earnings.
7	Statement of Cash Flows	Flexibility exists to use either (i) direct or (ii) indirect method.
8	Notes to the Financial Statements	Offers summary of significant accounting policies including (i) information about judgments and (ii) key sources of estimation uncertainty.

Contd

Section	Title	Remarks
9	Consolidated and Separate Financial Statements	Necessity of preparation of consolidated and separate financial statements arises when parent company controls both (i) financial and (ii) operating policies of other entity.
10	Accounting Policies, Estimates and Errors	If the IFRS for SMEs does not address an issue, policy is to be chosen that results in most relevant and reliable information. In order to correct prior period error, prior periods are required to be restated.
11	Basic Financial Instruments	Provides guidance for determination of fair values of financial instruments. Most reliable is the quoted price in an active market. If quoted price is not available, most recent transaction price provides evidence of fair value. If there is no active market, a valuation technique may be used.
12	Other Financial Instruments Issues	Financial instrument not covered by Section 11 comes under Section 12. It includes, forwards, futures, options, swaps and other derivatives. Hedge accounting involves matching gains and losses on a hedging instrument and hedged item.
13	Inventories	Inventory cost includes costs to purchase, costs of conversion and costs to bring the asset to present location and condition. Standard costing, retail method and most recent purchase price may be used only if the result approximates actual cost.
14	Investment in Associates	Significant influence over associates exists only with 20% or more the voting shares. Valuation may be done on the basis of any one of these three techniques, viz., (i) Cost-impairment model, (ii) Equity method, or (iii) Fair value through profit or loss.
15	Investment in Joint Ventures	Any one of the three options mentioned in Section 14 may be applied.
16	Investment Property	If fair value can be measured reliably without undue cost or effort, use the fair value through profit or loss model. Otherwise an entity must treat investment property as property, plant and equipment using Section 17.
17	Property, Plant & Equipment	The revaluation model (as in IAS 16) is not permitted. Measurement is initially at cost including cost to get the property ready for its intended use. Subsequent to acquisition, the entity uses the cost-depreciation impairment model which recognizes depreciation and impairment of the carrying amount.
18	Intangible Assets other than Goodwill	Revaluation of intangible assets is prohibited. If the entity is unable to estimate useful life, then use 10 years. Useful life of the asset is to be reviewed only if there is significant change in the asset or the way the same is used.
19	Business Combinations & Goodwill	Section 19 does not apply to combinations of entities under common control. Identifiable assets acquired and liabilities and provisions for contingent liabilities assumed are measured at their fair value.

Contd

Section	Title	Remarks
20	Leases	Leases are classified as either finance lease or operating lease. If a sale and leaseback results in a finance lease, the seller should not recognize any excess as a profit but recognize the excess over the lease term. On the other hand, if a sale and leaseback results in an operating lease and the transaction was at fair value, the seller shall recognize any profits immediately.
21	Provisions & Contingencies	Initially recognized at the best possible estimate at the reporting date. This value takes into time value of money if this is considered material. Subsequently, provisions are to be reviewed at each reporting date and adjusted to meet the best current estimate. So far as contingent asset and contingent liabilities are concerned, remote liabilities are not disclosed. Description of the nature and the financial effect of the contingent assets are disclosed.
22	Liabilities & Equity	Section 22 covers some material not covered by full IFRS. Shares are recognized as equity only when another party is obliged to provide cash or other resources in exchange for the instruments. Instruments are measured at the fair value of cash or resources received minus direct cost of issuing the equity instrument. However, if time value of money is significant, then initial measurement is to be done at the present value. The dividend liability is measured at the fair value of the assets to be distributed.
23	Revenue	IFRS for SMEs identified four sources of revenue, viz. (i) sale of goods, (ii) service being rendered, (iii) construction contract income by the contractor and (iv) use of assets by others. Some of the items like (i) biological assets, (ii) financial instruments, (iii) construction contracts, (iv) interest etc. are dealt with in some other sections.
24	Government Grants	Measured at fair value of the assets received or receivable. It excludes any grants in the form of income tax benefits.
25	Borrowing Costs	Borrowing costs include (i) interest and (ii) other cost arising from entity's financial liabilities and finance lease obligation. No borrowing costs are capitalized.
26	Share-based Payment	If possible to estimate reliably, transactions shall be recorded at fair value.
27	Impairment of Assets	Recoverable amount is the greater of fair value less costs to sell and value in use. If impairment indicator exists, the entity should review the useful life and the depreciation methods even though impairment may not be recognized.
28	Employee Benefits	Section 28 classifies employee benefits into (i) short time, (ii) post-employment, (iii) terminal benefits and (iv) other long-term benefits. Post-employment benefits are further classified into (a) defined contribution plan and (b) defined benefit plan.
29	Income Tax	Specific treatment has been suggested for current as well as deferred tax liability.

Contd

Section	Title	Remarks
30	Foreign Currency Translation	For monetary and non-monetary items translations, gains or losses are recognized when they were initially recognized—either in profit and loss for the period, comprehensive income or equity. Goodwill arising on acquisition of a foreign operation is deemed to be an asset of the subsidiary and translated at the closing rate at year end.
31	Hyperinflation	General price level adjusted financial statement is to be prepared when functional currency is hyperinflationary. The profit or loss on net monetary position is included in profit or loss.
32	Events after the end of the Reporting Period	Financial statement is to be adjusted to reflect events after the balance sheet date that provide further evidence of conditions that existed after the reporting date.
33	Related Party Disclosures	Government departments have been excluded. Information are required to be disclosed about (i) nature of the relationship, (ii) information about the transactions and outstanding balances, (iii) provisions for uncollectible receivables, etc.
34	Specialized Activities	Specific guidelines have been provided for (i) Agriculture, (ii) Extractive industries, and (iii) service concession arrangements.
35	Transition to the IFRS for SMEs	One prior period information disclosure is required. Exemptions are allowed for restating specific items.

10.6 IFRS for SMEs IFRSs and Full IFRSs—Similarities and Differences

IFRS for SMEs retains the fundamental principles on which the full version of IFRS is based. In many cases, it has been simplified keeping fewer complexities to reduce the cost and effort required for producing the financial statements. The options available under full IFRSs have been removed. There are five areas where options under full IFRSs have been removed. These are (i) For jointly controlled entities there is option to use proportionate consolidation; (ii) Investment properties must be measured under fair value. However, if fair value cannot be measured reliably without undue cost or effort, the same should be accounted for as property, plant and equipment. Cost model cannot be used; (iii) Property, plant and equipment (PP&E) must be measured at cost less depreciation and accumulated impairment loss. PP& E cannot be revalued; (iv) Like PP&E, intangible asset must be measured at cost less accumulated depreciation and accumulated impairment loss. They cannot be revalued; (v) Actuarial gains or losses must be recognized in full either through profit or loss or through comprehensive income.

Apart from the five such key areas, where options available in full IFRSs have been removed, there exist seven key areas where accounting for SMEs has been amended. (i) For intangible assets, it is imperative that they must have useful service life. Where useful service life can not be estimated reliably, it should be taken as 10 years. (ii) In business combination, acquisition costs are capitalized. Goodwill is tested for impairment, only where there are indicators of impairment. (iii) For valuation of financial instruments, entities have given choice to account for financial instruments in accordance with the IFRS for SMEs or to apply recognition and measurement provisions of IAS 39. The hedging rules have also been simplified to restrict the instances in which SMEs can apply hedge accounting and to reduce the criteria in order to apply hedge accounting. (iv) Accounting for borrowing cost has been made simple for SMEs. It must be expensed as incurred and cannot be capitalized in relation to qualifying assets. (v) For Government grants there could be two situations. It may come with or without performance conditions. All government grants must be recognized in profit and loss account either immediately or at the point such performance conditions are met. (vi) Share-based payments to be measured using directors' best estimate of fair value. (vii) The accounting for income tax differs significantly from the current requirement of full IFRS. The IFRS for SMEs provides guidance on recognition and measurement of uncertain tax positions brings in concepts of valuation of tax base which should be based on sale at the end of the period.

Accounting guidance included in full version of IFRSs has been reduced to the extent of 85 per cent in IFRS for SMEs. Much of the implementation guidance in full IFRSs has been omitted. Pricewaterhouse Coopers has undertaken an ongoing commitment to help companies to transit from local GAAP to IFRS for SMEs. Recently they have completed a project entitled 'Similarities and differences of full IFRSs and IFRS for SMEs.[5] Compared with full IFRSs, the IFRS for SMEs is less complex in a number of ways:

- Topics not relevant for SMEs have been omitted.
- Where full IFRS allows accounting policy choices, the IFRS for SMEs allows only the easier option.
- Many of the principles for recognizing and measuring assets, liabilities, income and expenses in full IFRSs are simplified for SMEs. Under IFRS for SMEs significantly fewer disclosures are required.
- Similarities and difference between IFRS and IFRS for SMEs have been highlighted under eight parameters, viz. (i) financial statements (format), (ii) business combinations, (iii) investment in associates and joint ventures, (iv) expense recognition, (v) financial instruments derivatives and hedging, (vi) non-financial assets and goodwill, (vii) employee benefits-defined plans, and (viii) income taxes.

Exhibit 10.3 depicts the key issues of that comparative study.

Exhibit 10.3: Full IFRSs and IFRS for SMEs—A Comparative Study

Parameters	Key Issues
1. Financial Statements	In the full IFRSs, a statement of changes in equity is required presenting a reconciliation of equity items between the beginning and the end of the period. In IFRS for SMEs, the requirement is same unless changes are occurring due to result of profit or loss, payment of dividend, corrections of prior period errors or changes in accounting policies. A combined statement of income and retained earnings can be presented instead of a statement of comprehensive income and a statement of changes in equity.

Contd

Parameters	Key Issues
2. Business Combinations	IFRS 3 has recently been revised. Transaction costs are excluded under this IFRS. Contingent consideration is recognized regardless of the probability of payment. In IFRS for SMEs, transaction costs are included in acquisition cost. Contingent considerations are included as part of the acquisition cost if it is probable that the amount will be paid and its fair value can be measured reliably.
3. Investment in Associates and Joint Ventures	In the full IFRSs, cost and fair value models are not permitted. In IFRS for SME, an entity may account for its investments in associates or jointly controlled entities using any one of the following: (i) the cost model, (ii) the equity method, (iii) the fair value through profit or loss model.
4. Expense Recognition	In the full IFRSs, research costs are expensed as incurred and development costs are capitalized and amortized only when specific criteria are met.
	In IFRS for SMEs, no distinction is made between research and development cost. All borrowing cost is capitalized.
5. Financial Instruments—derivatives & hedging	IAS 39 titled 'Financial instruments: Recognition and Measurement' distinguishes four measurement categories of financial instrument—that is (i) financial assets or liabilities at fair value through profit or loss, (ii) held to maturity investments, (iii) loans and receivables and (iv) available-for-sale financial assets.
	In IFRS for SMEs, most of the basic financial instruments are measured at amortized cost; the complex instruments are generally measured at fair value through profit or loss.
6. Non-financial Assets and Goodwill	Under full IFRSs, for tangible and intangible assets, there is an accounting policy choice between the cost model and the revaluation model. In IFRS for SMEs, only cost model is permitted.
7. Employee Benefits-defined Plans	In full IFRSs, under IAS 19 employee benefits, actuarial gain or loss can be recognized immediately or amortized into profit or loss over expected remaining working lives of participating employees. IFRS for SMEs requires immediate recognition and splits the expense into different components.
8. Income Taxes	In full IFRS, a deferred tax is only recognized to the extent that it is probable that there will be sufficient profit to enable recovery of the deferred tax asset.
	Under IFRS for SMEs, a valuation allowance is recognized so that the net carrying amount of the deferred tax asset equals the highest amount that is more likely than not to be recovered.

10.7 Conclusion

The need for having a common high quality and internationally accepted financial reporting framework for SMEs has long been felt. The IFRS for SMEs represents an attempt by the IASB's to respond to that long-felt need. This new IASB standard, which is a self-contained document, has been derived from full IFRSs. But its size has been considerably reduced. The standard provides a framework that generates high-quality comparable information in general purpose financial statements of the SME. The standard can be adopted even by countries that have not adopted full IFRSs. It is expected that the standard will reduce the compliance cost for many smaller entities and make the financial reports less complex. To promote better understanding of the standard, the IASC Foundation is developing training material and is making provisions for translation of the material in several languages. It is proposed to develop a separate training module for each section of the IFRS for SMEs. Meanwhile, the World Bank has published on their Web site a two-part webcast presentation by IASB member Paul Pacter entitled 'An Overview of the IFRS for SMEs'.[6] The presentation is based on the first of the 20 training modules used in the IASB's 'Train the trainer' workshops for IFRS for SMEs.

The process of implementation of the IFRS for SMEs has started. Initiatives are currently under way in many jurisdictions to implement the standard. Since the standard is principles-based requirements, implementation issues are likely to arise. A globally consistent approach is necessary to address those issues. The Trustees of the IASC Foundation have formed an SME Implementation Group that will consider implementation questions raised by users of the standard, decide which ones merit published implementation guidance, and develop and publish that guidance in the form of questions and answers. The IASB has indicated that it will take appropriate measures to modify the standard if significant implementation issues are encountered.

Appendix 10.1

List of IFRSs and IASs Currently in Force

IFRSs

IFRS 1, *First-time Adoption of International Financial Reporting Standards*
IFRS 2, *Share-Based Payment*
IFRS 3, *Business Combinations*
IFRS 4, *Insurance Contracts*
IFRS 5, *Non-current Assets Held for Sale and Discontinued Operations*
IFRS 6, *Exploration for and Evaluation of Mineral Resources*
IFRS 7, *Financial Instruments: Disclosures*
IFRS 8, *Operating Segments*
IFRS 9, *Financial Instruments*

IASs

IAS 1, *Presentation of Financial Statements*
IAS 2, *Inventories*

IAS 7, *Cash Flow Statements*
IAS 8, *Accounting Policies, Changes in Accounting Estimates and Errors*
IAS 10, *Events After the Balance Sheet Date*
IAS 11, *Construction Contracts*
IAS 12, *Income Taxes*
IAS 14, *Segment Reporting*
IAS 16, *Property, Plant, and Equipment*
IAS 17, *Leases*
IAS 18, *Revenue*
IAS 19, *Employee Benefits*
IAS 21, *The Effects of Changes in Foreign Exchange Rates*
IAS 23, *Borrowing Costs*
IAS 24, *Related-Party Disclosures*
IAS 26, *Accounting and Reporting by Retirement Benefit Plans*
IAS 27, *Consolidated and Separate Financial Statements*
IAS 28, *Investments in Associates*
IAS 29, *Financial Reporting in Hyperinflationary Economies*
IAS 31, *Interests in Joint Ventures*
IAS 32, *Financial Instruments: Presentation*
IAS 33, *Earnings per Share*
IAS 34, *Interim Financial Reporting*
IAS 36, *Impairment of Assets*
IAS 37, *Provisions, Contingent Liabilities and Contingent Assets*
IAS 38, *Intangible Assets*
IAS 39, *Financial Instruments: Recognition and Measurement*
IAS 40, *Investment Property*
IAS 41, *Agriculture*

Notes

1. When used collectively, IFRSs refer to the entire body of IASB pronouncements including standards and interpretations approved by the IASB, IFRIC, IASC and SIC (Ernst & Young 2010).

2. For details, see World Bank Webcasts on IFRS for SMEs Part 1. http://siteresources.worldbank.org/EXTCENFINREPREF/Resources/4152117-1276630882791/ifrs-webcast1.html

3. http://www.ifrs.org/News/Press Releases/IASB publishes IFRS for SMEs.htm

4. *The Chartered Accountant*, November, 2003.

5. The project report is available at PWC Web site www.pwc.com/ifrs

6. http://siteresources.worldbank.org/EXTCENFINREPREF Resources/4152117-1276630882791/ifrs-webcast1.html

References

D'Souza, D., Parikh, J., Spargo, E. and Bansal, V. (2010). *Step up to IFRS: An Ernst & Young Guide on First-time Adoption of IFRS in India*, Ernst & Yonng Pvt. Ltd.

Ernst & Young (2010). *Step up to IFRS: An Ernst & Young Guide on First Time Adoption of IFRS in India.* Ernst & Young Pvt. Ltd.

International Accounting Standards Board (IASB) (2001). *Framework for the Preparation and Presentation of Financial Statements.* IASB, London.

———(2007). *Exposure Draft: International Financial Reporting Standard for Small and Medium-sized Entities (IFRS for SMEs).* IASB, London.

———(2009). *International Financial Reporting Standard (IFRS) for Small and Medium-sized Entities (SMEs).* IASB, London.

———(2009a). *IFRS for SMEs Fact Sheet.* IASB, London.

Web sites

- www.iasb.org/current/dp_pv.asp
- http:// en.wikipedia.org/wiki/Accounting
- http:// go.iasb.org/IFRS for SME
- http:// www.iasb.org/current/dppv.asp
- http:// www.iasb.org/current/isab.asp

CHAPTER 11

Obstacles to the Development of Optimal Accounting Standards—Accounting and Political Issues

Arnab Deb Narayan Roy

ABSTRACT

Accounting regulation via standards has to be evolutionary because the scope of its improvement is always more than the actual improvement. Accounting standards have to be optimal standards. The optimal accounting standards should be based on fundamental accounting logic. The task of providing optimal standards for a society is associated with several problems such as conflicting interests of managers and shareholders, under-production of accounting data because it is a 'public good'. There are arguments for voluntary reporting and arguments for regulated reporting. There is paradox of regulation too. Indirect involvement of capital market in standard setting process is another major obstacle. This paper thoroughly examines the obstacles that stand in between the basic accounting logic and the accounting standard.

11.1 Relevance of Optimal Accounting Standards

Accounting standards need to be set mainly in controversial areas. Such issues involve interests of many parties having high socio-economic impacts. In order to maintain long run credibility of accounting, the standard setter has to be sensitive to the views of its diversified constituents so that ultimately the standards provide the society with adequate, relevant and reliable information about economic events and transactions of business entities. To say it more specifically, the approach of a standard should be to provide 'optimal' standards. The word 'optimal' may be used to indicate the best possible standard for (i) the constituents of the standard setting body; (ii) the preparers of the financial statements; and (iii) the users of accounting information. As the same standard might not be equally advantageous to all the parties, a standard can be treated as optimal when it creates minimum dissents among the external parties for their claiming that the new treatment is less favourable than the status quo.

Formulation of optimal standard has to take care of the reality that owing to the environmental influences, there has been radical change in the content of accounting information to be measured and communicated and in the environment within which the accounting should do its work. According to Gandhi (1976: 48), 'Although the basic accounting functions have not changed, the new content and the new environment are no longer responsive to the traditional accounting tools of measurement and communication'.

Gaa (1988) used the term 'best' to express concern not with the output of a standard setter, i.e., the form of standards, concepts, interpretations, etc. but with the underlying rationality of the standard setting process itself. If a standard setter thinks of the possibility that the accounting measurement techniques are subversible to produce supposedly beneficial social results, the credibility of accounting would quickly suffer.

The system of codifying accounting regulation via standards has to be evolutionary because it is expected to evolve and improve in a relatively open and democratic society, rather than in authoritarian societies. Since the scope of improvement of financial reporting by codified accounting regulation in a free democratic society is wider than actual improvement, it is expected that the accounting standard setting bodies shall make rational response to resolve difficult distributional problems like how benefits are distributed among competing groups. Such response may not be perfect, but the standard setter should have '… the ability, opportunity and desire to make a correct decision, or at least not the desire not to'. (Gaa 1988: 123)

This paper analyses the obstacles to the development of optimal accounting standard which may arise within the standard setting process of individual countries and also with regard to the efforts of the International Accounting Standards Board (IASB) for developing accounting rules to be duly adopted by many countries. The major obstacles standing on the way to develop accounting standards strictly on the basis of accounting logic have been the following:

(i) Uniform accounting system (UAS) that has been traditionally followed in many countries and that permits high level of government involvement in accounting regulation.
(ii) Lack of freedom that is necessary for doing accounting so that tax considerations cannot predominate over the accounting objective of fair presentation of the affairs of business enterprises.
(iii) Difficulties in internationalization and/or European harmonization of financial reporting.
(iv) Ambiguity in accounting rules that allows company managements for using discretions.
(v) Latitude given to the companies to take decisions about recognition and measurement of assets and liabilities.
(vi) Wide variety of disclosure requirements from country to country.
(vii) Irrationality of GAAP.
(viii) Dependence of the standard setter on historical values in response to the political sensitivity of standards.
(ix) Lack of accounting credibility for a number of reasons
(x) Reflexive intervention of capital market in accounting standard setting process.

11.2 Uniform Accounting System and Government Involvement in Accounting Regulation

A serious obstacle for standard setting is the uniform accounting system (UAS) that has been traditionally followed in France, Germany, Czech Republic, Romania, China, Hungary and Poland. In each of these countries, the level of government involvement in accounting regulation is very high.[1] In France, the explanatory detailed accounting rules are framed by French legislation and the very old French regulations (existing prior to 1940s) have been extended as essential elements of uniform accounting system in the form of charts of accounts for use by specific industries. In Germany, the Ministry of Finance sets law—Handelsgesetzbuch (HGB) and approves accounting standards prepared by German Accounting Standards Committee—Deutsches Rechnungslegungs Standards Committee (DRSC). The Ministry of Finance is itself the accounting regulator in Czech Republic, Romania and China. In Hungary, the National Accounting Committee is the accounting regulator. In Poland, the Accounting Act of the country prescribes the rules for financial recording and measurement.

Contrary to the above noted countries, governments in Australia, Canada, the UK and the USA are less involved in accounting regulation and the uniform accounting system is not traditionally followed in these countries. In case of Japan, UAS could not find its place although before 2001, the government remained highly involved in directing the accounting regulation—Business Accounting Deliberation Council (BADC), an advisor to the Ministry of Finance, was engaged in standard setting. The degree of government influence is being lowered in Japan since the establishment of the new Accounting Standards Board Japan (ASBJ) in 2001.

In case of China, UAS was imported to the country from former Soviet Union where the capitalist accounting system was hated as biased against the working class people (Xiao et al. 2004). The government of China wants to supplement uniform accounting system with International Accounting Standards (IAS) and to adopt the IAS-defined methods within its UAS. This is not like Romania where accounting standards have been supplemented with chart of accounts. However, the government of China does not intend to allow companies prepare consolidated accounts using international standards and individual accounts using UAS, as done in France. Xiao et al. (2004) identified three variables that determine coexistence of UAS and accounting standards in China—strong involvement of government in accounting regulation, underdeveloped equity market and the accounting tradition of relying on UAS. Why has not the government of China discarded the UAS and just focused on developing accounting standards? The answer found in an opinion collected by Xiao et al. 2004 in their analysis is that, 'Even now, a firm's operating and management mechanisms have not been totally transformed and thus there is still a lack of demand for accounting standards … Chinese accounting standards are mainly applicable to listed companies. Why does China need a UAS? Because the reform of state-owned enterprises has not reached the stage where only accounting standards are required.' A financial regulator in China (Feng 2001 in Xiao et al. 2004: 209) stressed that the practical outcome of the accounting system matters more than whether the treatment is prescribed in UAS or in accounting standards. However, the government seems to have underestimated the difficulty of setting and enforcing accounting standards.[2]

The following have been the characteristics of UAS adoption in the first group of countries (France, Germany, Czech Republic, Romania, China, Hungary, and Poland):

1. UAS is needed to support the macroeconomic control over accounting regulation. The government regulators are more concerned with macroeconomic issues and their involvement in accounting is high and it is always there in the sense that government directly issues detailed rules for financial recording and measurement. The accounting profession is weak and little involved in accounting regulation.
2. Capital market transactions in these countries are less sophisticated and doing them requires less professional judgement. Capital market forces in these countries do not require sophisticated information on investment risks and opportunities. A UAS does not focus on disclosure, but it only provides descriptions of accounts. It contains general rules of recording and measurement. The scope of professional judgement is restricted in a UAS because it contains only specific instructions for implementation, but not the concepts and principles to guide professional application of accounting methods. These rules are simply general rules; they are not advanced rules of implementation utilizing the 'fair presentation principle'. Because of this drawback, in these countries, the debate like 'principles versus rules' that is concerned with advanced rules did not arise at all. These two features confirm that the UAS is typically designed as a tool for administrative control and that is the motivation for government's involvement in revitalizing a prescriptive UAS while developing a set of professionally oriented accounting standards. It means it is felt unnecessary for UAS to provide information useful for investors. Hence, accounting profession gets no chance to gain experience in investor-oriented standard setting. This makes the accounting profession further weaker because it fails to demand self-regulation and resist government control.
3. Underdeveloped capital market imposes many technical constraints on standard setting. A less developed capital market requires more central planning because the market conditions are not conducive for standard setting. In these countries, an infrastructure suitable for UAS is evolved. Further, there are some inertial resistances to accounting standards that involve substantial judgement.

11.3 Contrast Between Financial Reporting and Tax Accounting

In some countries, the tax-code dictates the accounting policy. Periodic profit or loss is influenced by the changes in tax-rates and imposition of graduated tax-rates. For example, in Germany and France, book-profit and tax-profit are to conform as required by law. In the USA and the UK, financial reporting and tax accounting are allowed to follow their own way and accounting is developed without concern for what it may do to a business's tax burden. Solomons (1986: 19) opined that this freedom is necessary for doing accounting so that tax considerations cannot predominate over the accounting objective of trying fairly to present the affairs of an enterprise. The difference between accounting and taxable profit is widest when the enterprise uses cash basis for tax purpose and accrual basis for measurement of economic performance and its external reporting. Solomons (1986: 207) has used the phrase 'caricature of the accounting process' when accounting figures are changed retroactively to give a desired result, or the accrual basis coupled with the historical cost model results into profit manipulation.

11.4 Problems in Achieving International Harmonization in Financial Reporting

If it is not possible to embed the system of international accounting standards into the various national institutional structures, then the chances of success of international standardization of accounting are very bleak. A few relevant considerations in this regard are: (i) The role of national standard setting bodies to be played if conglomerates or group companies are permitted to publish their consolidated financial statements in accordance with international standards; (ii) The discrepancy that the groups and conglomerates prepare their financial statements according to international regulations while individual companies prepare their separate financial statements according to national rules; (iii) Violations of domestic rules are penalized by national laws, but violations of international standards are not yet dealt with.

Besides the contrast between national and international accounting regulatory requirements, harmonization of national accounting rules has also been a matter of apprehension. The European Union (EU) was least successful in harmonizing the accounting rules in those member states that have a long tradition of regulating accounting. National traditions conflicted with European Union directives. For example, in Germany, France, the UK, accounting has long been linked in many and diverse ways with other institutions. In the UK, the continental tradition of statutory regulation of accounting was not compatible with the British national tradition of regulation by the accounting profession or by a private standard setting body. Consequently, a particular status had to be bestowed upon the standards of the UK ASB.

Hussein and Ketz (1980) and Diggle and Nobes (1994) expressed the view that the process of transformation of the provisions of the fourth directive of the European Commission (EC) into national laws of the European countries was highly flexible. The fourth directive contained a large number of options so that at national level a country could choose from various alternative treatments. At the national level, several times the lobbyists put pressure for transformation of particular options developed within the framework of fourht directive into national laws. Hence that framework represented a significant external constraint on the national financial reporting regulatory systems.

11.5 Factors That Affect Standard Setter's Performance

Standard setter's performance is affected because ambiguity in accounting rules provides scope for using discretions by company managements. Latitude given to companies to take recognition and measurement decisions; wide variety of disclosure requirements from country to country; and irrationality of GAAP distorting the reported financial results have also been proved to be obstacles on the way to develop accounting standards strictly on the basis of accounting logic.

11.5.1 Ambiguity in Accounting Rules

Considerable judgement is required to pinpoint exactly when revenue has been earned, e.g., if customer takes delivery of the product but makes payments on it over several years. Revenue may be recognized to be realized on delivery or alternatively, the seller may consider the customer's ability to pay for commitment in future. But the latter option becomes complex if the customer dies before making full payment.

Judgement is also required to determine what constitutes revenue at different situations, e.g., when the seller is an auctioneer and earns commission in his business. In such case, the seller can treat the total sale proceed as revenue and the amount paid to the original owner as an expense. He can also count only the commission as revenue and show no expense. However, for disclosure of sales growth, the seller may adopt the first approach. Another example shows that there is lack of clarity in revenue recognition rules to determine revenue in an efficient logistic arrangement for a product which is to be shipped directly from the manufacturer to the customer. It is to be decided whether the sale price of the product should be taken as revenue or only the profit from the logistic arrangement. The decision tends to be more judgemental if the product is damaged in shipping.

Standards are not free from ambiguity regarding treatment of (i) Purchase of assets not for direct business purposes but for sale at a discount in future to the related companies or shareholders; (ii) Writing off loans to friendly parties in order to move corporate cash to the particular selected parties; (iii) Sale of products with discount or above market price to the related parties to transfer funds between them.

11.5.2 Latitude Given to Corporate Managers

Latitude is given to the companies to make either excess or short provision in accounts for uncertain future costs like product returns and bad debts, damages from product recalls, restructuring costs, obsolescence of inventory, etc. With the help of such latitude, companies can create hidden reserves so that the future profits are boosted, or they can diminish current provisions to raise current profits. Managers are allowed to take 'big bath' strategy to show large restructuring costs so as to flush out any probable impact on profits in future.

A variety of gains and losses are there whose true impact on profits is not yet certain and irreversible like: (i) Gains or losses from translation of financial statements of subsidiaries from local currencies to parent companies' currencies; (ii) Gains and losses from fluctuations in prices of financial securities invested. These gains and losses are allowed to be included in 'comprehensive income' appearing in shareholders' equity section in balance sheet, or reflected in the income statement.

Latitude is given to managements for purposeful revision of the estimates of useful life of depreciable assets. Such revisions create doubts about true desire of management—(i) is the adjustment made for any real change in useful life of the asset; (ii) is the revision made only to match competitor's accounting method; (iii) is there some other motivating factor?

11.5.3 Wide Variety in Disclosure Requirement of the Related-party Transactions

One of the objectives of standard setting is to enable the investors to benchmark the performance of a business against prior periods, budgets, domestic and global competitors. Performance comparisons require an understanding of how profits and assets are measured in domestic and foreign companies. However, Sherman and Young (2001) observed wide variety in financial reporting standards from country to country in relation to frequency, detail and audit requirements. Hence there may be an obstacle for standard setting in countries where regulation is poor over related-party transactions and their disclosure in financial statements. Standard setters of these countries find it difficult to reduce within the countries the differences in practices and disclosures that create misleading financial impression among competitors. This has been a field for potential manipulation by companies that are subsidiaries of the US and West European companies or by those companies that are being considered for merger or acquisition.

11.5.4 Irrationality of GAAP

Company managements may be asked to follow a number of irrational accounting rules due to which their financial results are distorted (Basu 1998). Some of the prevailing irrational accounting policies are mentioned here.

1. Companies are not allowed to revalue their long-term debts when there is significant difference between their market value and face value. The carrying value of corporate bonds issued at a fixed rate of interest shall have a steep fall if the market rate of interest rises much higher than the rate of interest applicable to such bonds. Companies obviously shall take the opportunity for liquidating these bonds in the market at a very low price. This is a cost-advantage enjoyed by the bond-selling company over its competitors. It tilts the balance in bond-market. But the prevailing accounting rules do not permit a company to adjust the carrying value of bonds to reflect fluctuations in market rate of interest.
2. In 1977, the US FASB issued SFAS 15: Accounting for Troubled Debt Restructurings. The standard conditionally exempted the banks and savings and loan institutions from writing down the loan receivables in balance sheet, i.e., recognizing the loss from bad loans in the published financial statements. The condition for such exemption was that the total cash flows receivable after restructuring of the troubled debts should not be less than the current balance in the loan receivable account. During the period of high interest rates, the banks had to accommodate their defaulting borrowers by reducing interest rates and/or extending the repayment periods and with the help of the accounting rule, the banks—which effectively became insolvent, could project apparent solvency in their balance sheets. Hence, the standard obscured the picture of the economic reality and quite deepened the financial crisis faced by banks and savings & loan institutions.
3. The US FASB issued SFAS 12: Accounting for Marketable Securities in 1975. The standard determined two separate places for disclosure of unrecognized holding gains/losses on current and non-current marketable equity securities. The accumulated gains and losses were ascertainable from the readily available market prices of both the current and non-current equity securities. The standard required the companies to include the gains and losses on current securities in earnings; but allowed the companies to park such gains and losses on non-current securities in shareholders' equity. Thus, the standard did not reflect the revaluations of the long-term marketable equity securities in earnings.
4. During periods of continuing inflation, the historical cost accounting method of valuation of assets understates the values of assets and consequently values of equities as well. Still then,

the prevailing accounting rules do not permit the companies to adjust their accounts for the effects of inflation. Owing to this serious drawback of current accounting rules, the published accounts fail to disclose the true gearing position of a company.

5. The traditional transaction approach of the historical cost accounting system fails to recognize the self-generated intangible assets like goodwill, brand name, management-team effort, etc. in balance sheet. These assets are recognized in books of accounts only if these are acquired from other parties at a cost. Managers often take the chance of manipulation of financial numbers with the help of this anomaly.
6. The total cost of production of a period is divided between cost of goods sold and closing stock of unsold goods. As per the prevailing system of accounting, this division can be made using any of the three basic methods for inventory valuation: Average cost, first-in first-out (FIFO), last-in first-out (LIFO). But the measures produced by the three methods will significantly differ from each other if cost of production changes rapidly over time. This is a critical situation for both the companies and the standard setters. The companies are directed to follow a procedure consistently. The standard setters are unable to stop the companies applying smart devices in order to adjust the procedures from period to period. But the key factor is the rapid change in cost of production over which neither the company nor the standard setter has any control.
7. Apart from latitude given to the managements for revision of useful life of depreciable assets, the 'most serious difficulty with depreciation is that no allocation method (straight line method, diminishing balance method, etc) is fully defensible' (Hendriksen and Breda 1992: 524), and 'depreciation computation involves a great degree of arbitrariness' (Naser 1993: 110). It provides temptation for switching from one method to another in order to charge desired amount of depreciation against revenue.
8. 'Goodwill is the difference between the value of an investment in a business and those assets of the business that happen to be separately identified and valued', (Pearce 1994: 97). This definition recognizes goodwill only when it is acquired along with other assets from the vendor. But controversy is there about how goodwill should be accounted for in the published company accounts. The efforts of the standard setting bodies for developing a single approach for accounting of goodwill have all been unsuccessful. This is mainly because there is no demonstrable method to ascertain the useful life of goodwill. How long the economic benefits will accrue from goodwill is highly uncertain. Sometimes, accounting bodies have argued that any goodwill (whether purchased or self-generated) should not at all be recognized in accounts. However, at present, the method of accounting of purchased goodwill leans heavily upon the desire of managers. They can write off goodwill immediately against reserves or over its useful economic life or carry it at cost without making any amortization on the plea that its economic life cannot be determined.
9. As in case of goodwill, there is a controversy regarding method of accounting for research & development (R&D) expenditures. It is difficult for many R&D activities to measure the expected future benefits. Sometimes those activities may be entirely futile. AS 8 of Institute of CAs of India (ICAI) mandated that only those R&D expenditures are to be capitalized that have created fixed assets. It indicates if there is lack of evidence of a direct relationship between R&D activities and specific future revenues, the R&D costs should be expensed when

incurred. But the matter of producing evidence is related not with the rule making power of the accounting bodies, but the discretion of company managements with regard to the choice of treatment of R&D costs.

10. Worldwide, the standard setting bodies are seriously concerned with methods for recognition, measurement and accounting of provisions. Standard setters from the UK, the USA, Australia, Canada and the IASC jointly published in 1995 a collaborative study on provisions. The joint study was a sign of the development of an international standard on provisions. The study formulated detailed proposals on recognition, measurement and accounting for provisions (UK Accounting Standards Board 1995). The matter has become serious because as per the prevailing accounting rules, companies create provisions not only when there is an obligation to do so, but also when there is intention of the management to incur expenditures in future. The obstacle to standard setting arises from allowing the companies to create provisions on the basis of their intents, which will be utilized for smoothing out profit fluctuations, if any, from period to period.
11. Company managements can use their discretionary power to identify the events and transactions as extraordinary or unusual. The US APB Opinion No. 30 stated that these events and transactions are distinguished by their unusual nature and by the infrequency of their occurrence. The qualitative guidelines for classifying the extraordinary or unusual events and transactions are flexible enough to permit company managements to apply their own judgements. They may want to show as many items of normal trading expenses and losses as extraordinary or infrequent as will be possible under given circumstances and make separate accounting for them. On the contrary, the unusual revenues and gains may be included in normal operating flows.
12. The cost of interest on loans taken for acquiring fixed assets can either be treated as cost of financing, or capitalized as part of cost of the asset. Company managements may decide as per their discretion how and when the borrowing costs will be capitalized. After capitalization, on a subsequent time, the borrowing can also be eliminated from the respective asset accounts on the plea that it will not be possible to recover the borrowing costs out of net cash flows of the asset in future. SFAS No. 34, 1979, set out the conditions under which capitalization of borrowing costs would be permitted. However, the US SEC placed a moratorium on capitalization of borrowing costs in new areas prior to this FASB standard. But SFAS 34 rescinded the moratorium.
13. Accounting standards have been issued in the UK, the USA, Canada, Australia and other countries also requiring capitalization of finance leases in the books of lessee. But in most of these countries, companies have been given latitude to structure the lease transactions in such a manner so that they need not satisfy the criteria that would require lease capitalization in balance sheet.
14. Ijiri (1975) proposed that the executory (unperformed) contracts can be recognized not only on the basis of present performance but also on the basis of commitment. He argued for extension of the transaction-recognition criteria from performance basis to commitment basis. However, the current accounting system exempts the companies to recognize the rights and obligations created by contracts that are less than half-executed.

11.5.5 An Example of Dependence of the Standard Setter on Historical Values

While discussing the political sensitivity of two American standards: SFAS 19—Oil & Gas Accounting and SFAS 8—Foreign Currency Translation, Solomons (1986) raised the following arguments:

Both standards were based on historical cost accounting and hence produced information that was deficient in relevance and representational faithfulness. Historical values were used instead of current values to provide information about assets, liabilities and results of operations. The latter could make the information more relevant. Similarly, the historical costs were taken for conversion into dollars at historical rates, instead of taking current costs and using current rates for conversion. The latter would provide more reliable and more faithfully represented financial conditions at the balance sheet date. Another deficiency of using historical values is that matching is made of costs and revenues separated by a time lag that extends to several months for inventories and several years for depreciable assets. But current cost numbers would be more reliable as they would match costs and revenues of the same current date.[3]

11.6 How Accounting Credibility May Suffer?

The task of providing 'best' standards for a society is associated mainly with three problems: (i) Conflicting interests of managers and shareholders; (ii) Under-production of accounting information because it is a 'public good'; (iii) Convergence of interests of the regulated parties having unified viewpoint and the regulatory body having need to survive.

11.6.1 Analysis of Conflicting Interests of Managers and Shareholders

The conflicting interests of managers and shareholders can be analysed on the basis of arguments for voluntary financial reporting and mandatory financial reporting.

11.6.2 Voluntary Financial Reporting Arguments

1. **Agency theory arguments:** The arguments against regulation of financial reporting, i.e., the arguments in favour of unregulated markets for accounting information, consider the incentives for reliable and voluntary reporting to the owners and capital markets. One of the incentives for voluntary disclosure of information to the capital market as suggested by 'Agency Theory' is that it improves firm's ability to raise capital. Even in absence of mandatory financial reporting requirements, the extensive, reliable, voluntary reporting to the capital market would reduce the firm's investment risk and cost of capital.[4] Capital is referred to here as risk capital and the term 'owners' in Agency Theory includes both debenture holders and stockholders (Jensen and Meckling 1976).
2. **Avoiding the information risk by quality reporting:** One of the free-market arguments says that the competitive pressure for capital induces the firms to report information about them. They cannot impose monopolistic prices for information; rather they have to report

freely in order to attract capital and to lower their cost of capital by being perceived as good reporting firms. The argument is that where there is perceived information risk due to poor quality reporting, investors require higher rate of return to compensate the additional risk that they think they are taking.

3. **Voluntary reporting initiatives taken by firms:** Voluntary reporting initiatives taken by good, moderate and bad performance firms (Ross 1979) can be summarized that in order to maintain continued investor interest in the firm, a firm of good performance and a firm of moderate performance, both will adopt the voluntary reporting practice. Since failure to report would be interpreted as bad news, a firm with neutral result would also like to disclose its performance to avoid being suspected of having bad result. And a firm of bad performance would also disclose its result in order to maintain its credibility in a competitive capital market. Ross (1979) remarked that the mandatory reporting requirements have not made any improvement in quality of the securities offered for public subscription since the mandated requirements were already being fulfilled on a voluntary basis.
4. **Avoiding more direct administrative regulation and control:** The concern of the US SEC towards the need for fair financial reporting and investor protection was severely criticized by Merino and Niemark (1982). They underrated the role performed by SEC by showing in an analysis that the US corporate community did accept disclosure and accounting regulation just to avoid more direct administrative regulation and control. Merino and Niemark observed that the politicians also did not think more than the accounting reforms in the belief that such regulatory reforms shall increase competition and reduce economic concentration. They opined that changes brought about by the Securities Acts have already been failed. The failure is to meet the real underlying need for corporate financial reporting regulation.
5. **Private contracting opportunities:** Another reason for having an unregulated market for financial information may be the private contracting opportunities. It is argued that any information not reported voluntarily could be obtained through private contracting. In a stock market, not only securities are traded, but also financial information. Investor-newsletters and investment-advices from the brokerage firms are the available pay-channels for private information. If information is truly desired beyond that, it is publicly available at free of cost, any party can get it by making private contracts with the firm itself or with the firm's owners, or indirectly with the information intermediaries such as stock analysts. Thus, this argument discards the necessity of mandatory disclosure rules. It suggests that the demand for financial information is optimally met when free market forces determine the production (supply) and disclosure of accounting information.

11.6.3 Mandatory Financial Reporting Arguments

After reviewing the arguments for voluntary reporting, the pro-regulation arguments are now being focussed. The arguments for regulation of financial reporting maintain that: (i) It prevents monopoly pricing for information supplies; (ii) It prevents failure of financial reporting and auditing too to protect public interest; and (iii) Deregulation is contrary to social goals.

1. **Benefits of mandatory public disclosure:** The business firms are monopoly suppliers of information about themselves restricting production of information, i.e., under reporting,

and charging monopolistic prices that could be viewed as market failure. On the other hand mandatory public disclosure would result in more information at a lower cost to the society. So it will be cheaper to the society to require mandatory free disclosure, rather than to have all investors privately contracting for the same information and paying higher monopolistic prices.

2. **Public interest argument:** Financial reporting has to protect public interest. It fails to do that when accounting and auditing standards are poor and the corporate financial statements or audit reports do not signal frauds and failures in advance. Hence in order to improve quality of financial reporting, extensive and better regulation is necessary. This will raise the confidence level of investors in the fairness of capital markets; they will take better investment decisions and it will lead to optimal capital allocation. However, there is a counterargument to the notion that a competitive capital market always produces reliable voluntary reporting. If capital market is competitive in nature, it provides an incentive for misleading reporting, at least in the short run. Managers are tempted to manipulate reporting in short term because they do not pay penalty for poor or misleading reporting. It also implies that the owners have not developed good mechanisms for monitoring agency contracts with the managers. Although the frauds and failures by themselves do not necessarily mean failure of corporate reporting system and investment risks cannot be totally eliminated as because risk is inherent to investment still then the increased regulation of financial reporting may reduce the likelihood of undetected frauds and failures.

When financial reporting is to be regulated to achieve social goals, it becomes a public interest argument and it involves a normative judgement about how society ought to allocate its resources. At this juncture, we can identify a paradox of regulation creating an obstacle to standard setting. The contradiction is being created because:

(i) The self-interested groups are allowed to involve in the deliberations for the sake of legitimacy of the regulatory process and a standard setting body for its political survival essentially adopts this method of operation. To a regulating body, more important may be how regulation is being conducted than what actual decisions it makes. In order to make standard setting a due process, in a democratic society, all parties—affected by standards are given opportunity to have input in to the standard setting process. Accounting policy-making cannot be neutral and apolitical as expected by Armstrong (1977) and Kirk (1978) but inevitably political because of its regulatory nature according to Horngren (1976) and Solomons (1978).

(ii) **Public interest not exactly known:** Although it is advocated that accounting regulation is undertaken in public interest, there is no criterion for determining what accounting policy will maximize the public interest. And what do we mean by 'public interest' is not exactly known due to impossibility to measure aggregate social preferences. These two factors have made standard setting a political process as much as an economic process. It is observed that individuals and groups are motivated to lobby for their vested interests, to form coalition with other groups to strengthen further their intervening influence over the standard setting process and to use the political system to their advantage.

(iii) **The impossibility to know social preferences:** A free market of voluntary reporting may fail to achieve the goal of utilization of resources to maximize social welfare. When the firms under-produce accounting information, treated as public good, the free reporting system fails and the standard setting becomes justified. But the paradox of regulation is that the problem unresolved in a deregulated market cannot also be solved optimally in a codified system of accounting regulation. This is explained with the help of Impossibility Theorem of Arrow (1963). In a free-market pricing system, the aggregate social preferences are revealed indirectly through supply/demand equilibrium and the resources are allocated according to the market prices. Once the free-market system is discarded, there is no means to determine aggregate social preferences and since there is no comparable rule in a regulated market, it becomes impossible to know if accounting standards are producing optimal quantity and quality of financial reporting (Demski 1973). The impossibility to know social preferences creates another problem of standards overload. Accounting information being of public good nature is overproduced in a regulated market due to its overstated demand. The real demand or preference for accounting information is over-projected because it is normally subsidized or even costless. Over-production of accounting information tends to create the problem of standards overload. A standard setting body can easily be misguided about the level of real demand for new or alternative accounting policies over-projected by the users since they do not directly pay for it. FASB paid more attention in this area particularly because it affects smaller and non-publicly traded companies; and consequently some closely held firms have been exempted by FASB from supplementary disclosures.[5]

(iv) **Social desirability of mandatory reporting:** Mandatory reporting is desirable on social grounds because it creates fairness of the capital market. The more public information is there (and the less that is private), the less wealth transfers between those who have information and those who do not.[6] Investors will spend less for they have not to buy private information. It saves waste of social resources because everyone has not to buy the same private information about firms. Production cost of mandatory public requirements is also quite small because most of the basic information is produced as a by-product of internal accounting system (Hakansson 1977).

The next issue raised is who bears the cost of producing free public disclosure. This is more significant if the cost is high. Firms will either absorb or pass on regulation costs to the consumers.

There are incentives for voluntary reporting. From the other angle, the focus of accounting regulation that could be kept on mandatory reporting has been mainly on improving the quality of accounting information. Accounting regulation is mainly concerned with refining and unifying the rules of recognition and measurement used in preparation of financial statements. If regulation is needed, the codification philosophy justifies the process of standard setting, though it does not guarantee that the output of the regulation process is always optimal. The accounting standards produced by the codification system can be evaluated on the basis of whether they provide information to the users at reasonable cost and if they fail, they can be amended. Hence, the attitude of the codification system has to be open-minded and satisfying.

The codification system does not always produce standards, which would necessarily be correct in terms of deductive logic. Quite surprisingly the pro-regulation arguments are largely deductively articulated, because very little is known about the costs and benefits of accounting regulation. On the other hand, the arguments for unregulated market are also deductive in nature, because empirical tests of the free-market position are rather difficult in a regulated environment.

All these imply that the accounting regulation requires a theoretical foundation—given that it is mainly the quality of information, which is being regulated. The lack of theoretical foundation was directly responsible for collapse of the Committee on Accounting Principles (CAP) and Accounting Principles Board (APB) as standard setting body. By contrast, FASB has developed a conceptual framework as the basis for standard setting.

11.6.4 Public Good Concept of Accounting Data

May and Sundem (1976) have advanced the idea that accounting information is a 'public good' that can be utilized by one without reducing the opportunity for its utilization by others. Accounting information can be freely passed from person to person; each person can consume the content of the information. This idea is true only in a regulated market. In an unregulated system, firms are not concerned to supply more information to meet the true market demand. It is because in an unregulated reporting system, the firms are not able to impose the cost of information on all users of information. Some people are able to utilize the financial data without paying any cost. They are called 'free riders'.

The modern financial disclosure system imposes costs on companies rather than on users of information. If it is assumed that the companies are able to recover the cost of producing information indirectly from the customers of their products or services, it shows one consequence of accounting regulation that there is wealth transfer from the non-users to the users of accounting information, i.e., the users get the benefits of free information while the non-users implicitly pay for the costs of producing such information. This means the cost of free riders is to be borne by the society as a whole if there is financial reporting regulation to meet the public demand. This is not a fair consequence of financial reporting regulation.

Owing to the failure of voluntary reporting system, the public good concept of accounting information happens to be appropriate only under codified accounting regulation. However, when there is a failure or abandonment of a free market, it becomes impossible to know whether resources are used optimally.[7]

11.6.5 Issue of Survival of a Standard Setting Body

The existence of a financial reporting standard setting body depends primarily on the quality of the due process in determination of its rules and on the nature of convergence of interests of the standard setting body itself and the interests of various interest groups of users of accounting information.

11.6.6 Due Process in Determination of Accounting Rules

The regulatory nature is associated with the issue of survival of the regulating body. Here comes the question of having an appropriate structure to ensure survival of the standard setting body. Its authority to regulate should be strong and legitimacy should persist in allowing the parties affected or would be affected, in deliberations. The two AICPA committees—CAP and APB—could not survive because they had only weak mandate to regulate financial reporting. Standard setting by these two private sector bodies was not officially endorsed by the US SEC prior to issue of Accounting Series Release (ASR) 150 in 1973. A tacit arrangement was made to provide SEC a shield from the political pressure of actually determining accounting policies except when it was expedient to do so.[8] Watts and Zimmermann (1978) expressed the view that SEC was in a position to use the private sector standard setter as a scapegoat if the US Congress were to challenge the work of SEC.

The point of weak regulatory authority of AICPA was coupled with lack of due process in its determining accounting rules. For this reason also, the affected parties did not accept those rules to any good extent. AICPA permitted a closed-door approach for policy making till late in the life of APB. Just before its death, APB started to gather informal facts and solicit views of interested parties. Throughout 1960s the accounting profession thought that the closed-door policy-making was a good approach to insulate the process from outside influence. But the functioning of the FASB has been much more successful than the AICPA committees. It has got its standards officially endorsed by SEC in ASR 150. It has got an organizational structure conducive for the mechanism of due process that is not a closed-door activity of identifying the normative accounting standards. Rather, the approach of FASB has been to achieve consensus through debates and evaluations of accounting standards by the affected parties.

The decision making under a due process may be extremely slow. Arrow (1963) referred to this tendency as 'democratic paralysis'. However, so long an egalitarian standard setting process does not serve the special-interest-groups to the detriment of the society as a whole, it is hopefully said that accounting standard setting produces net social benefit. But this cannot be conclusively asserted because there is paucity of hard evidence to support arguments either for or against standard setting due process.

11.6.7 Convergence of Interests of Regulated Parties and Regulator

An accounting rule shall no longer exist if a vested interest group captures standard setting. Capture Theory (Stigler 1971) argues that the group being regulated eventually comes to use the regulatory process to promote its own special interest. The report of Metcalf Committee of the US Senate, 1977 and Moss Committee of the US House of Representatives, 1976, alleged that the US accounting system was captured by Big Eight group of accounting firms which were predominant auditors of publicly listed companies and by this way this group occupied a large stake in the accounting regulation game. CAP and APB were heavily influenced by the Big Eight accounting firms, and after the recommendation of Metcalf Committee and Moss Committee, AICPA was restructured to lessen Big Eight dominance and to increase self-regulation by AICPA.

According to Life-Cycle Theory of Regulation (Bernstein 1955) although regulation starts with public-interest objective, after several phases, eventually it becomes an instrument for protecting the regulated group from competition. It becomes impossible for the regulator to remain truly independent because for its survival its policies are to be accepted by the group being regulated. Hence, both parties come to see that their interests converge.

Capture Theory and Life Cycle Theory cannot be applied to financial reporting because regulation of financial reporting and regulation of other industrial groups are not of same character.

The number of parties directly affected by accounting standards is much larger and diverse than in other regulated industries. That large number of affected parties shall have divergence of interests and as a result, the accounting regulator will remain in a more naturally neutral position than is possible for regulators of other industries. However, this is an expression about the codified accounting regulation as a whole, but not an analysis of the impact of specific standards prescribed individually. In the latter case, the number of affected parties would be small enough as in case of another single regulated industry. Hence, the key obstacle for independent standard setting is convergence of interests of the regulated parties having unified viewpoint and the regulatory body for its survival. Watts and Zimmermann (1978) found that the group of Big Eight firms could not dominate FASB's standard setting process as (i) FASB was independent; (ii) the Big Eight group did not have a unified viewpoint amongst the firms; and (iii) decision making at the FASB was pluralistic.

11.7 Complication from Reflexive Intervention by Capital Market in Standard Setting

This feature can be verified from the analyses of (i) capital market association of the accounting numbers, (ii) the power of predictive ability of the accounting method and (iii) use of capital market researches for standard setting.

11.7.1 Market Association Test of Representational Faithfulness of Accounting Numbers

Supplying accounting information and impounding that to security prices are two sides of the same coin. Hence the accounting numbers have to represent the economic reality of the enterprise that is seen by a capital market. This can be done by choice of accounting method for generating income numbers closely associated with security prices.

A closer association of accounting numbers and security prices proves the representational faithfulness of the accounting method. But cost of providing information is involved in the choice from amongst alternative reporting methods and the market can already obtain the information at lower cost from other sources (Beaver 1973). While the standard setter has to decide about representational faithfulness of a reporting method weighed against the cost of its producing data, there are examples when the requirement as per standard is different from what the capital market appears to treat. For example, R&D expenditure is mandatorily expensed as per FASB's SFAS No. 2, but the capital market appears to treat the expenditure as an asset with future economic benefits. This is evident from the fact that the changes in earnings for expensing R&D, which do not make any change in cash flows, do not affect share prices (Dukes 1976). Similarly, SFAS 13 required capitalization of certain leases in balance sheet, but it appeared to produce no significant market reaction (Martin et al. 1979).[9]

11.7.2 Independent Impact of Relevant Financial Information on Security Prices

Financial statements are widely used in lending decisions in a capital market. Accounting information can impress or depress stock prices and consequently can raise or lower credit rating and encourage or discourage the lender from wishing to lend. A capital market uses accounting information for allocation of financial resources.[10] However, one difficulty in standard setting is that as long as relevant information is disclosed, its impact on security prices seems to be independent of whether or not the information has any impact on earnings shown in financial statements. For example, while the Insurance Company stocks were valued by the market after treating the unrealized gains and losses of such securities as incomes, those unrealized items were not at all recognized in accounting (Foster 1977).

Capital market operations can significantly influence the standard setting process and its outcome and often create obstacles to move forward with accounting logic. A capital market, by its reaction to new information (i.e., the information not contained in past pattern of market prices) tells the accounting standard setter what it thinks is important and what it ignores. In a capital market, the accounting information is rapidly as well as fully impounded in security prices. For a major part of the capital markets in a highly developed economy like USA, prices reflect fully and without bias all publicly available information. At the same time, false information are also impounded as readily as correct information if there is no reason to believe it is false.

To a capital market what is disclosed is much more important than how it is disclosed.[11] Accounting non-issues, i.e., non-accounting social and political issues may also be significant to the capital market (Dyckman and Morse 1975) and hence the questions important to the companies and their accountants may not be considered at all by a capital market. A capital market is least bothered for accounting measurement problems (Solomons 1986). Solomons explained that a capital market sets the accountant free to use any of the alternative measurement methods so long the information is presented in a manner that enables the user to understand the fact and compare the positions, even by sidestepping the measurement problems, or converting one method to another. The accounting measurement problem and the substantive effect of accounting information on security prices, these two can have jurisdictional conflict. This is true because the task of an accounting standard setting body (like FASB) is related with measurement issues, but a security commission (like SEC) is concerned with disclosure issues that may have substantive impact on security prices.

11.7.3 Scope of Accounting Disclosure

Although financial disclosure is all-important, the investors and users are not supplied with 'data dump' from which they can pick up what they want. Solomons (1986) did not consider 'supplying data dump' as an acceptable alternative. Beaver (1976) declared it as an issue that has remained essentially unexamined. Major portion of data is aggregated in financial statements, and owing to this, loss of information might also occur. But income measurement is a useful job and the capital market researches have agreed to conclude that the income numbers and even the earnings forecasts made by managements and financial analysts have information content. The security prices are more closely associated with historical cost earnings numbers than with other performance measures such as cash flow or replacement-cost based income numbers (Foster 1973; May 1971).

Information disclosure must be made in such a way so that the capital market is able to derive the numbers it wants for its resource allocation purpose. According to Solomons (1986: 207) 'The central question of financial reporting has become how to make general purpose financial statements serve the diverse needs of a heterogeneous array of users, with the right balance of aggregation and disaggregation, stopping far short of data dump but going well beyond a mere bottom line'. At this point, it is understood that only a single set of financial statements cannot satisfy the information requirement of everyone equally and that is why the capital market researchers are mostly against mandating single set of numbers for everybody.

11.7.4 Power of Predictive Ability

Apart from representational faithfulness, the accounting method of measurement should possess predictive power (Beaver et al. 1968; Carsberg et al. 1977). The decision-usefulness parameter of an accounting method is judged by its predictive ability test because usefulness is compounded of relevance and reliability; and predictive value is an important factor of relevance. The relative predictive power of two or more alternative methods is to be measured. This proposal does not claim that the best predictions shall always lead to the best decisions because there are other factors and although all accounting are decision oriented, what is the best decision cannot be known without knowing a good deal about probable outcome of the decision.

Following are the other obstacles in using predictive value criterion in choosing the accounting method:

1. Many accounting measures are used for non-predictive purposes like accountability and reporting on stewardship.
2. One accounting method provides accounting input into a prediction model in a better way than the other method. Now, if different businesses use different models, they may well favour different accounting methods. This has been an important factor leading to proliferation of accounting methods where standards and other regulations permit them.

The broad criterion for selecting an accounting method is that accounting information should be useful for making decisions. In this context, the very fact that predictions lead to decisions shall mean that the purpose of a prediction is often to change an outcome in a desired way.

11.7.5 Capital Market Researches for Standard Setting

Accounting standard setting is aided by empirical researches on capital market, but they failed to give us a set of standards. Solomons (1986: 209) states one reason for this lapse as mere survey of current practices regarding any particular accounting problem and then selecting the majority practice (if there are different practices) for its approval by the standard setting body would not discharge it from its responsibility of standard setting. This is because any subjective unreliable research evidence is concerned with 'what is', but a standard is concerned with 'what should be'. If standards are set empirically, it will mean that a practice is declared to be 'right' because it was 'generally accepted', but it is not generally accepted as it was 'right'.

Empirical researches can provide descriptive information about: (i) How business decisions are taken and what information are used for taking those decisions; (ii) Impact of current standards on business behaviour and the probable effect (anticipated by implication) on business behaviour of a standard that is yet to be issued; (iii) Opinion of various interest groups on the actual and potential standards.

Thus, the result of research is only about assumptions upon which a standard may be based. But to get from assumptions to a standard, judgement is to be made about what kind of accounting is desirable, for whom it is desirable and who shall make the judgement that shall prevail. Hakansson (1978: 720) wanted normative model for the society to decide about desirability of accounting standards because, 'An empirical study per se can only yield descriptive knowledge. Desirability, in the public policy sense, is a strictly legal proposition and can only be evaluated in a normative model with a full set of assumptions including a posited criterion of "goodness".' May and Sundem (1976: 762) said, 'With our present state of technology in accounting research, there is no research method that will identify the most desirable accounting policy alternative. Nor is there any great likelihood that such a method will emerge, given the social choice dimension of accounting policy making.'

There is a wide gap that divides empirical findings from social policy. Kaplan (1978: 162) expressed as 'Preferences for alternative information systems ultimately require an analysis of social welfare considerations which cannot be decided merely by stock price associations. On a practical basis, accountants attempting to generate measures that have maximum association with market prices would eventually be driven to define accounting income as the change in market value over the period.'

Notes

1. With the objective to achieve uniformity, the uniform accounting system (UAS) typically consists of a chart of accounts and some rigid formats of financial statements applicable to all business entities in an industry or across all industries. To provide guidance, a UAS also normally explains how accounts are applied to typical economic transactions and how the financial statements are prepared.

2. The principle of prudence was thought in China as a source of manipulation for the interests of capitalists. The perception that it was a tool of capitalist exploitation was reinforced by numerous class struggle movements commissioned by people of China between 1950s and 1980s. The Maoist class struggle ideology was persisting and the UAS was adopted from the Chinese government's macroeconomic concerns. In China, the concept of conservatism or prudence has been included as a basic principle of financial reporting only in Accounting Standards for Business Enterprises (ASBE), 1992 because there was a fear that adoption of prudence principle and manufacturing costing in ASBE would reduce government revenues. The Finance Departments of the Ministry of Finance (MOF) did not agree till 1992 that the principle of prudence would not affect government's revenues in the long run. However, the enterprise accounting system (EAS) has been made compulsory only for the listed and unlisted joint stock companies. A remark of an academic contained in the analysis of Xiao et al. (2004), has clarified the attitude of Ministry of Finance, 'The main reason is that the Enterprise Accounting System is so conservative that a broadened scope of application would "create" more loss-making companies. Nobody in China can bear this additional loss'.

3. Solomons (1986: 224–228, 238) found one reason for not using the current values in place of historical values. That reason is the possible loss of verifiability that might result from the alleged greater subjectivity of the current cost numbers. But he anticipated that the gain from representational faithfulness would more than outweigh the loss of verifiability of the

accounting numbers. The argument has been extended with reference to Full Costing Method and Successful Efforts Method of Oil & Gas accounting, both of which were merely cost allocation methods. These methods could not faithfully represent the performance of oil & gas producing companies because they ignored the results obtained from the expenditures being allocated. But accounting is really meant for performance measurement. 'The measurement of changes in proved reserves, especially in value terms, is admittedly fraught with great difficulty, so that reliable performance measures using methods such as Reserve Recognition Accounting are elusive. But the accounting methods currently in use do not solve the problem either; they simply run away from it by leaving the value of reserves, except to the extent that they are represented by capitalized expenditures, off the balance sheet entirely. That kind of accounting simply turns its back on economic reality. Supplementary disclosures about reserves, now provided under SFAS No. 69 outside the financial statements, are better than nothing. But their very position outside the statements is an admission of the deficiencies of GAAP accounting'.

4. Agency Theory says that a firm is a nexus (i.e., an intersection) where an agency relationship is established mainly between owners and managers. Managers are hired by owners of a firm to administer its activities. Managers are agents of the owners. These two groups have potentially conflicting goals; owners are interested in maximizing the return on investments and managers in their compensation. Owners try to contract with managers in such a way as to minimize this conflict. Managers too want to keep the 'agency monitoring costs' as low as possible, by not being in conflict with owners, because such costs reduce their compensation. For this purpose, managers are motivated to make routine and reliable financial reporting to the owners. Accountants refer to this traditional type of reporting as stewardship or accountability to the owners of a firm. The managers are judged and rewarded by how well they report. When the owners perceive the accounting reports as reliable, the reputation of a manager is enhanced, agency monitoring costs are reduced and the manager is compensated with higher benefits.

5. In order to avoid the problem of standards overload, the non-purchasers must be debarred from using the public good accounting information. A provision should be kept so that only the purchasers can use accounting news. The financial reports of companies can be required to be filed with securities exchange or other like body and users can be asked to purchase copies of information. If this is done, the purchasers will not be motivated to pass on the information to the free riders.

6. This principle is behind regulation of 'insider trading' too.

7. Optimal use of resources in a more restrictive sense of pareto-optimality means that someone can gain only if some other one loses. This is an efficiency condition of a pareto-optimal economy. If it is possible to make someone better off at no cost of others, then the existing allocation of resources is inefficient and it involves a waste of resources due to sub-optimality.

8. The challenge raised by SEC on the specific standard on Investment Tax Credit can be referred.

9. While judging representational faithfulness of an accounting policy, the standard setter should remember that the accounting changes which were not mandated by the standard setter and which affected merely earnings, but not cash flows, did not also appear to affect market prices

of securities. For example, the change in method of depreciation from accelerated to straight line (Archibald, T. R., "The Return to Straight Line Depreciation: An Analysis of a Change in Accounting Methods", *Journal of Accounting Research, Empirical Research in Accounting: Selected Studies* (Supplement), 1967, 164–180), or change in treatment of investment tax credit from deferment to flow through (Kaplan, R. and Roll, R., "Investor Evaluation of Accounting Information: Some Empirical Evidence", *Journal of Business*, April 1972, 225–257) did not appear to affect the prices of securities.

10. Informational efficiency alone cannot ensure proper allocation of financial resources. Capital market of a less developed economy is not efficient in either sense. Even in a developed economy, capital market is efficient in respect of only publicly traded securities and it is little known how prices of private securities respond to the new information.

11. The information from audited financial statements are more reliable to the users; and cost of processing the information presented in an orderly manner in financial statements is much less than cost of processing other information.

References

American Institute of Certified Public Accountants (AICPA) (1973). *APB Opinion No. 30*, New York.

Armstrong, M. S. (1977). 'The Politics of Establishing Accounting Standards'. *Journal of February*, pp 76–79.

Arrow, K. (1963). *Social Choice and Individual Values*, John Wiley.

Basu, A. K. (1998). 'Creative Financial Reporting: An Overview'. In *Studies in Finance & Accounting*, Platinum Jubilee Commemorative Volume, Department of Commerce, Calcutta University, pp 166–183.

Beaver, W. H. (1973). 'What Should Be the FASB's Objectives?' *Journal of Accountancy*, August, p 55.

———(1976). 'The Implications of Security Price Research for Disclosure Policy and the Analyst Community'. In A. R. Abdel-Khalik and T. F. Keller (eds.), *Financial Information Requirements for Security Analysis*, Graduate School of Business Administration, Duke University, Durham NC, p 76.

Beaver, W. H., Kennelly, J. W. and Voss, W. M. (1968). 'Predictive Ability as a Criterion for the Evaluation of Accounting Data', *Accounting Review*, October, p 676.

Bernstein, M. H., (1955). *Regulating Business by Independent Commission*. Princeton University Press.

Carsberg, B., Arnold, J. and Hope, A. (1977). 'Predictive Value: A Criterion for Choice of Accounting Method'. In W. T. Baxter and S. Davidson (eds.), *Studies in Accounting*. Institute of CAs in England & Wales, London, pp 403–423.

Demski, J. S. (1973). 'The General Impossibility of Normative Accounting Standards', *The Accounting Review*, October, pp 718–723.

Diggle, G. and Nobes, C. (1994). 'European Rule-making in Accounting: The Seventh Directive as a Case Study'. *Accounting and Business Research*, 24, pp 319–334.

Ding, Y., Stolowy, H. and Tenenhaus, M. (2003). 'Shopping Around for Accounting Practices: The Financial Statement Presentation of French Groups'. *Abacus*, 39(1), February, pp 42–63.

Dukes, R. E. (1976). 'An Investigation of the Effects of Expensing Research & Development Costs on Security Prices', Schiff and Sorter (eds.), *Proceedings of the Conference on Topical Research in Accounting*, New York University Schools of Business, New York, pp 147–193.

Dyckman, T. R. and Morse, D. (1975). *Efficient Capital Markets and Accounting* (1e), Prentice-Hall, Englewood Cliffs, NJ, p 93.

Foster, G. (1973). 'Stock Market Reaction to Estimates of Earnings per Share by Company Officials'. *Journal of Accounting Research*, Spring, pp 25–37.

———(1977). 'Valuation Parameters of Property-Liability Companies'. *Journal of Finance*, June, pp 823–836.

Gaa, J. C. (1988). 'Methodological Foundations of Standard Setting for Corporate Financial Reporting', *Studies in Accounting Research*, American Accounting Association, 28, p 123.

Gandhi, N. M. (1976). *International Journal of Accounting*, spring.

Hakansson, N. H. (1977). 'Interim Disclosure & Public Forecasts: An Economic Analysis & Framework for Choice', *The Accounting Review*, April, pp 396–416.

———(1978). 'Where we are in Accounting: A Review of Statement on Accounting Theory and Theory Acceptance', *Accounting Review*, July, p 720.

Hendriksen, E. S. and Breda, M. F. V. (1992). *Accounting Theory* (5e). IRWIN, p 524.

Horngren, C. T. (1976). 'The Marketing of Accounting Standards'. *Journal of Accountancy*, October, pp 61–66.

Hussein, M. and Ketz, J. (1980). 'Ruling Elites of the FASB: A Study of the Big Eight'. *Journal of Accounting, Auditing and Finance*, 3, pp 354–367.

ICAI (1985). AS 8: *Accounting for Research & Development Costs*. ICAI, New Delhi, India.

Ijiri, Y. (1975). *Theory of Accounting Measurement*, American Accounting Association, p 129.

Jensen, M. and Meckling, W. (1976). 'Theory of the Firm: Managerial Behavior, Agency Costs, and Ownership Structure'. *Journal of Financial Economics*, October, pp 305–360.

Kaplan, R. S. (1978). 'The Information Content of Financial Accounting Numbers: A Survey of Empirical Evidence'. In A. R. Abdel-Khalik and T. F. Keller (eds.), *The Impact of Accounting Research on Practice & Disclosure*, Duke University Press, Durham, NC, p 162.

Kirk, D. J. (1978). 'How to Keep Politics Out of Standard Setting: Making Private Sector Rule-Making Work'. *Journal of Accountancy*, September, pp 92–94.

Martin, J. D., Anderson, P. F. and Keown, A. J. (1979). 'Lease Capitalization and Stock Price Stability: Implications for Accounting'. *Journal of Accounting, Auditing & Finance*, winter, pp 151–163.

May, R. (1971). 'The Influence of Quarterly Earnings Announcements on Investors' Decisions'. *Journal of Accounting Research, Empirical Research in Accounting: Selected Studies*, (Supplement), pp 119–163.

May, R. G. and Sundem, G. L. (1976). 'Research for Accounting Policy: An Overview'. *The Accounting Review*, October, pp 747–763.

Merino, B. D. and Niemark, M. D. (1982). 'Disclosure Regulation & Public Policy: A Sociohistorical Reappraisal'. *Journal of Accounting and Public Policy*, 1, pp 33–57.

Naser, K. (1993). *Creative Financial Accounting*, Prentice-Hall International (UK) Ltd., p 110.

Pearce, C. (1994). 'Wrong in Theory and Wrong in Practice'. *Accountancy*, June, p 97.

Report of the Moss Committee of the US House of Representatives, (The Sub-committee on Oversight & Investigations of the House Committee on Interstate & Foreign Commission) (1976).

Report of the Metcalf Committee of the US Senate, (The Sub-committee on Reports, Accounting & Management of the Senate Committee on Governmental Affairs) (1977).

Ross, S. A. (1979). 'Disclosure Regulation in Financial Markets'. In F. Edwards (ed.), *Issues in Financial Regulation*, McGraw-Hill, pp 177–202.

Sherman, H. D. and Young, S. D. (2001). 'Tread Lightly Through These Accounting Minefields'. *Harvard Business Review*, July–August, pp 129–135.

Solomons, D. (1978). 'The Politicization of Accounting'. *Journal of Accountancy*, November, pp 65–72.

———(1986). *Making Accounting Policy*. Oxford University Press, New York, Oxford, 207, pp 209, 228.

Stigler, G. J. (1971). 'The Theory of Economic Regulation', *Bell Journal of Economics & Management Science*, (Fall), pp 3–21.

UK Accounting Standards Board (1995). *Provisions*, Discussion Paper, London.

Watts, R. L. and Zimmermann, J. L. (1978). 'Toward a Positive Theory of the Determination of Accounting Standards', *The Accounting Review*, January, pp 112–134.

Xiao, J. Z., Weetman, P. and Sun, M. (2004). 'Political Influence and Coexistence of a Uniform Accounting System and Accounting Standards: Recent Developments in China'. *Abacus*, 40(2), June, p 194.

CHAPTER 12

The Philosophical Aspects of Accounting Ethics

Radhanath Pyne

ABSTRACT

The repeated occurrence of accounting irregularities made the accounting scholars to think about its ethicality, mainly during the last 20 years. Searching the root of the problem leads mainly towards its ethical foundation and the moral philosophies on which the ethical judgements are delivered. Efforts are also rendered to analyse the ways through which the conflicts are negotiated with the help of individual ethics which may not be equally compatible with the organizational ethics. Ethical disposition towards the stakeholders are also considered a point of imbalance in respect to protect one's own individual ethics. The major thrust is executed to understand the change in behavioural pattern of the accounting and auditing personnel in this consumer-culture oriented post-modern society. As accounting ethics is a part of professional ethics, the controlling role of professional bodies is questioned in the environment of financial failures arising out of irrational behaviour of accounting and auditing personnel. This paper is broadly divided into four parts. Different ethical theories and alignment of accounting ethics with its branches are dealt in the first part whereas the second part covers the applied areas along with the ethical treatment of the organization towards its stakeholders. The third part covers specifically the theories of moral behaviour as they relate to an individual who performs the role of an accountant or auditor. The fourth part develops a linkage of ethical intuition and accounting and finance. It also describes the role of steep consumerism as one of the major stimuli to germinate the unethical intuitions among the accountants. In the conclusion, an outline is provided as to the steps to be adopted to curb such unethical behaviour of the accountants for which it is necessary to measure the departure from the standard and the means of techniques to be followed to control the situation.

12.1 Ethical Theories and Accounting Ethics

Before studying the accounting and its relation with ethical theories, it will not be irrelevant to track the development of the different kinds of ethical concepts till date. Ethics is studied in three ways.

The normative way, which deals with the traditional approach, asks what is right and what is wrong. The descriptive way that is a form of anthropology that compares ethical beliefs without making value judgment and the meta-ethics which is a twentieth century approach that explores the meaning of ethical language such as 'good', 'bad', 'right' and 'wrong'. Normative ethical theories are again divided into two parts—deontological theories according to which acts are judged as intrinsically right or wrong and teleological theories through which the consequences determine the goodness of actions.

Ethics are also studied on the basis of absolutism and relativism. Absolutists believe in moral truths that are fixed for all times and all people. They believe that goodness itself exists beyond this world (Plato 5th–4th century BCE) in a divine law (Acquinas 1273), in a fixed part of a concrete universe (Bradley 1927). The relativists believe that moral truth varies depending on culture, time, place and religion. According to them, there is no fixed objective for moral reality; rather, it varies subject to the culture, religion, time and place.

There is a school that handles ethics with the natural moral law. Aristotle (4th century BCE) wrote that 'the natural is that which everywhere is equally valid. The Romanian lawyer Cicero (1841) in his book *On the Republic* wrote, 'true law is right reason in agreement with nature'. Thomas Aquinas (1273) in his natural moral law established it as a theory of absolutist and deontological which means that it is focused on the ethicacy of actions. But natural moral law should not be confused with ethical naturalism. Naturalists believe moral truths are facts like numbers or chemical properties. Naturalists believe that moral conclusions can be deduced from non-moral perceptions. We convert our sensual experiences to a logical premise and then draw our ethical conclusions. Such naturalistic theory is criticized by Moore (1903) by asserting that moral judgements are based on an infallible instinctive knowledge of good things. According to him 'good' is indefinable, because it is a simple idea. Complex ideas can be broken down into smaller ideas but a simple idea is not easily defined.

Influenced by David Hume, who believed that the sentiment was the source of right or wrong, two contributors, Ayer (1963; 1959) and Stevenson (1937; 1938; 1945) laid down the 'emotivism' in ethics. Ayer emphasized on verifying the knowledge in logical positivist way which excluded the possibility of moral facts. He emphasized that ethical statements and moral judgements are emotive responses to arouse feelings or express pains. Apart from saying that ethical statements are mere an expression of feelings like Ayer, Stevenson ultimately considered moral sentiments as being the result of subjective opinions, views or beliefs. At the time of developing the concept of emotivism, the language and meaning of ethical statements were considered seriously in the hands of Ayer and Stevenson.

Fletcher (1963) propounded the situational theory of ethics, which is constituted by three different ways of making moral decisions. Legalistic ethics has a set of pre-fabricated moral rules and regulations. Antinomian ethics is quite the reverse of legalistic ethics. The term 'antinomian' literally means 'against law'. Under it, a person enters an ethical decision by considering each occasion a totally unique and lastly, the situation ethics which agrees that reason is the instrument of moral judgements, but disagrees that the good is to be discerned from the nature of things. They repeat that love and justice are the same; for justice love is distributed.

Virtue theory of ethics asks how you can be a better person—it defines good people and the qualities that make them good. The roots of virtue theory are in Greek literature, especially, Aristotle, but MacIntyre (1966) has developed the new interest. He argues that modern ethics has lost sight of its roots. Keenan (1998) summarizes the virtue theory in three questions: Who am I? Who ought I to become? How do I get there? Virtues provide a way of estimating a character and suggest a direction in which you should go in order to become a good person. Virtue theory is person-centred and focused on our development. This theory has been discussed in later part of writing.

For our own interest, we have not discussed two main theories of ethics so far. One is Utilitarian and the other is Deontological. Accounting thinkers align their thoughts with either of the two. Consequential or teleological ethics judges the rightness or wrongness of an act by its consequences. The most elaborate consequentialist theory is that of utilitarianism as propagated by Bentham (1789). According to him the rightness or wrongness of an action is determined by the utility or usefulness of the amount of pleasure and happiness. An action is right if it produces greatest good for the greatest number. There may be *Act Utilitarianism and Rule Utilitarianism.* Act Utilitarianism says that good action is the one that leads to the greatest good whereas the Rule Utilitarianism emphasizes the course of action which when pursued by whole community leads to the greatest result. Utilitarianism has two advantages over the other ethical theories in business. Firstly, it relates self-interest with moral behaviour and secondly, the calculation of benefit and harm is similar to profit and loss accounting. Individual interest maximization in short term is a major issue in business. Question may arise whether accountants convey information without being bias to one group of individual. The opinions are different. Some say that accountants are not the key agents of change in society. Their information should be neutral or unbiased (Solomons 1991). Radical accountants like Tinker (1991) have questioned the neutrality from which an accountant reports and it is impossible for him to remain impartial in a social conflict. Whether accounting concepts are neutral or morally correct depends on how far it has touched the root of utilitarianism (Lovell 1995). But it is also criticized that utilitarianism offers democratic morality that promotes general happiness and opposes individual pursuits. To promote greatest good for the greatest number, the interest of the minorities may be neglected.

Kant's (1785; 1788; 1797) deontological theory is not based on consequences and, thus, not grouped under teleological theories. It is concerned with actions. It is deontological because it is based on duty. According to him, to act morally is to do one's duty, and one's duty is to obey the moral law. We should act out of duty and not emotion: Kant's ethic is reason based and not intuitive. Kant also distinguishes between duty and inclination. He laid down some categorical imperatives which prohibit acts that would commonly be considered immoral. Kantian Morality states that some actions are never permissible to one individual or society which achieves intentions through will of the agent and the deontologists praise his morality even if the results fall short of expectation.

Deontology works effectively on the regulatory parts of accountancy. According to Moizer (1995), the codes of the profession are based on either deontological or rule-utilitarian approaches. Auditor must not be consequential in attitude. But deontological approach does not force an auditor to ignore the circumstances. It will be relevant to discuss about virtues and accounting. Virtue ethics, as discussed earlier, considers both intention and outcome where duty-based ethics and utilitarianism see only one. A strong deontological understanding sometime means, *compliance with rules is 'moral'* which is not true. It is the virtuous behaviour of an accountant as a citizen and only in such capacity one can express concern over social issues (Solomon 1991). A social self-consciousness, a virtue, is to be developed by an accountant through which the conflict will be resolved (Tinker 1991).

Another type of ethics, the ethics of care, has been developed as a feminist critique of the traditional moral rights and rules. Feminist authors assess that the ethics of rights is essentially a male perspective and reflects male dominance in Western society and thought (Gilligan 1982). The ethics of care is applied directly to the accounting profession and in the concept of caring organization. It is felt that caring behaviour is needed to run the organization smoothly (Burton and Dunn, 1996). Rule-based independence of auditors seems arbitrary and care ethics help to develop a relationship between the auditor and the client keeping the mental separation intact (Reiter 1997). In the moral conflict, the choice between the resignation and hopeless compromise of integrity, the care perspective develops more positive approach to maintain relationship between the self and others. In accounting research too, care ethics does not believe that the research questions are appropriate in analysing the behaviour of the accountants which is reflected from the social cross currents (Oakes and Hammond 1995).

The moral issues of accounting do not attract one exclusive theory of ethics. Complex nature of moral issues necessitates a compound model of ethics. Moizer (1995) found that Kantian deontological and utilitarianism should be such as complementing each other and these two theories are dominating in accounting rule making. But Cavanagh et al. (1981) suggest a different version of compound model which they claim to be more handy than a practical businessman. They assert that an act would be unethical if it has violated any of the following principles: (i) to maintain the optimistic utility for all stakeholders involved, (ii) to respect the rights of the individuals concerned, (iii) to be consistent with norms of justice, and (iv) whether the act arises from an impulse to case, to a utility-rights-justice-care model.

Immediately after World War II, the field of ethics was dominated by the discussions of the meta-ethical theory known as 'emotivism'. The theory tells us that moral judgements are expressions of emotions and attitudes and not statement of facts about objective reality. The linguistic meaning of words and its justification were central to the idea. The words are not only a set of ideas or attitudes but they develop a 'tendency' to cause a person to say certain things and such tendencies are referred to as 'dispositions' which creates a constancy to develop an idea (Stevenson 1944).

One of the major contributors in this era is Rawls (1958; 1971), who proposed the method of 'reflective equilibrium' which is achieved by comparing the set of general principles and the particular judgement on intuitions about what to do in a specific circumstance where there is a high degree of confidence. Our principles can come to correct our personal beliefs just as our particular beliefs can function to correct our principles. In 'Justice of Fairness', Rawls showed the track of moving from 'original position', based on 'veil of ignorance' to an 'opted position' that would benefit everyone inclusive of the worst one. With this, the ethical relativism was propagated by Harman (1975) and Wong (1984) who asserts that what is right is only what is right for you in your society. Your norms and codes are valid for you just as moral codes of others are valid for them. Neither is valid or true for everyone. It is observed, that more the society is advancing with ages the more it is returning to its traditional thoughts, though after Second World War it started with departure from traditions. According to the theories explained above, the relation of accountancy is primarily close with two major normative branches, the Utilitarianism of Bentham and Mill and Kantian Deontology. But the justification of stating other theories above is to help the thinkers to develop a complex model of ethics required for accounting in the recent days.

12.2 Applied Areas of Accounting Ethics

Normative ethics remain insular in our day-to-day practical problems. The theoretical stronghold of such theories is becoming loose while it is logically framed at the point of application. The sterility of meta-ethics increased the dissatisfaction among the users to build a close link between the theory and practice in real life. In the late 1950s, the ramification of the theories was studied seriously for the ways we live our lives and resurgence of applied ethics was a neutral consequences. Ethics play a major role in three applied areas—bio-ethics, environmental ethics and business ethics. As all the three fields have certain common aspects like, whistle blowing, conscientious objectives, limits of professional responsibility, etc., professional ethics is a blend of all these. Accountancy, directly or indirectly, is related to two of the above areas, the environment ethics and the business ethics.

Armstrong (2002) divided accountants into three types as per employment status (see Fig. 12.1).

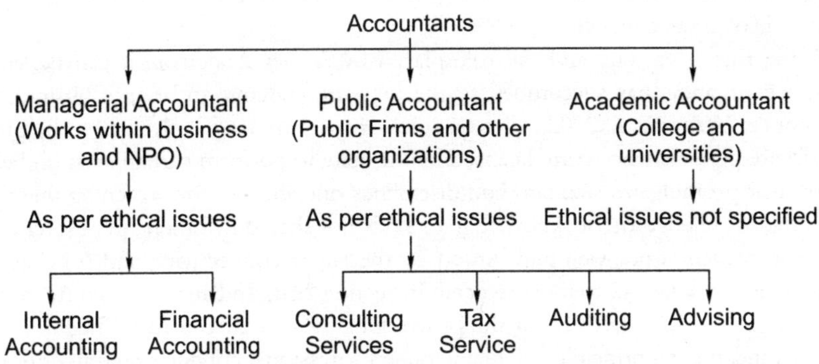

Figure 12.1 Ethical role of an accountant

These are the applied areas of accountants where ethical issues are raised and conflicts are resolved on the basis of the level of morality of an accountant. Internal accounting functions are grouped into three parts, namely, (i) budgeting, (ii) internal auditing, and (iii) internal reporting. In budgeting, the ethical conflict lies in the creation of 'slack' which is a provision created to meet the unforeseen contingencies. Though some scholars (Merchant and Van der Stede 2000) feel the necessity of creating slack, yet it is not ethically acceptable by many. In internal audit, there are five ethical themes as per Lemon and Wallace (2000). They are (i) organization structure, (ii) loyalty, (iii) independence, (iv) competition issues, and (v) conformity pressure. The loyalty of internal auditor cannot be judged properly as their performance is measured based on the structure designed by them. Auditors should never audit their own work. However, they are termed disloyal instantly if they report directly to the Audit Committee or Board of Directors. Conformity pressure forces an accountant to consider a partial judgement in case of earning management, which seems to be unethical to a group of stakeholders.

Four chief functions of public accountants are located among the various functions executed by them. In 1988, AICPA (American Institute of Certified Accountants) declared that the CPAs are expected to adopt some standard of care 'undoubtedly with the client'. If this function hints towards the consultation services, it will not be really possible that tax court will allow the treatment after consulting about the facts and services. Regarding the advising and auditing function in 1944, Public Oversight Board (POB), in accordance with GAAP and GAAS (auditing standards), published a report titled 'Strengthening the Professionalism of the Independent Auditor' where the chief observation was that that the Board of Directors, the representative of the shareholders, should be the client and not the corporate management. There is a possibility of developing a conflicting interest in performing the consulting and advising functions by the auditors where their independence may be impaired.

The AICPA Code of Professional Conduct (1992, ET, Section 55) describes independence as 'precluding relationships' that may be injured at the time of attestation. Independence deals with relationship and it has two sides—'in fact' and 'in appearance'. The independence is to be judged along with the objectivity (a state of mind) and integrity (an element of character). As the ethicality has a linkage with the independence, the Independence Standard Board (ISB) is engaged to develop a consistent rule of independence.

After the Enron episode and the role played by Arther Anderson, it can be said that the profession (accountancy) has succumbed to the pressure endemic to bring a business driven by the profit motive (Byrnes et al. 2002). Five qualities or traits are frequently cited to be professional. Professionals are persons who (i) are licensed by the state to perform certain acts; (ii) belong to an organization that promulgates standard and disciplines one another for breaching these standards; (iii) possess the so-called 'esoteric' knowledge or skills not shared by others; (iv) exercise autonomy over their work which is not well understood by the larger connectivity; and (v) publicly pledge themselves to render assistance to those in need. In Section 22 of Indian Chartered Accountants Act, 1949, it is discussed exhaustively about the professional misconduct in two schedules—Schedules I and II. The fundamental principles of maintaining professional conducts are integrity, objectivity, professional competence and due care, confidentiality, professional behaviour and technical standards. All those qualities are prevalent in the code of Professional Conduct of the AICPA. In addition, Article II of Section 53 highlights about Public Interest where the professionals should honour the public trust and demonstrate commitment to professionalism. In the ethical standard of the Institute of Management Accountants, more weightage has been unleashed on the 'confidentiality' where the accountant should refrain from disclosing the information unless it is legally compelled or it is necessary to disclose to the subordinates to monitor their activities.

The difference between the professional codes and the professional ethics should not be missed. The codes are laid down in the acts or set by an institute of the practitioners whereas the professional ethics are based on the compliance of the following points:

1. Trustworthiness—Professionals are thought to be trustworthy agents of clients either if (i) they are experts or (ii) they are service providers, who for a fee obey the clients' will. Generally, a professional is only an expert and he has no particular moral relation to the client. Expertise does not create any moral obligation. To preserve the trust of the client, the professional has to recognize who the client is and derive its principles from the clients' good. But the prevalent structural model often guides the clients to trust the professional.
2. Expertise—Handling the complexity proves the expertise of the professionals. According to sociologist Wilbert Moore, on ethical matters, complexity is more nearly the rule than the

exception and, thus, the judgement rather than merely routine compliance with unambiguous rules governs even the most scrupulous practitioner (Moore 1970).

3. Willingness—Professional is a trustee and the client a trustor and the trustee would have the willingness to do good for the client. There may not be a constant watch over the professional's job but their effort of rendering proper time and energy help them to do justice towards their goodwill.
4. Legitimacy—The relation between the professional and client is not morally legitimate just because it is trusting. The trustor grants power to the trustee but expects the trustee to exercise this discretion within the limits.

It is well known that stakeholder theory is a theory of organizational management and ethics. All theories of stakeholder management have some moral content though it is often implicit. Moral content is often ignored in the management scholarship. Such moral content is defeated due to the opportunistic behaviour of the manager in general and the accountant in particular. The ethical standing of the finance manager should not be restricted to the maximization of the shareholder's wealth; rather, attention needs to be directed towards the well-being of some non-shareholder stakeholders whose relation with organization is instrumental or derivative. But it has been claimed (Sternberg 2000) that the mangers who act in self-interest will satisfy one group of shareholders. It was opined that the business which is accountable to all is actually accountable to none. Normally, it is seen that the interest of the managers conflicts with the growth of organization and is also directed against the interest of the stakeholders. There may be conflict of interests among different groups, but all of them have a stake in the continued existence of the firm (Hill and Jones 1992). Apart from the interests stated above, an organization has its own ethics, which sometimes become authoritarian while it is imposed on the employees, especially on the accountants or managers.

12.3 Moral Behaviour of an Accountant

Agency theory works in two perspectives of accountancy—internal (within the organization) and external (to the public outside where accounting information has role in a democratic society). Human behaviour seldom works as a motivator. Instrumentalism and selfishness are the two common assumptions in the behaviour of an organizational individual. Accounting information helps assess the human effort and, thus, is the detector of financial inducement, the prime motivator of an individual. Accounting information becomes the transducer of individual and organizational performances subject to manipulation by all involved in its development, production and interpretation (Lovell 1996). The evaluation of an individual based on accounting information with manipulation makes an individual nervous and less confident (Roberts 1991).

Now, it is required to study the moral behaviour of an accountant in depth. There are numerous elements in the moral atmosphere through which an accountant has to move. The major areas are the socialization process of an accountant, the role of the professional bodies and the overall social, economic and political context within which the moral values are shaped. The socialization process of an accountant starts in a society where division of labour prevails. According to Giddens (1979), the integrity of local community is destroyed due to the opening up of occupational differences. The communication channels by which the organization opens up between its various component parts judge the character of a democratic state. Accountants being the information gatekeepers, have to perform a vital role to restore such democracy with their personal or collective value system. The professional bodies, of which they are loyal members, do not properly nurse their ethical injuries. In every step of accounting theory and practice, the human behaviour of an accountant is always considered negative as trust is disallowed and a likely outcome of accounting controls is a degree of dwarfing (Seedhouse 1988) of the individual and in this context, the individual can be both the controller and the controlled.

Professional bodies set the codes to monitor the activities of the members and to defend the society. Such codes enter in the normal society primarily at the time of recruiting the new entrants. A professional accountant has the idea of codes from the very beginning of his career but his strict adherence to the codes is flouted due to monetary gain and the non-supporting role of the body at the time of ethical conflict. But the accountants who are not the members of the professional bodies face the bureaucratic hegemony of the professional accountants because, in the opinion of Larson (1977), both profession and bureaucracy belong to the same historical matrix. Those ethical codes suffer from anachronism and are often used as a shield behind which various forms of behaviour can be tolerated (Lovell 1996). In the Kohlberg's classification of moral behaviour (Appendix 1), compliance of codes does not bring the individual within the principled stage. Kohlberg has argued that the general attitudes of rules, law, etc. can be heteronomous, semi-autonomous or autonomous, according to the manner in which an individual relates to moral standards. Here heteronomy means obedience to the adult, semi-autonomous means an advance to the rules itself and autonomy stands for feeling of an individual regarding the truthfulness necessary to the relations of sympathy and mutual respect. But the 'codes' are suffering from its participated or negotiated character, and it has a drawback of undue generality or conversely the specificity which is developed with assumptions or taken-for-granted notion. In the greater economical and political environment, the accountant has to face the conflict of his individual liberalism and contractualism. The social assumption concerning an accountant is that of an individual who is untrustworthy and requires constant control and monitoring. The modern organization today requires workers to do things they might not otherwise do (Jos 1988) and the workers are paid to obey (Benyon 1973). The social fabric between an individual and institution becomes loose in respect of an accountant. Denhardt (1981) contends that we originally need an institution to reflect our beliefs and values but now ominously our values reflect our institution, i.e., our life is structured by organization and we are locked in their group. The individualism when applied to the institution may embarrass the organization, and is instantly controlled by the codes and rules which was formed to support an accountant to resolve the conflict.

Accounting has the capacity to be a virtuous practice and the key to realizing virtue lies in the recognition that accounting is both a moral and discursive practice (Francis 1990). Francis also pointed out that accounting is a transformative practice and can affect the lived experiences in a very specific and particular way. The word 'discursive' means considering accounting as a 'discourse'. Discourse in social science is considered to be an institutionalized way of thinking that can be manifested through language and a social boundary defining what can be said about a specific topic. Accounting discourse is not the reporting of facts but what the accountants author. In such a discursive practice, accountants have to acknowledge their own personal involvement, their own moral agency and rhetorical role, in the production and creation of accounting reports. So the discursive character goes hand in hand with the moral character of the accountant.

If policies has to do with life in the 'polis', the communities in which we live, and the relation with each other in the communities, then accounting is a political practice. The mode of practice is also selected politically by not considering the cost of consuming the nature and infrastructure like roads and other civic amenities (Burchell et al. 1985). The orientation is framed around the capital and not around the labour, which is also a political selection. But in accounting ethics, virtues are not ignored. Virtue is defined as an acquired human quality, the possession and exercise of which enables us to achieve those goods which are internal to the practices and the lack of which effectively prevents us from achieving (MacIntre 1984). Primarily, five internal goods are suggested (Francis 1990):

1. Honesty—Accountants in general and auditor in particular are honest people (Mautz and Sharaf 1961).
2. Concern for Economic Status of Others—Concern for the economic status of others, which we have historically called stewardship or accountability, is an implicit purpose for which we do accounting.
3. Sensitivity to the Value of Cooperation and Conflict—Many accounting practices (transfer pricing, standard costing, cost centres and profit centres) operate in the edge of cooperation and conflict.
4. Communicative Character of Accounting—Accounting, in representing what we call 'reality', simultaneously construct our understanding of that what we call relit, simultaneously construct our understanding of that which we call real (Hines 1988; 1989).
5. Dissemination of Economic Information—Accounting is often characterized as a service function which proliferates economic information for decision making. It will be too restrictive if the information is disseminated to the suppliers of capital only.

The virtues stated above are threatened by the dominance of external rewards, corrupting power of institutions and the failure to distinguish between virtues and laws. The exercise of judgement is not merely abiding by the rules on laws. A virtuous person is not only a law-abiding-person. Too much application of technology may underestimate the individual's virtue and later on become dependent on machine rather than virtue. If accountancy is a virtuous practice, it becomes difficult to continue with that under pressure from the external affairs. This externality always poses a threat to the ethicality of accounting too. A point still stands unanswered. Is it only the external threats as discussed that are responsible to change a man into accountant? Do his intuitions at the back of his mind are also becoming unethical than previous years? The following section may help to seek the answer.

12.4 Ethical Intuition of an Accountant

So far, ethical intuitions of the accountants have not been considered in the literature of accounting ethics. Generally, we can accept that intuition is an inner longing of humans which have no logic itself. Audi (1996; 1998; 1999; 2004) and Shafer-Landau (2003) expressed the view that intuitions are self-evident propositions and are alone sufficient for justifications. This view has been contradicted by Huemer (2005; 2006; 2007; 2008) who is of opinion that intuitions are sui-generis (unique) seeming states, termed as intellectual seemings, which are like other kinds of seemings (e.g., those based on sensory experiences or memory) in the way they justify. 'Seeming' means 'as if' or 'as it appears'. That is a unique condition which occurs inside oneself before taking an action. But there is an opinion (Bedke 2008) that the contribution of Heumer is an improvement on Audi.

However, intuitions are becoming an issue to accountancy. Whether it is a 'self-evident proposition' or a 'sui-generis seemings', the intuitions applied, instead of logical process of thinking, in ethical issues are prevalent in the current scenario. But the telling result at the end regarding such issues is not acceptable. It proves the claim of Bedke (2008) that the 'self evident' entails defeasibility which means it is open to debate. The ethical stand of an accountant based on intuition is fallible in many respects. Though the intuition is based on 'intellectual seemings', it is not a belief. A belief may be characterized as stronger than mere ungrounded opinion but weaker than full knowledge. In case of ethical conflict, the intuition applied by an accountant is presumed captured from his belief which actually is not. Now the question is, Where from such 'intellectual seemings' are originated if it is not from any belief? A common opinion is that it may come from the 'attitude' of the person or from the 'content' of the subject or from the phenomenology of attitude–content pair effect. For example, the non-disclosure of expenses to inflate profit for earning credit by an executive is an ethical issue. The intuitive act may vary due to the attitudinal outlook of the executive or the content (inflated profit) may influence the executive to earn credit or it is the reality to accept the manipulation (object) but in the hands of the executive (subject) who does or does not apply the intuition based on the attitude and content pair of application. Here it should not be overlooked that though both intuitions about logic and intuitions about the ethics are intellectual seemings, their content and structure are distinct from one another. Again if we look back at the origin of seemings, it can be said that the 'sensory seeming' is based on the content whereas the 'intellectual seeming' may be related to competence. In case of any ethical dilemma, this 'intellectual seeming' based on competence or skill becomes effective in accountancy. It requires a technical knowledge to adopt any off-balance sheet treatment. The question of ethicality of doing that addresses the role of ethical intuition. These ethical intuitions are of different types. There are intuitions about particular cases, about mid-level moral principles (like fidelity, reparation, gratitude, justice, etc) and about the most general moral principles, such as act utilitarianism. Whatever may be the type of ethical intuition, they are nothing but the phenomenological variety of seeming. Phenomenological variety stands as the variability in consciousness towards something. Different intuitional objects like perception, memory retention and protention, signification, etc. constitute such consciousness.

Though it is claimed by Audi that intuitions are self-evident and by Huemer that it comes from intellectual seemings in accountancy, the phenomenological effect of intuitions are difficult to ignore. Accountants are social human beings. They have to go through several socio-economical changes. One of them is post-modern culture of consumerism which creates a heavy impact on their intentional object to influence their intellectual seemings which affect the ethical intuition to act accordingly. It is normally prominent that his role towards stakeholder carries a defeated logic by some intuitive deliberation which proved unethical in justificatory bearings.

12.5 Conclusion

Though an exhaustive philosophical background of accounting ethics is narrated above, there could be more philosophical openings of the issue. As it is seen, right from the Aristotelian ethics to meta-ethics, the applied part has drawn enough blood from the theoretical concepts. It has also nourished the professional part which is a special form of applied one. But the study on the philosophical part of accounting ethics remains ineffective if it does not show the impact of improvement in the ethical standard applied in accounting. Thus, the necessity of measuring the unethical behaviour of accountants is becoming imperative day by day. Nowadays, scholars use the Newstrom and Ruch's (1975) method of measurement despite its limitation of scope. Though researchers (Kaptein 2008) are working to cover wider aspect through the method, still the limitations like specificity problem, risk in the subjectivity of respondents' interpretations and risk of social desirability response bias which create snag in the findings. The definition of 'unethical behaviour' also varies from individual to organization to country level to make the finding less reliable in the process of measurement (Greenberg 1996). The risks like social desirability response originated from the anonymity or absence of the respondent creates bias to the result (Fernandes and Randall 1992).

Scholars (Schwartz and Weber 2006) have also developed A Business Ethics National Index (BENI) taking data from different sectors, like academia, business, social or ethical investment, business ethics organizations, government activity, social activist group and media coverage. This measurement technique may be helpful for accounting ethics which will help to guide the future direction of research and to compare with the other cross-national ethical activity. It can also help to prepare a global directory of accounting ethics which will guide the cross-national investors.

Lastly, a major burning issue of the subject is how to control such unethicality in finance. The views differed. One view is to include the ethical issues in the curriculum whereas others are prone to a strict adherence of professional codes at the time of application. While some are in favour of developing the individual ethical qualities during the training period inside an organization, the alternative view is that the responsibility is to be shared by the professional bodies at the time of ethical conflict. However, researches are after exploring the most apt way to control the unethical issues of accounting and finance throughout the globe.

Appendix 12.1: Kohlberg's Classification of Moral Behaviour

Level One—The Pre-conventional Level

The individual is responsive to cultural rules and labels (e.g., good, bad, right and wrong) but interprets the labels in terms of either physical or hedonistic consequences (i.e., the decision criteria are the avoidance of pain or personal gain). As with the other levels, the pre-conventional level is subdivided into two stages

- **Stage one:** The punishment and obedience orientation—The physical consequences of actions determine its goodness or badness, irrespective the consequences of the actions. There is an unquestioning deference to power and reference to any underlying moral order is absent.
- **Stage two:** The instrumental relativist orientation—The right action is that which satisfies ones own needs. Human relations are viewed as those of the market place. Fairness, reciprocity and equal sharing is present but not in good terms. Reciprocity means 'you scratched my back I shall scratch yours'.

Level Two—The Conventional Level

At this level, the maintenance of the expectation of family group or nations is judged as valuable in its own right, regardless of immediate and obvious consequences. The level is associated with conforming social order and contains the following stages:

- **Stage three:** The interpersonal concordance of good boy/nice girl orientations: behaviour is directed at pleasing or helping others. There is conformity to stereotypical images of natural behaviour. Approval is achieved by being nice.
- **Stage four:** The law and order orientation—the orientation at this stage is towards authority, in an unquestioning way. The maintenance of rules and social order assume importance over other considerations.

Kohlberg identifies a stage between stage four and five which is post-conventional, but not yet principled. It is a stage at which individual picks and chooses between obligations where some notions of a broader social perspective is evident but not in a coherent, consistent and principled way. Kohlberg interprets it as a transitory stage between four and five (Kohlberg 1973).

Level Three—The Post-conventional and Principled Level

At this level, there is a clear effort to define moral values and principles of behaviour which recognize and respect the sovereignty of other individuals. This recognition move from contractual notion of social relationship and involves:

- **Stage five:** The social contract, legalistic orientations—This stage of moral reasoning tends to display utilitarian overtones. There is a compliance with standards which have been societally determined although not necessarily enshrined in statute.
- **Stage six:** The universal ethical principles orientations—this stage assumes guidance by universal ethical principles which all humanity should follow. Usually this means, keeping within existing laws because these will have been socially determined and presumably just. However, where inequities exist, where justice has been violated then laws can be broken. Justice is regarded as having higher status than unjust laws. 'The prospective is that of any rational individual recognizing the nature or the basic moral premise of respect for the persons as end not means' (Kohlberg 1981).
- **Stage seven:** The post-conventional or principled level of moral development—it takes the debate increasingly towards the philosophical dimension. Stage seven embraces the spiritual spheres of human existence more forcibly than stage six.

References

Aquinas, St. T. (1273). *Summa Theologica*. Translated by the Fathers of English Dominican Province. Benzigar Brothers, USA, 1947.

Aristotle (4th Century BCE). *The Nicomachean Ethics*. Translated with an introduction by W. D. Ross. OUP, Oxford, 1980.

Armstrong, M. B. (2002). 'Ethical Issues in Accounting'. In E. B. Norman (ed.), *The Blackwell Guide to Business Ethics*. Blackwell Publishing, Chapter 7, p 145.

Audi, R. (1996). *Intuitionism, Pluralism and the Foundation of Ethics, in Moral Knowledge*? Ed. Waltor Sinnott–Armstrong and Mark Timmons–OUP, pp 101–136.

———(1998). 'Moderate Intuitionism and Epistemology of Moral Judgement'. *Ethical Theory and Moral Practice*, 1(1), pp 15–44.

———(1999). 'Self Evidence'. *Philosophical Perspection*, 13, pp 205–228.

———(2004). *The Good in the Right*. Princeton University Press, Princeton, NJ.

Ayer, A. J. (1936). *Language, Truth and Logic*. Victor Gallary, London.

———(1959). *Philosophical Essays*. Macmillan, London.

Bedke, M. S. (2008). 'Ethical Intuitions: What They Are, What They Are Not and How They Justify'. *American Philosophical Quarterly*, 45(3), July, pp 253–270.

Bentham, J. (1789). 'Introduction to the Principles of Morals and Legislations'. In M. Warnock (ed.), *Utilitarianism*. Fontana.

Benyon, H. (1973). *Working for Ford*. Penguin, Harmondsworth, UK.

Bradley, F. H. (1927). *Ethical Studies* (2e). OUP, Glasgow, UK, Published in 1876.

Burchell, S., Clubb, C and Hopwood, A. (1985). 'Accounting in Its Social Context: Towards a History of Value Added in the United Kingdom'. *Accounting Organisation and Society*, 10(4), pp 381–341.

Burton, B. K. and Dunn, C. P. (1996). 'Feminist Ethics as Moral Grounding for Stakeholder Theory'. *Business Ethics Quarterly*, 6(2), pp 133–147.

Byrnes, N., Mcnamee, M., Brady, D., Lavelle, L. and Palmeri, C. (2002). 'Accounting in Crisis'. *Business Week*, January 28, pp 44–48.

Cavanagh, G. F., Moberg, D. J. and Valesquez, M. (1981). 'The Ethics of Organisational Politics'. *Academy of Management Review*, 6, pp 363–374.

Cavanagh, G. F., Moberg, D. J. and Velasquez, M. (1995). 'Making Business Ethics Practical'. *Business Ethics Quarterly*, 5, pp 389–418.

Cicero, M. T. (1841). *The Political Works of Marcus Tullius Cicero: Comprising His Treatise on the Common Wealth and His Treatise on the Laws*. Translated from the original with dissertation and notes in two volumes by Francis Barham Esq, vol. I, Edmund Spettigue, London.

Denhardt, R. B. (1981). *In the Shadow of Organisation*. Regent Press, Lawrence, KS.

Fernandes, M. F. and Randall, D. M. (1992). 'The Nature of Social Desirability Response Effects in Ethics Research'. *Business Ethics Quarterly*, 2, pp 183–205.

Fletcher, J. (1963). *Situation Ethics: The New Morality*. Westminster Press, Philadelphia, PA.

Francis, J. R. (1990). 'After Virtue? Accounting as a Moral and Discursive Practice'. *Accounting, Auditing and Accountability Journal*, 3(3), pp 5–16.

Giddens A. (1979). *Central Problems in Social Theory: Actions, Structure and Contradiction in Social Analysis*. Macmillan, London.

Gilligan, C. (1982). *In a Different Voice*. Harvard University Press, Cambridge, MA.

Greenberg, J. (1996). *The Quest for Justice on the Job Essays and Experiments*. Sage Publications, Thomas Oaks, CA.

Hammond, T. A. and Oakes, L. S. (1995). 'Biting the Epistemological Hand: Feminist Perspectives on Science and Its Implication for Accounting Research'. *Critical Perspectives on Accounting*, 6(1), pp 49–75.

Harman, G. (1975). 'Moral Relativism Defended'. *Philosophical Review*, 84, pp 3–22.

Hill, C. W. L. and Jones, T. M. (1992). 'Stakeholder Agency Theory'. *Journal of Management Studies*, 29, pp 131–154.

Hines, R. D. (1988). 'Financial Accounting in Communicating Reality, We Construct Reality'. *Accounting Organisations and Society*, 13(3), pp 251–261.

Hines, R. D. (1989). 'The Sociopolitical Paradigm in Financial Accounting Research'. *Accounting Auditing and Accountability Journal*, 2(1), pp 52–76.

Huemer, M. (2005). *Ethical Intuitionism*. Palgrave Macmillan, New York.

———(2006). 'Phenomenal Conservatism and the Internalist Intuition'. *American Philosophical Quarterly*, 43, pp 147–158.

———(2007). 'Compassionate Phenomenal Conservatism'. *Philosophy and Phenomenological Research*, 74, pp 30–55.

———(2008). 'Revisionary Intuitionism'. *Social Philosophy and Policy*, 25, pp 368–392.

Jos, P. H. (1988). 'Moral Autonomy and Modern Organisation, Polity'. *The Journal of the North-Eastern Political Science Associations*, XXI(2), winter.

Kant, I. (1785). *Groundwork for the Metaphysics of Moral.* Translated by H. J. Paton, Routledge, London, 1948.

———(1788). *Critique of Practical Reason.* Translated by L. W. Beck, Bobbs Merrill, Indianapolis, IN, 1977.

———(1797). *The Metaphysics of Moral.* Cambridge University Press, Cambridge, 1996.

Kaptein, M. (2008). 'Developing a Measure of Unethical Behaviour in the Workplace: A Stakeholder Perspective'. *Journal of Management*, 34(5), October, pp 978–1008.

Keenan, J. F. (1998). 'Virtue Ethics'. In B. Hoose (ed.), *Christian Ethics: An Introduction.* Cassell, London, pp 84–94. See also Dialogue, *A journal for Religious Studies and Philosophy*, PO Box 1098, Bircham, Kings Lynn PE 316XA, 15 Nov., 2000.

———(1981). 'Essays on Moral Development'. *The Philosophy of Moral Development: Moral Stages and the Idea of Justice*, vol. 1. Harper & Row, San Francisco, CA.

Kohlberg, L. (1973). 'Continuities in Childhood and Adult Moral Development Revisited'. In P. B. Baltes and K. W. Schaline (eds.), *Life Span Development Psychology: Personality and Socialisation.* Academic Press, New York.

Larson, M. S. (1977). *The Rise of Professionalism: A Sociological Analysis.* University of California Press, Berkeley, CA.

Lemon, W. M. and Wallace, W. A. (2000). 'Ethical Issues facing Internal Auditors and Their Profession'. *Research on Accounting Ethics*, 6, pp 189–203.

Lovell, A. (1995). 'Moral Reasoning and Moral Atmosphere in the Domain of Accounting'. *Accounting Auditing and Accountability Journal*, 8(3), p 60.

Lovell, A.. (1996). 'Morals Reasoning and Moral Atmosphere in the Domain of Accounting'. *Accounting, Auditing and Accountability Journal*, 8(3), pp 60–80.

———(1997). 'Some Thoughts of Kohlberg's Hierarchy of Moral Reasoning and Its Relevance of Accounting Theories'. *Accounting Education*, 6(2), pp 147–162.

MacIntyre, A. (1966). *A Short History of Ethics.* Routledge, London.

MacIntyre, A. (1984). *After Virtue: A Study in Moral Theory* (2e). Notre Dame University Press, South Bend, IN.

Mautz, R. K and Sharaf, H. A. (1961). *The Philosophy of Auditing.* American Accounting Association, Sarasota, FL.

Merchant, K. S and Van der Stede, W. A. (2000). 'Ethical Issues Related to "Result Oriented" Management Control Systems'. *Research on Accounting Ethics*, 6, pp 153–169.

Moizer, P. (1995). 'An Ethical Approach to the Choices Faced by Auditor'. *Critical Perspectives on Accounting*, 6(5), pp 415–431.

Moore, G. E. (1903). *Principia Ethica.* Cambridge University Press, Cambridge, 1993.

Moore, W. E. (1970). *The Professions: Roles and Rules.* Russell Sage Foundation, New York, p 111.

Newstrom, J. W. and Ruch, W. A. (1975). 'The Ethics of Management and Management of Ethics'. *MSU Business Topics*, 23, pp 29–37.

Oakes L. S. and Hammond T. A. (1995). 'Biting the Epistemological Hand: Feminist Perspectives on Science and their Implications for Accounting Research'. *Critical Perspectives on Accounting*, 6(1), pp 49–75.

Plato (5th–4th century BCE). *The Republic.* Translated by Desmond Lee 2e, Penguin Hermon's Worth, 1979.

Rawls, J. (1958). 'Justice as Fairness'. *Philosophical Review*, 67, pp 164–194.

———(1971). *A Theory of Justice.* Harvard University Press, Cambridge, MA.

Reiter, S. (1997). 'The Ethics of Care and New Paradigms for Accounting Practice'. *Accounting Auditing and Accountability Journal*, 10(3), pp 299–324.

Roberts, J. (1991). 'The Possibility of Accountability'. *Accounting, Organization and Society*, 16(4), pp 355–368.

Seedhouse, D. (1988). *Ethics: The Heart of Health Care.* John Wiley & Sons, New York, NY.

Schwartz, M. S and Weber, J. (2006). 'A Business Ethics National Index (BENI): Measuring Business Ethics Activity Around the World.' *Business and Society*, 45(3), pp 182–405.

Shafer-Landau, R. (2003). *Moral Realism: A Defence.* Clarendon Press, Oxford.

Solomon, D. (1991). 'Accounting and Social Change: A Neutralist View'. *Accounting Organisations and Society*, 16(3), pp 287–295.

Sternberg, E. (2000). *Just Business.* OUP, New York.

Stevenson, C. L.(1937). 'The Emotive Meaning of Ethical Terms'. *Mind*, pp 14–31.

———(1938). 'Persuasive Definitions'. *Mind*, pp 45–57.

———(1944). *Ethics and Language.* Yale University Press, New Heaven, CT.

Stevenson, C. L. (1945). *Ethics and Language.* Yale University Press, New Haven CT; OUP, Landon.

Solomons, D. (1991). 'Accounting and Social Change: A Neutralist Value'. *Accounting Organisation and Society*, 16(3), pp 287–295.

Tinker, T. (1991). 'The Accountant as Partisan'. *Accounting Organization and Society*, 16(3), pp 297–310.

Wong, D. (1978). *Reason and Morality.* University of Chicago Press, IL.

Wong, D. (1984). *Moral Relativity.* University of California Press, Berkeley, CA.

CHAPTER 13

A Note on Global Financial Crises (From an Indian Perspective)

Syamal K. Ghosh

ABSTRACT

Economic history is replete with instances of financial crises or financial meltdown of various kinds and sheds in different parts of the world. The current financial crisis which originated in the United States in 2007 following a crash in real estate prices has affected many economies across the globe. However, there is indication suggesting that the acute phase of the crisis is over and that recovery is in sight. Although, India has been affected by the global financial meltdown, we have been able to avert any major crisis. In fact, despite several odds, we have been able to maintain positive growth rate and also able to register progress in various walks of life. India's relatively favourable situation is due to several factors. These include inner strength of the economy, strong financial architecture, limited exposure to foreign trade and timely actions by the government. India has great economic opportunity ahead and there is every reason to believe that we will be able to explore that opportunity, given our track record of resilience, dynamism and prudence.

13.1 Introduction and Background

Since 2007, when the first tell-tale signs of global financial meltdown reared their ugly heads, we have hardly ever been able to breathe easy. While some palliative measures adopted in different countries have yielded some limited dividends, as a whole, we have not completely succeeded in addressing the crisis. The World Bank Web site http://www.worldbank.org/financialcrisis/succinctly describes the current situation as follows: 'Though the most acute phase of the global financial crisis has passed, recovery remains fragile. Persistent risks to economic health include high unemployment and low growth in developed countries and scarce international financing for developing countries'.

Economic history is replete with instances of financial crises or financial meltdown of various kinds and shades in different parts of the world. Some of these have even had a global reach.

However, the fact that we have not only survived these, but also managed to register progress in various walks of life stands as a testimony to the indomitable human spirit.

Let us cite a few major examples of such crises which we have witnessed since the beginning of the twentieth century. We are witness to the havoc wrought by the Great Depression of the 1930s, the Latin American Debt Crisis of the 1980s, the United States Savings & Loan Crisis of the late-1980s and the early 1990s, the bursting of the Japanese Asset Price Bubble in the 1990s, the crisis following speculative activity in the European Exchange Rate Mechanism in the early 1990s, the resurgence of debt crisis in Latin America in the mid-1990s, Asian Financial Crisis of 1997–98, Russian Financial Crisis of 1998, the crisis in Argentina between 1999 and 2002 when its banking system broke down, the bursting of the United States DotCom Bubble in the early 2000s and so on.

The reasons for our concern over the global financial meltdown are well-founded, indeed. The rate of unemployment is on the rise almost all over the world; industrial production has been declining; there is a conspicuous slowing down of the growth rate of the gross domestic product throughout the world and even the emerging economies are no exception.

The third largest economy in the world, China, is growing at its slowest in recent years. Here, in India, we are unlikely to reach the nearly double-digit growth rate that we experienced over the past few years. There is now a conspicuous concern about the *2010 Euro Crisis*. Understandably, the likelihood of a sovereign debt crisis in some parts of Europe, e.g., Greece, Spain, Portugal, is worrisome, indeed.

When the trough is deep and the recession lingers for a few years, it can certainly be worrisome, and this is making people wonder as to whether another Great Depression is in the making.

Alice M. Rivlin has rightly pointed out that: 'In the Great depression of the 1930s, millions of workers lost their jobs as the unemployment rate reached 25 percent of the labor force. Hunger and malnutrition were widespread. A large fraction of the population lacked adequate food, shelter, clothing and medical care…when President Franklin D. Roosevelt spoke of "a third of a nation ill-housed, ill-clad, ill-Fed" he reflected the scale of the destitution by the standards of the time" (Rivlin 1994).

We, all, know from the data available to us that 'the Great Depression was a worldwide economic downturn starting in 1929 and ending at different times in the 1930s or early 1940s…the depression had devastating effects on virtually every country, rich or poor. International trade plunged by half to two-thirds, as did personal income, tax revenue, prices and profits. Cities all around the world were hit hard, especially those dependent on heavy industry. Construction was virtually halted in many countries. Farming and rural areas suffered as crop prices fell by roughly 60 percent'.[1]

Bourses typically process all available information and investors react to signals, and this is one of the reasons behind the disastrous market crash (Wall Street crash of 1929) that came on the heels of the bursting of bubbles in housing. Bank runs occurred and a banking panic was in evidence. According to a source,[2] industrial production in the United States plunged by about 45 per cent between 1929 and 1932; homebuilding dropped by 80 per cent; around 5,000 banks went out of business; by 1933, around 11,000 out of the 25,000 banks in the United States had failed; between 1929 and 1933, the gross domestic product (GDP) in the United States fell around 30 per cent; over 1 million families lost their farms between 1930 and 1934; corporate profits dropped from $10 billion 3 years ago to $1 billion in 1932. The rest of the world suffered as well and global economy seemed to shake off the stupor to a large extent during the World War II years.

13.2 Financial Crisis or Financial Meltdown—Definition

During a financial crisis, people, as a whole, begin losing faith in the financial system in the country and there may be a variety of ways in which this may happen. Banking panics and bank runs occur, as people lose faith in the banking and financial system and are wary about losing their deposits. When all or most of the depositors scramble for withdrawing their deposits at the same time, banks collapse. When unsustainably high prices in any market crash and go for a correction, this is perceived as the bursting of a bubble. Understandably, people feel shaky as bubbles in the real estate market or stock market or for that matter even in commodity markets or other markets burst, causing players in such market/s to lose substantial sums of money, and making potential players shy of the market/s.

Primary (IPOs or initial public offerings) and secondary (bourses or stock exchanges) capital markets are important for they help channel savings into investment. Both investors and speculators participate in the markets and as we do have a predominance of the corporate form of business organization all over the world, stock market crashes can and do have a tendency of dampening spirits and eroding faith in the financial system. In today's spaceship, earth stock market crashes spread like a contagion throughout the world and depress sentiments. We have ample evidence of this phenomenon. When a country is faced with a currency crisis, following mismanagement of the economy on account of endogenous or exogenous reasons, people lose faith in the currency and the financial system as a whole.

Citizens of a country as well as foreigners become restive when the domestic economic situation in that country worsens to such a degree that the country concerned is unable to honour its international payment obligations and there is sovereign default. When credit becomes scarce and the cost of credit keeps rising, when banks and financial institutions are wary of lending, popular disillusionment with the system can hardly be ruled out. Business cycles are a fact of life and can hardly be wished away.

After a boom or a period of relative economic prosperity, when the trade cycle turns downward, recession sets in, the rate of unemployment goes up, the rate of growth of the GDP tapers off, consumers restrain their spending, export markets are lost and producers worry about disposal of unsold inventories and cut back on output and usage of labour, thus, aggravating the problem further, people begin to worry for good reasons. This certainly erodes confidence in the existing financial system, particularly so, if the recession is not short-lived, as expectations are influenced.

13.3 Where Are We Now?

We are witnessing manifestations of all the malaise listed above in various parts of the world. Are we, indeed, threatened by the spectre of another Great Depression or is it more likely that we shall succeed in taming this recession. What parallels do we see from history? Are there lessons that we failed to learn? David Hume had suggested that: 'Mankind are so much the same, in all times and places, that history informs us of nothing new or strange in this particular' (Hume, 1935). He seems to suggest that innate human behaviour is invariant to time and place. He further adds, 'should a traveler, returning from a far country, bring us an account of men…who were entirely divested of avarice, ambition or revenge, who knew no pleasure but friendship, generosity and public spirit; we should immediately…prove him a liar, with the same certainty as if he stuffed his narration with stories of centaurs and dragons, miracles and prodigies'. Well, Hume seems to be right. The quest for a fast buck, unethical and shady business deals, greed and avarice, indiscipline in the financial system have accompanied financial crises in the past and these very same factors seem to have been the causal influences behind the present debacle. The financial system in the West is in a state of disarray. During the Great Depression, bank runs were there in the United States. Only 10 years ago, in March 1999, the Ecuadorian banking sector suffered a series of highly devastating bank runs (Eiteman et al. 2007). In the recent past, in 2007, Great Britain has suffered its first bank run since the nineteenth century.

Bubbles have burst in many parts of the world. The Great Depression had visited us on the heels of the bursting of the South China Seas bubble. As we know now, the prospect of making windfall gains prompted avaricious middlemen to hawk non-existent real estate in the South China Seas. Eventually, this real estate price bubble burst. The Savings & Loan crisis in the United States in the 1980s also was related to the bursting of a bubble. The East Asian Financial crisis of the late-1990s was also related to bursting of a real estate bubble. 'Crony capitalism' led to 'friends' of influential bankers and politicians making investment in dubious real estate. Obviously, the euphoria over escalating property prices could not last forever as such prices were unsustainable. Crisis ensued as the bubble burst.

The financial crisis that has been unveiling since 2007 also follows a crash in real estate prices in the United States. For around 3 years preceding 2007, the United States economy enjoyed relatively low rates of inflation and unemployment. However, the bursting of the bubble changed the scenario.

13.4 How Does the Bursting of a Bubble Hurt?

Let us take the case of the bursting of a real estate bubble and examine how the economy as a whole is affected by it. A fall in the demand for real estate leads to a fall in real estate prices. As a consequence construction activity is put on a slow burner. Some construction jobs are lost. This again reduces consumer spending as a whole. People who borrow on the strength of their real estate holding and finance a part or the whole of their consumer spending thereby find it difficult to borrow as financial institutions become apprehensive about default and delinquency. Consumer spending shrinks further. Lower consumer spending prompts consumer goods producers to cut down on output and retrench labour, thus depressing aggregate demand further. As the producers of consumer goods find the going tough, they place fewer orders for capital goods. Thus, the producers of capital goods start experiencing problems and as they react, demand gets depressed all the more. A recession sets in. A prolonged recession can lead to a depression.

The United States economy is the largest economy in the world and has extensive trade relations with the rest of the world. Decline in demand (consumer spending) in the United States will mean loss of export markets for other countries, thus propelling them towards an economic downturn. Moreover, financial crisis of any kind in a major economy can very well spread to other economies like a contagion, unless adequate preventive measures are in place.

13.5 Curative Measures

Measures, such as the nationalization of sick banks or covering banks through insurance by staking taxpayers' funds, however, politically hazardous that may be, may yet remain, a solution to the malaise. Sanitization of non-performing and toxic assets in the banking system is necessary in order to restore confidence. Similarly, use of public funds for bailing out sick firms in other industries cannot be ruled out, if we intend to stem the rot. Based on their cost–volume–profit analysis, accountants will readily point out the fact that the closure of sick firms would mean leaving fixed costs therein uncovered. This would adversely affect societal morale as people lose jobs and effective demand, i.e., demand backed by purchasing power declines thus precipitating an economic downturn. Bailing out of banks and insurance houses and business firms of other hues ought to be viewed in this context.

There is no denying that the financial system the world over lacks discipline. The Great Depression came on the heels of the stock market crash of 1929. Here, in India, we have witnessed near-crashes. We are quite familiar with stock scams by now. Even when the Harshad Mehta episode has not yet faded out of memory, we now have to contend with the Satyam scandal! Plenty of instances of stock market scams can be cited in the global context: the Xerox case, the Adelphia Communications case, the AOL Time Warner case, the Enron case, Parmalat case, etc., to name a few. These have certainly raised issues of financial indiscipline, failures of the regulatory mechanisms, laxity in norms of professional conduct, lacunae in current disclosure practices and so on. It goes without saying that these events definitely corrode one's faith in the financial system.

Researchers (Ghosh and Budhia 2005) had mentioned that, 'Only time will tell whether… moves towards better corporate governance and more adequate and effective legislation will succeed in preventing scams'. It does seem now that there is enough scope for improvement in corporate governance practices in firms engaged in sub-prime lending without adequate proof of creditworthiness, in firms covering the risks of such loan defaults and delinquencies, in firms resorting to creative accounting, in those getting into a mad rush for the use of collateralized debt obligations (CDOs) and so on. It is undeniably true that corporate governance practices need to be looked into. No business can survive in a vacuum and it is in the interest of business and industry to adopt such practices as would inspire public confidence.

Legislation and rigorous implementation of such legislation to address the real issues involved is called for. In the United States where the present crisis originated, the Financial Services Modernization Act[3] (Gramm–Leach–Bliley Act), which was adopted by the US Congress in 1999, may have, to an extent, contributed to the crisis. Under the new rules which came into vogue, commercial banks, brokerage firms, institutional investors and insurance companies were allowed to freely invest in each other's businesses and fully integrate their financial operations. This Act repealed the Glass–Steagall Act of 1933, which was put in place by President Roosevelt to put a check on corruption, financial jugglery and insider trading which resulted in the failure of several banks in the years following the 1929 Wall Street Crash.

In the United States, this issue has been hotly debated. For instance, Eliot Spitzer, former governor of New York had forewarned that a crisis is looming. Spitzer had cautioned about the predatory lending practices of mortgage lenders. He had pointed out that some of these lenders were misrepresenting the terms of the loan, some loans were being offered without regard for the customer's ability to repay, there were 'teaser' rates in some loans which ballooned astronomically, loans were packed with undisclosed charges and fees, and even illegal kickbacks. However, in the light of hindsight it would seem that these warnings went virtually unheeded. It appears that the problems were compounded when in 2003 in the United States, the Office of the Comptroller of Currency (OCC) invoked a clause from the National Bank Act of 1863 to issue formal opinions, thus pre-empting all state predatory lending laws.[4] The end result is now on the surface: with insider information, prior knowledge and skilful manipulation and an obvious disdain for ethical values, financial institutions seem to have misled investors. Markets began to crash as investors realize their mistakes and the 'herd' mentality takes over.

It is all in the public knowledge now that there has been widespread betting in derivatives, stocks, currencies and commodities, not all of which can be termed scrupulous and rational. The events are appalling, indeed: Lehman Brothers have gone bankrupt; Merrill Lynch has changed hands; Fannie Mae and Freddie Mac, the mortgage giants, have been taken over; Bear Stearns has collapsed; value of shares in AIG, America's largest insurance house, has taken a nosedive and it was gasping for breath till the bailout.

A number of economies in the West have been hit by liquidity crunch and bank runs. Economies like ours are also experiencing a credit crunch. Banks still in reasonably good shape are justifiably wary about lending money as they are concerned about possible delinquency. This has raised the cost of borrowing and thus the cost of capital. To cite an instance, right now in India, banks are going slow on real estate financing and financing of non-banking financial companies (NBFC), and even on financing of manufacturing and trading operations. In a bid to reverse the process, we can see various measures being taken now to soften, among others, home loan rates. The logic behind this move is obviously to encourage construction activity and to stimulate demand.

There have been several cases of sovereign default over the past decade or so. A few examples would suffice to underscore the gravity of the situation: during November 1998, Pakistan defaulted on $1,627 million; in August 1998, Russia defaulted on $72,709 million and we eventually witnessed a devaluation of the 'Ruble'; Ukraine defaulted on $1,271 million in September 1998; in July 1998, Venezuela defaulted on $270 million; in August 1999, Ecuador defaulted on $6,604 million; in September 2000, Peru defaulted on $4,870 million; Ukraine once again defaulted on $1,064 million in January 2000; in November 2001, Argentina defaulted on $82,268 million; in June 2001, Moldova defaulted on $145 million; in April 2003, Uruguay defaulted on $5,744 million; in April 2005, Dominican Republic defaulted on $1,622 million; and as recently as December 2006, Belize defaulted on $242 million.[5]

The risk of sovereign default remains as long as domestic economies in various countries fail to perform according to expectations. Global financial crises, indeed, have the potential of adversely affecting the behaviour of domestic economies and increasing the risk of sovereign default. In such a case, problems will get compounded. We have seen how the Latin American Debt Crisis of the 1980s led to devaluation of the currency in several cases. The role of the international lending agencies in monitoring the economic behaviour of debtor countries can hardly be overemphasized. As of 2010, we are worried about the prospect of sovereign default in Greece and debt problems in Spain and Portugal in the European Union.

In a currency crisis, the value of a currency becomes unstable, making it difficult for the currency to be used as a reliable medium of exchange. This is also termed as a balance-of-payments crisis. Currency and sovereign default crises which have surfaced rather frequently since the Latin

American Debt Crisis of the 1980s have prompted a good deal of academic research in this area. While the first generation of economic models in this area began with the work by Krugman (1979), the second generation of models begin with the work by Obstfeld and Rogoff (1986), and the third generation of models, which seem more relevant in the light of today's circumstances begin with the contributions by Chang and Velasco (2000; 2001). They have sought to draw our attention to the manner in which problems in the banking system may interact with currency crises and such crises may have real effects on the rest of the economy. They have, very convincingly, argued that a currency crisis may cause a banking crisis if domestic banks have debts denominated in foreign currency. Other economists, in particular, Burnside et al. (2001; 2004; 2008), have argued that, 'a government guarantee of the banking system may offer banks the incentive to take on foreign debt, making both the currency and the banking system vulnerable to attack.' For a thorough discussion on this topic, interested readers are requested to visit the relevant Wikipedia site.[6]

There was a crisis with the European Exchange Rate Mechanism in the early 1990s and several currencies were devalued and some withdrew from the system. In the late-1990s we saw the Asian currency crisis, although we, in India, escaped relatively unscathed by it. This time around, the credit crisis started initially in the United States. An overview of the crisis given in the following by the *New York Times*[7] serves to highlight the linkages between the credit crunch following the sub-prime mortgage crisis and its aftermath:

> In the fall of 2008, the credit crunch which had emerged a little more than a year before, ballooned into Wall Street's biggest crisis since the Great Depression. As hundreds of billions in mortgage-related investments went bad, mighty investment banks that once ruled high finance have crumbled or reinvented themselves as humdrum commercial banks. The nation's largest insurance company and largest savings and loan were both seized by the government. The channels of credit, the arteries of the global financial system, have been constricted, cutting off funds to consumers and businesses, small and large. In response, the federal government adopted a $700 billion bailout plan meant to reassure the markets and get credit flowing again. But the crisis began to spread to Europe and to emerging markets, with government scrambling to prop up banks, broaden guarantees for deposits and agree on a coordinated response.

They trace the origin of the present crisis as follows:

> The roots of the credit crisis stretch back to another notable boom and bust: the tech bubble of the late 1990s. When the stock market began a steep decline in 2000, and the nation slipped into recession the next year, the Federal Reserve sharply lowered interest rates to limit the damage. Lower interest rates make mortgage payments cheaper, and demand for homes began to rise, sending prices up. In addition millions of home-owners took advantage of the rate drop to refinance their existing mortgages. As the industry ramped up, the quality of mortgages went down. And turn sour, they did, as home buyers had to leverage themselves to the hilt to make a purchase. Default and delinquency rates began to rise in 2006, but the pace of lending did not slow. Banks and other investors had devised a plethora of complex financial instruments to slice up and resell the mortgage-backed securities and to hedge against any risks- or so they thought.

The events that hastened the present financial crisis can be traced to the collapse of two hedge funds owned by Bear Stearns in June 2007. They had invested heavily in the sub-prime market. Several banks discovered to their utter discomfort that securities they had considered so far to be safe, were, indeed, tainted with toxic mortgages. Now, as loan defaults led to foreclosures, real estate prices started declining and cases of default started soaring up. The central bank of the United States intervened to bolster the stock market, but the downward movement continued unabated, and in March 2008 the Federal Reserve staved off a Bear Stearns bankruptcy by assuming $30 billion in liabilities and engineered a sale to J P Morgan Chase at almost a throwaway price. We also witnessed, as the stock prices of mortgage moguls, Fannie Mae and Freddie Mac, slid sharply downward; on 7 September 2008, the US Treasury Department announced a government takeover. However, the downhill journey did not seem to get arrested. On a fire-fighting mission, on 12 September 2008, officials gathered for talks to fend off bankruptcy for Lehman Brothers, considered to be a giant in the financial market. However, as we know, the talks fell through and the government declined to bail out Lehman Brothers the same way as it had bailed out Bear Stearns. The collapse of Lehman Brothers has sent shock waves through the global financial markets. Another giant in distress, Merrill Lynch sold itself to Bank of America. Understandably, insurance firms also suffered on account of their exposure to exotic financial instruments like the credit default swaps, as defaults piled up, and on 16 September 2008, the American insurance giant, AIG (American International Group), which was on the verge of failure was bailed out by the Federal Reserve in an $85 billion deal. But this, too, has so far failed to address the gloom in the stock markets to any substantial extent.

The chronology of events has made bankers all over the world wary about lending. National governments in a host of countries have announced monetary and fiscal measures to inspire confidence, but so far the results have been muted at best. Some examples: Brazil's central bank cut its benchmark interest rate by one percentage point to 12.75 per cent on 21 January 2009; a day earlier, i.e., on 20 January 2009, Canada reduced its main rate from 1.5 per cent to 1 per cent; the Hungarian central bank trimmed its base rate by half a percentage point to 9.5 per cent;[8] Taiwan's central bank cut interest rates by half a point to 1.5 per cent in the face of a steep fall in the country's exports;[9] in November 2008, China announced a 4 trillion yuan (nearly $600 billion) fiscal stimulus package, its central bank has already cut rates several times since September 2008,[10] and as we know, India announced a fiscal stimulus package of Rs. 200 billion ($4 billion) on 7 December 2008 and on 6 December 2008, the Indian central bank, the Reserve Bank of India had cut its policy rate by a percentage point to 6.5 per cent and this was the third reduction in less than 2 months.[11] Lowering of interest rates to provide supply-side stimulus to encourage investment is the kind of policy still being pursued in India in spite of the rate of inflation going up.

Cyclical activity in the economy, the movement from booms to recession, depression and recovery leading to a boom or prosperity once again seem to have dominated our economic lives for as long as data have been collected. In simple terms, business cycles involve shifts over time between periods of relatively brisk growth of output (recovery and boom) and periods of relative stagnation and/or slower growth of output (contraction or recession). Economists have debated over the causation, some arguing in favour of demand side factors and some in favour of supply side factors and some have cited other causal influences. There has been a good deal of research into the duration of the phases of a business cycle. Joseph A. Schumpeter provided a typology according to the periodicity of the cycle, and in that light, we classify Kitchin cycle (after Joseph Kitchin) inventory cycle of 3–5 years, Jugler cycle of 7–11 years (after French economist, Clement Jugler), Kuznets (after Simon Kuznets) infrastructural investment cycle of 15–25 years, Kondratieff (after Nikolai Kondratieff) technological cycle of 45–60 years, Forrester (after Jay Wright Forrester) cycles of 200 years and so on (Schumpeter 1954). Interested readers may refer to the informative article[12] in the Wikipedia on this subject area. Though major depressions have not occurred since the Great Depression of 1929, we have been experiencing the other phases of business cycles throughout this period. In the capitalist system of production that is followed almost throughout the world, business cycles remain a fact of life.

13.6 How Are We Doing Here, in India?

Our financial system is under a great deal of pressure. A credit crunch is already here. Some job losses following the meltdown have been reported. Reports indicate that hundreds of Indians employed in the Middle East are returning home, as the global economic slowdown has hit that area. Reportedly, there have been wage cuts and job losses there as their real estate, construction, tourism sectors are under strain and oil prices have been on the decline. However, so far this is a trickle and not a tide, but it certainly is a reason for concern. Out of 5 million non-resident Indian workers, 90 per cent hold jobs in the Gulf and in South East Asia.[13] As the crises hit us, there have been some job losses in the domestic economy as well. A sample survey conducted by the Labour Ministry disclosed that 5 lakh workers lost their jobs between October and December 2008. The affected work-force belonged to 20 sectors, including textiles, metals, gems and jewellery, automobile, etc., in 11 states and union territories.[14]

The Labour Ministry at the Federal level, which conducted the sample survey referred to above, has urged the state governments and the employers to ensure social security for the jobless. As we launched liberalization and globalization programs, the need for providing a social security net for our workforce assumed a great deal of significance. The current scenario merely underscores that need. This is so, as we are not insulated from shocks, and given the current scheme of things, it is well nigh difficult to insulate the country from such shocks.

However, the world-at-large pins its hopes on the two large emerging economies in Asia, China and India. According to the International Monetary Fund (IMF), these two countries were expected to record growth rates of more than 5 per cent in 2008–09 while advanced economies were projected to record a decline of 2 per cent in output.[15] Apparently, the forecasts have not been very far from the truth.

Chances of bank runs and banking panics occurring in India are remote, as deposit insurance has been in place since 1962. The Deposit Insurance Corporation of India was created following bank failures, such as the failure of Travancore National and Quilon Bank in 1938, failure of Laxmi Bank and Palai Central Bank in the early 1960s, and banking crises in Bengal between 1946 and 1948. Because of deposit insurance, the vulnerable section of bank depositors, particularly, the small depositors are protected to a certain extent through this mechanism.[16] Moreover, because of prudent policies pursued by the Central Bank, the exposure of banks in India to toxic assets has been rather limited.

Our financial system now comprises 27 nationalized banks, 32 private sector banks, 45 foreign banks and 96 regional rural banks, apart from other financial institutions and co-operative banks. The Reserve Bank of India regulates the banking scene in this country. As Raju (2008) rightly points out, RBI, as the super regulator has 'proved its resilience during the Asian financial crisis that had a contagion effect on the whole of Asia, except India and the subprime crisis of 2007 that is still alive and causing flutter and furor'. The rate of growth of our GDP still remains robust. Our foreign exchange reserves stand at a healthy level. Indications are available to suggest that the government will make use of Keynesian policy prescriptions, i.e., make use of monetary and fiscal policy measures to stem the rot. In fact, a recent news report[17] suggests as much. Commerce Secretary G. K. Pillai said that the positive impact of the packages to stimulate the economy will be seen from June 2009 and 'we will turn the corner and start to grow'. As we know, since October 2008, government has announced a number of measures, such as reduction in excise duties and investments in infrastructure, to stimulate effective demand. The Reserve Bank has been quite active on the monetary policy front and has been adopting measures to lower the interest rates and ease the credit crunch. In fact, the focus on lowering interest rates on home loans needs to be viewed in this context. This has the potential of boosting demand for home loans and housing, thus providing a boost to the real estate sector, promoting construction activity and generating demand for cement, steel and other construction materials and creating more aggregate demand as employment goes up.

As par data released by the Central Statistical Organisation (CSO), Government of India, on Monday, 9 February 2009, the Indian economy was expected to grow at 7.1 per cent during the financial year 2008–09. This rate is lower than the rate of around 9 per cent achieved over the past 3 consecutive years, it is remarkably good considering the financial meltdown that has been haunting us since 2007.[18] We may, in reality, have achieved a growth rate somewhat lower than that expected by optimists, but even then, it is remarkable considering the state of other economies, and taking into account the fact that exports have dipped. According to a report in *Times of India* (2 April, 2009), latest government data released on 1 April 2009 showed exports coming down to almost $12 billion in February from a little over $15 billion in the corresponding period last year.

Another report on the same day in the *Times of India* ('Inventory Levels Come Off-peak') notes that a 'sense of feel-good seems to be returning to key industry sectors like steel, cement and textiles, if diminishing inventory levels are anything to go by. The sectors which witnessed a severe liquidity crunch in the December quarter, leading up to February this year are now breathing easy. Not only are inventory levels back to normal but demand generation has also prompted companies to raise their production levels'. According to the Web site http//www.theodora.com/wfbcurrent/India/India_economy.html, '...India escaped the brunt of the global financial crisis because of cautious banking policies and a relatively low dependence on exports for growth'.

We have every reason to believe that the Company Law Administration and the Securities & Exchange Board of India will try to bring to book errant management teams and instil a sense of financial discipline. We have seen how the Satyam episode has been handled. Restoring investor confidence and ensuring transparency and accountability are certainly prime concerns in any economy. Indian firms on their own are likely to improve their corporate governance practices so as to be able to address investors' concerns. It is in their own interest.

A further reason why the effects of the global economic downturn will be muted in India is that our exposure to international trade is rather limited and as a result, the shocks transmitted through trade are likely to be muted as well. The track record in meeting international debt obligations has been quite good. The state of our foreign exchange kitty is also quite healthy and should allow us to fund several months of imports.

Considering the total foreign investment in this country and the strength of the domestic economy, the chances of hot money flows from foreign institutional investors (FIIs) do not seem to be so very worrisome as of now. Moreover, it is not at all unlikely for FIIs to invest in our capital market considering our relative strength in the present context. The domestic economy is very large and we have weathered several recessions in the past. The Indian economy has displayed a great deal of resilience, for instance, in the face of oil price shocks of the 1970s and even the Asian financial crisis of the late 1990s. Given the sensible policies and firm implementation thereof, there is hardly any reason to brook pessimism.

Hopefully, professional accounting bodies will prevail upon their membership and deter them from aiding and abetting creative accounting and thus hurting our confidence in the financial system. While it is true that global phenomena affect the sentiments on our bourses, it is also true that our economy has the requisite strength to bounce back. For instance, capital issues (in billion rupees) moved from 494.1 in 2001–02 to 441.7 in 2002–03, then climbed to 541.5 in 2003–04 and continued to climb to reach 1786.6 in 2007–08; we see nearly the same story in terms of the market capitalization as a percentage of the GDP. The state of the global economy does affect us to some extent, as is evident from the quantum of GDRs/ADRs/ECBs/(floatations). From ($ million) 494.9 in 2001–02, these slid to 188.3 in 2002–03, then increased to 993.2 in 2003–04, rising further to 3406.4 in 2004–05, then to 9028.4 in 2005–06, then sharply declining to 2334.1 in 2006–07 and again rising to 7921.8 in 2007–08. However, the strength of our domestic economy is undeniable, especially if nature is bountiful.

Economic Survey 2009–10 which preceded Union Budget 2010–11[19] notes that, 'The fiscal year 2009–10 began as a difficult one. There was a significant slowdown in the growth rate in the second half of 2008–09, following the financial crisis that began in the industrialized nations in 2007 and spread to the real economy across the world. The growth rate of the gross domestic product in 2008–09 was 6.7%, with growth in the last two quarters hovering around 6%. There was apprehension that this trend would persist for some time, as the full impact of the economic slowdown in the developed world worked through the system'.

The Survey talks about the policy measures adopted to address the fallout of the global financial meltdown. We find in the final analysis based on Central Statistical Organization (CSO) data quoted by the Survey that the rate of growth at factor cost at 2004–05 prices was 9.5 per cent in 2005–06, 9.7 per cent in 2006–07, 9.2 per cent in 2007–08, 6.7 per cent in 2008–09, and 7.2 per cent in 2009–10. This was remarkably good considering the fact that monsoons were not quite as charitable as we would have liked them to be during 2009–10. Foreign Exchange Reserves initially declined from $309.7 billion in 2007–08 to $252 billion in 2008–09, and again moved up to $283.5 billion in 2009–10, indicating that there is hardly much reason to worry. However, the rate of inflation is on the rise, especially after the recent revision in the prices of petroleum products (i.e., the revision which became effective on 26 June 2010). Inflation needs to be contained on a priority basis in order to alleviate the suffering of the common man.

13.7 Concluding Observations

Ours is the land of 'Jugaad', there is no limit to Indian ingenuity and we may quite succeed in converting this into an era of opportunity, given our track record of resilience, dynamism and prudence.

Notes

1. http:en.wikipedia.org/wiki/Great_Depression
2. http:en.wikipedia.org/wiki/Great_depression#Facts_and_figures)
3. http:en.wikipedia.org/wiki/Gramm-Leach-Bliley- Act
4. http://www.truthout.org/article/eliot-spitzer-predatory-lenders-partner-crime-0)
5. http://www.tu-dresden.de/wwvwlgkw/Downloads/Events/Past%20Events/Workshops Workshops%20Countryrisk%20and%20FDI/Moodys_zu_workshop.pdf
6. http://en.wikipedia.org/wiki/Currency_Crisis
7. http://topics.nytimes.com/topic/reference/timestopic/subject/c/credit_crisis/index.html?WT.srch=I&WT.mc_ev=click&WT.mc_id=BI-S-E-GG-NA-CT-subprime
8. *The Economist*, London, 24 January 2009, p 97.
9. *The Economist*, London 10 January 2009, p 81.
10. *The Economist*, London, 13 December, p 13.
11. *The Economist*, London, 13 December, p 101.
12. http://en.wikipedia.org/wiki/Business_cycle.
13. *The Times of India*, Kolkata, 5 February 2009, p 7.
14. *The Times of India*, Kolkata, 5 February 2009, p 7.
15. *The Times of India*, Kolkata, 10 February 2009.
16. http://www.rbi.org.in/scripts/fun_deposit.aspx.
17. *The Times of India*, Kolkata, 6 February 2009.
18. *Monthly Review of the Indian Economy*, February 2009, Centre for Monitoring the Indian Economy, Mumbai.
19. http://indiabudget.nic.in/es2009-10/chapt2010/chapter01.pdf

References

Burnside, C., Eichenbaum, M. and Rebelo, S. (2001). 'Hedging and Financial Fragility in Fixed Exchange Rate Regimes'. *European Economic Review*, 45, pp 1151–1193.

———(2004). 'Government Guarantees and Self-fulfilling Speculative Attacks'. *The Journal of Economic Theory*, 119, pp 31–63.

———(2008). 'Currency Crisis Models'. *New Palgrave Dictionary of Economics* (2e), edited by Durlanf and Blume, Palgrave Macmillan.

Chang, R. and Velasco, A. (2000). 'Financial Fragility and the Exchange Rate Regime'. *The Journal of Economic Theory*, 92, pp 1–34.

———(2001). 'A Model of Currency Crises in Emerging Markets'. *Quarterly Journal of Economics*, 116(2), pp 489–517.

Eiteman, D. K., Stonehill, A. I., Moffett, M. H. and Pandey, A. (2007). *Multinational Business Finance* (10e). Pearson Education, New Delhi, India, p 46.

Ghosh, S. K. and Budhia, S. (2005). 'Corporate Governance: How Effective is it?' *Indian Accounting Review*, 9(2), December, pp 57–72.

Hume, D. (1935). *An Enquiry Concerning Human Understanding*. Open Court, Chicago, pp 85–86.

Krugman, P. (1979). 'A Model of Balance-of-payments Crises'. *Journal of Money*, Credit and Banking, 11, pp 311–325.

Obstfeld, M. and Rogoff, K. (1986). 'Rational and Self-fulfilling Balance-of-payments Crises'. *The American Economic Review*, 76(1), pp 72–81.

Raju, B. Y. (2008). 'Guest Column'. *The Financial Express*, 25 August.

Rivlin, A. M. (1994). *Reviving the American Dream*. Affiliated East-West Press, New Delhi, India, pp 46–47.

Schumpeter, J. A. (1954). *History of Economic Analysis*. George Allen & Unwin, London.

CHAPTER 14

M–M Hypothesis of Dividend Irrelevance in the Backdrop of Taxation in India

Snehamay Bhattacharyya

ABSTRACT

Traditionally, it is believed that dividend, among other factors, has a bearing on the market price of shares. Modigliani and Miller (M–M), in their model (known as M–M hypothesis), established the irrelevance of dividend, i.e., dividend has no effect on the value of the firm. M–M assumed non-existence of tax. Alternative assumption that they forwarded is equality of tax on dividend paid and that on capital gains. The intention is to make the shareholders indifferent between earnings in the form of dividend and earnings in the form of capital gains. In other words, they support the fact that if there is no difference in tax rate on dividend and tax rate on capital gains, shareholders will remain indifferent. But they (M–M) could never imagine a system of dividend distribution tax payable by the company declaring or paying dividend. The present study finds that even on testing M–M's model of dividend irrelevance in a situation prevailing in India with no tax differential between dividend earnings and capital gains does not hold good as a company paying dividend is required to pay tax on dividend payments.

14.1 Introduction

A company can utilize the profits earned by it in two ways: for reinvestment in the business and/or for distribution of dividend. The scale of preference between reinvestment and dividend varies from firm to firm. A firm with an opportunity for expansion will prefer retention whereas a firm that has reached the phase of stagnation may find dividend payment as the better alternative.

When individuals or institutions invest in firms, they give up cash in hope of a higher return of cash in future (Penman 2008). Return consists of two components: dividends and capital gains. Dividend policy has a direct influence on these two components of return (Pandey 2008). Dividend increases are often greeted as good news, an indicator that the firm will earn more in future, and cuts in dividends are greeted as bad news. These information effects—dividend signalling effects—occur when dividends are announced (Penman 2008). Dividend is the reward for shareholders' participation in the ownership of the company. It is the release of accumulated profit in favour of shareholders, the return that shareholders earn for their risk perception in the company. Traditionally, it is the expectation for dividend that guides a firm in the determination of cost of equity fund and this, in turn, implies that shareholders expect dividend and this expectation for dividend has, among other factors, a bearing on the market price of shares.

Modigliani and Miller, in their model (known as M–M hypothesis), tried to establish the irrelevance of dividend, i.e., dividend has no effect on the value of the firm.

14.2 Modigliani and Miller (M–M) Hypothesis

The objective of a dividend policy like other two financial decisions (financing and investing) is to maximize value of the firm. M–M claims that value of the firm, which is the present value of sum of dividend and capital gains, is independent of dividend policy. In other words, dividend policy has no role in influencing the market price of share and hence the value of the firm (which is the product of number of shares and market price of shares).

14.2.1 Assumptions

M–M's theory of irrelevance is based on the following assumptions:

- The firm operates in perfect capital markets where all investors behave rationally.
- Taxes do not exist or there is no tax differential between dividends and capital gains.
- The investment policy of the firm is fixed.

The crux of M–M's argument is that the effect of dividends on wealth of the shareholders is offset exactly by the effect of other means of financing. Thus, the shareholders would be indifferent between dividends and retained earnings (Banerjee 1999).

Proof

$$P_0 = (D_1 + P_1)/(1 + k) \tag{14.1}$$

where, P_0 is the market price per share at time 0

k is the cost of capital

D_1 is the dividend per share at time 1

P_1 is the market price per share at time 1.

When there is no external financing, the value of the firm (V) would simply be the number of shares (n) times the price of each share (P_0). Thus,

$$V = n\,P_0 = n\,(D_1 + P_1)/(1 + k) \tag{14.2}$$

If new shares are to be issued to finance investment programme at time 1 at a price of P1, the value of the firm at time 0 will be:

$$\begin{aligned} V &= [n\,P_0 = n\,(D_1 + P_1) + m\,P_1 - m\,P_1]/(1 + k) \\ &= [n\,D_1 + n\,P_1 + m\,P_1 - m\,P_1]/(1 + k) \\ &= [n\,D_1 + (n + m)\,P_1 - m\,P_1]/(1 + k) \end{aligned} \tag{14.3}$$

Now, total value of new shares issued is

$$m P_1 = I - (E - n D_1) \tag{14.4}$$

where I is the total new investments during period 1.
E is the earnings of the firm for the period.

By substituting Eq. (14.4) into Eq. (14.3), M–M shows below that the effect of dividend payment is cancelled out:

$$\begin{aligned} n P_0 &= [n D_1 + (n + m) P_1 - m P_1]/(1 + k) \\ &= [n D_1 + (n + m) P_1 - I - (E - n D_1)]/(1 + k) \\ &= [n D_1 + (n + m) P_1 - I - E + n D_1)]/(1 + k) \\ &= [n D_1 + (n + m) P_1 - I + E - n D_1)]/(1 + k) \\ &= [(n + m) P_1 - I + E)]/(1 + k) \end{aligned} \tag{14.5}$$

Equation (14.5) shows that the value of the firm is independent of its dividend policy.

The dividend irrelevance notion says that the dividends themselves will not affect (cum-dividend) shareholder value (when the stock goes ex-dividend). The return to the shareholder is made up of a dividend and a capital gain. A dividend adds to the return but capital gain is reduced by the amount of the dividend, leaving the return unaffected. Some investors might prefer dividends to capital gains because they need cash. But they can sell some of their shares to convert capital gains into dividends. Other investors might prefer no dividends; they can achieve this by buying the stock with the cash from dividend. This ability to make what are called home-made dividends means that investors do not care if their return comes from dividends or capital gains (Penman 2008).

To understand M–M's argument that dividend policy is irrelevant, recognize that any shareholder can in theory construct his or her own dividend policy. For example, if a firm does not pay dividends, a shareholder who wants a 5 per cent dividend can 'create' it by selling 5 per cent of his or her stock. Conversely, if a company pays a higher dividend than an investor desires, the investor can use the unwanted dividends to buy additional shares of the company's stock. If investors could buy and sell shares and, thus, create their own dividend policy without incurring costs, then the firm's dividend policy would truly be irrelevant (Brigham and Errhaedt 2004).

14.2.2 Tax Non-existence Assumption of M–M

M–M assumed non-existence of tax. Alternative assumption that they forwarded is equality of tax on dividend paid and that on capital gains. The intention is to make the shareholders indifferent between earnings in the form of dividend and earnings in the form of capital gains. In other words, they support the fact that if there is difference in tax rate on dividend and tax rate on capital gains, shareholders will not remain indifferent.

14.3 World Scenario on Dividend Taxation

There is significant international diversity in the sphere of taxation of dividends. A brief description of taxation of dividends in some selected countries is provided below.

- In USA dividends are taxed at a 15 per cent rate for most individual taxpayers. Dividends received by low income individuals are taxed at 5 per cent rate until 31 December 2007.

- In *Canada*, there is taxation of dividends, but tax policy attempts to compensate for this through the Dividend Tax Credit or DTC for personal income in dividends from Canadian corporations.
- In the *Netherlands*, there is a tax of 1.2 per cent per year on the value of the *share*, regardless of the dividend, as part of the *flat tax on savings and investments*.
- In *Czech Republic*, there is a tax of 12.5 per cent on dividends.
- In *Bulgaria*, there is a tax of 5 per cent on dividends.
- In *Romania*, there is a tax of 16 per cent on dividends.
- In *Poland*, there is a tax of 19 per cent on dividends. This rate is equal to the rates of capital gains and other taxes.
- In the *UK*, companies pay *corporation tax* on their profits and the remainder can be paid to shareholders as dividends. Basic rate tax payers have no further tax to pay as the dividend is deemed to have been received a net of 10 per cent tax. For higher-rate taxpayers, additional tax must be paid at 22.5 per cent of the net dividend received (32.5 per cent less the 10 per cent deemed tax deduction, calculated on the deemed gross payment of the dividend).
- In the *Republic of Ireland*, companies paying dividends must generally withhold tax at the standard rate (*as of 2007*, 20 per cent) from the dividend and issue a tax voucher to include details of the tax paid. A person not liable to tax can reclaim it at the end of the year, while a person liable to a higher rate of tax must declare it and pay the difference.
- In *Australia*, dividends are taxed at the recipient's marginal tax rate (up to 46.5 per cent from 1 July 2006). Australia (like *New Zealand*) has a *Dividend Imputation* system which allows *franking credits* to be attached to dividends. This allows recipients of franked dividends to impute (or credit) the corporate tax paid by the paying company. A recipient of a fully franked dividend on the top marginal tax rate will effectively pay only about 23 per cent tax on the cash amount of the dividend. (en.wikipedia.org)

14.4 History of Dividend Tax in India

There are four phases in the history of dividend taxation in India. All these four phases have centred around the question: What is the taxable event—dividend earning or dividend declaration? Let us have a look at all such phases.

Phase I (Upto 31st May 1997)

Taxable event: Earning of dividend

Assessee: The shareholder

Up to 31 March 1997, the company was not liable to pay any income tax on the amount of dividends declared, distributed or paid by such company. However, such dividend was included in the income of the shareholders under the head 'income from other sources'. For 'domestic company'-investor, Section 80M provided for deduction on account of dividend income from investee-domestic-company. For 'individual'-investor, 80L provided for such deduction.

Phase II (From 1 June 1997 to 31 March 2002)

Taxable event: The declaration or payment of dividend

Assessee: The company declaring or paying the dividend

To quote Mr. Chidambaram, the then Union Finance Minister, while introducing the Finance Bill 1997:

> In order to encourage investment in the shares of domestic companies,[1] the Bill proposes to exempt from income-tax, dividends received from domestic companies on or after 1st June, 1997. Consequently, deductions under section 80L and 80M in respect of corporate dividends have been discontinued. The provisions relating to tax deduction at source from dividends have also been suitably modified (indiabudget.nic.in).

Under Section 115-O of the Income Tax Act, 1961, a domestic company shall be liable to pay additional income tax on any amount declared, distributed or paid by such company by way of dividend (whether interim or otherwise) on or after 1 June 1997, whether out of current or accumulated profits. Such additional income tax shall be payable at a flat rate on the amount so distributed. This additional tax shall be payable even if no income tax is payable by such company on its total income. Further, under Sub-section 4 of Section 115-O of the Income Tax Act, 1961, any dividend, tax paid by a Dividend Distributing Company (DDC) is treated as a final payment of tax in respect of the amount declared, distributed or paid as dividends and no further credit may be claimed by the DDC or by any other person in respect of the amount of tax so paid. In view of the income tax now payable by the domestic company, any dividends declared, distributed or paid by such company, on or after 01-06-1997 shall be exempt in the hands of the shareholders. [Section10(34)].

Phase III (From 1 April 2002 to 31 March 2003)

Taxable event: Earning of dividend

Assessee: The shareholder

Dividend distribution tax withdrawn and deductions to shareholders under Sections 80L and 80M reintroduced, i.e., the pre-1997 days came back. Again the shareholders were considered as assesses. But the journey did not last for a long time and ended on 31 March 2003.

Phase IV (From 1 April 2003)

Taxable event: The declaration/payment of dividend

Assessee: The company declaring/paying the dividend

The fourth phase started on 1 April 2003 and is continuing till now. Again tax on account of divided payment is imposed on the dividend distributing company and exemption to shareholders reintroduced.

Specialities in India: At a glance

For the shareholders

Dividend income exempt from tax under Section 10(34) of the Income Tax Act, 1961

Long-term capital gains (i.e., shares held for more than 12 months) exempt from tax under Section 10(38) of the Income Tax Act, 1961.

---

1 '*Domestic Company*': means an Indian company, or any other company which in respect of its income liable to tax under this act, has made the prescribed arrangements for the declaration and payment within India, of the dividends (including dividends on preference shares) payable out of such income. [Section 2(22A) of the Income Tax Act 1961].

For the dividend distributing company

Company declaring or paying dividend is required to pay tax at 16.995 per cent (i.e., 15 per cent + surcharge + education cess secondary and higher education cess) on dividend distributed or paid by it.

14.5 Testing of Validity of M–M Hypothesis

In their dividend irrelevance, hypothesis M–M assumed the non-existence of personal income tax payable by a shareholder or equality of tax on dividend and that on capital gains payable by a shareholder, to remove the possibility of tax differential that may set a scale of preference between dividend earnings and earnings from capital gains for the shareholder. But they (M–M) could never imagine a system of dividend distribution tax payable by the company declaring/paying dividend. In the light of such a system, let us test how far their model is competent to prove the irrelevance of dividend policy.

Giving effect to the dividend tax (t_d) payable by dividend distributing company in Eq. (14.4) we get,

$$m P_1 = I - \{E - n D_1 (1 + t_d)\} \tag{14.6}$$

where I is the total new investments during period 1.
E is the earnings of the firm for the period.
t_d is the tax on dividend payable by the dividend distributing company.

By substituting Eq. (14.6) into Eq. (14.3), we see that

$$\begin{aligned} nP_0 &= [n D_1 + (n + m) P_1 - mP_1]/(1 + k) \\ &= [n D_1 + (n + m) P_1 - [I - \{E - n D_1 (1 + t_d)\}]]/(1 + k) \\ &= [n D_1 + (n + m) P_1 - I + \{E - n D_1 - n D_1 t_d\}]/(1 + k) \\ &= [n D_1 + (n + m) P_1 - I + E - n D_1 - n D_1 t_d]/(1 + k) \\ &= [(n + m) P_1 - I + E - n D_1 t_d)]/(1 + k) \end{aligned} \tag{14.7}$$

A comparison between Eqs. (14.5) and (14.7) gives

$$nP_0 = [(n + m) P_1 - I + E)]/(1 + k) \tag{14.5}$$

$$\begin{aligned} nP_0 &= [(n + m) P_1 - I + E - nD_1 t_d)]/(1 + k) \\ &= [(n + m) P_1)]/(1 + k) + E/(1 + k) - I/(1 + k) - (n D_1 t_d)/(1 + k) \end{aligned} \tag{14.7}$$

When $D_1 = 0$

$$nP_0 = [(n + m) P_1)]/(1 + k) + E/(1 + k) - I/(1 + k) \ldots (V_{Zd})$$

When D_1 is other than 0

$$nP_0 = [(n + m) P_1)]/(1 + k) + E/(1 + k) - I/(1 + k) - (n D_1 t_d)/(1 + k) \ldots (V_{NZd})$$

$(V_{NZd}) - (V_{Zd}) = - (n D_1 t_d)/(1 + k)$, indicating that in case of dividend payment, value of the firm will decrease by the present value of cash outflow on account of dividend distribution tax.

14.6 Observations

1. In the dividend distribution tax era in India, a non-zero dividend payment will generate a negative impact on value of the firm. So the value of the firm will vary from a zero payout

to a non-zero payout policy, i.e., the value of the firm becomes dependent on its dividend policy.

2. Even when there is no tax differential between dividend earnings and capital gains, we find that the dividend distribution tax alone proves that M–M hypothesis of dividend irrelevance does not hold good in India.
3. Investors who want additional dividends must incur brokerage costs to sell shares, and investors who do not want dividends must first pay taxes on the unwanted dividends and then incur brokerage costs to purchase shares with the after-tax dividends. Because taxes and brokerage costs certainly exist, dividend policy may well be relevant (Brigham and Errhaedt 2004).
4. If making home-made dividend is difficult because of illiquidity in the market for shares, lack of dividends might reduce the value of an investment (known as liquidity discount) to a shareholder who desires dividend (Penman 2008).

14.7 Conclusion

James E. Walter's dividend model suggests that when the return on investment earned by a firm is equal to its cost of capital, the market price of its shares become insensitive to its dividend policy. But actual determinants of dividend policy in any company emerge from more pragmatic considerations than theoretical difference between rate of return and cost of capital. Because of the existence of uncertainty, individual shareholders prefer current dividend. Stability of dividend rate also has favourable impact on share market (Das 2006). But, if a firm forgoes value creating projects to pay dividends, it will destroy value. But given a ready availability of financing, sensible management will borrow or issue shares to pay dividends rather than affecting good investments (Penman 2008).

There are three tax-related reasons for thinking that investors might prefer a low dividend payout to a high payout. They are discussed below:

Long-term capital gains are taxed at a rate lower than that on dividends. Therefore, wealthy investors (who own most of the stock and receive most of the dividends) might prefer to have companies retain and plough earnings back into the business. Earnings growth would presumably lead to stock price increases, and thus, lower-taxed capital gains would be substituted for higher-taxed dividends.

Taxes are not paid on the gain until a stock is sold. Due to time value effects, taxes paid in the future has a lower effective cost than taxes paid today.

If a stock is held by someone until he or she dies, no capital gains tax is due at all. The beneficiaries who receive the stock can use the stock's value on the death day as their cost basis and, thus, completely escape the capital gains tax. Because of these tax advantages, investors may prefer to have companies retain most of their earnings (Brigham and Errhaedt 2004).

As a consequence, the value of shares should be higher in the internal financing case than in the external financing one. Thus, the tax advantage of capital gains over dividends strongly favours a low-dividend payout policy. This implies that investors in high tax brackets should own low-payout shares, and those in low-tax bracket shou!d own high-payout shares (Pandey 2008).

M–M argued that all economic theories are based on simplifying assumptions, and that the validity of a theory must be judged by the empirical tests and not by the realism of its assumptions (Brigham and Errhaedt 2004).

But, even on testing M–M's model in a situation prevailing in India with no tax differential between dividend earnings and capital gains, the M–M hypothesis of dividend irrelevance does not hold good as companies paying dividends are required to pay tax on their dividend payments.

References

Banerjee, B. (1999). *Financial Policy and Management Accounting*. World Press, India.

Brigham, E. and Errhaedt, M. (2004). *Financial Management: Theory and Practice*. Thomson, U.S.A.

Das, P. K. (2006). 'Dividend Policy in Selected Company—An Empirical Analysis'. *The Management Accountant*, April, India.

Pandey, I. M. (2008). *Financial Management*. Vikas Publishing House, Noida, India.

Penman, S. H. (2008). *Financial Statement analysis and Security Valuation*. TMH, India.

(2007). *Income Tax Act*, 1961, Taxman, India.

Web sites

en.wikipedia.org
indiabudget.nic.in

CHAPTER 15

Performance of NGOs—A Study on Some Selected Districts in West Bengal

Dhrubaranjan Dandapat and Bhaskar Bagchi

ABSTRACT

Evaluation is the term most commonly used to describe the process of assessing performance against objectives. At their best, evaluation techniques should be able to assess performance results against objectives, and benefits against costs. In West Bengal, for NGOs working in the development field, evaluation is still very new and the vast majority of projects and programmes funded by donors are neither subject to any sort of formal evaluation nor bound to specified cycles of expenditure for committed support. Most NGOs do not carry out any assessment of the impact of the projects and programmes beyond simple project report back-up and financial audit.

This paper scans the performance of NGOs in selected districts in West Bengal with respect to prominent activities undertaken by the NGOs.

15.1 Introduction

In common parlance, the term NGO is used to encompass a whole range of organizations which differ in size, function and geographical location. Thus, the term can be used to describe small, locally based and loosely established voluntary and largely grass-root types of associations, as well as large national and transnational voluntary associations with formal constitutions, employing hundreds of staff. They may be engaged in relief, emergency or longer term development work or a mixture of all three (Bennett 1997). In most developing countries, NGOs are central actors in anti-poverty policies and programmes. The social and educational background of many NGO staff enables them to interact easily with the staff of national institutions and they can help create bridges between these institutions, outside agencies and grass-root organizations. NGOs can also be very effective in delivering assistance to poor people (Bennett 1997). Sometimes, NGOs reflect the political system in which they thrive or local interest groups and, thus, may not serve the interest of the poor people. However, it is important that they should be accountable for their actions, especially to the poor groups that they seek to represent (Riddell and Robinson, 1995).

In India, voluntary actions by individuals, communities and organizations existed from ancient days. Ancient rulers of India developed a unique tradition of social work through the inbuilt mechanism of providing security to the common people through joint family system, kinship and other supporting social structures. Indian voluntary organizations had been influenced by the economic structures of *Zamindari* system and by the religious values of *Karma* and *Dharma*. During the British period, some eminent political and social leaders set up a network of voluntary agencies mostly geared towards removing the social divisions and discrepancies and later on during the Gandhian era, these agencies become more active and powerful (Sengupta 2006).

This paper focuses on the general topic of impact assessment, and considers several important issues. Section 15.2 delineates the major activities of NGOs. Section 15.3 summarizes performance evaluation techniques that can be adopted by NGOs. Section 15.4 shows the methodology of the study. Section 15.5 highlights the performance of selected NGOs. Section 15.6 briefly analyses the results of the survey and Section 15.7 ends with concluding observations.

15.2 Activities of NGOs in West Bengal

Voluntary agencies in West Bengal have a history of involvement in a wide range of social welfare and developmental work which stretches back to the last century. Over the past quarter century, and especially during the past two decades, there has been a rapid growth in the number of NGOs involved in the developmental works, the number of people working for NGOs and the amount of money which flows into voluntary agencies. Perhaps, the greatest growth has been in the thousands of new grass-root organizations, sometimes referred to simply as 'groups' and sometimes as 'peoples' organizations (UNDP 2004), which have grown up locally—some extending no further than one or two villages. A survey conducted by a voluntary organization, Society for Participatory Research in Asia (PRIA), New Delhi, reveals that as many as 20 million people are associated with Non-profit Organizations (NPOs) as paid or volunteer staff in India. The survey titled 'Invisible: Yet *Wide Spread*: *The Non-profit Sector in India*' also revealed that more than 60 percent of NPOs are engaged in religious, community service and education related activities. Every eighth person in the non-agricultural workforce is engaged in the NPO sector.

In a state like West Bengal, with differences between individual districts and regions, NGOs are characterized by a rich diversity of approaches, traditions and activities rendering the task of generalization difficult, if not impossible. They cover most areas of the state and their activities affect a significant proportion of the population living in poverty. Our study has identified a particular set of attributes with which they are associated across 19 districts of the state of West Bengal.

The fundamental objectives of NGO activity in rural West Bengal are *poverty alleviation* and the *empowerment of the poor*, primarily through small-scale development projects. Some NGOs have chosen to *tackle the symptoms of poverty manifested in low educational standards, ill-health, poor sanitation and inferior housing* by means of social welfare programmes. Others, among 46 NGOs examined in the present study, which are operating across the districts of Coochbehar, Murshidabad, Purulia,

TABLE 15.1

Activities of NGOs in West Bengal—A Case Study of Six Districts

Activities \ Districts	Cooch-behar	Murshida-bad	Purulia	Birbhum	Purba Medinipur	24 Parganas (South)	Total	Percentage
Health and Family Welfare	3	5	7	8	4	6	33	71.74
Sanitation	3	3	3	4	3	4	20	43.49
Welfare of Women and Children	1	4	7	9	3	7	31	67.39
Help for Poor, Aged and Destitute	4	4	6	8	4	4	30	65.22
Care of Orphans		2	5	6	3	3	19	41.30
Running of High Schools			2	2		2	6	13.04
Housing			2				2	04.35
Research						1	1	02.17
Stipends/ Scholarships						1	1	02.17
Vocational/ Technical Training	2	4	4	7	5	6	28	60.87
Education/Literacy Programme	3	5	6	9	3	6	32	69.57
Seminar/ Conference/ Meetings		1	3	4		4	12	26.09
Religious Functions			2			1	3	06.52
Publications of Religious Books			1			1	2	04.35
Agricultural Activities	1		4	2	2		9	19.57
Animal Husbandry	1	2	4	4	2		13	28.26
Environmental Programme	2		2	1			5	10.87
Rural Development	2	5	6	8	3	5	29	63.04
Cultural Programme					1	1	2	04.35
Relief for Natural Calamities						1	1	02.17
Others	2	3	4	1	1	2	13	28.26

Source: Field Survey.
Note: Figures indicate number of NGOs performing particular activities.

Birbhum, Purba Medinipur and 24 Parganas (South) have concentrated on *enhancing the asset position* and *income earning potential of the poor* through *land-improvement schemes*, *credit* and *vocational and technical training*.

Districtwise activities of these 46 NGOs are shown in Table 15.1.

From Table 15.1 it is evident that '*Health and Family Welfare*' programme receives highest attention from the NGOs across six districts of the State. About 71.74 per cent of the selected

NGOs receive grants to run this scheme, followed by 'Education and Literacy' programme (69.57 per cent) and '*Welfare of Women and Children*' (67.39 per cent). The project like '*Help for Poor, Aged and Destitute*' comes next with 65.22 per cent of the selected NGOs opted to undertake this scheme, while '*Vocational/Technical Training*' programme is a close follower (60.87 per cent).

15.3 Performance Evaluation Techniques

Any organization dependent upon voluntary contributions attempts to assess the extent to which its goals are being achieved, and to do so as efficiently and openly as possible. NGOs are no exception (Armstrong and Bridger 1986). In fact, the NGOs would rate themselves highly in all these respects, but the benefits of assessment are both broader and deeper than this (Bowmann et al. 1989). Furthermore, if voluntary organizations are able to show that the funds made available to them are well spent, support will tend to be strengthened and funding will be based on a firmer footing, while, at the same time, criticisms of poor performance can be more substantially met (Armstrong and Bridger 1986). Evaluation can also be used to highlight weaknesses in current monitoring practices, as well as to provide a wider perspective on different types or clusters of projects or programmes (Armstrong and Bridger 1986).

15.3.1 Criteria for an Appropriate Performance Measurement Tool

Duvel and Rumbel (1998) recommend that performance measurement be approached in a holistic manner and adhere to the following pre-defined measurement criteria:

- *Relevance*: Does the measure reflect the most important results for the organization?
- *Integration*: Can the measure be cascaded downward from the corporate level to the operating units?
- *Sustainability*: Can the measure accurately forecast the trend in future results?
- *Measurability*: Can the measure be calculated from readily available data?
- *Reliability*: Would different judges make the same calculations?
- *Manageability*: Can the individual control the results?
- *Communicability*: Can the measure be explained easily and clearly to internal and external audiences?
- *Timeliness*: Can the measure be adopted annually even if it were designed for use in the longer term?
- *Consistency*: Can the measure be related to past performance and competitive performance?
- *Credibility*: Is the measure resistant to manipulation?
- *Differentiation*: Do the results vary sufficiently so that people know which specific goal has been achieved?

15.3.2 Application of the Balanced Scorecard

Kaplan and Norton (1996) describe the balanced scorecard as a management system that enables organizations to clarify their vision and strategy and translate them into action. The balanced scorecard combines both short and long-term objectives to improve management's ability to gauge the attainment of strategic goals. The balanced scorecard enables organizations to bridge the gap between ambiguous goals and day-to-day operations. It creates a process, which encourages strategic focus by shifting the organization's focus from programmes to the outcomes, for which the programmes were designed to accomplish.

In developing a balanced scorecard for NGOs, we have modified some key terms to show the selected dimensions and associated goals, measurement indicators and activities using the original diagram of the balanced scorecard.

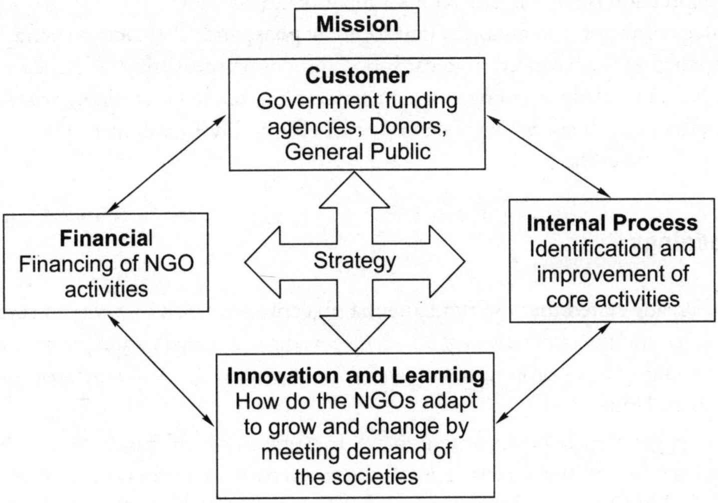

Figure 15.1 Balanced scorecard adapted for NGOs

Once the relevant perspectives are selected, the strategic goals are defined for each perspective. The next step is to illustrate the goals and key success factors through cause-and-effect links. The result is a cohesive map of organization's functioning and strategy, indicating how the strategy is to be implemented. Finally, a matrix provides an overview of the dimensions, goals and variables which can be actively influenced.

In Fig. 15.1, it is illustrated that the balanced scorecard is a measurement system for not-for-profit entities that provides feedback on both internal business processes and external outcomes to improve performance and results (Averson 2004). The following four dimensions are selected in a balanced scorecard: *financial perspective, customer perspective, internal process perspective* and *innovation and learning perspective.*

- *Financial perspective*: The financial perspective is usually the most important dimension. After all, like any other organization, NGOs cannot be sustainable if their activities cannot be financed.
- *Customer perspective*: The main aim is to determine customer segments and the key factors to customer satisfaction. Customers (governments, funding agencies, donors, sponsors, members of the NGOs, the public, etc.) finance the organization in some form or other through their demand.

- *Internal process perspective*: Identification of the core activities of the organization and continuous improvement of those activities enhances efficiency and effectiveness of the NGOs and increases customer satisfaction.
- *Innovation and learning perspective*: It focuses on the learning and innovation capability of the NGOs and how does it build and retain know-how in order to implement strategy. Learning processes and innovations are a pre-requisite for a process environment.

The balanced scorecard differs from a loose collection of indicators in that the key figures are mapped onto cause–effect relationships between as well as within the perspectives, providing a clear and concrete expression of the organization's function and strategy.

The strategy of the organization, the development phase and other factors such as organizational culture dictate whether the balanced scorecard should focus on measuring efficiency, effectiveness or impact. If the NGO is relatively young, it will be most interested in determining whether the internal processes are effective. Once this has been established, the NGO will gain more effectiveness by functioning more efficiently.

15.4 Methodology

As it has been already stated that the fundamental objectives of NGO activity in rural West Bengal are *poverty alleviation* and the *empowerment of the poor*, so we have decided to analyse the performance of the NGOs in reaching the poor in terms of *utilization of funds by the NGOs for below poverty line* (*BPL*) section of the population.

In order to get first-hand information on the utilization of funds by the NGOs for the underprivileged section of the society, a *primary survey* across six districts in West Bengal has been conducted on 60 NGOs selected on stratified random sampling basis (Kothari 1995), out of the listed 1214 NGOs in West Bengal (DAINET 2000) administering structured questionnaire. Amongst 60 selected NGOs, questionnaires relating to 14 NGOs had to be cancelled due to disorganized or incomplete responses. Thus, the *final sample* stood at 46.

For the purpose of the study, we have identified two *major activities* like, *Health and Family Welfare* and *Education and Literacy Programme*; which are being undertaken by the NGOs in West Bengal (Table 15.1). Accordingly, we have selected six districts (one-third of the total population) in West Bengal on random sampling basis. The grand average of all the six districts taken together in respect of utilization of funds for BPL sector for 3 years (2003–06) for each respective programme has been calculated. Similarly, the district average for the above 3 years with respect to utilization of funds for BPL sector is obtained for each respective programme of each six districts of the state. Then the district average figure has been compared with the grand average figure of six districts taken together and the differences have been shown accordingly.

15.5 Performance Evaluation of Selected NGOs

In this section, we present the data collected through primary survey in respect of performance of NGOs across six different districts of West Bengal in Tables 15.2 through 15.10.

TABLE 15.2

Districtwise Receipt and Utilization of Funds for BPL Category Project—Health and Family Welfare (2003–06)

Districts	Funds Utilized for BPL Category (Percentage) (2003–04)	Funds Utilized for BPL Category (Percentage) (2004–05)	Funds Utilized for BPL Category (Percentage) (2005–06)
Coochbehar	73.2	72.3	60.1
Murshidabad	68.33	73.88	72.33
Purulia	73.25	86.61	65.7
Birbhum	85.6	80.05	63.25
Purba Medinipur	60.00	66.3	61.09
24 Parganas (South)	76.4	80.2	66.7
Total	**77.91**	**81.41**	**65.84**

Source: Field Survey.

TABLE 15.3

Districtwise Receipt and Utilization of Funds for BPL Category Project—Education and Literacy Programme (2003–06)

Districts	Funds Utilized for BPL Category (Percentage) (2003–04)	Funds Utilized for BPL Category (Percentage) (2004–05)	Funds Utilized for BPL Category (Percentage) (2005–06)
Coochbehar	63.48	50.8	66.6
Murshidabad	70.09	63.25	75.00
Purulia	69.7	77.77	70.19
Birbhum	76.75	68.39	78.92
Purba Medinipur	55.75	66.1	71.11
24 Parganas (South)	71.56	56.2	72.00
Total	72.63	69.40	70.99

Source: Field Survey.

TABLE 15.4 Districtwise Receipt and Utilization of Funds for BPL Category Project—Welfare of Women and Children (2003–06)

Districts	Funds Utilized for BPL Category (Percentage) (2003–04)	Funds Utilized for BPL Category (Percentage) (2004–05)	Funds Utilized for BPL Category (Percentage) (2005–06)
Coochbehar	66.75	64.2	60.11
Murshidabad	59.8	73.25	70.00
Purulia	71.19	75.5	83.83
Birbhum	70.05	80.9	77.75
Purba Medinipur	60.19	60.08	66.66
24 Parganas (South)	66.25	66.1	79.2
Total	68.55	73.62	79.94

Source: Field Survey.

TABLE 15.5 Districtwise Receipt and Utilization of Funds for BPL Category Project—*Help for Poor, Aged and Destitute* (2003–06)

Districts	Funds Utilized for BPL Category (Percentage) (2003–04)	Funds Utilized for BPL Category (Percentage) (2004–05)	Funds Utilized for BPL Category (Percentage) (2005–06)
Coochbehar	68.9	73.6	70.7
Murshidabad	68.33	73.29	64.37
Purulia	63.28	84.5	78.9
Birbhum	76.7	82.3	79.8
Purba Medinipur	70.1	63.5	68.9
24 Parganas (South)	74.5	75.6	66.00
Total	**63.4**	**80.42**	**73.02**

Source: Field Survey.

TABLE 15.6

Districtwise Receipt and Utilization of Funds for BPL Category—Average for 3 Years (2003–06)
Project: Health and Family Welfare

Districts	Average Funds Received (Rs. in Crores)	Average Funds Utilized (Rs. in Crores)	Average Funds Unutilized (Rs. in Crores)	Average Funds Utilized for BPL Category (Rs. in Crores)	Average Funds Utilized for BPL Category (Percentage)
Coochbehar	0.0101	0.0101	–	0.0068	67.33
Murshidabad	0.5791	0.5748	0.0043	0.4175	72.64
Purulia	5.472	5.4488	0.0232	3.9027	71.63
Birbhum	3.5215	3.512	0.0095	2.7365	77.92
Purba Medinipur	0.3494	0.3493	0.0001	0.2170	62.13
24 Parganas (South)	2.7651	2.7587	0.0064	2.7026	75.13

Source: Field Survey.

TABLE 15.7

Districtwise Receipt and Utilization of Funds for BPL Category—Average for 3 Years (2003–06)
Project: Education and Literacy Programme

Districts	Average Funds Received (Rs. in Crores)	Average Funds Utilized (Rs. in Crores)	Average Funds Unutilized (Rs. in Crores)	Average Funds Utilized for BPL Category (Rs. in Crores)	Average Funds Utilized for BPL Category (Percentage)
Coochbehar	0.0088	0.0088	–	0.0053	60.23
Murshidabad	0.219	0.2174	0.0016	0.1537	70.70
Purulia	2.6155	2.6003	0.0152	1.8789	72.26
Birbhum	3.3444	3.3367	0.0077	2.4752	74.18
Purba Medinipur	0.1137	0.1122	0.0016	0.0725	64.62
24 Parganas (South)	1.374	1.3706	0.0034	0.9290	67.78

Source: Field Survey.

TABLE 15.8

Districtwise Receipt and Utilization of Funds for BPL Category—Average for 3 Years (2003–06)
Project: Welfare of Women and Children

Districts	Average Funds Received (Rs. in Crores)	Average Funds Utilized (Rs. in Crores)	Average Funds Unutilized (Rs. in Crores)	Average Funds Utilized for BPL Category (Rs. in Crores)	Average Funds Utilized for BPL Category (Percentage)
Coochbehar	0.0021	0.0021	–	0.0013	61.91
Murshidabad	0.0849	0.0842	0.0007	0.0582	69.08
Purulia	0.5393	0.5266	0.0127	0.4147	78.75
Birbhum	0.4939	0.4807	0.0132	0.3701	77.00
Purba Medinipur	0.0445	0.0439	0.0006	0.0267	60.74
24 Parganas (South)	0.4029	0.3976	0.0053	0.2808	70.63

Source: Field Survey.

TABLE 15.9

Districtwise Receipt and Utilization of Funds for BPL Category—Average for 3 Years (2003–06)
Project: *Help for Poor, Aged and Destitute*

Districts	Average Funds Received (Rs. in Crores)	Average Funds Utilized (Rs. in Crores)	Average Funds Unutilized (Rs. in Crores)	Average Funds Utilized for BPL Category (Rs. in Crores)	Average Funds Utilized for BPL Category (Percentage)
Coochbehar	0.0443	0.0443	–	0.0317	71.56
Murshidabad	0.0666	0.065	0.0016	0.0465	71.59
Purulia	0.2608	0.2593	0.0015	0.2023	78.02
Birbhum	0.3776	0.3736	0.004	0.3002	80.34
Purba Medinipur	0.0549	0.0546	0.0003	0.0379	69.41
24 Parganas (South)	0.3599	0.3561	0.0039	0.2481	69.68

Source: Field Survey.

TABLE 15.10 **Utilization of Funds for BPL Category—Comparison Between Grand Average of Six Districts and District Average**

Districts	Health and Family Welfare	Education and Literacy Programme	Welfare of Women and Children	Help for Poor, Aged and Destitute
Total Average	75.05	71.01	74.04	72.43
Coochbehar	–7.72	–10.78	–12.13	–0.87
Murshidabad	–2.41	–0.31	–4.96	–0.84
Purulia	–3.42	+1.25	+4.71	+5.59
Birbhum	+2.87	+3.17	+2.96	+7.91
Purba Medinipur	–12.92	–6.39	–13.3	–3.02
24 Parganas (South)	+0.08	–3.23	–3.41	–2.75

Source: Field Survey, Results computed.

Note: The positive (+ve) an negative (–ve) figure indicates how much more or less is the district average than the grand average.

All Figures are in Percentage.

15.6 Findings of the Study

Coochbehar: The district average for *Education and Literacy Programme* is the lowest amongst the districts selected with 60.23 per cent allocation of funds to the BPL category. The average is also disappointing for the rest of the programmes and the performance of the NGOs is below the grand *average.*

Murshidabad: Generally, the NGOs functioning in this district show overall *agreeable* performance. Their spending pattern for the underprivileged classes is marginally less than that of grand *average* for all the sectors selected.

Purulia: There is a far-reaching prospect for the NGOs operating in the fallow and barren lands of Purulia, and *social mobilization* through NGOs is inevitable for *economic empowerment* and *poverty alleviation*. The average utilization of funds for BPL category for programmes like *Education and Literacy Programme*, *Welfare of Women and Children* and *Help for Poor, Aged and Destitute* is *greater* than the *grand average.*

Birbhum: The district average with respect to utilization of funds for BPL category is higher than the grand average figure in case of programmes like *Health and Family Welfare, Education and Literacy Programme* and *Help for Poor, Aged and Destitute.* This is a remarkable performance and hence, it can be concluded that *Birbhum district is the best performer* among all the six districts in terms of reaching the target groups and working for the underprivileged classes of the society.

Purba Medinipur: The Tenth Five Year Plan viewed the role of government and non-government sector as complimentary. But this does not hold good for the case of Purba Medinipur. The district average *falls short* of the *grand average* irrespective of all programmes, and immediate intervention by the government and donors/funding agencies is necessary. According to our study results, amongst the six districts of the State, Purba Medinipur is the *worst performer.*

24-Parganas (South): Our observations on the performance of the NGOs operating in West Bengal ends with the findings of the 24 Parganas (South) district. Interestingly, here the NGOs demonstrate *better than* the grand *average* only in the case of *Health and Family Welfare*, while the rest of the other projects exhibit marginally *poor performance* which calls for urgent attention from the NGOs' end.

15.7 Conclusion

The increase in public funding of NGO activities in India has raised the prominence of evaluation within NGOs, increased the pressure to undertake more evaluations and encouraged the examination of more rigorous methods of evaluations (Riddell and Robinson 1995).

The more significant is the allocation of public funds to NGOs, and greater is the pressure from governments to justify their projects and programmes (Robinson 1991). Greater amount of public money channeled to NGOs, growing income from individual sources and a greater public attention given to NGOs have all combined to raise the profile of NGOs as agencies which work to alleviate poverty by aiming at long-term development (Bowmann et al. 1989). Thus, not only is the government putting pressures on NGOs to prove their effectiveness, but the public is also becoming increasingly concerned to know whether NGOs are effectively and efficiently achieving their objectives or not (Cameron and Cocking 1991).

NGOs have various objectives and roles based on their communities and missions. Therefore, evaluation of NGOs should not be focused on the comparison of different organizations, but on the continuous improvement of each organization. Evaluation should be done at least from two perspectives: *performance measurement of programs* and *organizational evaluation.* In this paper, only the first one has been considered. The second one, i.e., organizational evaluation, contains two viewpoints: one from outside to measure organization's credibility, such as fair process of decision-making or financial sustainability, and the other from inside to assess organizational social capital, such as teamwork or Human Resource Development.

References

Armstrong, G. A. and Bridger, G. A. (1986). *Cost Effectiveness: Appraising Projects with Non-Quantifiable Benefits.* Crown Agents, London.

Bennett, J. (1997). *NGO Coordination at Field Level.* INTRAC/ICVA, Oxford, UK.

Bowmann, A., Baanante, J., Dichter, T., Londner, S. and Reiling, P. (1989). *Measuring Our Impact: Determining Cost-effectiveness of Non-governmental Organization Development Projects.* Technoserve, Norwalk, CT.

Cameron, C. and Cocking, J. (1991). *The Evaluation of NGO Activities, Organizations, Methodology and Results.* Overseas Development Agency, London.

Kaplan, R. S. and Norton, D. (1996). *The Balanced Scorecard.* Boston: Harvard Business School Press.

Riddell, R. C. and Robinson, M. (1995), *Non-governmental Organizations and Rural Poverty Alleviation.* Overseas Development Institute/Clarendon Press, London.

Robinson, M. (1991). 'Evaluating the Impact of NGOs in Rural Poverty Alleviation: India Country Study'. Working Paper No. 49. Overseas Development Institute, London.

Sengupta, D. (2006). *Academic-NGO Collaboration-Social Responsibility*. Jadavpur University, Kolkata.

United Nation Development Programme (2004). *Human Development Report 2004*. Oxford University Press, Oxford.

Web sites

www.balancedscorecard.org/default.html
www.lbl.ch/internat
arminbarandun@datacomm.ch

CHAPTER 16

Personal Carbon Trading—A Lifestyle-based Carbon Control Mechanism

K. C. Paul

ABSTRACT

Global warming is the lethal cause for the living beings on the earth. In turn, it is caused by emission of greenhouse gases (GHGs). Of the six constituents of GHGs, carbon dioxide is the dominant one. Combustion of carbon, contained mainly in fossil fuels, contributes to carbon dioxide emissions. Imposition of tax on the carbon content of the fuel used—known as Carbon Tax—is the most formidable 'Economic Policy Measure' to reduce carbon dioxide emission. But it is definitely not without some limitations which give rise to the search for other measures. Kyoto Protocol (2005) provided for three alternative trade-based marketing mechanisms: (i) Carbon Trading through 'Cap-and-Trade' system, (ii) Clean Development Mechanism (CDM), and (iii) Joint Implementation (JI). The largest ever initiative on emission trading under Kyoto Protocol is European Union's Emission Trading System (EU ETS) which completed its first phase during 2005–07. But it is designed mainly for application in industrial sector. Considering it important not to ignore the domestic or personal sector, The Environmental Audit Committee (2007–08) appointed by the House of Commons (UK) opted for 'Personal Carbon Trading' or PCT to bring about the desired behavioural change necessary to meet the '2050-global target'. It provides for rewards (monetary savings) for less-polluters and penalties for more-polluters at individual level. Though PCT has certain limitations, it is expected that after gradual overcoming of the limitations during implementation, it may emerge as a better and sustainable alternative mechanism to contain GHG emissions within limit necessary to avoid any atmospheric catastrophe. Based on the fact that there is huge scope of reducing carbon dioxide emissions significantly in individual and household sector through lifestyle changes, this paper advocates mingling of the concepts of carbon trading and lifestyle-based carbon control mechanism to derive twin benefits from them.

16.1 Introduction

Irrational human activities cause disproportionate emission, *inter alia,* of carbon dioxide (CO_2) in the atmosphere. Fossil carbon stored in coal, oil or gas when taken out of the ground and used by combustion for meeting various energy needs builds up in the atmosphere mainly in the form of carbon dioxide. There are six most dangerous gases including carbon dioxide, which together are called 'greenhouse gases', or GHGs, that are responsible for creating greenhouse effect. Other major gases included in the group are methane, nitrous oxide and chlorofluorocarbon. Earth receives heat from the sun through ultraviolet (UV) light but most of the heat, thus, received is radiated back from the earth and only the insignificant residual part of the heat left in the earth makes it habitable for living beings. But GHG traps the heat so radiated back causing global warming and threat to the humankind. Though carbon dioxide is the most intensively emitted man-made greenhouse gas, methane, nitrous oxide and chlorofluorocarbons all absorb far more radiation than carbon dioxide; thankfully, methane stays in the atmosphere for only 12 years before it breaks down but nitrous oxide stays for over 120 years and chlorofluorocarbons stay there much longer than that (Kyriakides 2008). Studies revealed that per capita GHG emissions is strongly correlated with economic prosperity and developing countries can hardly pursue their socio-economic goals sans GHG emissions or alternatively adopting appropriate technology options. Under this predicament, it is now well acknowledged that to avoid any imminent atmospheric catastrophe, urgent action is required to cut GHG emissions significantly—to the tune of 50–80 per cent globally by 2050.

16.1.1 Global Warming

Global warming is now a fact which is beyond doubt and debate. Global average temperatures have increased by only 0.7°C since the mid-1800s. Significant changes in the climate and the results are already being observed. During the last quarter of the last century, the proportion of global population affected by weather-related disasters doubled. But that is only the tip of what is waiting for us in the present century, i.e., the iceberg. According to an estimate, on current trends, this planet which has been so far providing favourable conditions for the living beings would warm up by between 1.4°C and 5.8°C by the turn of the century. It is beyond one's imagination whether this planet would still find favourable conditions for the living beings to exist.

There is a growing consensus about the disastrous effects of global warming; the severest of them may come from the effect of climate change as hinted above. Some of the other environmental and economic consequences of global warming as described in an IMF Working Paper (Cuervo and Gandhi 1998) are: fall in agricultural production and consequential rise in prices, rise in sea level, loss of forests, water shortage, cooling and heating needs, air and water pollution, health hazards, etc.

The severity and the urgency of the problems may be gauged from the following estimates about the growth of carbon dioxide emissions and the consequential damages as presented in the Working Paper referred to above, quoting various sources. According to it, the carbon dioxide concentration is projected to double around 2065, as compared to the levels of the pre-industrial era, in a business-as-usual scenario (OECD 1995 on '*Global Warming: Economic Dimensions and Policy Response*'). Intergovernmental Panel on Climate Change (IPCC 1996) estimated that damages from doubling of carbon dioxide concentrations in the global atmosphere could be as high as 1.5–2 per cent of world GDP, for world impact, 1–1.5 per cent of GDP of developed countries, and 2–9 per cent of GDP of developing countries.

Having realized the severity of the problems, it is now a well-recognized phenomenon to pay immediate attention to reduce carbon dioxide (being the major component of the GHGs) emissions. It is worth mentioning that any action involving combustion of carbon (contained mainly in fossil fuels like coal, oil, and natural gas and also in woods), either by any individual or any organization, would contribute to carbon dioxide emissions. At the present stage and age of industrial production-based civilization, we cannot think of a decent living without carbon consumption. It has also become a necessity of life to the poor. Thus, the sources of global warming may be individual or institutional, local or regional. But its effects are not confined within the creators or their localities; it may affect anyone and everyone ignoring any social, political or geographical boundaries, irrespective of whether one is responsible for its creation or not. So, any single *local source* of carbon dioxide emissions may have *global effects* of global warming.

The generic issue have already been introduced in Section 16.1, after which, the rest of the paper is organized as follows. Section 16.2 deals with the two basic approaches available as measures to mitigate the basic problem of reducing carbon dioxide emissions. It also gives a cosmetic touch to the Kyoto Protocol and the European Union Emission Trading Scheme (EU ETS) which is so far the largest emission trading programme. Section 16.3 introduces lifestyle-based carbon control mechanism in no-less-significant household sector. The concept of Personal Carbon Trading (PCT) is the subject matter of discussion in the penultimate section, i.e., Section 16.4. It also discusses the various models of PCT together with a comparative analysis of their respective merits and demerits. The last section i.e., Section 16.5 presents conclusion of the discussion.

16.2 Approaches to Mitigating Measures

The issue of rising temperature of the atmosphere is a global one since the location of the cause, i.e., GHG emissions, does not create any location-specific effect; rather, the effect is location-independent or global. So, any scheme undertaken by anybody, be it an individual or an organization of local, regional, national or international base in the public or private sector, to mitigate the global-natured problem must effectively have a global-level effect. It may be mentioned that in view of the enormity and spread of the crises, no individual action at a local level or even at a national level appears to be in commensurate with the need. What is actually needed is a concerted effort with a sound mechanism on the part of almost all the nations together. Environmental legislations enacted in different countries mainly addressed to the industrial sector assuming it to have a major role in polluting the environment. Well, while that is true, the global environmental situation is now so critical that we can hardly afford to ignore the role of an individual citizen in the global crises.

Almost in every problem-solving situations there are two approaches: preventive and curative. Again, we also know theoretically that '*prevention is better than cure*'. In case of the present problem-solving situation of searching out a solution, preventive approach, i.e., finding out ways and means to reduce carbon dioxide emissions, appears to be an incomparably better approach than the curative approach, which ultimately is a damage-control mechanism. Considering the severity, enormity, and global spread of the damages done by the effects of global warming, the curative approach, being infeasible, is mostly rejected.

Under preventive approach, the two major types of measures are economic policy measures and market-based measures.

Economic Policy Measures: Of the various types of economic policies that may be adopted, important ones are: imposition of taxes, charging user-fees, etc. Some examples of such taxes, charges or fees may be carbon tax, tax on traded pollution permits, royalties on minerals mined, tax on international aviation, tax on kerosene, charges for dumping at sea, etc. Among all these economic measures, carbon tax is the most relevant, formidable, and popular one. We may, therefore, have a brief discussion on carbon tax in Section 16.2.1.

Market-based Measures: 'Market instruments have advantages in reducing emissions across diverse activities because they provide flexibility: those subject to such instruments can pay the cost of the instrument, or change their activities to avoid it, whichever is least costly to them. Such instruments also provide a continuous incentive for innovation or improvement over time, as every additional abatement of emissions saves a cost for the emitter. This contributes to dynamic efficiency in the economy' (Report to Business New Zealand 2007). Under this mechanism, carbon emissions by any people, industrial organization, or a nation are 'capped' or restricted, upper limit of emissions being fixed and the rights, permits or allowances measured in equivalent units of one metric ton of CO_2 are issued to the capped entities. The measuring unit is commonly called '*Carbon Credit*' or simply called 'Carbon' or 'Credit'. 'Carbon' is given an economic value just like a tradable commodity. A market is also created to facilitate trading where the entities can buy carbon if they are under compelling situation to emit more than their caps from those which are 'credit surplus' in the sense that they can go on with emissions being less than their caps. The total emission is thus kept confined within the pre-determined reduced emission target. Market forces, i.e., the demand for and the supply of carbons, ultimately determine the price of the carbons. 'The value of the carbon would be based on the ability of the country owning the carbon to store it or to prevent it from being released into the atmosphere. (The better you are at storing it, the more you can charge for it.)' (*Web site of Investopedia*). The biggest carbon trading mechanism is run under 'Cap and Trade' system which is discussed in the following.

16.2.1 Carbon Tax

Policy Perspective

The policy issue is based on the premise that the tax would have a direct impact on the price. So, charging carbon tax on coal at the highest rate (based on the carbon-richness) would lead to a steeper price increase of coal. Following natural economic laws, consumption of coal would decline and so also the carbon-emissions (GHGs). Over a longer time horizon and the wider spread, it may ultimately reduce the level of global warming. Thus, the outcome of a policy to levy carbon tax is generally progressive in nature. Because by checking the increase in global warming, it saves the poor people more than the riches since the poor are more prone to the hazardous effects of global warming.

Mechanism

It is a tax on the carbon content of commercial fuels as a means to stop global warming (Paul and Wahlberg 2002). Since tax is charged on the carbon content of the fuel, not directly on the quantity of the fuel used, the rate of tax on different carbon emitting fuels will be different; in fact, the tax rates will be in proportions of the carbon contents in such fuels. Accordingly, coal being the most carbon-rich fuel, would have to bear the highest load of carbon tax and natural gas the least load.

Revenue-earning Potential

Carbon tax is a '*double dividend*' measure. It acts to reduce carbon-emissions, as discussed above, and at the same time it is a revenue-earner. The revenue so earned may be used in running other emission-reduction programmes. But the effectiveness of a carbon-tax scheme depends on its ultimate capacity to reduce carbon-emissions, which rate of carbon tax would impact how much emission-reduction. Two factors interplay in it: (i) the rate of tax, and (ii) the time horizon to measure the impact. An estimate by Intergovernmental Panel on Climate Change (IPCC) shows that a tax rate of $100 per ton of carbon could reduce the emission up to 5 billion tons by 2020. If the rate is doubled to $200 per ton, it could reduce emissions by 50 per cent of the present level and could also earn revenue of $630 billion per year after a 15-year phase-in period. In fact, revenue potential of carbon tax will show an upward trend to reach its peak till the carbon use remains high. At the initial stages of a long phase-in period, the tax effect may not be sufficient to outweigh the normally increasing use of carbon due to population pressure, etc. With the gradually increasing impact of tax on carbon use, a time comes when real impact in terms of reduced carbon use comes to the surface. Naturally, the revenue earning rate would then take a declining path.

Redistribution Effect

Taxes are charged to collect revenues. This part of the process involves a transfer of wealth from the tax-payers primarily to the collector, i.e., the government. But the government imposes tax with the ultimate objective of canalizing the collected revenues to the planned programmes. In this latter part, the earned revenues are redistributed. So, overall, taxation is a redistribution strategy.

A redistribution strategy may have either a regressive or a progressive effect. Surely, the latter effect is the preferred one. A regressive effect means having adverse impacts. For example, charging carbon tax to reduce carbon emission may increase the poor men's sufferings through increased cost burden for carbon use even for different essential purposes which they cannot avoid. A small burden of increased cost, however small it may be, on small income-earners may result in a greater distress and lessened well-being to the latter marginal income-earners. 'Cost burden to income' ratio is higher among low-income earners than it is for high-income earners. 'It is argued that because low-income families spend a larger proportion of their income on energy-related products, a carbon tax would unfairly impose a higher burden on them (Cuervo and Gandhi 1998). Regressive effect also depends on a country's adaptability to more efficient energy use. Countries with high adaptability can easily switch over to other more efficient 'carbon-less fuel' or to 'fuel with less carbon content' to avoid or lessen the load of carbon tax. Generally, poor countries' adaptability is low and they have to bear the brunt to carry with heavy load of carbon tax failing to switch over. Thus, charging carbon tax may fail to reduce carbon use; rather it puts additional financial pressure on the economy of a country. Regressive effects may be lessened by adopting various other measures like allowing exemptions, subsidies, etc. To ensure a more progressive effect of carbon tax, it may be levied on a multi-tier basis, i.e., levying higher rates in rich countries and lower rates in poor countries (Paul and Wahlberg 2002).

16.2.2 Carbon Trading

Policy Perspective

The fundamental idea behind carbon trading is that businesses will pollute less if they have to pay for polluting (Patterson, Websearch). Carbon trading aims at reducing emissions by setting 'caps' on the emitters, i.e., not allowing them to emit more than the permitted amount at no cost (meaning emission cost only). If the emitters need to overstep the capped amount of emissions, they can do so by buying the 'credit'—the permission to emit more—from those who can save 'credits' by containing their emissions below the 'capped' amount. Thus, the credit savers are financially rewarded by way of 'credit selling' for reduced emissions. On the other hand, since more emissions involve cost, the credit-deficit emitters will also be induced to keep their additional emission requirement at as low a level as possible in order to save cost.

Mechanism

Trading in carbon is quite similar to securities trading or commodity trading in the common marketplace. The system that is followed is called '*Cap & Trade*' system. A Cap and Trade programme '*caps*' the quantity of a pollutant that can be emitted, and allows the regulated parties to '*trade*' reductions in emissions of that pollutant (Edick, Websearch). It may be mentioned that a policy-guided global target for a specified target period is set at a level of emission, which is then distributed amongst the agreed nation-states in the form of national quotas. The target level of emissions is to be set surely at a level lower than the current level of emissions. Every nation redistributes its quota amount of emissions amongst the emitters in the form of 'credits' such that every subsequent emission is backed by pre-allocated credit—no matter whether emission is from a credit-deficit or a credit-surplus emitter, whether it is within the 'cap' or outside. Thus, the total national (or for that matter global) emissions can never cross the pre-determined target level. Once the reduced emission target is achieved in a target period, the next target is then further lowered and the process is continued to lead the world towards a safer and greener one with lower rate of global warming.

16.2.3 Kyoto Protocol

The Kyoto Protocol is an agreement under the United Nations Framework Convention for Climate Change (UNFCCC), signed in Kyoto, Japan, by some 180 countries in December 1997; it calls for 38 industrialized countries to reduce their greenhouse gas emissions between the years 2008 to 2012 to levels that are 5.2 per cent lower than those of 1990. The countries ratifying this protocol actually commit to reduce their emissions to the agreed level.

The Kyoto Protocol provides for a *flexible mechanism* which actually provides flexibility in the manner of achieving the target of reduced emission. In doing this, all the countries have been divided into two: (1) Annex 1 countries, i.e., the countries listed in Annexure 1; these are mostly the developed countries which have undertaken the obligation to reduce their emission level. (2) Non-Annex 1 countries, i.e., those countries that are not under any emission reduction obligation.

A party (may be an emitting company) in an Annex 1 country may transition to a more carbon-efficient technology to contain its emission within the cap. But in the short run, this transition may not be affordable or preferable in terms of cost. In such a situation, the party may go for any one or more of the other alternatives available in meeting the target. The alternatives are: (1) *Participating in Carbon Trading*—A party can meet its target by buying the 'credit' from credit-surplus parties or from the carbon credit market. (2) *Financing Projects under 'Clean Development Mechanism'* (CDM Projects)—A party in an Annex 1 country may finance an emission-efficient project in a Non-Annex 1 country so that the latter is rendered credit-surplus and the former can buy the surplus credit to meet its target. 'In order to qualify as CDM projects, they have to show that they are "additional", which means that they would not happen without funding from carbon trading. However, there are significant questions about whether this critical principle is being adhered to effectively. If the projects are not additional, then the sale of credits from them leads to an actual increase in carbon emissions' (Kumar 2007). (3) *Financing in Joint Implementation Project*—This is a scheme similar to CDM; the only difference is that investment may be made in projects in Annex 1 countries. This provides an opportunity to a carbon-deficit company in an Annex 1 country with high cost emission reduction technology to find a country with low cost emission reduction technology even within the same Annex 1 group of countries.

16.2.4 European Union's Emission Trading Scheme (EU ETS)

The 'Cap-and-Trade' is not a new concept; it is already in operation in different countries including US in various other forms with different other objectives. However, the largest ever initiative on Emission Trading under Kyoto Protocol is European Union's Emission Trading System (EU ETS) which commenced its first phase in 2005 and the second phase in 2008 while the third phase is scheduled to commence in 2013 and proposed to continue up to 2020. On the basis of the performance of the first phase, the EU ETS is now under severe criticism on different counts like 'failure to cut emissions', 'an excuse to avoid real emissions reductions', 'undermines individual responsibilities', 'institutionalizes social inequities and rewards largest polluters', 'considers only selected business sectors and not applicable at individual household level', 'puts disproportionate emphasis on individual lifestyles', etc.

Carbon trading is claimed to have a win–win situation since it helps reduce the carbon emissions (ultimate target being GHG emission reduction) on the one hand and on the other, in doing this some of the emitters can also derive some financial benefits by selling credits.

16.3 Lifestyle-based Carbon Control

Individual and household sector is significantly important in India as also in almost all the countries. Because it is found that there is huge scope for reduction of CO_2 emissions through savings in household energy consumption by lifestyle changes. A recent report (Niyogi 2009b) reveals the following shares of energy consumption in household electrical appliances: lighting—34 per cent, air conditioners (ACs) and geysers—35 per cent, pumps—9 per cent, computers—14 per cent and fans—7 per cent. The report also reveals the feasibility of following energy saving in the form of cut in electricity bills through prudent lifestyle practices: lights and fans—15 per cent, ACs—12–15 per cent, TV/VCD, etc.—8 per cent. Energy saving may be further enhanced by introducing various improved technologies like energy saving appliances. Average household consumption of electricity in Kolkata is 130 units per month or a carbon-footprint of 130 kg per month. Based on a household-consumer base of 20 lakhs in Kolkata, the above consumption level of electricity may translate into an emission reduction equivalent to 2.35 lakh tonne per year (Niyogi 2009b).

On the other hand, tapped water supply for household consumption involves huge energy consumption—first for filtration, then for distribution to store water in household underground reservoirs, and finally for lifting water from underground reservoirs to overhead reservoirs. According to a survey, the above report dated 16 December 2009 says, '35–50% of treated water supplied to households in Kolkata is wasted. Citywide (in Kolkata), 100 million gallons of treated water is wasted daily.' So, there is also huge scope for energy saving by plugging treated water wastage through desired lifestyle practices. Other areas of energy saving sources may be tapped equally to reduce CO_2 emissions at household level.

The concept of carbon control through lifestyle change initiatives at household level has been uniquely implemented at Raj Bhavan (Kolkata), the office-cum-residential campus of the Governor of West Bengal. With a view to converting Raj Bhavan into a carbon-neutral campus, a report on 'Climate Responsible Lifestyle Initiative at Raj Bhavan' (Niyogi 2009a) was prepared and submitted by a research team led by Professor Joyashree Roy of Jadavpur University (West Bengal) to the then Governor (2004–09) of West Bengal, Gopalkrishna Gandhi, who readily accepted the report for implementation. It may be mentioned that he is the grandson of Mahatma Gandhi. The twin tools—'voluntary actions' and 'technological interventions'—that were used yielded immediate results. Initiating actions on 7 April 2008 (World Health Day) when carbon-footprint of Raj Bhavan was 408 tonne (2005–06), CO_2 emissions could be brought down by 73 tonne (18 per cent)—59.7 tonne through voluntary actions and the balance 13.3 tonne through technological interventions. Voluntary actions include reducing the convoy size (from 5 to 3, obviously without diluting the safety protocol requirements), observing voluntary power cuts, etc. Technological interventions include replacing high wattage incandescent bulbs with compact fluorescent lamps, replacing old AC machines by more efficient ones, installing devices using solar power, etc. The study of the research team claims that 'the voluntary action led six times as much saving as achieved by technological interventions'. Such type of individual but voluntary initiatives is highly potential in rendering financial benefits in the form of slashing electricity bills significantly. This may be an effective incentive to sensitize individuals and households. Governor Gandhi, however, felt and also called for the need to 'institutionalize' the individual initiatives to realize its worldwide impact on global warming and climate change.

With an eye to institutionalize the concept and to provide more impetus to incentivize individuals, the concept of carbon trading can be mingled with the above concept of lifestyle-based carbon control mechanism. Personal carbon trading is rightly a concept that combines them prudently.

16.4 Personal Carbon Trading

Personal carbon trading or PCT is a concept by which the carbon trading mechanism is tried to be applied at an individual level on an equal per capita basis. PCT is variously described as individual carbon trading, personal carbon allowances, domestic tradable quotas, personal carbon rations, carbon credits, etc. (Roberts and Thumim 2006). It is the brainchild of David Miliband, the then Secretary of State in the Department of Environment, Food and Rural Affairs (DEFRA), UK. In July 2006, Mr. Miliband initiated a study on the viability and feasibility of PCT under the Environmental Audit Committee appointed by the House of Commons, UK. The Committee submitted its report in May 2008. In June 2008, a House of Commons committee suggested that the UK Parliament should create a personal carbon-trading scheme for all citizens of the United Kingdom.

16.4.1 Need for PCT

Carbon emissions from household and personal transport *account for 40 per cent* of total carbon emissions in UK. Being aware of this factual information, the UK government was apprehensive of meeting its committed target of reducing emissions to 20 per cent below 1990 level by 2010 and to 60 per cent by 2050 under Climate Change Bill. Reductions in carbon emissions from business and industry will be meaningless unless accompanied by significant and equal reductions from households and individuals (*Report of the Environmental Audit Committee* 2008).

Since the source of a significant portion of carbon emissions (for example in UK) can be traced to individual and household sectors, we can hardly afford to ignore these sectors from the purview of emission reduction scheme. Reducing emissions by these sectors requires a *behavioural change* among the individuals—a favourable attitude is to be created about the need and individuals' roles thereto. Existing models of emission reduction schemes like carbon taxes, carbon trading, etc. are basically meant for application in the business sector and do lack in sufficient motivational elements required to bring about that behavioural change at personal level.

16.4.2 Mechanism

Like carbon trading, under PCT also a cap on an *equal per capita basis* is placed on the total emissions per year, not on the business unit but on the individuals and households.

'Allowances', i.e., the emission entitlements equal to the value of such caps, are distributed (may be on a monthly basis) to the individuals and households. It may be mentioned that an emission measuring unit is variously called either for various definitions given under various emission reduction schemes or simply for convenience. For example, 'Carbon Credit', 'Carbon', 'Credit', 'Carbon Unit', 'Permit', 'Allowance', 'Entitlement', etc. are some such units in use. Again, all these units may not be equivalent also in terms of the volume of emissions defined in a unit. For example, while one unit of 'Carbon Credit' in 'Cap and Trade' system under Kyoto Protocol worth 1 tonne of carbon dioxide equivalent, one unit of 'Carbon Unit' under PCT (specifically in DTQs discussed below) worth only 1 kg of carbon dioxide equivalent. We, however, have been using these terms interchangeably to mean an emission measuring unit with corresponding definition as to the volume of emissions per unit.

Individuals and households have then to surrender those allowances whenever they purchase fossil fuel–based energy for household consumption and transport over the accounting period (a month when issued on a monthly basis). The fossil-fuel suppliers would collect the allowances surrendered by the consumers and they will ultimately surrender back the allowances to the Registry which issued them.

Normally, allowances are issued to the individuals free of charge. But anybody who is in need of more emissions than that of his entitlements has to buy allowances from the market. Conversely, an allowance-surplus individual can sell their surplus allowances either in the market or into a central bank and derive financial gain out of his effort to save carbon emissions. The price for a unit of 'carbon credit' is the on-time rate as determined by the market forces in the carbon market; it is just like how currency exchange rate is determined in the foreign exchange market.

An individual is, however, allowed to opt out of the whole process by selling his allowances immediately after initial distribution and to depend on spot buying whenever he needs buying carbon; this is essentially a leaning to the principle of 'pay as you go'.

16.4.3 Practicalities

Individual accounts are maintained in a Register of accounts maintained by a separate specialized agency. System of maintaining accounts is similar to that of a credit card of a Bank. One proposal was for personal carbon credits to be stored on a credit card—similar to a store loyalty card—which could be swiped at the point of purchase of carbon credits. However, there was a lot of concern amongst participants about the loss or theft of these cards. One key factor driving negative responses to the concept of PCT was the idea of Government intervening in people's everyday lives exerting influence over how they lived and clamping down on their freedom of choice. In addition, participants were opposed to PCT (compared to other proposed schemes) on the grounds that it could be quite carbon intensive—because of paperwork and computer power—to implement, which they saw as contradictory and hypocritical (Final report to the DEFRA 2008).

16.4.4 Alternative Proposals

There are three major alternative proposals which differ from one another based on the differences in some characteristics like participation (i.e., who can participate, whether only individuals or along with organizations), allocation (i.e., to whom allowances are allocable, whether only to individuals or along with children), and scope (i.e., which type/s of emissions are included in the scheme, whether or not personal air travel and/or public transport are to be included). The alternative models of PCT are: (i) Tradable Energy Quotas (TEQs) proposed by David Fleming, (ii) Domestic Tradable Quotas

(DTQs) proposed by Richard Starkey and Kevin Anderson at the Tyndall Centre (a development of Fleming's work), and (iii) Personal Carbon Allowances (PCAs) proposed by Mayer Hillman, Tina Fawcett and Brenda Boardman's team at Oxford's Environmental Change Institute.

Commonalities Among the Alternative Models

The following are the common characteristics among the three models:

1. All the three models are *quantity-based* rather than price-based since all are proposed to be run under 'Cap and Trade' system.
2. All of them are to pursue *downstream carbon trading* scheme since they target the individual end-users of energy. The EU ETS also targets the end-users but since it involves only the large users and power companies it may be called a *mid-stream carbon trading* scheme. In contrast, the *upstream carbon trading* scheme addresses the energy suppliers.
3. All the three models involve only the *personal carbon emissions* from energy use like household activities, personal transport including personal aviation, and even public transport. There is, however, a debate on whether public transport should come under personal or non-personal category. Non-personal category includes carbon emissions from fossil fuel–based energy use by businesses, industries, services and infrastructures.

Differences Among the Models

The Centre for Sustainable Energy summarized the differences between the schemes as follows (Table 16.1):

As we find from Table 16.1, DTQs are models slightly developed over the basic model of TEQs proposed by Fleming. So these are more or less similar, the only difference being that DTQs include personal aviation within the fold. Again, while TEQs or DTQs consider public transport (included in road fuels) as personal, PCAs consider it to be non-personal and keep them outside

TABLE 16.1 **Models of PCT: A Comparison**

Models	Participation	Allocation	Scope
TEQs	Individuals: 40% free Organizations: 60% tendered (principally to market makers from whom organizations then buy as required)	Allocation on weekly rolling basis to— Adults only: Equal per capita Organizations: Through tender as mentioned	Coal, oil, gas, electricity (fossil-fuel based), road fuels
DTQs	Same as TEQs	Same as TEQs	As for TEQs plus personal aviation
PCAs	Individuals only (Organizations to be covered by another unspecified scheme). At least 40% of UK emissions (i.e., all domestic plus aviation)	Adults: Full allowance; Children (under 18): Half an allowance	As for TEQs (not public transport)

Source: Roberts and Thumim (2006).

the fold. However, according to the Workshop Summary Report (Bottrill 2006a) of the UK Energy Research Centre, under transport category DTQs consider carbon emissions only from private vehicle use and both the sources of public transport and personal air travel are excluded. According to it, PCAs to include all the sources of emissions from transport like private vehicle use, public transport, and personal air travel.

Apart from the distinguishing characters, the schemes are more or less governed by the common mechanism as described above.

16.4.5 Superiority of PCT over Other Similar Existing Schemes

Progressivism: PCT is a progressive scheme in the sense that it discourages over-emitters (must be richer) for their emissions beyond the cap by involving payment for buying allowances and encourages less-emitters (must be poorer) to save emissions and sell the allowances gainfully. It, thus, redistributes money from the rich to the poor. On the contrary, carbon tax is regressive since it imposes tax equally on the less-emitters as on rich-emitters (Roberts and Thumim 2006).

Guaranteed emission reduction: It enforces personal responsibility to reduce emissions and does not allow emissions to exceed overall cap; thus total emission always remains within the national carbon budget which is set at a level lower than the current level of carbon footprint. Carbon tax provides incentives to reduce emissions but cannot ensure such reduction. Thus, under carbon tax regime rich people are free to increase emissions by simply paying taxes. The overall global emission level may, thus, go up in the absence of any 'cap'.

Cost effectiveness: Being governed by trading, the PCT should result in emission reduction at the lowest cost. Why, the theory asks, would anyone buy allowances to emit carbon dioxide from someone else if it were cheaper for them to reduce their own emissions (Roberts and Thumim 2006)? However, in terms of transaction costs, it is revealed that PCT involves higher costs: Setup cost may be somewhere between £700 million–£2 billion and estimated running costs between £1 billion–£2 billion per annum (Starkey 2008). But at the same time, it is worth mentioning that the income to Government generated by the scheme would be around £6 billion per annum. (*DEFRA's Pre-feasibility Study into Personal Carbon Trading—A Missed Opportunity* 2008).

16.4.6 Major Debatable Issues

Equal per capita allowance: Distributing allowances on an equal per capita basis brings about equity in having equal right of emissions among individuals but it disregards the inevitable inequality found in the differential needs of individuals depending on the circumstances of the case. For example, disabled or chronically sick people, or the elderly people may have higher per capita needs; even the poor people may have higher needs to meet their basic needs of life in the form they are used to and they can afford to. In such cases, a fair distribution based on equity needs unequal allocation since these people need more allocations for a welfare level similar to other common people (*DEFRA's Pre-feasibility Study into Personal Carbon Trading—A Missed Opportunity* 2008). Though not a perfect solution, equal per capita allowance is considered to be the better one in comparison to having distribution with varying allowances. Varying allowances means allowing extra allowances to some individuals. That raises a host of some other problems like to whom to allow extra allowances, how much extra to be allowed and on what basis, etc. and above all it leads to an impossible situation of satisfying everybody taking adequate care of all of their interests. One attitudinal study (Jagers et al. 2009) revealed that individuals who agree to any of the three fairness principles—equity, equality and need—are more likely to be positive towards the PCA scheme than those who do not agree to the principles.

Inclusion of children: Children do contribute to the increase in carbon emissions of a household. So their exclusion from the list of eligible allottees takes the households with children to a disadvantaged situation. On the other hand, their inclusion means widening of the distribution base and consequential reduction in the per capita share of distributed allowances. This brings about an adverse distributional impact on the households without children. A compromise formula with half the per capita allowance for children has been accepted in Personal Carbon Allowances or PCAs.

Exclusion of public transport: Public transport is excluded for various reasons. Reasons include: Only 1.6 per cent of individual's carbon emissions comes from ground public transport; its exclusion reduces the number of transactions significantly; difficulty in computing share of emissions from public transport in the total emissions of an individual; it motivates individuals for switching away from driving private vehicles; etc. (Bottrill 2006b).

16.4.7 Evaluation

PCT is yet a proposal waiting to be implemented. Thus, there is no question of any evaluation on its practical application. However, on the basis of theoretical analyses under various research efforts, it appears that PCT is tested satisfactory at least comparatively, may be not absolutely, in all the 3Es of the evaluation criteria, i.e., equity, efficiency and effectiveness. It is common to have certain difficulties at the initial stage of implementation. Those difficulties can be overcome gradually with the progress in its application. For example, for implementation of any scheme among the common people, political and public support is very important. For the purpose, while implementing the PCT initial cap must be leniently set at not-too-low a level so that the common mass is not antagonized. The caps may be gradually lowered as the scheme gains public acceptability.

However, carbon-focused emission reduction schemes, be it carbon tax or carbon trading, are criticized on different counts. Firstly, it is argued that all these measures ignore other GHGs like methane, nitrous oxide and chlorofluorocarbons, more powerful in warming the earth. Secondly, these measures would fare badly against countries like China, Mexico, Taiwan and South Korea that emit carbon to run industries for manufacturing goods to meet the demand in countries like the USA and the UK (Kyriakides 2008). By the by, China is now emitting on an average of one tonne per person per year while India still manages with just one-third of a tonne per person.

16.5 Conclusions

As stated earlier, PCT needs a behavioural change in carbon usage by the downstream consumers. But bringing about a behavioural change depends on (i) social and cultural factors, i.e., the society we live in, (ii) financial factors, i.e., costs and the benefits, (iii) personal internal factors, i.e., personality, motivation, habits, etc., (iv) effort factors, i.e., routines, needed effort, expected gain (Yael Parag 2008). The barriers in bringing about behavioural change include a common human trait of 'unwillingness to give up personal comfort'. But at the same time it is so argued that PCT captures a feeling of involvement, public engagement, feeling of empowerment and control from having the emissions entitlement as a right (Hufnagel 2007). In fact, bringing about a change in the behaviour of the common people about reduction in carbon emission is not an easy task. This is because there is no immediate cause-and-effect relationship between carbon emission by individuals and its ultimate effect—the global warming. A huge time gap makes it difficult for the common people to digest the ideological arguments in substantiating their roles in hampering inter-generational equity. Even then, we must not delay further leaving our future to plunge into an uncertainty. However, the *Report of the Environmental Audit Committee* submitted to the House of Commons (UK) said, 'While personal carbon trading remains a potentially important way to engage individuals, and there are no insurmountable technical obstacles to its introduction, it would nonetheless seem that it is an idea currently ahead of its time in terms of its public acceptability and the technology to bring down the costs.' Accordingly, on the basis of the pre-feasibility study into personal carbon trading, the Government of UK has decided to wind down its work in this area on the grounds of high implementation costs and public resistance to the concept.

Fifteenth World Conference in Copenhagen in Denmark (7–18 December 2009) is grossly a failure as most of the developing and less developed countries criticize the 'Copenhagen Climate Accord' by four BASIC countries (Brazil, South Africa, India and China) and the USA to be a 'sideline deal'. Debates are going on around the world on various counts of the Deal. In that context, PCT may ultimately emerge as a better and sustainable alternative mechanism to contain GHG emissions within a limit (a dream) necessary to avoid any atmospheric catastrophe (a reality).

Notes

1. Full Text of *What is the Carbon Trade?* is available at www.investopedia.com/ask/answers/04/060404.asp
2. The research team at Jadavpur University is led by Professor Joyashree Roy, Coordinator, Global Change Programme, Jadavpur University. Professor Roy is also a member of the Nobel Prize-winning Inter-government Panel on Climate Change (IPCC) team.
3. Full Text of *A Rough Guide to Individual Carbon Trading: The Ideas, the Issues and the Next Steps* is available at www.defra.gov.uk
4. Full Text of 'Personal Carbon Trading', *Report of the Environmental Audit Committee (2008)* is available at http://www.publications.parliament.uk/pa/cm200708/cmselect/cmenvaud/565/565.pdf
5. Full Text of 'Personal Carbon Trading: Public Acceptability', *Final Report to the DEFRA* (2008) is available at www.defra.gov.uk
6. Full Text of *DEFRA's Pre-feasibility Study into Personal Carbon Trading—A Missed Opportunity* (2008) is available at www.teqs.net/DEFRAPFSresponse.pdf

References

Bottrill, C. (ed.) (2006a). 'Personal Carbon Trading: An Exploratory Research and Policy Workshop'. *Workshop Summary Report*, 24th October, UK Energy Research Centre, p 12.

Bottrill, C. (2006b). 'Personal Carbon Trading: Excluding Public Transportation'. Working Paper, December, UK Energy Research Centre.

Cuervo, J. and Gandhi, V. P. (1998). 'Carbon Taxes: Their Macroeconomic Effects and Prospects for Global Adoption—A Survey of the Literature'. IMF Working Paper No. WP/98/73, May.

Hufnagel, K. (2007). 'Individual Carbon Trading—A Suitable Policy Instrument to Curb Greenhouse Gas Emissions from Households and Consumers'. 15th Ph. D. Workshop on International Climate Policy, 12–13 October, Lund University, Environmental and Energy System Studies.

Jagers, S C., Löfgren, A. and Stripple, J. (2009). 'Attitudes to Personal Carbon Allowances: The Effect of Trust in Politicians, Perceived Fairness and Ideology'. Working Papers in Economics (No. 360), April, University of Gothenburg, School of Business, Economics and Law, ISSN 1403-2465 (online).

Paul, J. A. and Wahlberg, K. (2002). 'Global Taxes for Global Priorities'. *Global Policy Forum, the World Economy, Ecology and Development Association (WEED) and the Heinrich Böll Foundation*, March.

Kumar, S. (2007). 'Emission Impossible for Carbon Trading'. EU ETS Coordinator, WWF News Centre, WWF European Policy Office. skumar@wwfepo.org

Kyriakides, R. (2008). 'Why Personal Carbon Allowances Will Not Reduce Carbon Emissions'. Robert Kyriakides's weblog: Ideas about the Environment, posted on 8 July.

Niyogi, S. (2009a). 'Carbon Control, the Gandhi Way'. *Times of India*, 17 June, p 2.

Niyogi, S. (2009b). 'Plug Wastage, You have the Power'. *Times of India*, 16 December, p 2.

Report of the Environmental Audit Committee (2008). 'Personal Carbon Trading'. *House of Commons*, UK, May.

Roberts, S. and Thumim, J. (2006). 'A Rough Guide to Individual Carbon Trading: The Ideas, The Issues and The Next Steps'. Centre for Sustainable Energy, November, www.defra.gov.uk

Starkey, R. (2008). 'Personal Carbon Trading: An Overview', *Tyndall Centre for Climate Change Research*. A presentation at The University of Manchester, 16 May.

Yael P. (2008). 'Personal Carbon Allowances: Tying Economic, Social and Psychological Mechanisms Together for Emissions Reduction in the Domestic Sector'. A presentation in *Behavior Energy and Climate Change Conference*, 16–19 November, Sacramento, CA, Environmental Change Institute, University of Oxford.

CHAPTER 17

GARCH Models—A Key to Capture Volatility of Financial Data

J. K. Das and Sharad Nath Bhattacharya

ABSTRACT

The paper discusses various statistical properties and models that a researcher dealing with various types of financial data sets would come across. It emphasizes on models useful for financial data with heavy tails and volatility clustering. Various models including ARMA and GARCH family models have been discussed with their applications pertaining to risk analysis, volatility forecasting, portfolio selection and derivative pricing. The paper concludes that volatility forecasting models are extremely data specific and it may not be possible to identify any particular model with superior forecasting power than the others.

17.1 Introduction

Financial markets always lure money makers as well as policy makers. For long time, academia has also engaged in the study of financial variables. Statistical properties of stock prices, commodities prices, market indexes and exchange rates are being studied using data from various markets and instruments. Availability of high-frequency financial databases and an increase in the processing power of computer have opened new horizons to researchers in empirical finance in the last decade and have contributed to the reinforcement of data-based approach in financial modelling. Many market analysts take an event-based approach in which one attempts to 'explain' or rationalize a given market movement by relating it to an economic or political event or announcement/news. However, we can easily understand that different assets are not necessarily influenced by the same events or information sets. Price data series obtained from different assets and from different markets will exhibit different properties. There are no theoretical reasons to believe that properties of commodity futures are similar to those of equity shares or foreign exchange rates such as the rupee/dollar exchange rate. However, empirical studies on financial time series indicate that this might be the case if one examines their properties from a statistical point of view: the apparently random variations of asset prices do share some quite non-trivial statistical properties.

In this paper, we provide various statistical properties and models that a researcher in social science dealing with various types of financial data sets would come across. Study and analysis of existence of these properties have become relevant with the increased use of computer-aided research techniques. Recent developments in financial econometrics require the use of mathematical models that are able to explain the attitude of investors not only towards expected returns and risks, but also towards volatility. Market participants should be aware of the need to manage risks associated with volatility. Volatility measures the size of the errors made in modelling financial variables. For studying volatility, the key issue is the variance of the error terms and its amplitude. This is specially the case where the dependent variable is the return on an asset or portfolio and the variance of the return represents the risk level of those returns. Initially, the research in this field revolved around autoregressive moving average processes (ARMA), which were easy to implement. AR is autoregressive process where the outcome is modelled as a weighted average of past observations plus a white noise term and MA is moving average processes where outcome is expressed as a moving average of the past values of the white noise term. In ARMA models, the value of the series at any point is written as a linear function of its lagged values and past values of some noise processes. However, ARMA process showed limitations in the field of finance and monetary forecasting. This was because financial time series exhibits diverse form of non-linear dynamics, the crucial one being the strong dependence of variability of the series on its own past. This spawned the research to specify how the information could be used to forecast the mean and variance of the return, conditional on the past information. The primary descriptive tool for this was the rolling standard deviation, which is calculated using a fixed number of the most recent observations. However, it bears an unattractive assumption that the variance of tomorrow's return is an equally weighted average of the squared residuals from the fixed number of the observations. The ARCH model proposed by Engle (1982) allowed the data to determine the best weights to use in forecasting the variance. The ARCH and GARCH models, which stand for autoregressive conditional heteroskedasticity and generalized autoregressive conditional heteroskedasticity, respectively, are designed to deal with the above issue. The most widely used GARCH specification asserts that the best predictor of the variance in the next period is a weighted average of the long-run average variance, the variance predicted for this period, and the new information in this period that is captured by the most recent squared residual. Applications of the ARCH/GARCH approach are widespread in situations where the volatility of returns is a central issue. The goal of such models is to provide a volatility measure—like a standard deviation—that can be used in financial decisions concerning risk analysis, volatility forecasting of returns from stocks, commodities and foreign exchanges, portfolio selection and derivative pricing.

The paper begins with a description of various statistical characteristics which are common to a wide set of financial assets and is followed by discussions on modelling volatility clustering and non-linear dependence through application of various GARCH models.

17.2 Characteristics of Financial Data—A Discussion

17.2.1 Heavy Tails

For years, researchers assumed that the empirical distribution of changes in exchange rates and other financial variables was best described by either a normal or lognormal probability distribution. Some studies and many current tests 'automatically' apply the logarithmic transformation (Das 2006) to returns from spot, forward, futures and exchange rate changes. This transformation assumes that the transformed data produces returns that are normally distributed. However, Mandelbrot (1963) pointed out the insufficiency of the normal distribution for modelling the marginal distribution of asset returns and their heavy-tailed character. Since then, the non-Gaussian character of the distribution of price changes has been repeatedly observed in various market data. Empirical results are not sufficient for identifying the distribution of returns and leave a considerable margin for the choice of the distribution. Fitting various functional forms to the distribution of stock returns and stock price changes has become a popular pastime. Normal distribution, stable distributions, the Student's *t* distribution, hyperbolic distributions, normal inverse Gaussian distributions, exponentially truncated stable distributions are some of the parametric models which have been proposed in the literature. The choice among these classes is a matter of analytical and numerical tractability. Probability distribution for asset returns often exhibit fatter tails than the Gaussian distribution. It is now well known that log returns exhibit two specific kinds of departure from a Gaussian: kurtosis and fat tails. A high kurtosis means that the model distribution is more peaked than a Gaussian around the mean. Fat tails mean that crashes and huge increases appear far more often than predicted by the normal law. The (unconditional) distribution of returns generally display a power-law (A power law relationship between two scalar quantities x and y is any such that the relationship can be written as $y = ax^k$ where a and k are constants) or Pareto-like tail (A random variable x with a Pareto distribution has a probability density function given by $f(x) = ak^a x^{-(a+1)}, x \geq k$ where a and k are positive constants), with a finite tail index. The precise form of the tails is difficult to determine although it excludes distributions with infinite variance and the normal distribution. In finance, fat tails are considered undesirable because of the additional risk they imply. When data arises from a fat tail distribution, fitting the normal distribution model of risk and an estimate of the corresponding risk from a finite sample size generally understate the true risk. Normal distributions that emerge in finance generally do so because the factors influencing an asset's value or price are mathematically 'well-behaved', and the central limit theorem provides for such a distribution. However, 'real-world' events (such as an information shock, a large corporate bankruptcy, or an abrupt change in a political situation) are usually not mathematically well behaved.

Existence of non-Gaussian character of the distribution led researchers to focus on higher order moments as measures of dispersion and variability in order to model variability of returns. However, such moments need to be well defined. The tail index k of a distribution may be defined as the order of the highest absolute moment that is finite. The higher the tail index, the thinner the tail; for a Gaussian or exponential tail, $k = +\infty$ (all moments are finite), while for a power-law distribution with exponent α, the tail index is equal to α. But, a distribution may have a finite tail index α without being a power-law distribution. Measuring the tail index of a distribution gives a measure of how heavy the tail is. Mandelbrot (1963) represented the sample moments (or cumulants) as a function of the sample size n while studying the variation of cotton prices. He observed that the sample variance did not converge to a particular value as the sample size increased and continued to fluctuate persistently indicating that the theoretical variance may not be finite. If the theoretical moment is finite, then the sample moment should converge to a region defined around its theoretical limit and fluctuate around that value.

Modelling heavy tail distributions have become an area of interest especially with the use of extreme value theory, which takes into consideration the probabilities of extreme events. Jansen and de Vries (1991), followed by Longin (1996) and others, were the first to apply the extreme value theory to financial time series. The variability in financial time series as revealed by finite probability of occurrence of violent market movements and its magnitude makes this modelling important for calculating Value-at-Risk (VaR), which has its application in risk management, risk measurement, financial control, financial reporting and computing regulatory capital.

17.2.2 Loss/Gain Asymmetry

In financial data series, one observes that the time interval needed for stock prices and stock index values to change is different for downward movements than for upward movements. This property is particularly observed in stock market data and is generally not true for exchange rates where there is generally higher symmetry in up/down movements.

17.2.3 Skewness

The distribution that is not symmetrical is called skewed. Skewness can be mathematically defined as the averaged cubed deviation from the mean divided by the standard deviation cubed. If the result of the computation is greater than zero, the distribution is positively skewed. If it is less than zero, it is negatively skewed and equal to zero means it is symmetric. Interpretation and analysis of skewed distribution generally focus on downside risk. Negatively skewed distributions have what statisticians call a long left tail, which for investors can mean frequent gains where as positively skewed distribution would mean frequent negative outcomes. The presence of both positive and negative skewness in individual and portfolio stock return distributions is well documented in the literature (Aggarwal and Aggarwal 1993; Alles and Kling 1994; Badrinath and Chatterjee 1991; Beedles 1979; Bekaert et al. 1998; Schwert 1990).

17.2.4 Aggregational Gaussianity

It has been observed that long-term aggregation of financial asset returns, in the sense of summing the returns over longer periods, will lead to approximately normally distributed variates. If one increases the timescale over which returns are calculated, their distribution looks more and more like a normal distribution.

17.2.5 Intermittency

Intermittency is the alternation of phases of apparently periodic and chaotic dynamics. In the apparently periodic phases, the behaviour is not absolutely periodic, but only nearly periodic.

17.2.6 Volatility Clustering

Volatility clustering can be thought of as clustering of the variance of the error term over time: if the regression error has a small variance in one period, its variance tends to be small in the next period, too. It suggests that large shocks in asset returns tend to be followed by large shocks (of either sign) and small shocks tend to be followed by small shocks, indicating a positive autocorrelation over several time periods. It has now been well established in the empirical finance literature that returns on many financial assets display fat tail, spiked peaks, persistence in the variance structure and exhibits the phenomenon of volatility clustering (Pagan and Schwert 1990). Time-variation in the conditional variance of financial time-series is important when pricing derivatives, calculating measures of risk, and hedging against portfolio risk. Therefore, there has been an enormous interest amongst researchers and practitioners to model the conditional variance.

17.2.7 Conditional Heavy Tails

This generally refers to the existence of heavy tails in GARCH filtered residuals. After adjusting financial data series for volatility clustering, the residual time series may still exhibit heavy tails. However, the tails are generally less heavy than in the unconditional distribution of returns.

17.2.8 Slow Decay of Autocorrelation in Absolute Returns

This essentially means that the autocorrelation function of absolute returns may decay slowly as a function of the time lag. The persistence of volatility is often interpreted with the presence of long-term memory in absolute returns and the main feature of a long-memory process is that its autocorrelation function decays slowly.

17.2.9 Leverage Effect

It has been observed in many financial markets that bad news often have a more prominent effect on volatility than good news. This is known as volatility asymmetry and it was first discussed by Black (1976) who observed that the amplitude of relative price fluctuations (volatility) of a stock tends to increase when its price drops. This effect is particularly important for option markets as option prices indeed reflect the fact that a negative volatility–return correlation induces a negative skew in the distribution of returns on longer timescales. Many measures of volatility of an asset are negatively correlated with the returns of that asset.

17.2.10 Volume–Volatility Correlation

We may observe that trading volume is correlated with all measures of volatility. This observation needs to be modelled to capture the volatility dynamics in a given financial market.

17.2.11 Dependence Properties of Returns

It is generally observed that linear correlation is absent in price increments and asset returns and is well documented in literature (Fama 1971). If price changes exhibit significant correlation, statistical arbitrage will eventually reduce correlations except for very short timescales, which represent the time the market takes to react to new information. Mandelbrot (1963) articulated this property by stating that 'arbitrage tends to whiten the spectrum of price changes'. This property implies that traditional tools of signal processing which are based on second-order properties, in the time domain—autocovariance analysis, ARMA modelling—or in the spectral domain—Fourier analysis, linear filtering—cannot distinguish between asset returns and white noise. This points out the need for nonlinear measures of dependence in order to characterize the dependence properties of asset returns (Cont 2001).

17.3 Modelling Volatility Clustering and Non-linear Dependence

Several activities such as valuation of assets, asset management, calculation of expected returns, portfolio selection, hedging and pricing are related to their volatility, or risk. For derivatives markets, volatility is an even more explicit input into the pricing models used. Volatility models target peculiar properties possessed by financial series. Hence this work is aimed at exploiting the usability of these models in market prediction.

The absence of autocorrelations in return generally provides support for 'random walk' models of prices in which the returns are considered to be independent random variables. However, simple non-linear functions of returns, such as absolute or squared returns, exhibit significant positive autocorrelation or persistence. This is in fact a quantitative assertion of the well-known phenomenon of volatility clustering where large price variations are more likely to be followed by large price variations. Volatility clustering is commonly measured by the autocorrelation function of the squared returns (Karmakar 2007). Empirical studies using returns from various indices and stocks indicate that this autocorrelation function remains positive and decays slowly. This is sometimes called the 'ARCH effect' in the econometric literature and is a feature of GARCH models; but it is important to bear in mind that it is a model-free property of returns which does not rely on the GARCH hypothesis. This persistence implies some degree of predictability for the amplitude of the returns as measured by their squares. The volatility-clustering feature indicates that asset returns are not independent across time; on the other hand, the absence of linear autocorrelation shows that their dependence is non-linear. Whether this dependence is 'short range' or 'long range' has been the object of many empirical studies.

There has been considerable volatility (and uncertainty) in the past few years in mature and emerging financial markets worldwide. Most investors and financial analysts are concerned about the uncertainty of the returns on their investment assets, caused by the variability in speculative market prices (and market risk) and the instability of business performance. Market participants should be aware of the need to manage risks associated with volatility. This requires models that are capable of dealing with the volatility of the market (and the series). Due to unexpected events, uncertainties in prices (and returns) and the non-constant variance in the financial markets, financial analysts started to model and explain the behaviour of stock market returns and volatility using time series econometric models.

The prominent tools for capturing such changing variance were the ARCH and GARCH models developed by Engle (1982), and later extended by Bollerslev (1986). Two important characteristics within financial time series, the fat tails and volatility clustering (or volatility pooling), can be captured by the GARCH family models. ARCH imposes an autoregressive structure on conditional variance, allowing volatility shocks to persist over time. This persistence captures the propensity of returns of like magnitude to cluster in time and can explain the well-documented non-normality and non-stability of empirical asset return distributions (Fama 1965). Volatility clustering implies that the error exhibits time-varying heteroskedasticity (unconditional standard deviations are not constant).

We will now focus on various ARCH/GARCH models that are useful for social science research. Let us consider a univariate time series. If Ω_{t-1} is the information set at time $t-1$, we can define its functional form as follows:

$$y_t = E\left(\frac{y_t}{\Omega_{t-1}}\right) + \varepsilon_t \quad \text{(This is called mean equation)} \tag{17.1}$$

where E (./.) denotes the conditional expectation operator and ε_t is the disturbance term with $E(\varepsilon_t) = 0$ and $E(\varepsilon_t\,\varepsilon_s) = 0$, for all $t \neq s$. ε_t is the innovation of the process expressed as

$$\varepsilon_t = \sigma_t\, z_t \tag{17.2}$$

where z_t is an independently and identically distributed (i.i.d.) process with $E(z_t) = 0$ and var $(z_t) = 1$. By definition, ε_t is serially uncorrelated with a mean equal to zero but its conditional variance equals σ_t^2 and therefore may change over time (heteroskedastic). The models discussed hereafter are AR, ARMA and various ARCH/GARCH type processes. ARCH/GARCH type processes will essentially have the same mean equation as in Eqs. (17.1) and same innovation as in (17.2) unless specified separately, but they will differ depending on the functional form of σ_t^2. Henceforth, we shall explain models based on variance equation, i.e., based on the functional form of σ_t^2, bearing in mind that Eqs. (17.1) and (17.2) remain valid and are essential for the models unless stated otherwise.

17.3.1 Autoregressive Method (AR)

An autoregressive model expresses a forecast as a function of previous values of the time series. A pth order autoregressive model takes the form

$$y_t = \alpha_0 + \sum_{i=1}^{p} \alpha_i\, y_{t-i} + \varepsilon_t$$

where, y_t is the response (dependent) variable at time t.

$y_{t-1}, \ldots, y_{t-p}$ are response variable at time lags $t-1, t-2, \ldots, t-p$, respectively.

$\alpha_0, \alpha_1, \alpha_2, \ldots, \alpha_p$ are the coefficients to be estimated.

ε_t is the error term at time t that represents the effects of variables not explained by the model.

AR (p) models have been applied by many researchers while dealing with financial data sets. For applications, one may refer to Das and Basu (1992; 1993; 1995; 1997a; 1997b; 1999; 2002) among others.

17.3.2 ARMA

This is a model where autoregressive terms combine with a model having moving average terms resulting in an autoregressive moving average model. An ARMA (p, q) model has the general form

$$y_t = \alpha_0 + \sum_{i=1}^{p} \alpha_i \, y_{t-p} + \varepsilon_t - \beta_1 \varepsilon_{t-1} - \beta_2 \varepsilon_{t-2} - \cdots - \beta_q \varepsilon_{t-q}$$

where $\varepsilon_{t-1}, \varepsilon_{t-2}, \ldots, \varepsilon_{t-q}$ are errors in previous time periods that at time t are incorporated in the response Y. Alternatively using back shift operator, ARMA (p, q) model may be expressed as $\phi(B)y_t = \theta(B)\varepsilon_t$ where $\phi(B) = 1 - \alpha_1 B - \alpha_2 B^2 - \cdots - \alpha_p B^p$, $\theta(B) = 1 - \beta_1 B - \beta_2 B^2 - \cdots - \beta_q B^q$ and back-shift operator B is defined by $B^k y_t = y_{t-k}$. When q equals zero, it becomes a pure AR (p) process and when p equals zero, it becomes a pure MA (q) process. For applications of ARMA models one may refer to Box and Jenkins (1970) and Das and Basu (1991; 1994).

17.3.3 ARCH

In the year of 1982, to capture the serial correlation of volatility, Engle proposed a model for variance $\{\sigma_t^2\} : \sigma_t^2 = \alpha_0 + \sum_{i=1}^{q} \alpha_i \varepsilon_{t-i}^2$ with mean equation similar to Eq. (17.1) and innovation similar to Eq. (17.2). This model is called the autoregressive conditional heteroskedasticity (ARCH (q) process where the 'autoregressive' property in principle means that old events leave waves behind a certain time after the actual time of the action. The process depends on its past. The terms 'conditional heteroskedasticity' means that the variance (conditional on the available information) varies and depends on old values of the process. One can resemble this with the process having a short-term memory and that the behaviour of the process is influenced by this memory. However, empirical evidence shows that high ARCH order has to be selected in order to catch the dynamic of the conditional variance. The high ARCH order implies that many parameters have to be estimated and the calculations get burdensome. Some areas of empirical application of the ARCH specification are (i) effects of shocks on the variance of stock market returns, (ii) effects of increases in the variance of excess returns of bonds on risk premiums. For more discussions, one may refer to Gourieroux (1997).

17.3.4 GARCH (p, q)

Bollerslev (1986) provided a parsimonious alternative and introduced the GARCH model that restricts the conditional variance of a time series to depend upon past squared residuals of the process. Such a model is represented as

$$\sigma_t^2 = \alpha_0 + \sum_{i=1}^{q} \alpha_i \varepsilon_{t-i}^2 + \sum_{j=1}^{p} \beta_j \sigma_{t-j}^2$$

where ε_t denotes a real-valued discrete-time stochastic process and the α_i's and the β_j's are non-negative parameters, and $p > 0,\ s \geq 0,\ \alpha_0 > 0,\ \alpha_i \geq 0$.

In Bollerslev's (1986) GARCH model, the conditional variance is a linear function of past squared innovations and earlier calculated conditional variances. With these models there are two types of return distribution to be considered; the conditional return distribution (where the conditioning is the current volatility) and the marginal or stationary distribution of the process. There is huge application of GARCH models to stock return data (French et al. 1987), to interest rate data (Engle et al. 1987) and to foreign exchange data (Giovannini and Jorion 1989; Hsieh 1988). In the Indian context, GARCH model and its various extensions have been used by Karmakar (2005; 2006), Kaur (2002; 2004), Pandey (2005), Pattanaik and Chatterjee (2000) and Thomas (1995; 1998). There is a growing literature of the implications of non-linear dynamics for financial risk management (Bollerslev et al. 1992; Brock et. al 1996; Engle 2000; Hsieh 1993; Manfredo et al. 2001; Ng and Pirrong 1994; Susmel and Thompson 1997; etc). De Gooijer and Hyndman (2006) provide good summary of experiments and development happened with volatility models in last 25 years.

We shall now provide a description of GARCH family of models.

17.3.5 GARCH-M

Engle et al. (1987) introduced GARCH-in-mean (GARCH-M) model where the relationship between return and time-varying risk is established by including a function of the conditional variance in the model for the conditional mean. GARCH-M model is considered useful to model the return of a security that depends on its volatility. The model specifies the conditional mean and variance of stock returns (r_t) as follows:

$$r_t = \mu + \gamma\sigma_t + \varepsilon_t, \qquad \varepsilon_t = \sigma_t z_t$$

$$\sigma_t^2 = \alpha_0 + \sum_{i=1}^{q} \alpha_i \varepsilon_{t-i}^2 + \sum_{j=1}^{p} \beta_j \sigma_{t-j}^2$$

where μ represents the conditional mean of stock returns at time t and σ_t is the standard deviation of the conditional variance, which reflects the risk premium. The parameter γ is called the risk premium parameter. A positive γ indicates that the return is positively related to its past volatility. The formulation of the GARCH-M model implies that there are serial correlations in the return series r_t. These serial correlations are introduced by those in the volatility process $\{\sigma_t^2\}$. The existence of risk premium is, therefore, another reason that some historical stock returns have serial correlations. Many attempts have been undertaken to test Merton's (1973) Inter-temporal capital asset pricing model prediction by using various formulations of the GARCH-M model. Most empirical studies on the risk–return relation using GARCH-M model led to controversial findings: some studies such as by French et al. (1987), Campbell and Hentschel (1992) and Li (2003) indicate a positive relationship; some studies such as by Glosten et al. (1993), Pagan and Hong (1990), Li et al. (2005) or Guedhami and Sy (2005) indicate a negative relationship; while other studies such as by Bodurtha and Mark

(1991), Baillie and De Genarro (1990) or Shin (2005) do not find a significant relationship at all. French et al. (1987) estimate GARCH-M models on the daily excess returns of the S&P composite portfolio for the period 1928 to 1984. Using both the conditional variance and the conditional standard deviation specification, they provide evidence for a significant positive relationship between excess returns and risk. Beck (2001) used GARCHM process to investigate risk–return relationship in agricultural commodities and found mixed evidence of positive and negative relationship. Li (2003) models daily S&P500, FTSE100 and DAX30 return as GARCH-M using the skewed *t*-distribution and allowing the conditional skewness to influence the mean equation. For all three indices, the parameter estimates suggest a positive and significant relation between the conditional variance and the expected excess return. In Indian context, Kumar and Singh (2008) investigated the risk–return relationship and seasonality in risk-return through GARCHM modelling in which seasonal dummies are used for return as well as volatility equation. The stock and commodity markets returns show persistence as well as clustering and asymmetric properties. Risk–return relationship is positive though insignificant for Nifty and Soybean where as significant positive relationship is found in the case of gold. Seasonality in risk and return is also found which suggests the asymmetric nature of return, i.e., negative correlation between return and its volatility.

17.3.6 log-GARCH

Logarithmic GARCH: The log-GARCH (p, q) model, which was suggested independently in slightly different forms by Geweke (1986), Pantula (1986) and Milhoj (1987), parameterizes the logarithmic conditional variance as a function of the lagged logarithmic variances and the lagged logarithmic squared innovations. The variance equation is

$$\log(\sigma_t^2) = \alpha_0 + \sum_{i=1}^{q} \alpha_i \log(\varepsilon_{t-i}^2) + \sum_{j=1}^{p} \beta_j \log(\sigma_{t-j}^2)$$

17.3.7 EGARCH (Exponential GARCH)

The symmetric volatility models like GARCH model as discussed in Section 17.3.4 is characterized by a symmetric response of current volatility to positive and negative lagged return. This is because, the GARCH expression for conditional variance shows that it considers square of return terms. The empirical literature on returns of risky assets shows that, future volatility of stock returns is much more affected by negative news compared with positive news (Black 1976). The EGARCH model developed by Nelson (1991) explicitly allows for asymmetries in the relationship between return and volatility. With Eqs. (17.1) and (17.2), the variance of EGARCH (p, q) model may then be expressed as

$$\ln(\sigma_t^2) = \alpha_0 + \sum_{i=1}^{q} \alpha_i\, g(z_{t-i}) + \sum_{j=1}^{p} \beta_j \ln(\sigma_{t-j}^2)$$

where $g(z_t) = \phi z_t + \gamma(|z_t| - E(|z_t|))$.

For $\phi < 0$, negative shocks will obviously have a bigger impact on future volatility than positive shocks of the same magnitude. This effect, which is typically observed in equity index returns, is often referred to as a 'leverage effect,' although it is now widely agreed that the apparent asymmetry has little to do with actual financial leverage. The EGARCH model has been commonly used to examine the interest rates, interest rate futures markets, to model foreign exchange rates and to analyse stock returns (see, e.g., Brunner and Simon (1996), Hu et al. (1997), Koutmos and Booth (1995) and Tse and Booth (1996)). Using EGARCH models, Floros (2008) found leverage effects on returns for Egypt and Israel stock market. Koulakiotis et al. (2006) showed that EGARCH-M model provides more accurate results with respect to the relationship between stock price returns and volatility. Miyakoshia and Jalolovb (2005) investigated how money-income causality in the Asia is influenced by US interest rates and the money supply and which policy variable has a stronger impact on Asia using an EGARCH model. Appiah-Kusi and Menyah (2003) used EGARCH-M model to investigate the weak-form pricing efficiency of 11 African stock markets. Chen et al. (2001) investigated the presence of asymmetric relations between the stock market returns and volatility in nine countries (Canada, France, Hong Kong, Italy, Japan, Netherland, USA, UK and Switzerland). Results show evidence of asymmetry as the leverage factor is statistically significant. Kobayashi and Shi (2005) used EGARCH model to evaluate it against other stochastic volatility models in equity market.

17.3.8 IGARCH

For the GARCH model discussed in Section 17.3.4, a weakly stationary solution exists if and only if $\sum_{i=1}^{q} \alpha_i + \sum_{j=1}^{p} \beta_j < 1$. If we allow for $\sum_{i=1}^{q} \alpha_i + \sum_{j=1}^{p} \beta_j = 1$, the GARCH (p, q) model becomes ntegrated in variance and we have Integrated GARCH (IGARCH) model of Engle and Bollerslev (1986). IGARCH models are persistent in variance because current information remains important for forecasts of the conditional variance for all the horizons. Choudhry (1995) studied the persistence of stock return volatility in five European markets during the 1920s and 1930s using the IGARCH model. Results show that for the bulk of the series, shocks to volatility are permanent, implying a significant impact of volatility on stock prices. Morana (2002) showed how IGARCH effects could arise as an artefact of unaccounted structural change. Using daily returns for the DM/US$ and Yen/US$ exchange rates, the finding is shown to have empirical relevance. IGARCH models appear to be useful approximations, for short-term forecasting, to data-generating process, which shows time-varying conditional variance due to switching heteroskedasticity. Kumar and Supriya (2007) studied the functional relationships between the trading value and the trading price of Nifty Futures. Through the IGARCH (1, 1) two stage modelling, futile trading is observed in all the economic situations, causing disequilibria in the market.

17.3.9 FIGARCH

Fractionally Integrated GARCH: The model may be seen as natural extension of the IGARCH model, allowing for fractional orders of integration (I) in the autoregressive polynomial in the corresponding ARMA representation. The FIGARCH model proposed by Baillie et al. (1996) encompasses the possibility of persistent but not necessarily permanent shocks to volatility. In contrast to GARCH and IGARCH models, FIGARCH model allows fractional orders of integration and therefore response of the conditional variance to the past shocks can decay slowly. Rewriting the GARCH (*p*, *q*) equation from Section 17.3.4 as $\sigma_t^2 = \alpha_0 + \alpha(L)\varepsilon_t^2 + \beta(L)\sigma_t^2$, where *L* is the backshift operator, the variance equation for FIGARCH (*p*, *d*, *q*) model can be expressed as

$$[1-\beta(L)]\sigma_t^2 = \alpha_0 + [(1-\beta(L)) - \phi(L)(1-L)^d]\varepsilon_t^2$$

where $\beta(L) = 1 + \beta_1 L + \cdots + \beta_p^p$ and $\phi(L) = 1 + \phi_1 L + \cdots + \phi_q L^q$ are the lag polynomials of orders *p* and *q*, respectively and all roots of $\phi(L)$ and $[1-\beta(L)]$ lie outside the unit circle. α_0, β's ϕ's and *d* are the parameters to be estimated with *d* being the fractional integration parameter. As in standard ARIMA type models, the fractional differencing parameter, *d*, indicates the speed at which shocks to ε_t^2 die out over time. For values of $d = 0$, the model reduces to standard GARCH model; for $d = 1$, it is IGARCH and for $0 < d < 1$, it becomes FIGARCH. Using a daily time series of the German mark/US dollar exchange rate, they show that the FIGARCH (1, 1) model is superior to both the GARCH (1, 1) and the IGARCH (1, 1). FIGARCH class of models has the resemblance to the fractionally integrated class of processes for the conditional means and is flexible in modelling the persistence of shocks to the conditional variance process. The FIGARCH model has been successfully applied in several areas of empirical finance. Bollerslev and Mikkelsen (1999) investigate the economic value of FIEGARCH forecasts of volatility, while Brunetti and Gilbert (2000) extend the model to a bivariate framework, and Baillie et al. (2000) and Beltratti and Morana (1999) studied high frequency data with the model. In the light of this topic, some researchers have extended the work for the application of time-varying volatility models, specifically ARCH-type models, in VaR estimations (Brooks et al. 2000a; Giot 2005; Manfredo et al. 2001). Most of these findings enhance the use of time-varying models in risk management applications using VaR. In Indian context, Banerjee and Sarkar (2006) evaluated long memory property in SENSEX and compared GARCH, FIGARCH and EGARCH models. The results show a strong evidence of long memory in conditional variance and they found that FIGARCH is the best-fit model.

17.3.10 FIEGARCH (Fractionally Integrated EGARCH)

The FIEGARCH model imposes a fractional unit root in the autoregressive polynomial in the ARMA representation of the EGARCH model. If $\varepsilon_t = \sigma_t z_t$ denote the standardized innovations, rewriting EGARCH equation in terms of backshift operator as $\ln(\sigma_t^2) = \alpha_0 + [1-\beta(L)]^{-1}[1+\gamma(L)]\, g(z_{t-1})$ where $g(z_t) = \theta z_t + \alpha[|z_t| - E|z_t|]$ and factorizing the autoregressive polynomial $1-\beta(L) = \phi(L)(1-L)^d$, Bollerslev and Mikkelsen (1996) proposed the FIEGARCH model as

$$\ln(\sigma_t^2) = \alpha_0 + \phi(L)^{-1}(1-L)^{-d}[1+\gamma(L)]\, g(z_{t-1})$$

For $0 < d < 1$, this representation implies fractional integrated slowly decaying hyperbolic dependencies in $\log \sigma_t^2$. This is generally used to study long memory properties of volatility. Ruiz and Veiga (2008) found that the kurtosis and autocorrelations of squares of daily returns of the S&P500 and DAX indexes increase with the asymmetry but autocorrelations decreases with persistence in case of FIEGARCH model.

17.3.11 NGARCH (Non-linear GARCH)

The NGARCH (p, q) model proposed by Higgins and Bera (1992) parameterizes the conditional standard deviation raised to the power δ as a function of the lagged conditional standard deviations and the lagged absolute innovations raised to the same power. The variance equation for the model may be expressed as

$$\sigma_t^\delta = \alpha_0 + \sum_{i=1}^{q} \alpha_i |\varepsilon_{t-i}|^\delta + \sum_{j=1}^{p} \beta_j \sigma_{t-j}^\delta$$

Sometimes referred to as a Power ARCH or Power GARCH model, the NGARCH model reduces to standard GARCH (p, q) model for $\delta = 2$. This model is a slightly different version of the NGARCH model $\sigma_t^2 = \alpha_0 + \alpha|\varepsilon_{t-1}|^\delta + \beta\sigma_{t-1}^2$ estimated by Engle and Bollerslev (1986). With most financial rates of returns, the estimates for δ are found to be less than two, although not always significantly so. Lanne and Saikkonen (2005) used non-linear GARCH model for an empirical application to exchange rate return series and showed that the new models can be superior to conventional GARCH models especially in longer term forecasting.

17.3.12 AGARCH (Asymmetric GARCH)

The AGARCH model (Engle 1990) allows asymmetric effects of negative and positive innovations. The AGARCH (p, q) model is defined by

$$\sigma_t^2 = \alpha_0 + \sum_{i=1}^{q} (\alpha_i \varepsilon_{t-i}^2 + \gamma_i \varepsilon_{t-i}) + \sum_{j=1}^{p} \beta_j \sigma_{t-j}^2$$

where negative values of γ imply that positive shocks will result in smaller increases in future volatility than negative shocks of the same absolute magnitude. Caporin and McAleer (2006) developed the dynamic asymmetric GARCH (or DAGARCH) model that generalizes asymmetric GARCH models and presented an application to daily stock market indices to demonstrate the practical usefulness of the new model. McMillan and Speight (2007) analysed the daily index data for eight emerging stock markets in the Asia-Pacific region, in addition to US and UK benchmark comparators, and found both asymmetric and long memory features to be important considerations in providing improved VaR estimates that minimize occasions when the minimum capital requirement identified by the VaR methodology would have fallen short of actual trading losses.

17.3.13 APARCH (Asymmetric Power ARCH)

The APARCH, or APGARCH, model of Ding et al. (1993) nests several of the most popular univariate parameterizations. In particular, the APGARCH (p, q) model,

$$\sigma_t^\delta = \alpha_0 + \sum_{i=1}^{q} \alpha_i (|\varepsilon_{t-i}| - \gamma_i \varepsilon_{t-i})^\delta + \sum_{j=1}^{p} \beta_j \sigma_{t-j}^\delta$$

reduces to the standard linear GARCH (p, q) model for $\delta = 2$ and $\gamma_i = 0$, the TS GARCH (p, q) model for $\delta = 1$ and $\gamma_i = 0$ and the NGARCH (p, q) model for $\gamma_i = 0$. The applicability of the

Power ARCH class of model to stock market data has been well documented in papers such as Ding et al. (1993) and Hentschel (1995). Tse and Tsui (1997) applied the APGARCH model to daily Malaysian–US and Singapore–US exchange rate data. The authors find that the model adequately describes the data, Further, whilst no evidence of asymmetry is found for the Singapore dollar, it was present in the Malaysian currency. Brooks et al. (2000b) analyse the applicability of these power ARCH (PARCH) models to national stock market returns for 10 countries plus a world index. They find the PARCH model to be generally applicable once GARCH and leverage effects are taken into consideration. In addition, they also find that the optimal power transformation is remarkably similar across countries. Tully and Lucey (2007) investigated macroeconomic influences on gold using the asymmetric power GARCH model. They suggest that APGARCH model provides the most adequate description for the data, with the inclusion of a GARCH term, free power term and unrestricted leverage effect term. The role of the dollar in gold was confirmed but few other macroeconomic variables had an impact.

17.3.14 GJR-GARCH

Glosten, Jagannathan and Runkle (1993) showed how to allow the effects of good and bad news to have different effects on volatility by allowing the conditional variance to react differently to the past negative and positive innovations. The GJR (p, q) model may be expressed as

$$\sigma_t^2 = \alpha_0 + \sum_{i=1}^{q} \alpha_i \varepsilon_{t-i}^2 + \sum_{i=1}^{q} \gamma_i \varepsilon_{t-i}^2 I_{t-i}(\varepsilon_{t-i} < 0) + \sum_{j=1}^{p} \beta_j \sigma_{t-j}^2$$

where I (•) denotes the indicator function such that it equals 1 if $\varepsilon_{t-1} < 0$ and is equal to zero otherwise. The model is also sometimes referred to as a Sign-GARCH model. The GJR formulation is closely related to the Threshold GARCH, or TGARCH, model proposed independently by Zakoian (1994) and the asymmetric GARCH, or AGARCH, model of Engle (1990). When estimating the GJR model with equity index returns, a positive γ indicates that the negative shocks have larger effects on volatility than positive shocks. This asymmetry, as already discussed in Section 17.2.9, is referred to as the 'leverage effect,' although it is largely different from actual financial leverage. Engle and Ng (1993) studied the impact of news on volatility and concluded that GJR model is the superior parametric model. Li et al. (2008) used GJR GARCH (1,1) to study whether the widely documented momentum profits can be attributed to time-varying risk. Das et al. (2008) used this model for VaR computation with NSE data.

17.3.15 QGARCH (Quadratic GARCH)

This model by Sentana (1995) is used to model asymmetric effects of positive and negative shocks. Sentana's QGARCH (p, q) model can be expressed as

$$\sigma_t^2 = \alpha_0 + \sum_{i=1}^{q} \gamma_i \varepsilon_{t-i} + \sum_{i=1}^{q} \alpha_i \varepsilon_{t-i}^2 + 2\sum_{i=1}^{q} \sum_{k=i+1}^{q} \alpha_{ik} \varepsilon_{t-i} \varepsilon_{t-k} + \sum_{j=1}^{p} \beta_j \sigma_{t-j}^2$$

with mean equation similar to Eq. (17.1) and the innovation similar to Eq. (17.2). If all γ_i and α_{ik} are equal to zero, the above model reduces to GARCH (p, q) model. The additional term

$\gamma_i \varepsilon_{t-i}$ makes it possible for positive and negative shocks to have different effects on conditional volatility. The condition for covariance stationary is same as GARCH (1, 1) model. Franses and van Dijk (1996) showed that the asymmetric model (QGARCH) is the best when the estimation sample does not contain extreme observations.

17.3.16 TS-GARCH (Taylor–Schwert GARCH)

The TS-GARCH (*p*, *q*) model of Taylor (1986) and Schwert (1989) parameterizes the conditional standard deviation as a distributed lag of the absolute innovations and the lagged conditional standard deviations,

$$\sigma_t = \alpha_0 + \sum_{i=1}^{q} \alpha_i |\varepsilon_{t-i}| + \sum_{j=1}^{p} \beta_j \sigma_{t-j}$$

This formulation is a special case of the more general Power GARCH, or NGARCH model. This model mitigates the influence of large (in an absolute sense) observations relative to the traditional GARCH (*p*, *q*) model. The TS-GARCH model is also sometimes referred to as an Absolute Value GARCH, or AVGARCH, model, or simply an AGARCH model. Canarella and Pollard (2008) applied TSGARCH to model the volatility of the London gold market.

17.3.17 TGARCH (Threshold GARCH)

The TGARCH (*p*, *q*) model proposed by Zakoian (1994) extends the TS-GARCH (*p*, *q*) model to allow the response of volatility to news with different coefficients for good and bad news. The TGARCH (*p*, *q*) model may be expressed as: $\sigma_t = \alpha_0 + \sum_{i=1}^{q} \alpha_i |\varepsilon_{t-i}| + \gamma_i \varepsilon_{t-i} d_{t-i} + \sum_{j=1}^{p} \beta_j \sigma_{t-j}$

where $d_t = 1$ if $\varepsilon_t < 0$ and $d_t = 0$ otherwise.

Generally, $\varepsilon_{t-1} = 0$ is the threshold such that shocks greater than the threshold have different effects than shocks below the threshold. The TGARCH model is also sometimes referred to as the ZARCH, or ZGARCH, model. The basic idea behind the model is closely related to that of the GJR-GARCH model developed independently by Glosten et al. (1993). Longin (1997) used this process to model information flow to measure expected volatility. Floros (2007) used TGARCH model along with others for the calculation of minimum capital risk requirements in US and European market.

17.3.18 STGARCH (Smooth Transition GARCH)

A recent development in GARCH modelling has been the use of smooth transition models. The essence of these models is that at least one parameter is modelled as a continuous function of a transition variable. Franses and van Dijk (2000: Ch. 4) provide a useful review of smooth transition GARCH models. The logistic smooth transition (LSTGARCH) model of González-Rivera (1998) enables a smooth transition between the α and γ coefficients of the lagged squared error terms in the GJRGARCH model. The ST-GARCH (1,1) model of González-Rivera (1998) allows the impact of the past squared innovations to depend upon both the sign and the magnitude of ε_{t-1} through a smooth transition function,

$$\sigma_t^2 = \alpha_0 + \alpha\varepsilon_{t-1}^2 + \delta\varepsilon_{t-1}^2 F(\varepsilon_{t-1}, \gamma) + \beta\,\sigma_{t-1}^2$$

where $F(\varepsilon_{t-1}, \gamma) = (1+\exp(\gamma\varepsilon_{t-1}))^{-1}$ so that the value of the function is bounded between 0 and 1.

One may consult Lundburgh and Terasvirta (2000) for details. Also if one replaces the logistic function with exponential function, we have what is called ESTGARCH. For application one may refer to Taylor (2004).

17.3.19 STAR-GARCH (Smooth Transition Autoregressive GARCH)

Combining various smooth transition autoregressive (STAR) type models with GARCH has become popular in the financial volatility literature. STAR models are proposed for diagnostic control, forecasting and impulse response analysis. This combination has resulted in two highly flexible non-linear models of financial volatility, STAR-GARCH and STAR-STGARCH. One may consult Terasvirta (1994) and Lundburgh and Terasvirta (2000) for details.

17.3.20 HGARCH (Hentschel GARCH)

Based on a Box-Cox transformation of the conditional standard deviation, Hentschel (1995) proposed HGARCH model that nests some of the most popular univariate parameterizations. The HGARCH (1, 1) model may be expressed as

$$\sigma_t^\delta = \alpha_0 + \alpha\delta\sigma_{t-1}^\delta(|\varepsilon_{t-1}\sigma_{t-1}^{-1} - \kappa| - \gamma(\varepsilon_{t-1}\sigma_{t-1}^{-1} - \kappa))^\upsilon + \beta\sigma_{t-1}^\delta$$

The model reduces to the GARCH (1, 1) model for $\delta = 2$, $\nu = 2$, $\kappa = 0$ and $\gamma = 0$ but it also nests the APARCH, AGARCH, EGARCH, GJR, NGARCH, TGARCH, and TS-GARCH models as special cases. This model is also known as fGARCH (family GARCH).

17.3.21 HYGARCH (Hyperbolic GARCH)

The HYGARCH model proposed by Davidson (2004) nests the GARCH, IGARCH and FIGARCH models (see GARCH, IGARCH and FIGARCH). The model is defined in terms of the ARCH (∞) representation

$$\sigma_t^2 = \alpha_0 + \left[1 - \frac{\delta(L)}{\beta(L)}(1+\alpha((1-L)^d - 1)\right]\varepsilon_{t-i}^2$$

where $\delta(L)$ and $\beta(L)$ denotes appropriately defined lag parameters. The standard GARCH and FIGARCH models correspond to $\alpha = 0$, and $\alpha = 1$ and $0 < d < 1$, respectively. For $d = 1$, the HYGARCH model reduces to a standard GARCH or an IGARCH model depending upon whether $\alpha < 1$ or $\alpha = 1$. The HYGARCH shares with the GARCH model the desired property of covariance stationarity while at the same time it obeys hyperbolically decaying impulse response coefficients as the FIGARCH. Moreover, it provides a natural framework for testing geometric versus hyperbolic decay. Niguez and Rubia (2006) apply the HYGARCH model to a portfolio of five exchange rates and report that it clearly outperforms simpler GARCH variants in terms of out-of-sample forecasting. Tang and Shieh (2006) compare the performance of FIGARCH and HYGARCH models in predicting VaR for three stock index futures markets. Their empirical results show that for the S&P500 and Nasdaq 100 futures prices, the HYGARCH (1, *d*, 1) models with skewed Student-t distribution perform better based on the Kupiec (1995) LR tests.

17.3.22 ATGARCH (Asymmetric Threshold GARCH)

The ATGARCH (1, 1) model of Crouhy and Rockinger (1997) allows the threshold used in characterizing the asymmetric response to differ from zero. The formulation combines and extends the TS-GARCH (1, 1) and GJR (1, 1) models and can be expressed as:

$$\sigma_t = \alpha_0 + \alpha|\varepsilon_{t-1}| I(\varepsilon_{t-1} \geq \gamma) + \delta|\varepsilon_{t-1}| I(\varepsilon_{t-1} < \gamma) + \beta\sigma_{t-1}$$

Higher order ATGARCH (*p*, *q*) models may be defined analogously. Chen et al. (2006) used this model with US financial market news as threshold variable and observed that it performs better than GJR GARCH and TGARCH.

17.3.23 GARCH-X

Lee (1994) provides an extension of the standard GARCH model linked to an error-correction model of co-integrated series on the second moment of the bivariate distributions of the variables. This model is known as the GARCH-X model. If short-run deviations affect the conditional mean, they may also affect conditional variance, and a significant positive effect may imply that the further the series deviate from each other in the short run, the harder they are to predict. If the error correction term (short-run deviations) from the co-integrated relationship between company index and market index affects the conditional variance (and conditional covariance), then conditional heteroskedasticity may be modelled with a function of the lagged error correction term. If shocks to the system that propagate on the first and the second moments change the volatility, then it is reasonable to study the behaviour of conditional variance as a function of short-run deviations (Lee 1994).

$$\sigma_t^2 = \alpha_0 + \sum_{i=1}^{q} \alpha_i \varepsilon_{t-i}^2 + \sum_{j=1}^{p} \beta_j \sigma_{t-j}^2 + \gamma_1 z_{t-1}^2$$

The short-run deviations are presented by the squared and lagged error-correction term z_{t-1}^2. The parameter γ_1 indicates the effects of the short-run deviations from a long-run co-integrated relationship on the conditional variance. Brenner et al. (1996) applied this model and its extension on short-term interest rates.

17.3.24 CGARCH (Component GARCH)

The component GARCH model of Engle and Lee (1999) was designed to better account for long-run volatility dependencies. Rewriting the GARCH (1,1) model as $\sigma_t^2 - \sigma^2 = \alpha(\varepsilon_{t-1}^2 - \sigma^2) + \beta(\sigma_{t-1}^2 - \sigma^2)$

where $\sigma^2 = \omega/(1-\alpha-\beta)$ refers to the unconditional variance, the CGARCH model is obtained as $\sigma_t^2 - \zeta_t^2 = \alpha(\varepsilon_{t-1}^2 - \zeta_{t-1}^2) + \beta(\sigma_{t-1}^2 - \zeta_{t-1}^2)$ with the corresponding long run variance parameterized by a separate equation of the form $\zeta_t^2 = \omega + \rho\zeta_{t-1}^2 + \varphi(\varepsilon_{t-1}^2 - \sigma_{t-1}^2)$. Substituting this expression into the former equation, the CGARCH model may alternatively be expressed as a restricted GARCH (2, 2) model. Wei (2009) studied the spillover effects of the unexpected exchange rate shock of the USD, Yen, and Eurodollar to the China Renminbi (RMB) within the domestic and Chinese stock markets.

17.3.25 EVT-GARCH (Extreme Value Theory GARCH)

The EVT-GARCH of McNeil and Frey (2000) originates from extreme value theory for i.i.d. random variables and corresponding generalized Pareto distributions for more accurately characterizing the tails of the distributions of the standardized innovations from GARCH models. This model may be used in the calculation of low-probability quantile, or VaR type predictions. Bhattacharyya and Ritolia (2008) used this model to construct a robust VaR measure for the Indian stock markets by combining two well-known facts about equity return time series—dynamic volatility resulting in the well-recognized phenomenon of volatility clustering, and non-normality giving rise to fat tails of the return distribution.

17.3.26 GARCH-Γ/GARCH-Δ (GARCH Gamma/Delta)

The delta of an option is the first derivative of the option price with respect to the price of the underlying asset. The gamma of an option is defined as the second derivative of the option price with respect to the price of the underlying asset. Options delta/gamma play an important role in hedging volatility risk embedded in options positions. GARCH-Γ refers to the gamma obtained under the assumption that the return on the underlying asset follows a GARCH process. Engle and Rosenberg (1995) parameterized the volatility process as GARCH, and utilizing risk-neutral valuation, they estimated hedging parameters (delta and gamma) using Monte-Carlo simulation. They estimated hedging parameters for options on the Standard and Poor's 500 index, a bond futures index, a weighted foreign exchange rate index, and an oil futures index. They find that Black–Scholes and GARCH deltas tend to be fairly close for all the options considered, while GARCH gammas are significantly higher than Black–Scholes gammas for all options.

17.3.27 Structural GARCH

The Structural GARCH approach named by Rigobon (2002) relies on a multivariate GARCH model for the innovations in an otherwise unidentified structural VAR to identify the parameters through time-varying conditional heteroskedasticity. Closely related ideas and models have been explored by Sentana and Fiorentini (2001) among others.

17.3.28 F-ARCH/F-GARCH (Factor GARCH)

The multivariate factor ARCH model developed by Diebold and Nerlove (1989) and the factor GARCH model of Engle et al. (1990) undertakes temporal variation in the $N \times N$ conditional covariance matrix for a set of N returns, which can be described by univariate GARCH models for smaller set of $K < N$ portfolios,

$$\Omega_t = \Omega + \sum_{k=1}^{K} \lambda_k \lambda_k' \sigma_{kt}^2$$

where λ_k and σ_{kt}^2 refer to the time invariant $N \times 1$ vector of factor loadings and time t conditional variance for the kth factor, respectively. Specifically, the F-GARCH (1, 1) model may be expressed as

$$\Omega_t = \Omega + \lambda\lambda'[\beta\omega'\Omega_{t-1}\,\omega + \alpha(\omega'\varepsilon_{t-1})^2]$$

where w denotes an $N \times 1$ vector, and α and β are both scalar parameters. Diebold and Nerlove (1989) used this model to capture the dynamics of exchange rate volatility, the ARCH effects to capture volatility clustering and the factor structure to captures the commonality in volatility movements across exchange rates.

17.3.29 AR (*p*)/ARCH (*p*)

From the definitions of AR and ARCH processes, we know that an AR process has a non-constant conditional mean but a constant conditional variance while ARCH process is just the reverse. However, there may be cases where we need both the conditional mean and variance of a process to depend on the past, i.e., we may need a model that has features of both AR and ARCH models. Therefore there may be cases where in order to explain the data characteristics we may combine AR and ARCH or any ARMA model with any GARCH model. Application of these types of models are well documented in Francq and Zakoıan (2004), Ling and McAleer (2003) and Ling and Li (1998).

17.4 Multivariate GARCH

It is now widely accepted that financial volatilities move together over time across assets and markets. Incorporating this feature in a multivariate modelling framework leads to more relevant empirical models than working with separate univariate models that were discussed earlier. The relations between the volatilities and co-volatilities of several markets can be studied by using MGARCH (multivariate GARCH) models. Are volatilities across markets integrated? Is the volatility of an asset transmitted to another asset directly (through its conditional variance) or indirectly (through its conditional covariances)? Does a shock on a market increase the volatility on another market, and by what extent? Do shocks with different signs but of the same amplitude have same impact? A related issue is whether the correlations between asset returns change over time. Are they higher during periods of higher volatility (sometimes associated with financial crises)? Does globalization of financial markets causes these correlations to increase in the long run? Further, asset-pricing models relate returns to 'factors', such as the market return in the capital asset pricing model. A specific asset excess return (in excess of the risk-free return) may be expressed as a linear function of the market return. Assuming its constancy, the slope, or β coefficient, may be estimated by OLS. Like in case of hedge ratio, since β is the ratio of a covariance to a variance, an MGARCH model can be used to estimate time-varying β coefficients (Bollerslev et al. 1988; De Santis and Gerard 1998; Hafner and Herwartz 1998). Given an estimated univariate GARCH model on a return series, one knows the return conditional distribution, and one can forecast the VaR of a long or short position. When considering a portfolio of assets, the portfolio return can be computed directly from the asset shares and returns. A GARCH model can be fit to the portfolio returns for given weights. If the weight vector changes, the model has to be estimated again. On the contrary, if a multivariate GARCH model is fitted, the multivariate distribution of the returns can be used directly to compute the implied distribution of any portfolio. There is no need to re-estimate the model for different weight vectors. It is probably simpler to use the univariate framework if there are many assets, but we suppose that using a multivariate specification may become a feasible alternative. Whether the univariate 'repeated' approach is more adequate than the multivariate one is an open question.

Multivariate GARCH (VECTOR ARCH) models were first analysed and estimated empirically by Bollerslev et al. (1988). The unrestricted linear MGARCH (p, q) model is defined by:

$$vech\ (\Omega_t) = A_0 + \sum_{i=1}^{q} A_i\ vech(\varepsilon_{t-i}\ \varepsilon'_{t-i}) + \sum_{j=1}^{p} B_j\ vech(\Omega_{t-j})$$

where vech (.) denotes the operator that stacks the lower triangular portion of a symmetric $N \times N$ matrix into an $N(N+1)/2 \times 1$ vector of the corresponding unique elements, and the A_i and B_i matrices are all of compatible dimension $N(N+1)/2 \times N(N+1)/2$. This vectorized representation is also sometime referred to as a VECH GARCH model. The general vech representation does not guarantee that the resulting conditional covariance matrices Ω_t are positive definite. Also, the model involves a total of $N(N+1)/2 + (p+q)(N^4 + 2N^3 + N^2)/4$ parameters, which is too many from computational point of view. Much of the research on multivariate GARCH models has been concerned with the development of alternative more parsimonious, yet empirically realistic, representations, that easily ensure the conditional covariance matrices are positive definite. The trivariate vech MGARCH (1, 1) model estimated in Bollerslev et al. (1988) assumes that the A_1 and B_1 matrices are both diagonal, so that each element in Ω_t depends exclusively on its own lagged value and the product of the corresponding shocks. This diagonal simplification, resulting in 'only' $(1 + p + q)(N^2 + N)/2$ parameters to be estimated, is often denoted as a diag MGARCH model or diagonal GARCH.

17.5 Conclusion

We have discussed various statistical properties that one may come across while working with financial data series. Since most of the financial data series show volatility implicitly or explicitly, we presented a set of models, which a researcher may try to fit in with the concerned data sets. Emphasis was laid on univariate GARCH type models that takes into account conditional variance and is useful when ordinary regression analysis fails due to the presence of heteroskedasticity. However, from the plethora of volatility models, which models is most suitable is still a controversial topic. In the literature, many researchers focus on financial market volatility of different countries

(Appiah-Kusi and Menyah 2003; Bollerslev and Zhou 2006; Bollerslev et al. 2006; French et al. 1987; Kayahan et al. 2002; Schwert 1989), but the best-forecast volatility model is controversial. Some empirical studies have emphasized the power of historical GARCH models (McMillan et al. 2000). For instance, Brailsford and Faff (1996) stress the ARCH class of models provide superior forecasts of volatility. Additionally, Ederington and Guan (2002) compare the forecasting ability of some volatility models and conclude that GARCH (1, 1) generally yields better forecasts than the historical standard deviation and exponentially weighted moving average models. In the contrast, some empirical studies have emphasized the power of asymmetries on the forecast performance of GARCH models (Loudon et al. 2000; Maris et al. 2004). For example, Awartani and Corradi (2005) investigate the out of sample predictive ability of different GARCH models and conclude the GARCH (1, 1) is beaten by the asymmetric GARCH models. Additional to that, Franses and van Dijk (1996) study the performance of the GARCH model and two of its non-linear modifications to forecast weekly stock market volatility. They conclude that the asymmetric model (QGARCH) is the best when the estimation sample does not contain extreme observations. We feel the success of any volatility forecasting model is extremely data specific and it may not be possible to conclude that any particular type of model is able to predict future better.

References

Aggarwal, R. and Aggarwal, R. (1993). 'Security Return Distributions and Market Structure: Evidence from the NYSE/AMEX and the NASDAQ Markets'. *Journal of Financial Research*, 76(3), pp 209–220.

Alles, L. and Kling, J. (1994). 'Regularities in the Variation of Skewness in Stock Index Returns'. *Journal of Financial Research*, 77, pp 427–438.

Appiah-Kusi, J. and Menyah, K. (2003). 'Return Predictability in African Stock Markets'. *Review of Financial Economics*, 12(3), pp 247–270.

Awartani, B. M. A. and Corradi, V. (2005). 'Predicting the Volatility of the S&P-500 Stock Index via GARCH Models: The Role of Asymmetries'. *International Journal of Forecasting*, 21(1), pp 167–183.

Badrinath, S. G., and Chatterjee, S. (1991). 'A Data-Analytic Look at Skewness and Elongation in Common Stock Return Distributions'. *Journal of Business and Economic Statistics*, 9, pp 223–233.

Baillie, R. T. and De Gennaro, R. P. (1990). 'Stock Returns and Volatility'. *Journal of Financial and Quantitative Analysis*, 25, pp 203–214.

Baillie, R. T., Bollerslev, T. and Mikkelsen, H. (1996). 'Fractionally Integrated Generalized Autoregressive Conditional Heteroscedasticity'. *Journal of Econometrics*, 74(1), pp 3–30.

Baillie, R. T., Cecen, A. A. and Han, Y. (2000). 'High Frequency Deutsche Mark-US Dollar Returns: FIGARCH Representations and Non Linearities'. *Multinational Finance Journal*, 4(3–4), pp 247–267.

Banerjee, A. and Sarkar, S. (2006). 'Long Memory Property of Stock Returns Evidence from India'. *Indian Accounting Review*, 10, pp 48–62.

Beck, S. (2001). 'Autoregressive Conditional Heteroscedasticity in Commodity Spot Prices'. *Journal of Applied Econometrics*, 16(2), pp 115–132.

Beedles, W. L. (1979). 'Return, Dispersion and Skewness: Synthesis and Investment Strategy'. *Journal of Financial Research*, 2(1), pp 71–80.

Bekaert, G., Erb, C., Harvey, C. and Viskanta, T. (1998). 'Distributional Characteristics of Emerging Market Returns and Asset Allocation'. *The Journal of Portfolio Management*, 24(2), pp 102–116.

Beltratti, A. and Morana C. (1999). 'Computing Value at Risk with High Frequency Data'. *Journal of Empirical Finance*, 6(5), pp 431–455.

Bhattacharyya, M. and Ritolia, G. (2008). 'Conditional VaR Using EVT—Towards a Planned Margin Scheme'. *International Review of Financial Analysis*, 17(2), pp 382–395.

Black, F. (1976). 'Studies in Stock Price Volatility Changes'. *Proceedings of the 1976 Business Meeting of the Business and Economics Statistics Section*, American Statistical Association, pp 177–181.

Bodurtha, J. N. and Mark, N. C. (1991). 'Testing the CAPM with Time-Varying Risks and Returns'. *Journal of Finance*, 46(4), pp 1485–1505.

Bollerslev, T. (1986). 'Generalised Autoregressive Heteroscedasticity'. *Journal of Econometrics*, 31(3), pp 307–327.

Bollerslev, T. and Mikkelsen, H. O. (1996). 'Modelling and Pricing Long Memory in Stock Market Volatility. *Journal of Econometrics*, 73, pp 151–184.

Bollerslev, T. and Mikkelsen, H. O. (1999). 'Long-term Equity Anticipation Securities and Stock Market Volatility Dynamics'. *Journal of Econometrics*, 92, pp 75–99.

Bollerslev, T. and Zhou, H. (2006). 'Volatility Puzzles: A Simple Framework for Gauging Return-Volatility Regressions'. *Journal of Econometrics*, 131(1), pp 123–150.

Bollerslev, T., Engle, R. F. and Wooldridge, J. (1988). 'A Capital Asset Pricing Model with Time-Varying Covariances'. *Journal of Political Economy*, 96(1), pp 116–131.

Bollerslev, T., Chou, R. Y. and Kroner, K. F. (1992). 'ARCH Modelling in Finance: A Review of the Theory and Empirical Evidence'. *Journal of Econometrics*, 52, pp 5–59.

Bollerslev, T., Litvinova, J. and Tauchen, G. (2006). 'Leverage and Volatility Feedback Effect in High-Frequency Data'. *Journal of Financial Econometrics*, 4(3), pp 353–384.

Box, G. E. P. and Jenkins, G. M. (1970). *Time Series Analysis Forecasting and Control*. Holden-Day, San Francisco, CA.

Brailsford, T. J. and Faff, R. W. (1996). 'An Evaluation of Volatility Forecasting Techniques'. *Journal of Banking and Finance*, 20(3), pp 419–438.

Brenner, R. J., Harjes, R. H. and Kroner, K. F. (1996). 'Another Look at Models of the Short-term Interest Rate'. *Journal of Financial and Quantitative Analysis*, 31, pp 85–107.

Brock, W., Dechert, D., Sheinkman, J. and LeBaron, B. (1996). 'A Test for Independence Based on the Correlation Dimension'. *Econometric Reviews*, pp 197–235.

Brooks, C., Clare, A. D. and Persand, G. (2000a). A Word of Caution on Calculating Market based Minimum Capital Risk Requirements. *Journal of Banking and Finance*, 24(10), pp 1557–1574.

Brooks, R. D., Faff, R. W., Michael D., McKenzie, M. D. and Mitchell, H. (2000b). 'A Multi-Country Study of Power ARCH Models and National Stock Market Returns'. *Journal of International Money and Finance*, 19(3), pp 377–397.

Brunetti, C. and Gilbert, C. L. (2000). 'Bivariate FIGARCH and Fractional Cointegration'. *Journal of Empirical Finance*, 7, pp 509–530.

Brunner, A. D. and Simon, D. P. (1996). 'Excess Returns and Risk at the long End of the Treasury Market: An EGARCH-M Approach'. *The Journal of Financial Research*, 14(1), pp 443–457.

Campbell, J. and Hentschel, L. (1992). 'No News is Good News: An Asymmetric Model of Changing Volatility in Stock Returns'. *Journal of Financial Economics*, 31, pp 281–318.

Canarella, G. and Pollard, S. K. (2008). 'Modeling the Volatility of the London Gold Market Fixing as an Asymmetric Power ARCH Process'. '*The ICFAI Journal of Applied Finance*', 14(5), pp 17–43.

Caporin, M and McAleer, M (2006). 'Dynamic Asymmetric GARCH'. *Journal of Financial Econometrics*, 4(3), pp 385–412.

Chen, G. M., Firth, M. and Rui, O. L. (2001). 'The dynamic Relation Between Stock Returns, Trading Volume, and Volatility'. *The Financial Review*, 38, pp 153–174.

Chen, C. W. S., Gerlach, R. and So, M. K. P. (2006). 'Comparison of Nonnested Asymmetric Heteroskedastic Models'. *Computational Statistics & Data Analysis*, 51(4), pp 2164–2178.

Choudhry, T. (1995). 'Integrated-GARCH and Non-stationary Variances: Evidence from European Stock Markets during the 1920s and 1930s'. *Economics Letters*, 48(1), pp 55–59.

Cont, R. (2001). 'Empirical Properties of Asset Returns: Stylized Facts and Statistical Issues'. *Quantitative Finance*, 1, pp 223–236.

Crouhy, H. and Rockinger, M. (1997). 'Volatility Clustering, Asymmetric and Hysteresis in Stock Returns: International Evidence'. *Financial Engineering and the Japanese Markets*, 4, pp 1–35.

Das, J. K. (2006). 'Business Forecasting Techniques: An Appraisal for Managers'. *Business Studies*, 27, pp 1–32.

Das, J. K. and Basu, A. K. (1991). 'On Estimation and Asymptotic Properties of the Parameters of ARMA(p, q) Process in the Stable Case'. *Calcutta Statistical Association Bulletin*, 41, pp 45–64.

Das, J. K. and Basu, A. K. (1992). 'Optimality of Maximum Likelihood Estimator in AR(p) Model Under a General Set-up of the Roots'. *Calcutta Statistical Association Bulletin*, 42, pp 18–41.

Das, J. K. and Basu, A. K. (1993). 'On Random Coefficient Autoregressive Model with Infinite Variance'. *Journal of Indian Statistical Association*, 31, pp 5–19.

Das, J. K. and Basu, A. K. (1994). 'Bayesian Approach to Kalman Filter for Elliptically Contoured Distribution with Application in Time Series Models'. *Calcutta Statistical Association Bulletin*, 44, pp 11–28.

Das, J. K. and Basu, A. K. (1995). 'Sequential Least Square Estimation and Shrinkage Estimation of the Autoregressive Parameters in AR(P) Model'. *Proceedings of XVth ISPS Conference*, Tirunelveli, India, pp 6–21.

Das, J. K. and Basu, A. K. (1997a). 'Sequential Shrinkage Estimation of the Autoregressive Parameters in AR(P) Model'. *Journal of Applied Statistical Science*, 5, pp 267–282.

Das, J. K. and Basu, A. K. (1997b). 'Sequential Estimation of the Autoregressive Parameters in AR (P) Model'. *Sequential Analysis*, 16, pp 1–24.

Das, J. K. and Basu, A. K. (1999). 'A Lower Bound for the Variance of Fixed Accuracy Estimator of AR(1) Parameter'. *Stochastic Modeling and Application*, 2, pp 67–71.

Das, J. K. and Basu, A. K. (2002). 'Sequential Estimation of the Autoregressive Parameters in an Explosive AR(p) Process'. *Journal of Statistical Theory and Application*, 1, pp 223–231.

Das, A., Basu, P. N. and Das, S. C. (2008). 'A Relook at the VaR Computation Method Recommended by National Stock Exchange of India'. *The ICFAI Journal of Applied Finance*, 14(9), pp 45–53.

Davidson, J. (2004). 'Moment and Memory Properties of Linear Conditional Heteroskedasticity Models, and a New Model'. *Journal of Business and Economic Statistics*, 22, pp 16–29.

De Gooijer, G. J. and Hyndman, R. J. (2006). '25 years of Time Series Forecasting'. *International Journal of Forecasting*, 22(3), pp 443–473.

De Santis, G. and Gerard, B. (1998). 'How Big is the Premium for Currency Risk'. *Journal of Financial Economics*, 49, pp 375–412.

Diebold, F. X. and Nerlove, M. (1989). 'The Dynamics of Exchange Rate Volatility: A Multivariate Latent Factor ARCH Model'. *Journal of Applied Econometrics*, 4, pp 1–21.

Ding, Z., Granger, C. W. J. and Engle, R. F. (1993). 'A Long Memory Property of Stock Market Returns and a New Model'. *Journal of Empirical Finance*, 1, pp 83–106.

Ederington, L. H. and Guan, W. (2002). 'Is Implied Volatility an Informationally Efficient and Effective Predictor of Future Volatility?'. *The Journal of Risk*, 4(3), pp 29–46.

Engle, R. F. (1982). 'Autoregressive Conditional Heteroscedasticity with Estimates of the Variance of United Kingdom Inflation'. *Econometrica*, 50(4), pp 987–1007.

Engle, R. F. (1990). 'Discussion: Stock Market Volatility and the Crash of 87'. *Review of Financial Studies*, 3, pp 103–106.

Engle, R. F. (2000). 'The Econometrics of Ultra High Frequency Data'. *Econometrica*, 68(1), pp 1–22.

Engle, R. F. and Bollerslev, T. (1986). 'Modelling the Persistence of Conditional Variances'. *Econometric Reviews*, 5, pp 1–50.

Engle, R. F. and Lee, G. G. J. (1999). 'A Permanent and Transitory Component Model of Stock Return Volatility'. In R. F. Engle and H. White (eds.), *Cointegration, Causality, and Forecasting: A Festschrift in Honor of Clive W. J. Granger*. Oxford University Press, Oxford, UK, pp 475–497.

Engle, R. F. and Ng, V. K. (1993). 'Measuring and Testing the Impact of News on Volatility'. *Journal of Finance*, 48(5), pp 1749–1778.

Engle, R. F., Ng, V. K. and Rothschild, M. (1990). 'Asset Pricing with a Factor-ARCH Covariance Structure: Empirical Estimates for Treasury Bills'. *Journal of Econometrics*, 45(1–2), pp 213–237.

Engle, R. F. and Rosenberg, J. (1995). GARCH Gamma. *Journal of Derivatives*, 17, pp 229–247.

Engle, R., Liben, D. and Robins, R. (1987). 'Estimating Time Varying Risk Premia in the Term Structure: The ARCH-M Model. *Econometrica*, 55, pp 391–407.

Fama, E. F. (1965). 'The Behavior of Stock Market Prices'. *Journal of Business*, 38, pp 34–105.

Fama E. F. (1971). 'Efficient Capital Markets: A Review of Theory and Empirical Work'. *Journal of Finance*, 25(2), pp 383–417.

Floros, C. (2007). 'The Use of GARCH Models for the Calculation of Minimum Capital Risk Requirements: International Evidence'. *International Journal of Managerial Finance*, 3(4), pp 360–371.

Floros, C. (2008). 'Modeling Volatility Using GARCH Models: Evidence from Egypt and Israel'. *Middle Eastern Finance and Economics*, 2, pp 31–41.

Francq, C. and Zakoıan, J. (2004). 'Maximum Likelihood Estimation of Pure GARCH and ARMA-GARCH Processes'. *Bernoulli*, 10(4), pp 605–637.

Franses, P. H. and van Dijk, D. (1996). 'Forecasting Stock Market Volatility Using (Non-linear) GARCH Models'. *Journal of Forecasting*, 15(3), pp 229–235.

Franses, P. H. and van Dijk, D. (2000). *Non-linear Time Series Models in Empirical Finance*. Cambridge University Press, Cambridge, UK.

French, K. R., Schwert, G. W. and Stambaugh, R. F. (1987). Expected Stock Returns and Volatility. *Journal of Financial Econometric*, vol. 19, pp 3–29.

Geweke, J. (1986). 'Exact Inference in the Inequality Constrained Normal Linear Regression Model'. *Journal of Applied Econometrics*, 1(2), pp 127–141.

Giot, P. (2005). 'Implied Volatility Indexes and Daily Value at Risk Models'. *Journal of Derivatives*, 12, pp 54–64.

Giovannini, A. and Jorion, P. (1989). 'The Time Variation of Risk and Return in the Foreign Exchange and Stock Markets'. *Journal of Finance*, 44(2), pp 307–325.

Glosten, L. R., Jagannathan, R. and Runkle, D. E. (1993). 'On the Relation between the Expected Value and the Volatility of the Nominal Excess Return on Stocks'. *Journal of Finance*, 48 (4), pp 1779–1801.

González-Rivera, G. (1998). 'Smooth Transition GARCH Models'. *Studies in Nonlinear Dynamics and Econometrics*, 3(2), pp 61–78.

Gourieroux, C. (1997). *ARCH Models and Financial Applications*. Springer, New York.

Guedhami, O. and Sy, O. (2005). 'Does the Conditional Market Skewness Resolve the Puzzling Market Risk-Return Relationship?'. *The Quarterly Review of Economics and Statistics*, 45, pp 582–598.

Hafner, C. M. and Herwartz, H. (1998). 'Structural Analysis of Portfolio Risk Using Beta Impulse Response Functions'. *Statistica Neerlandica*, 52, pp 336–355.

Hentschel, L. (1995). 'All in the Family: Nesting Symmetric and Asymmetric GARCH Models'. *Journal of Financial Economics*, 39, pp 71–104.

Higgins, M. L. and Bera, A. K. (1992). 'A Class of Nonlinear ARCH Models'. *International Economic Review*, 33, pp 137–158.

Hsieh, D. (1988). 'The Statistical Properties of Daily Exchange Rates: 1974–1983'. *Journal of International Economics*, 1–2, pp 129–145.

Hsieh, D. A. (1993). Implications of Nonlinear Dynamics for Financial Risk Management. *Journal of Financial and Quantitative Analysis*, 28, pp 41–64.

Hu, M. Y., Jiang, C. X. and Tsoukalas, C. (1997). 'The European Exchange Rates Before and After the Establishment of the European Monetary System'. *Journal of International Financial Markets*, Institutions and Money, 7, pp 235–253.

Jansen, D. W. and de Vries, C. G. (1991). 'On the Frequency of Large Stock Returns: Putting Booms and Busts into Perspective'. *The Review of Economics and Statistics*, 73(1), pp 18–24.

Karmakar, M. (2005). 'Modeling Conditional Volatility of the Indian Stock Markets'. *Vikalpa*, 30(3), pp 21–37.

Karmakar, M. (2006). 'Stock Market Volatility in the Long Run, 1961–2005'. *Economic and Political Weekly*, 41(18), pp 1796–1802.

Karmakar, M. (2007). 'Asymmetric Volatility and Risk Return Relationship in the Indian Stock Market'. *South Asia Economic Journal*, 8(1), pp 99–116.

Kaur, H. (2002). *Stock Market Volatility in India.* Deep & Deep Publications, New Delhi, India.

Kaur, H. (2004). 'Time Varying Volatility in the Indian Stock Market'. *Vikalpa*, 29(4), pp 25–42.

Kayahan, B., Stengos, T. and Saltoglu, B. (2002). 'Intra-Day Features of Realized Volatility: Evidence from an Emerging Market'. *International Journal of Business and Economics*, 1(1), pp 17–24.

Kobayashi, M. and Shi, X. (2005). 'Testing for EGARCH Against Stochastic Volatility Models'. *Journal of Time Series Analysis*, 26(1), pp 135–150.

Koulakiotis, A., Papasyriopoulos, N. and Molyneux, P. (2006). 'More Evidence on the Relationship between Stock Price Returns and Volatility: A Note'. *International Research Journal of Finance and Economics*, 1, pp 21–28.

Koutmos, G. and Booth, G. G. (1995). 'Asymmetric Volatility Transmission in International Stock Markets'. *Journal of International Money and Finance*, 14, pp 747–762.

Kumar, B. P. and Singh, P. (2008). 'Volatility Modeling, Seasonality and Risk-Return Relationship in GARCH-in-Mean Framework: The Case of Indian Stock and Commodity Markets'. Conference paper in *The 5th Conference of Asia-Pacific Association of Derivatives*, Busan, Korea.

Kumar, B. P. and Supriya, M. V. (2007). 'S&P CNX Nifty Futures at NSE, India: An Empirical Analysis'. *Asia-Pacific Business Review*, 3(1), pp 67–90.

Kupiec, P. (1995). 'Techniques for Verifying the Accuracy of Risk Management Models'. *Journal of Derivatives*, 3, pp 73–84.

Lanne, M. and Saikkonen, P. (2005). 'Non-linear GARCH Models for Highly Persistent Volatility'. *The Econometrics Journal*, 8(2), pp 251–276.

Lee, T. H. (1994). 'Spread and Volatility in Spot and Forward Exchange Rates'. *Journal of International Money and Finance*, 13, pp 375–383.

Li, H. (2003). 'Mean/Variance Relation and the Conditional Distribution'. Working Paper, Swedish School of Economics and Business Administration.

Li, Q., Yang, J., Hsiao, C. and Chang, Y. J. (2005). 'The Relationship between Stock Returns and Volatility in International Stock Markets'. *Journal of Empirical Finance*, 12, pp 650–665.

Li, X., Miffre, J., Sullivan, N. and Brooks, C. (2008). 'Momentum Profits and Time-Varying Unsystematic Risk'. *Journal of Banking and Finance*, 32(4), pp 541–558.

Ling, S. and Li, W. K. (1998). 'Limiting Distributions of Maximum Likelihood Estimators for Unstable ARMA Models with GARCH Errors'. *The Annals of Statistics*, 26, pp 84–125.

Ling, S. and McAleer, M. (2003). 'Asymptotic Theory for a Vector ARMA-GARCH Model'. *Econometric Theory*, 19, pp 280–310.

Longin, F. M. (1996). 'The Asymptotic Distribution of Extreme Stock Market Returns'. *The Journal of Business*, 69(3), pp 383–408.

Longin, F. M. (1997). 'The Threshold Effect in Expected Volatility: A Model based on Asymmetric Information'. *Review of Financial Studies*, 10(3), pp 837–869.

Loudon, G. F., Watt, W. H. and Yadav, P. K. (2000). 'An Empirical Analysis of Alternative Parametric ARCH Models'. *Journal of Applied Econometrics*, 15(2), pp 117–136.

Lundburgh, S. and Terasvirta, T. (2000). 'Forecasting with Smooth Transition Autoregressive Models'. SSE/EFI Working Paper Series in Economics and Finance, no. 390.

Mandelbrot, B. (1963). 'The Variation of Certain Speculative Prices'. *The Journal of Business*, 36(4), pp 394–419.

Manfredo, M., Leuthold, R. M. and Irwin, S. H. (2001). 'Forecasting Cash Price Volatility of Fed Cattle, Feeder Cattle and Corn: Time Series, Implied Volatility and Composite Approaches'. *Journal of Agricultural and Applied Economics*, 33(3), pp 523–538.

Maris K., Pantou, G., Nikolopoulos, K., Pagourtzl, E. and Assimakopoulos, V. (2004). 'A Study of Financial Volatility Forecasting Techniques in the FTSE/ASE 20 Index'. *Applied Economics Letters*, 11(7), pp 453–457.

McMillan, D. G. and Speight, A. E. H. (2007). 'Value-at-Risk in Emerging Equity Markets: Comparative Evidence for Symmetric, Asymmetric, and Long-Memory GARCH Models'. *International Review of Finance*, 7(1–2), pp 1–19.

McMillan, D. G., Speight, A. and Gwilym, O. (2000). 'Forecasting UK Stock Market Volatility: A Comparative Analysis of Alternate Methods'. *Applied Financial Economics*, 10(4), pp 435–448.

McNeil, A. J. and Frey, R. (2000). 'Estimation of Tail-Related Risk Measures for Heteroskedastic Financial Time Series: An Extreme Value Approach'. *Journal of Empirical Finance*, 7, pp 271–300.

Merton, R. C. (1973). 'An Intertemporal Capital Asset Pricing Model'. *Econometrica*, 41(5), pp 867–887.

Milhoj, A. (1987). 'A Conditional Variance Model for Daily Deviations of an Exchange Rate'. *Journal of Business and Economic Statistics*, 5, pp 99–103.

Miyakoshia, T. and Jalolovb, M. (2005). 'Money-Income Causality Revisited in EGARCH: Spillovers of Monetary Policy to Asia from the US'. *Journal of Asian Economics*, 16(2), pp 299–313.

Morana, C. (2002). 'IGARCH Effects: An Interpretation'. *Applied Economics Letters*, 9, pp 745–778.

Nelson, D. (1991). 'Conditional Heteroscedasticity in Asset Returns: A New Approach'. *Econometrica*, 59, pp 347–370.

Niguez, T. M. and Rubia, A. (2006). 'Forecasting the Conditional Covariance Matrix of a Portfolio under Long-run Temporal Dependence'. *Journal of Forecasting*, 25, pp 439–458.

Ng, V. K. and Pirrong, S. C. (1994). 'Fundamentals and Volatility: Storage, Spreads, and the Dynamic of Metals Prices'. *Journal of Business*, 67, pp 203–230.

Pagan, A. R. and Hong, Y. S. (1990). 'Nonparametric Estimation and the Risk Premium'. In W. A. Barnett, J. Powell and G. E. Tauchen (eds.), *Nonparametric and Semiparametric Methods in Econometrics and Statistics: Proceedings of the Fifth International Symposium in Economic Theory and Econometrics*, Cambridge: Cambridge University Press, pp 51–75.

Pagan, A. and Schwert, W. (1990). 'Alternative Models for Conditional Stock Volatility'. *Journal of Econometrics*, 52, pp 245–266.

Pandey, A. (2005). 'Volatility Models and their Performance in Indian Capital Markets'. *Vikalpa*, 30(2), pp 27–46.

Pantula, S. G. (1986). 'Comment: Modeling the Persistence of Conditional Variances, by Engle and Bollerslev'. *Econometric Reviews*, 5, pp 71–74.

Pattanaik, S. and Chatterjee, B. (2000). 'Stock Returns and Volatility in India: An Empirical Puzzle'. *Reserve Bank of India Occasional Papers*, 21(1), pp 37–60.

Rigobon, R. (2002). 'The Curse of Non-Investment Grade Countries'. *Journal of Development Economics*, 69, pp 423–449.

Ruiz, E. and Veiga, H. (2008). 'Modelling Long-Memory Volatilities with Leverage Effect: A-LMSV versus FIEGARCH'. *Computational Statistics & Data Analysis*, 52(6), pp 2846–2862.

Schwert, G. W. (1989). 'Why does Stock Market Volatility Change Over Time'? *Journal of Finance*, 44(5), pp 1115–1153.

Schwert, G. W. (1990). 'Indexes of U.S. Stock Prices from 1802 to 1987'. *Journal of Business*, 63(3), pp 399–426.

Sentana, E. (1995). 'Quadratic ARCH Models'. *Review of Economic Studies*, 62, pp 639–661.

Sentana, E. and Fiorentini, G. (2001). 'Identification, Estimation and Testing of Conditional Heteroskedastic Factor Models'. *Journal of Econometrics*, 102, pp 143–164.

Shin, J. (2005). 'Stock Returns and Volatility in Emerging Stock Markets'. *International Journal of Business and Economics*, 4, pp 31–43.

Susmel, R. and Thompson, R. (1997). 'Volatility, Storage and Convenience Evidence from Natural Gas Markets'. *Journal of Futures Markets*, 17(1), pp 17–43.

Tang, T. L. and Shieh, S. J. (2006). 'Long Memory in Stock Index Future Markets: A Value-At-Risk Approach'. *Physica A: Statistical Mechanics and its Applications*, 366, pp 437–448.

Taylor, S. J. (1986). *Modeling Financial Time Series*. John Wiley, New York.

Taylor, J. W. (2004). 'Volatility Forecasting with Smooth Transition Exponential Smoothing'. *International Journal of Forecasting*, 20, pp 273–286.

Terasvirta, T. (1994). 'Specification, Estimation and Evaluation of Smooth Transition Autoregressive Models'. *Journal of American Statistical Association*, 89, pp 208–218.

Thomas, S. (1995). 'An Empirical Characterization of the Bombay Stock Exchange'. PhD. Thesis, University of Southern California, Los Angeles, California.

Thomas, S. (1998). *Volatility Forecasting in Indian Financial Markets: Derivative Markets in India.* Tata McGraw Hill, New Delhi.

Tse, Y. and Booth, G. G. (1996). 'Common Volatility and Volatility Spillovers Between U.S. and Eurodollar Interest Rates: Evidence from The Futures Market'. *Journal of Economics and Business*, 48, pp 299–312.

Tse, Y. K. and Tsui, A. K. C. (1997). 'Conditional Volatility in Foreign Exchange Rates: Evidence for the Malaysian Ringgit and Singapore Dollar'. *Pacific-Basin Finance Journal*, 5, pp 345–356.

Tully, E. and Lucey, B. M. (2007). 'A Power GARCH Examination of the Gold Market'. *Research in International Business and Finance*, 21(2), pp 316–325.

Wei, C. C. (2009). 'Using the Component GARCH Modeling and Forecasting Method to Determine the Effect of Unexpected Exchange Rate Mean and Volatility Spillover on Stock Markets'. *International Research Journal of Finance and Economics*, 23, pp 62–74.

Zakoian, J. (1994). 'Threshold Heteroskedastic Models'. *Journal of Economic Dynamics and Control*, 18, pp 931–995.

Index

A

AASB. *See* Australian Accounting Standards Board (AASB)
absolutism, 182
accountability, 21–23, 82–84, 145
  issues of, 22
accountants, 20–21, 185–190
  applied areas of, 185
  ethical intuition of, 189–190
  ethical role of, 185
  moral behaviour of, 187–189
accounting disclosure, 175–176
accounting ethics, 181–190
accounting for amalgamation, 128–131
accounting for financial instruments, 60–77
  controversial issues on, 68–73
  evolution of, 62–64
accounting information, 21, 171, 187
  public good concept of, 172
accounting regulation, 161–162
  uniform accounting system and government involvement in, 161–163
accounting standards, 159–165
  ambiguity in accounting rules, 163–164
  convergence of interests of regulated parties and regulator, 173–174
  determination of accounting rules, 172–173
  issue of survival of a standard setting body, 172
  latitude given to corporate managers, 164
  obstacles to, 160
  public good concept of, 172
  related-party transactions and, 164–165
  relevance of, 159–160
  standard setters and, 163, 166, 167, 168
acquire, 132
acquirer, 132
acquisition, 127
Africa, 12
AFS. *See* Available-for-Sale Financial Assets (AFS)
AGARCH. *See* asymmetric GARCH (AGARCH)
Agency Theory arguments, 168
aggregational Gaussianity, 252
AICPA Code of Professional Conduct, 186
AICPA committees, 173
AICPA. *See* American Institute of Certified Accountants (AICPA)
A-IFRS. *See* Australian equivalents of IFRS (A-IFRS)
amalgamation, 128–131
American Institute of Certified Accountants (AICPA), 185–186
amortization, 55–56
APARCH. *See* asymmetric power ARCH (APARCH)
ARCH effect, 254
ARMA model, 250, 254–255, 256
AS 14, 127–132
Asia, 11–12
asymmetric GARCH (AGARCH), 261
asymmetric power ARCH (APARCH), 261–262
atmosphere
  approaches to mitigating measures, 235–239
  economic policy measures, 236
  global warming, 234–235
  lifestyle-based carbon control, 240–241
  market-based measures, 236
Australia, 13–14, 214
Australian Accounting Standards Board (AASB), 13–14
Australian equivalents of IFRS (A-IFRS), 13–14
autoregressive model, 255–256
available-for-sale financial assets (AFS), 64, 65, 66

B

BAC. *See* Business Accounting Council (BAC)
balanced scorecard, 222–224
  customer perspective, 223
  financial perspective, 223
  innovation and learning perspective, 224
  internal process perspective, 224

Bear Sterns, 202, 204
Birbhum, 229
Birla Committee, 90
Birla, Kumar Mangalam, 90
Black–Scholes–Merton (BSM) model, 112
Blue Ribbon Committee, 87
BSM model. *See* Black–Scholes–Merton (BSM) model
Bulgaria, 214
Business Accounting Council (BAC), 11

C

Cadbury Committee, 86–87
Canada, 12, 31, 214
Cap-and-Trade, 239
capital market transactions, 162
capital market, 174–176
Capture Theory, 173
carbon tax, 236–238
  mechanism, 237
  policy perspective, 236
  redistribution effect, 237–238
  revenue-earning potential, 237
carbon trading
  mechanism, 238
  policy perspective, 238
Cartwright, Brian G., 103
CGARCH. *See* component GARCH (CGARCH)
China, 12, 101–102, 103, 161
cogeneric merger, 127
Combined Code on Corporate Governance, 89
Commons committee, 241
complex transactions, 147
component GARCH (CGARCH), 265–266
conditional heavy tails, 253
conglomerate merger, 127
conventional financial accounting, 136
Coochbehar, 229
corporate governance, 81–95
  benefits of, 84–85
  concept of, 83–84
  definition of, 83
  evolution of, 85–89
  overview of, 81–83
  synoptic view of the genesis of, 90–92
corporate reporting, 92–95
corporate restructuring, 126
corporation, definition of, 82
Cox, Christopher, 98
currency crisis, 202
Czech Republic, 214

D

democratic/accountability approach, 29
deregulation of economies, 125
direct intellectual capital method (DICM), 49
disclosure, 115–122
  of earning per share, 121–122
  of stock option value by Indian companies, 116–122
  valuation assumptions and, 119–120
dividend policy, 212–213, 216–217
dividend taxation, 213–214

E

earning per share (EPS), 121–122
East Asian Financial crisis (late-1990s), 199
EDINET, 102
EGARCH. *See* exponential GARCH (EGARCH)
emotivism, 184
employee stock option (ESO), 109–122
employee stock option plan (ESOP), 109–122
  accounting, 110–111
  Black–Scholes–Merton (BSM) model, 112
  disclosure of stock option value by Indian companies, 116–122
  lattice model, 112–113
  literature review, 113–114
  regulatory framework of accounting in India, 114–116
  valuation, 111–112
enlightened capitalism, 20
Enron, 88, 91, 92
enterprises, 146
environmental accountability, 21
environmental legislations, 235
environment-related management accounting, 24
EPS. *See* earning per share (EPS)
ESO. *See* employee stock option (ESO)

ESOP. *See* employee stock option plan (ESOP)
ethics, 181–190
 applied areas of, 185–187
 descriptive way, 182
 normative way, 182
 professional ethics, 186–187
 virtue theory, 182–183
ethics of care, 184
EU ETS. *See* European Union's Emission Trading Scheme (EU ETS)
EU. *See* European Union (EU)
Europe, 10
European Exchange Rate Mechanism, 203
European Union (EU), 2, 6, 52, 93, 163
European Union's Emission Trading Scheme (EU ETS), 239
EVT-GARCH. *See* extreme value theory GARCH (EVT-GARCH)
exponential GARCH (EGARCH), 258–259
eXtensible Business Reporting language (XBRL), 94, 97–103
 adoption by different countries, 101–103
 advantages of, 101
 concepts of related terminologies, 99–100
 definition of, 97
 evolution of, 98–99
 taxonomy, 99
 tools used in, 100–101
eXtensible Markup Language (XML), 98
extreme value theory GARCH (EVT-GARCH), 266

F

factor GARCH (F-GARCH), 267
fair value, 110
 definition of, 135
 recognition of, 136–137
fair value accounting, 110, 135–141
 definition of, 135
 problems with, 141
fair value measurement, 138–139
Fannie Mae and Freddie Mac, 202, 204
FASB. *See* Financial Accounting Standards Board (FASB)
FCA. *See* full cost accounting (FCA)
F-GARCH. *See* factor GARCH (F-GARCH)
FIEGARCH. *See* fractionally integrated EGARCH (FIEGARCH)
FIGARCH. *See* fractionally integrated GARCH (FIGARCH)
financial accounting, 136
Financial Accounting Standards Board (FASB), 62, 65, 66, 73, 75
financial crisis, 199–200
financial disclosure, 175–176
financial instruments, 60–77
 controversial issues on, 68–73
 measurement principles for, 65
 reform initiatives taken by standard-setting bodies, 73–77
 treatment of gains and losses, 65–66
 treatment of impairment losses, 66
financial reporting, 162
 problems in achieving international harmonization in, 163
financial services agency (FSA), 11
Financial Services Modernization Act (1999), 201
fractionally integrated EGARCH (FIEGARCH), 260
fractionally integrated GARCH (FIGARCH), 259–260
France, 161
free riders, 172
free-market pricing system, 171
FSA. *See* financial services agency (FSA)
full cost accounting (FCA), 19–37
 business case for, 28–29
 definition and nature of, 27
 goal of, 27–28
 implemenatation, 29–30
 methodology for adoption, 31–37
 as pre-requisite for mainstream sustainability reporting practice, 22–25
 objectives of, 21
 traditional *versus* emerging views of, 25–27
full IFRSs, 152–154
full privatization approach, 30

G

GARCH model, 250, 254–255, 256–260
GARCH-M model, 257–258
GARCH-X model, 265
GARCH-Γ, 266

Gaussian distribution, 251
Germany, 161
GJR-GARCH, 262
Glass–Steagall Act (1933), 201
global accounting standards, 2–4
global financial crises, 197–207
global warming, 234–235
goodwill, definition, 166
Gramm–Leach–Bliley Act (1999), 201
Gray, Rob, 24
Great Depression (of 1930s), 198–201, 203, 205
Greenbury Committee, 86–87
Greening of Accountancy: The Profession After Pearce, 24

H

HaFV. *See* Held at Fair Value through Profit or Loss (HaFV)
Hampel Committee, 87
heavy tail, 251–252
hedge accounting, 66–67
Held at Fair Value through Profit or Loss (HaFV), 64, 65
held for trading (HFT), 64
held-to-maturity investments (HTM), 64
Hentschel GARCH (HGARCH), 264
HFT. *See* held for trading (HFT)
HGARCH. *See* Hentschel GARCH (HGARCH)
HTM. *See* held-to-maturity investments (HTM)
HTML. *See* Hyper Text Markup Language (HTML)
Hume, David, 182, 199
Hungary, 161
HYGARCH. *See* hyperbolic GARCH (HYGARCH)
Hyper Text Markup Language (HTML), 98
hyperbolic GARCH (HYGARCH), 264–265

I

IAS 32, 62–63
IAS 36, 50, 51, 55
IAS 38, 50, 51, 52, 54–55
IAS 39, 62–63, 65, 66, 67
IASB. *See* International Accounting Standards Board (IASB)
IASC. *See* International Accounting Standards Committee (IASC)
ICAI. *See* Institute of Chartered Accountants of India (ICAI)
IFAC. *See* International Federation of Accountants (IFAC)
IFRS. *See* International Financial Reporting Standards (IFRS)
IFRS 3, 50, 51, 127, 131–133
IFRS 5, 50
IFRS 7, 63
IGARCH. *See* Integrated GARCH (IGARCH)
income statement, modification of, 140–141
Income Tax Act (1961), 215
India, 11, 102, 205–207, 220
    history of dividend tax in, 214–216
instance document, 99
Institute of Chartered Accountants of India (ICAI), 102, 114–115, 127
intangible assets, 43–56
    accounting and reporting of, 51–56
    acquisition as part of business combination, 54
    amortization and impairment, 55–56
    awareness for, 43–44
    definition and recognition of, 45–48
    importance of, 43
    literature review, 44–45
    measurement and valuation of, 48–51
integrated GARCH (IGARCH), 259
intermittency, 253
internal accounting functions, 185
International Accounting Standards Board (IASB), 1–2, 4–6, 8–9, 14–15, 73, 75, 138–139, 143–149
    conceptual foundation of, 8–9
International Accounting Standards Board (IASB), 62
International Accounting Standards Committee (IASC), 4–5, 62
International Federation of Accountants (IFAC), 144
International Financial Reporting Standards (IFRS), 1–2, 6–8, 9–14, 93–94, 140
    first-time adoption of, 9–10
    focus of, 7
    for small and medium-sized entities, 147–154
    worldwide adoption of, 10–14
intrinsic value, 110
irrational accounting policies, 165–167

J

James E. Walter's dividend model, 217
Japan, 11, 102, 103. 161
Joint Working Group (JWG), 73
Justice of Fairness, 184
JWG. *See* Joint Working Group (JWG)

K

Kant's ethic, 183
Kantian Morality, 183
Kohlberg's classification of moral behavior, 188, 191
Korea, 11
Kyoto Protocol, 238–239

L

Latin American Debt Crisis (1980s), 198, 202
lattice model, 112–113
Leeladhar, V., 102
legalistic ethics, 182
Lehman Brothers, 202, 204
leverage effect, 253
Life-Cycle Theory of Regulation, 173
lifestyle-based carbon control, 240–241
Loans & Receivables (L&R), 64
log-GARCH, 258
logistic smooth transition (LSTGARCH), 263
London Stock Exchange, 86, 87
long-term capital gains, 216, 217
LSTGARCH. *See* logistic smooth transition (LSTGARCH)

M

mandatory financial reporting arguments, 169–172
mandatory public disclosure, 169–170
market capitalization method (MCM), 49
marking to market (MTM), 64–65
Mehra, Dr Madhav, 92
mergers, 127
    cogeneric, 127
    conglomerate, 127
Merrill Lynch, 202, 204
Metcalf Committee, 173
MGARCH. *See* multivariate GARCH (MGARCH)
mitigating measures, 235–239
modern financial disclosure system, 172
Modigliani and Miller (M–M) hypothesis, 212–213
    assumptions, 212–213
    observations, 216–217
    tax non-existence assumption of, 213
    testing of validity of, 216
moral behavior, 187–189
Moss Committee, 173
MTM. *See* Marking to Market (MTM)
multivariate GARCH (MGARCH), 267–268
Murshidabad, 229
Murthy, N. R. Narayana, 91

N

Naresh Chandra Committee, 91
NASSCOM. See National Association of Software and Service Companies (NASSCOM)
National Association of Software and Service Companies (NASSCOM)
National Bank Act (1863), 202
Netherlands, 102, 214
New Zealand, 14
NGARCH. *See* non-linear GARCH (NGARCH)
NGO, 219–230
    activities in West Bengal, 220–222
    balanced scorecard for, 222–224
    performance evaluation of, 224–229
non-linear GARCH (NGARCH), 261
normal distribution, 251
normative ethics, 185
North America, 12–13

O

OECD. *See* Organisation for Economic Cooperation and Development (OECD)
OLAP. *See* on-line analytical processing (OLAP)
On the Republic, 182
on-line analytical processing (OLAP), 98–99
Ontario Hydro, 31, 33–37

achievements with FCA during 1980–95, 34
external environmental costs, 35
FCA approach, 34
internal environmental costs, 35
optimal accounting standards, 159–160
Organisation for Economic Cooperation and Development (OECD), 88

P

Pareto-like tail, 251
PCT. *See* personal carbon trading (PCT)
performance comparisons, 164
personal carbon trading (PCT), 241–245
alternative Proposals, 242–243
evaluation, 245
major debatable issues, 244–245
mechanism, 241–242
need for, 241
practicalities, 242
superiority over other similar existing schemes, 244
Pillai, G. K., 206
place of disclosure, 117–118
Poland, 161, 214
pooling of interests method, 129
predictive value, 176
private contracting, 169
private environmental costs, 28
Proctor and Gamble, 32
professional ethics, 186–187
professionals, 186–187
property, plant and equipment (PP&E), 152
public environmental costs, 28
public interest argument, 170
Purba Medinipur, 229–230
purchase method, 129
Purulia, 229

Q

quadratic GARCH. (QGARCH), 262–263

R

reflective equilibrium, 184
relativism, 182
Republic of Ireland, 214
Reserve Bank of India, 206
return on assets method (ROA), 49
returns, dependence properties of, 254
risk-free interest rate, 119
Rivlin, Alice M., 198
Romania, 214
Roosevelt, Franklin D., 198
Russian Financial Crisis (1998), 198

S

Sarbanes–Oxley Act (SOX), 88, 91
Satyam Computer Services, 83, 92
Schumpeter, Joseph A., 204
SEBI. *See* Securities and Exchange Board of India (SEBI)
Securities and Exchange Board of India (SEBI), 90, 91, 115–116
SFAS 8, 168
SFAS 19, 168
SFAS 105, 62
SFAS 107, 62
SFAS 115, 62, 63
SFAS 119, 62, 63
SFAS 123, 62, 111
SFAS 133, 62, 63, 67
SFAS 157, 75–76, 138, 139
SFAS. *See* Statements of Financial Accounting Standard (SFAS)
SGML. *See* Standardised General Markup Language (SGML)
shadow price approach, 30
skewness, 252
small and medium-sized entities (SMEs), 143–154
choices of accounting, 147
evolution of IFRS for, 147–148
exposure draft (ED), 147
IASB definition, 145
ICAI definition of, 146
IFRS and, 147–154
SMEs. *See* small and medium-sized entities (SMEs)
Smith, Adam, 82
smooth transition GARCH (STGARCH), 264–265
social environmental costs, 28
South America, 13

SOX. *See* Sarbanes–Oxley Act (SOX)
Spain, 102
Spitzer, Eliot, 201
standard setters, 163, 166, 167, 168
standard setting, 170–175
    capital market researches for, 176–177
Standardised General Markup Language (SGML), 98
statement of cash flows, 7
statement of comprehensive income, 7
statement of the financial position, 7
Statements of Financial Accounting Standard (SFAS), 62
STGARCH. *See* smooth transition GARCH (STGARCH)
stock option plans, 109–110
structural change approach, 30
structural GARCH, 266
sustainability
    corporate evolution towards, 20
synergy, 126

T

tail index of a distribution, 251–252
tax accounting, 162
tax-code, 162
Taylor–Schwert GARCH (TS-GARCH), 263
TBL. *See* triple bottom line (TBL)
TGARCH. *See* threshold GARCH (TGARCH)
threshold GARCH (TGARCH), 263
Times of India, 206
traditional accounting, 21, 25–26, 137
transferee company, 127
triple bottom line (TBL), 23–24
TS-GARCH. *See* Taylor–Schwert GARCH (TS-GARCH)
Turnbull Committee, 87
24 Parganas, 230
Tweedie, David, 3, 11, 144

U

UAS. *See* uniform accounting system (UAS)
uniform accounting system (UAS), 161–162
    characteristics of, 162
United Kingdom, 86, 87, 102
United States (US), 12, 102, 103, 198, 200–204
United States Savings & Loan Crisis (late-1980s and the early 1990s), 198, 200
US Financial Accounting Standards Board (FASB), 12
US GAAP, 12–13, 43, 111, 137, 139
USEPA, 36
Utilitarian, 183

V

valuation model, 118
Virtue theory of ethics, 182–183
volatility asymmetry, 253
volatility clustering, 253, 254–255
voluntary financial reporting arguments, 168–169
voluntary reporting initiatives, 169

W

West Bengal, 220–221, 224
whistle blower policy, 92

X

XBRL Composer, 100
XBRL International, 100
XBRL reporting system, 101
XBRL Viewers, 101
XBRL. *See* eXtensible Business Reporting language (XBRL)
XML. *See* eXtensible Markup Language (XML)